Explorers and Their Quest
for North America

To Joyce

Out of dreams you came to me on golden wings
Blown by the soft breath of the night winds
You flew across moonlit skies into my heart
Gliding through the white clouds and over the crest
   of the mountains
You brush against my lips with the kiss of tenderness
Bringing joy and love through the emptiness of time, while
Softly whispering once alone now forever together.

Explorers and Their Quest for North America

Philip J. Potter

PEN & SWORD
HISTORY

First published in Great Britain in 2017 by
PEN AND SWORD HISTORY
an imprint of
Pen and Sword Books Ltd
47 Church Street
Barnsley
South Yorkshire S70 2AS

ISBN 978 1 52672 053 5

Printed and bound in England
by TJ International Ltd. Padstow

Typeset in Times New Roman by
CHIC GRAPHICS

Pen & Sword Books Ltd incorporates the imprints of Pen & Sword
Archaeology, Atlas, Aviation, Battleground, Discovery,
Family History, History, Maritime, Military, Naval, Politics, Railways,
Select, Social History, Transport, True Crime, Claymore Press,
Frontline Books, Leo Cooper, Praetorian Press, Remember When,
Seaforth Publishing and Wharncliffe.

For a complete list of Pen and Sword titles please contact
Pen and Sword Books Limited
47 Church Street, Barnsley, South Yorkshire, S70 2AS, England
E-mail: enquiries@pen-and-sword.co.uk
Website: www.pen-and-sword.co.uk

Contents

Preface

The exploration and colonization of North America began in the late tenth century when Norsemen from Greenland set sail to the west, discovering unknown lands. According to *The Saga of the Greenlanders*, as the Norse merchant, Bjarni Herjolfsson, was returning to Greenland in 985, his ship was blown westward by a violent storm, causing his Greenlanders to land on the coast of a new continent, North America. Shortly after making landfall, he sailed his vessel along the coastline of modern-day Canada, becoming the first European to explore the New World over 500 years before Christopher Columbus reached the Bahama Islands in 1492. Following Herjolfsson's exploration of the territory, he returned to Greenland to report his discovery.

Around 1000, Norse chieftain Leif Eriksson led a crew of thirty-five men to find the new land in the west reported earlier by Herjolfsson. The Norse seamen rowed and sailed their small vessel toward the setting sun in the freezing waters of the northern Atlantic Ocean, and after several weeks spotted land in the distance. After making landfall at several inhospitable sites, Eriksson navigated further south, finally encountering a warm forested area at the northern tip of Newfoundland. He assembled an armed landing party and went ashore to explore the new discovery. During his exploration, the Northmen found the region was full of wild grape vines, calling the site Vinland. With winter now approaching, Eriksson decided to remain on the island and built several small cabins for protection against the cold weather, which became the first European settlement in the New World. After wintering at Vinland, in the spring the Norsemen loaded their ship with grapes, fish and timber, returning to Greenland. Following the expedition of Leif Eriksson, two other voyages to the territories in the west were reported in the sagas, but there was no interest in building a permanent colony and the discoveries were largely forgotten.

In twelfth-century Europe, little was known about Asia beyond the eastern lands of the Byzantine Empire. Knowledge about the continent of Africa was limited to the region along the shoreline of the Mediterranean, and information about its western Atlantic coast was highly fragmented and derived from ancient maps and legends. Knights returning to the courts of Europe from the Crusades in the Holy Lands created interest in the products of the region, encouraging trade and commercial ties. Later, the Italian firms' earlier connections to the Middle East stimulated further commercial lure and curiosity about the unknown kingdoms in the east. In the early thirteenth century, emboldened by the prospects for highly profitable commercial activities, merchants from the Maritime Republics, primarily Venice and Genoa, began opening overland trading routes to the Far East.

As interest in Africa and Asia expanded, European regimes and wealthy merchants began sending expeditionary parties to collect information on these unknown lands and establish trading relationships. In May 1291, patronized by a powerful mercantile organization from Genoa, the Vivaldi brothers, Vadino and Ugolino, set sail from the city to attempt the first exploration of the Atlantic Ocean in two galleys, but disappeared along the coastline of Morocco, provoking stories of huge horrible sea monsters that devoured whole ships. Despite the dangers, numerous merchants ventured overland to the east to trade for the area's silks, spices, herbs and opium. Spices were highly prized by the European courts and their strong demand stimulated trade deeper into the Asian continent. Many of the traders published books about their travels and adventures, which were used as reference guides and added to the allure of Africa and China. After the reconquest of Portugal from its Muslim occupiers, Portuguese King Afonso IV encouraged maritime commerce and sponsored the first exploration along the African coast, leading to the regime's claim to the Canary Islands.

By the mid-thirteenth century, Europe was slowly emerging from the instability and turmoil of the Dark Ages. As the economy and governmental stability improved, the merchants of Venice were increasingly looking to expand trade to the east to the rich markets of China. The Polo family owned a highly successful Venetian trading enterprise, and in 1271 Marco Polo travelled overland to the court of Kublai Khan to establish a business relationship. He remained in the Orient for over seventeen years, travelling extensively throughout the region studying the culture, economy and demographics of the population. Following his return to Venice, he wrote a detailed account of his journeys entitled *The Travels of Marco Polo*, which was read throughout Europe and inspired generations of adventurers with its descriptions of the wealth and wonder of the Far East.

The merchants of Europe were eager to trade with the Orient, but were compelled to make the arduous and dangerous journey overland. To find a faster and shorter route to the east, Portuguese sailors began steering down the unknown western coastline of Africa, searching for a sea passage around the tip of the continent. To better prepare his sea captains for navigating in the dangerous waters of the Atlantic Ocean, in 1418 Prince Henry of Portugal established a centre for navigation, bringing cartographers, geographers, instrument makers and navigators to his small court to teach and improve the skills of exploration, seamanship and sailing. The prince personally financed numerous expeditions for the journey south along the African shoreline, searching for the passageway into the Indian Ocean. Following Prince Henry's death, the Portuguese regime continued its quest for the sea route to China, navigating the uncharted waters of the Atlantic Ocean, slowly steering further down the coast. Finally, in 1488, Bartolomeu Diaz rounded the tip of the continent, sailing into the Indian Ocean and opening an eastern water route to the riches of India and Cathay.

As the Portuguese court pressed its search for the eastern water route to the Far East, Christopher Columbus became increasingly convinced through his studies of maps, charts and captains' logs that it was possible to reach China faster by sailing to the west. With financial backing from Queen Isabella and King Ferdinand II of Spain, three ships under the command of Columbus departed from Palos in September 1492, sailing to the west. When Columbus left Spain for his voyage into the unknown waters of the Atlantic, he carried with him a Bible, maps and a copy of Marco Polo's book about his years in the Far East. After navigating west for over two months, in the early morning moonlight of 12 October, the lookout saw in the distance a new continent, igniting the Age of Exploration. Columbus' first voyage to the west was the beginning of a wave of exploratory expeditions by Portuguese, Spanish, English and French mariners in search of the fabled North-west Passage to the riches of China.

Explorers of North America traces the history of the discovery, exploration and settlement of a new continent through the biographies of fourteen explorers who had the courage and inquisitiveness to search the limits of the New World and unveil its unknown secrets. The book is organized chronologically, beginning with the transatlantic voyage of Columbus in 1492 and ending in 1806 with Meriwether Lewis' epic journey through the Louisiana Purchase to the Pacific Ocean to begin the mass migration across the Mississippi River into the American west.

Late Sixteenth Century Map Illustrating the
Assembly of an Exploration Fleet

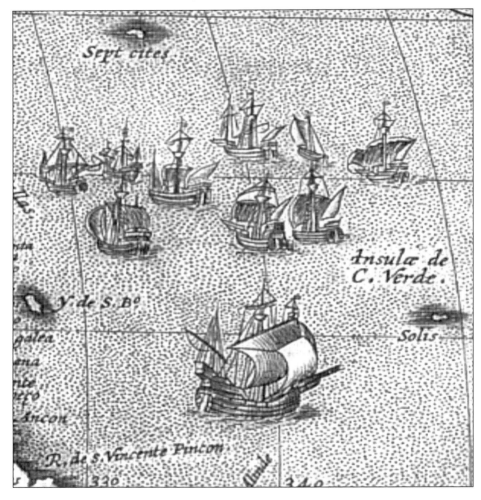

Christopher Columbus

In April 1492, Christopher Columbus was issued a charter by the Spanish crown for an expedition to reach the riches of China by sailing to the west. After recruiting his crews and preparing his fleet, on 3 August 1492 his small ships departed from the port of Palos in south-west Spain, heading into unknown seas that many Europeans believed were occupied by horrible monsters. By early October, the crewmen on Columbus' vessels had been out of sight of the land for over twenty days and were growing increasingly mutinous. As the seamen talked of turning back to Spain, on 7 October large flocks of birds were seen flying overhead. Encouraged by the sightings of the birds, Columbus altered his western course, steering his ships south-west. The trade winds blew stronger two days later, and there were the first signs of land when the sailors spotted tree branches with green leaves. The Spanish flotilla ploughed forward into the pitching deep blue ocean. On 11 October, the sun set on a clear horizon and the night was cloudless, with a late rising moon. As the lookouts high in the riggings strained their eyes into the golden light of the moon, around two in the morning, Rodrigo de Triana onboard the *Pinta* shouted out, 'Land, land'. In the morning, the white beach was clearly visible and Columbus went ashore in the early afternoon, naming the island in the Bahama chain San Salvador to ignite the age of discovery and exploration in the New World.

Christopher Columbus was born in the independent Italian Republic of Genoa in the second half of 1451, the first son of Domenico and Susanna Fontanarossa Columbus. He was raised in a middle class tradesman's family with his three younger brothers and one sister. Domenico was a master weaver and owned a prosperous wool business in Genoa. He was a member of the local weaver's guild and was active in the city's politics. In recognition of his political loyalty, Domenico was appointed warden for the Porta dell Olivella Gate. Christopher received little if any formal education and was occupied working in his father's shop as a weaver. As a Genoese boy living on the coast of the Mediterranean, he had frequent contacts with sailors, ships' captains and travellers from foreign lands, and was drawn to the sea. Around age 10, Columbus began making short voyages close to Genoa, while continuing to work in the family's weaving business. Several years later, he started taking longer journeys, gaining an education and experience in seamanship and navigation. In 1470, when King Rene II of Anjou hired a mercenary fleet for his war against John II, king of Aragon, Columbus served as a seaman on a Genoese warship taking part in a brief naval battle against the Spanish.

While Columbus continued to work in his father's cloth shop, in late May 1476, he was employed as a seaman on the Flemish ship *Bechalla* as part of an armed convoy carrying valuable cargo to England and the Low Countries. As the fleet passed the southern coast of Portugal, it was attacked by French pirates. During the ensuing sea battle, the *Bechalla* was sunk and Columbus thrown into the sea. He grabbed a large piece of floating debris, making his way to shore. After reaching land, he was found by local Portuguese and provided with food and shelter. There was a large community of Genoese immigrants in Lisbon, and Columbus soon travelled to the city. He settled with his compatriots, while continuing to sail on merchant vessels.

At the time of Columbus' arrival in Lisbon, the kingdom of Portugal was at the centre of discovery and exploration along the west coast of Africa, and its sailors were exposed to the latest techniques in navigation and map-making. From these seamen and his associations with Genoese merchants, Columbus studied mathematics and astronomy, learning to read and write Portuguese, Castilian and Latin. He expanded his education by reading books on geography, history, philosophy and geometry, while becoming skilled in cartography. In Portugal, he renewed his commercial sea voyages, becoming involved in the Iberian trade network. Columbus made numerous journeys in the Mediterranean region and later travelled to the known western limits of the Atlantic Ocean at Iceland. By 1478, Columbus had risen to the rank of captain and first piloted a merchant vessel to Maderia in the eastern Atlantic off the coast of Morocco. As Columbus continued to sail for various Genoese and Portuguese tradesmen, he served as ship's officer on a voyage down the western shores of Africa to the fortified trading enclave at St George of the Mine on the Gold Coast, increasing his knowledge of seamanship, currents, winds, weather and navigation during the long journey.

In 1479, Columbus expanded his influence and access to the Portuguese royal court with his marriage to Dona Filipa de Perestrelo Moniz, who was from a minor noble family with hereditary rights to the island of Porto Santo in the Madeira chain. Shortly after the marriage, they moved to Porto Santo, where their only child, Diego, was born. Dona Filipa died of unknown causes in Porto Santo in 1484.

CHRISTOPHER COLUMBUS

Before Christopher Columbus' arrival in Lisbon, Portuguese sea captains had been steadily pushing down the west coast of Africa in search of an eastern passage to the trading riches of the Indies, which in the fifteenth century included China, Japan and India. As Columbus continued to sail the waters of the South Atlantic, expanding his knowledge of seamanship and navigation, talking to Portuguese sailors and map-makers and studying the writings of ancient and medieval geographers, he became convinced that a shorter route to the Indies was possible by navigating west. Beginning with Prince Henry in 1418, the monarchy of Portugal had financially supported and encouraged voyages of discovery to Asia down the west African coast, and in 1484, Columbus was granted an audience with King John II to promote his Indies expedition. During his discussions with the king, Columbus requested vessels to sail west to the island of Japan. John II referred him to his maritime committee, which dismissed his petition as folly.

Undeterred by his first rejection, Columbus was now totally committed to securing financial support for his Indies expedition. In May 1485, he sailed to Spain to seek ships and crews from Queen Isabella of Castille. After entering the kingdom, he stayed at a Franciscan monastery and through a monk received a letter of introduction to the Duke of Medina Sidonia, who referred him to a relative, Luis de la Cerda, Count of Medina Celi. After discussing his expedition with the count, he was sent to meet Queen Isabella at Cordova. When Columbus arrived in the town, he was compelled to wait for the queen's return to court. Cordova had a large Genoese enclave, and Columbus made friends with many of his compatriots. He met Diego de Harane, and through him was introduced to his cousin, Beatriz Enriquez. Columbus and Beatriz were attracted to each other, and she soon became his mistress. As a result of this relationship, she bore Columbus his second son, Ferdinand. Columbus remained in Cordova for over four months before the queen arrived in May 1486, and with his recommendation from Luis de la Cerda, he was received at court. He met with Isabella, promoting his voyage to the Indies, but she deferred a decision to a special commission. The members of the committee debated their answer for over six months, failing to reach a judgment. While the board continued its deliberations, Columbus was granted a retaining fee, enough to support himself.

As the Castilian commission continued its talks, Columbus wrote to king John II of Portugal in 1488, again promoting his Indies expedition. When Columbus was granted a second audience with the king, he travelled back to Lisbon. While he waited to meet with the king, Bartholomew Diaz returned to Portugal after rounding the southern tip of Africa and sailing up the coast to open the eastern trade route to the Indies. Following Diaz's successful voyage, John II quickly lost interest in Columbus' project and the Genoese captain was forced to return to Spain.

By 1489, Columbus had returned to Spain and his quest for the Indies expedition with the Castilian crown. While he waited for a reply from the queen's commission, his brother, Bartholomew, sailed to England and later France to promote the venture. During the following year, Columbus continued to expand his knowledge of cosmology, reading numerous works on astronomy, geography and geology, while supplementing his income by selling books and for a short period serving in the Spanish Army against the Moors at the siege of Baza. Late in 1490, the committee finally issued its report, rejecting Columbus' proposal. However, the queen sent a message to Columbus, telling him he could reapply after the Moors were defeated. Columbus spent another year without an interview before deciding to join his brother in France. Before leaving, he wrote to Isabella asking for an audience, and she replied by summoning him to court. In late December 1491, Columbus appeared at court with his maps, diagrams and exhibits to promote his Indies expedition again. A new commission reviewed the proposal, which was again rejected as too costly. The Genoese captain had demanded the title of admiral, appointment as governor for the new lands discovered and 10 per cent of the trade. He refused to lower his demands and prepared to join Bartholomew in France. As Columbus left the queen's court at Santa Fe, he was overtaken by a royal messenger with the news that the throne was finally prepared to finance the voyage to prevent him from sailing under the flag of England or France.

After the charter with the crown was signed and sealed in April 1492, Columbus travelled to the port of Palos on the Rio Tinto River in south-western Spain to assemble his crews and vessels. Under the agreement with Isabella, the expedition was promised three equipped ships and provisions for two months. The town of Palos was under orders from the Castilian regime to provide two caravels, and the inhabitants delivered the *Nina* and *Pinta,* while Columbus chartered the *Santa Maria*. The *Santa Maria* was a 100-ton carrack with three masts, developed by the Portuguese for use in the Atlantic, and the two caravels were around 70 tons each, also with three masts. After first arriving in Spain, Columbus had become friends with the Pinzon family of Palos, who were shipowners and builders of caravels. They were experienced sailors and well-respected sea captains and navigators. Columbus appointed Martin Alonso Pinzon as captain for the *Pinta* and his brother, Vicente Pinzon, captain of the *Nina*, while he took command of the

Santa Maria. The expedition's ninety-man crew was recruited with the help of the Pinzon brothers from the towns of Andalusia, and soon began to gather in Palos. By early August 1492, the small fleet of three vessels was ready to navigate west and ignite the age of discovery in the New World.

As the orange glow of the morning sun began to spread its light over the harbour on 3 August, the three vessels left Palos, heading down the Rio Tinto River to the Atlantic Ocean and the sailors' first destination, the Canary Islands. During the voyage, the *Pinta* encountered rudder problems and, after reaching the islands, repairs were made, while the sail riggings on the *Nina* were changed to a three-masted square and lateen combination. Before leaving the Canaries, the crews took on additional provisions and the water barrels were refilled. On 6 September, the small fleet steered west into the Atlantic under the royal flag of Castile and the expedition's banner of a white background with a green cross in the centre, and the letter F for the queen's husband, Ferdinand II of Aragon, on the left side, and Y for Isabella on the right, topped with two crowns. Sailing into unknown waters posed new problems for Columbus with the navigation and control of the flotilla. The ships travelled at different speeds, and the captain-general ordered his two captains to close up on the *Santa Maria* at sunrise and sunset to prevent losing contact with them. Columbus and the pilots of the two caravels navigated by dead reckoning, using compasses, time and estimated speed to determine their position and distance navigated, while meeting frequently to compare calculations.

They steered into fair weather, with calm seas and constant winds. Life on the ships was monotonous for the crews, with the daily routine of keeping the decks clear and clean, setting sails, scrubbing the rails, repairing gears and ropes and standing watch, while enduring cramped space and poor food. On the evening of 25 September, an island was sighted and Columbus altered his direction to the south-west. However, by the next morning, without finding land, he ordered his flotilla to resume its western course. The seamen had been out of sight of land for over twenty days, and on 3 October the men on the *Santa Maria* began demanding the captain-general turn back for Spain. To quell the growing dissent, Columbus met with the Pinzon brothers, asking their opinion. The Pinzons were totally supportive of continuing the journey, and the three vessels kept sailing to the west. Columbus was highly religious and strongly believed God had given him the mission to bring His word to the heathen people of the Indies. He was obsessed by the quest to explore the west and open Asia to Christianity.

As the three ships ploughed through the blue waters of the Atlantic and the seamen talked increasingly about returning to Spain, during the evening of 7 October, large flocks of birds were seen flying toward the south-west. Believing the sightings to be an indication of nearby Asia, Columbus ordered his vessels to change course to the south-west. After three days there was still no land and the sailors became more mutinous. To subdue the growing unrest, Columbus agreed to turn back after several more days if the Indies were not discovered. With the assistance of the Pinzon brothers, the crews agreed and the expedition continued into the unknown.

The eastern winds now blew stronger, carrying the fleet faster through the pounding dark blue waters as the sailors began to see the first signs of land when tree branches with green leaves were sighted. In the twilight of 11 October, the sun set on a clear horizon as the north-eastern winds continued to blow harder. As the evening watches took their posts, Columbus encouraged them to keep a sharp lookout. The night was cloudless, with a late-rising moon. The ships pushed forward through the tossing and battering sea as the lookouts high in the riggings strained their eyes in the golden light of the moon. Around 2 am on 12 October, Rodrigo de Triana on the *Pinta* saw a white sandy beach and shouted, 'Land, land'. In the early morning light, the island was plainly visible to the crewmen, while Columbus guided his flotilla around the southern tip of the landmass, finding a shallow bay on the western coast to anchor his vessels. The newly discovered island was located at 74° 40' west longitude and 24° north latitude in the Bahama Archipelago. As the captain from Genoa prepared to set foot on a New World, he believed his expedition had reached the outer islands of Asia.

Columbus assembled a landing party and in the early afternoon was rowed ashore carrying the royal flag of Castile, while the Pinzon brothers held the expedition's banner. Reaching the beach, Columbus claimed the island in the Bahamas chain for the Spanish crown and named it San Salvador, while assuming the title Admiral of the Ocean Sea. The land was inhabited by natives from the Arawak tribe, who slowly came out of the tropical forest to greet the strange foreigners. Columbus assumed he was near India and called the naked inhabitants with bodies painted red, white or black, Indians. The Arawaks were friendly and eager to trade any of their possessions. The Spanish took special notice of the natives' gold ear ornaments. For two days, the Spaniards explored San Salvador, while trading glass beads and hawks' bells with the Arawaks. The land was flat and covered by a dense forest of trees and underbrush, but no gold or spices were discovered. Columbus needed to take back to the queen's court large amounts of gold or tradeable commodities to make his voyage a success, and the Indians assured him by sign language that there were sizeable quantities of the precious metal on other islands.

After spending two days exploring San Salvador, on 14 October the Spanish fleet departed with six local guides to search for other lands. During the next several days, as the seamen sailed south, additional islands were found, but they were similar to San Salvador. The Indians kept assuring the admiral that the next one would have great quantities of gold. As the flotilla continued looking for the precious metal, Columbus learned of a large island called Cuba and became convinced that it must be Japan or part of China. With the Arawaks guiding his ships, he made his way to the large island, and on 23 October anchored in a beautiful harbour ringed with trees covered with flowers and fruits. He sent a landing party ashore to look for signs of the Japanese or Chinese and gold, but the Spanish were unsuccessful. The next day he renewed his quest, steering along the eastern shoreline and stopping at present-day Puerto Gibara. The expedition remained on the Cuban coast for the next twelve days as Columbus searched for the Asians. The admiral continued to talk with the local natives through sign language, and believed he had been told that the Great Khan could be found in the interior. He sent a small delegation to the imperial city with his royal letters from the Spanish monarchs and gifts to announce his presence. While his men were gone, the crews were ordered to collect plants that could be used for trading. The sailors gathered specimens of what they thought were aloe, cinnamon and gum mastic. Following a four-day wait, the members of the embassy returned on 5 November, reporting they had only located a village of about fifty huts but no signs of the Khan or gold.

Undeterred by the report of his ambassadors, Columbus renewed his search for gold, which the Cubans said was in large quantities on an island called Babeque to the east. As he explored the coast of Cuba, Martin Alonso Pinzon took the *Pinta* without authorization, sailing to look for Babeque. The admiral continued along the shoreline with his two vessels, stopping in numerous harbours reconnoitring for gold and signs of the Asians. Throughout his explorations, Columbus found the local Taino tribe to be friendly and noted in his diary that 'the Indians ought to make good and skilled servants and can easily be made Christians for they seem to have no religion'. Early in the morning of 5 December, the two ships reached the easternmost point of Cuba and Columbus pushed on, crossing the Windward Passage to discover the large island of Hispaniola On 6 December, he anchored the *Santa Maria* and *Nina* at the harbour of modern-day St Nicolas.

Following a brief stay at St Nicolas, Columbus resumed his voyage, reconnoitring the northern shoreline, while observing the beautiful tropical forest and vegetation. The westward wind carried the Spanish into Moustique Bay, where Columbus anchored his two ships. A search party was sent ashore and found a large village with over 1,000 inhabitants, but no gold. As the Spanish renewed their exploration, on 16 December, Columbus was visited by the local chief, escorted by hundreds of his natives. The chief boarded the *Santa Maria* to meet Columbus while the vessels remained moored off the beach. They shared some food and exchanged gifts of friendship in the admiral's cabin, Columbus being impressed by the noble behaviour and dignity of the chief.

The *Santa Maria* and *Nina* renewed their explorations, anchoring on 20 December at Acul Bay. As the ships stayed in the bay, Columbus received a message from Guacanagari, chief of the Cacicazgo tribe in the Marien region of modern-day north-western Haiti, inviting the Spanish to visit him in his capital at Caracol Bay. Guacanagari was one of five chiefs who ruled and governed the island. On 24 December, the two vessels set out for the chief's village. However, the winds were calm and little progress was made. During the night, disaster struck the expedition when the *Santa Maria* drifted into a coral reef, becoming grounded. As the ship remained on the reef, holes were ripped into its bottom, with water rushing in. The crews, with help from the warriors sent by Guacanagari, tried to free the *Santa Maria* from the reef, but could only salvage some equipment, supplies and stores.

Columbus believed the loss of his flagship was a message from God telling him to establish a colony in Hispaniola, and on 26 December preparations were begun for part of the crew to remain in the new settlement. He met with Guacanagari, and while dining with him received his approval to erect a fort near his village. Before leaving the island, Columbus ordered his sailors to fire a small cannon to impress the chief with the power of European weapons and ensure his continued loyalty and friendship. Construction of the fort, named La Navidad, began, and thirty-nine men volunteered to stay on the island. The stockade was quickly built with timber from the *Santa Maria*, while the volunteers were issued instructions to search Hispaniola for gold and locate a site for a future permanent settlement. Following a final meeting with Guacanagari and a festive celebration, at sunrise on 4 January 1493, the *Nina* set sail for Spain, leaving the first European colony in the New World.

The wind pushed the Spaniards east along the northern coast of what Columbus still believed was Japan, and on 6 January the lookout spotted the *Pinta* ahead. The two caravels anchored close to each other and the admiral met with Martin Alonso Pinzon, who offered several excuses for his insubordinate conduct during the past three weeks. To prevent dissent among his crews jeopardizing the return voyage, Columbus did not press the issue with Pinzon. While waiting for the breeze to change direction, Columbus left the *Nina* to explore the Rio Yaque del Norte River by boat, finally finding quantities of gold upriver. On 8 January, with a favourable wind, the small flotilla headed home, the admiral carrying back to the Spanish court specimens of gold, pods of chilli, cinnamon, tobacco and natives from the Taino tribe.

In mid-January 1493, Columbus left the coast of Hispaniola, setting a course east by north-east for Spain. He was forced to sail farther north before finding a constant wind from the west. During the journey, the crews had only bread and sweet potatoes to eat, with wine to drink, and there were worrisome periods of calm, while the *Pinta* had problems with its mainmast. In early February, the weather turned bitterly cold, with winds gusting at gale strength smashing large white-capped waves dangerously against the vessels. As the two captains fought to keep their ships from capsizing, the caravels became separated during the night of 14 February, compelling Pinzon to find his own way to Spain with the *Pinta*. As the winds blew stronger, the mariners on the *Nina* vowed to make a pilgrimage to a holy shrine if they survived the voyage. The winds slowly diminished, and early on 15 February the lookout sighted land.

Contrary winds kept the Spanish at sea for three more days, but finally on 18 February 1493, Columbus reached land. He sent his boat ashore, where his crewmen learned from the inhabitants they were on the island of Santa Maria in the Portuguese-controlled Azores chain. While the *Nina* anchored in the harbour at Our Lady of the Angels, officials from the town brought fresh supplies to the caravel and told Columbus that their captain would meet with him in the morning. Early the next day, Columbus sent half of his seamen ashore to the local chapel to give thanks and penitence for their survival. In the church, the men were arrested by the Portuguese captain and put in prison. When the island commander approached the *Nina*, threatening the remainder of the crew with seizure, Columbus ordered the ship to sail out to sea. Three days later he returned to Santa Maria, agreeing to talk with a delegation from the captain, which examined his papers and vessel, determining that the Spanish had not been on an illegal trading expedition to western Africa. The captured sailors were released and the caravel reprovisioned by the Portuguese.

The homeward voyage was renewed on 24 February, the northern breeze driving the *Nina* toward St Vincent Cape on the south-western coast of Portugal. As the admiral moved closer to Spain, the wind shifted from the north-east, blowing the caravel in the wrong direction for three days. Finally, late on 2 March, the wind came from the north again, putting the ship back on course, but during the night the crew was hit by a fierce storm. The force of the squall ripped the foresail to pieces, compelling Columbus to continue with a bare mast. The vessel rolled and pitched in the violent ocean, driving the seamen dangerously close to the shoreline of Portugal as streaks of lightning lit the sky. Columbus manoeuvred the *Nina* on a southerly heading, and as day broke found the entrance to Lisbon via the Tagus River. While the men of the *Nina* battled the storm, Martin Alonso Pinzon avoided the worst of the squall and made his way to landfall in north-western Spain at Bayana. He rejoined Columbus at Palos in mid-March.

By mid-morning on 4 March, the caravel was safely anchored near Lisbon. Columbus sent a message to King John II, asking permission to remain and refit his ship. Four days later he received the king's reply, which invited him to court and agreed to provide any necessary supplies and equipment. Columbus travelled to the royal residence with several crew members and the six Indians, meeting John II and dispelling his suspicions that the new discoveries were made in lands claimed by the Portuguese throne. Following several days at court discussing his expedition and the recently found lands, the admiral and his escort returned to the refitted *Nina*, and on 13 March sailed south down the Portuguese coastline, past St Vincent Cape and up the Rio Tinto River, dropping anchor at Palos two days later to end his historic seven-month venture of discoveries in the New World.

From the region of Andalusia, Columbus wrote to Queen Isabella and King Ferdinand II in Barcelona, announcing his return and describing his expedition and discoveries. While he waited for his summons to court, the monarchs sent envoys to the Vatican, asking Pope Alexander VI to recognize their sovereignty over Columbus' newly found lands. The pope issued four bulls granting the Spanish crown control over all the area Columbus had explored, and extended its claims to the region along the meridian 300 miles from the Azores, with all territories to the west belonging to Spain. Columbus stayed in Palos for a short time with several officers and sailors from the *Nina*, along with the six Indians from Hispaniola, before establishing his residence in Seville. In early April, he received a letter from Ferdinand II and Isabella ordering him to appear at their court in Barcelona. The admiral travelled across Spain, with the six Tainos, crewmen and caged green parrots attracting large crowds at each town. They reached the royal court in mid-

April, entering the great hall at the Alcazar Palace with the Indians dressed in their native clothing. Columbus approached the throne in a ceremony of great pomp and splendour, kneeling before the two sovereigns. He discussed his journey and explorations with Isabella and Ferdinand II, describing the beauty of the islands, available trading opportunities and friendliness of the natives, while answering their multitude of questions, before retiring to the royal chapel to give thanks for the success of the venture. Columbus remained with the Spanish monarchs for over a month, attending state dinners and private banquets and taking part in religious festivals, while making plans for his second voyage. Before leaving Barcelona, Columbus was further rewarded by the crown with the grant of letters patent recognizing him as a nobleman, with a coat of arms adorned by the castle of Castile, lion of Leon and symbols of an archipelago, along with the five anchors of an admiral.

While in Barcelona, Columbus began planning his second voyage to Hispaniola. He was eager to establish a permanent colony on the island, relieve the thirty-nine seamen left behind and continue his search for gold. Isabella and Ferdinand fully supported his return to the newly discovered lands, issuing instructions to Columbus for the governing of the settlement, treatment and conversion to Christianity of the Indians and the creation of a royal monopoly for all trading activities. In mid-June, he travelled to Seville to assemble his mariners and ships. With news of the success of the first expedition quickly spreading throughout Spain, Columbus had little difficulty recruiting the 1,200 men needed for the second venture. As his fleet of seventeen ships gathered at Cadiz, the colonists brought horses, cows and sheep along with wheat seeds and apple and citrus trees to establish a farming community. The flotilla was made up of carracks, caravels and some small barques for coastal water exploration. Columbus chose another carrack, *Santa Maria the Gallant,* as his flagship. On 25 September 1493, the sailors, soldiers, farmers, traders, gentlemen adventurers and six clerics boarded the vessels, departing from Cadiz to the south and sailing to their first destination in the Canary Islands.

On 5 October, the fleet anchored at the island of Gomera in the Canary Islands chain, replenishing provisions before beginning the Atlantic crossing eight days later. Columbus set his course to the south-west, encountering fair weather throughout the voyage across the open sea of deep blue waters. After twenty-one days at sea, the lookout sighted land on 3 November, which Columbus named Dominica. A second island, Santa Maria la Galante, was discovered later in the day. When Columbus sent a landing party ashore to explore, the men found a small village of the Carib tribe. As the mariners searched the huts, they found human remains. During his first expedition, Columbus had heard stories of the cannibalistic Carib tribe, and the discoveries of his sailors and soldiers confirmed the rumours.

Columbus continued his expedition, finding additional islands to the north-west. On 14 November, the flotilla anchored at Salt River Bay on the island named Santa Cruz by the admiral. He sent twenty-five men to explore the island in the afternoon, and while reconnoitring inland they clashed with four Carib warriors, who held two Arawak boys prisoner. The Spanish fired their arquebuses and drew their swords, attacking the cannibals, killing them and freeing their captives. Following the encounter with the Caribs, Columbus changed his course to a more northerly direction, discovering a large chain of islands he called the Eleven Thousand Virgins, the present-day Virgin Islands.

The admiral explored the Virgin Islands using the small caravels and barques, sending them east into shallow waters, while the bigger carracks sailed into deeper seas to the north, reconnoitering two larger islands, St Thomas and St John. On 19 November, the fleet was reunited near St Thomas, resuming its voyage to the west and discovering modern-day Puerto Rico. Columbus travelled along the mountainous southern coast of the island, anchoring at Ariasco Bay. A search party was sent ashore but found only a deserted Taino village. The fierce Caribs occupied the eastern region of Puerto Rico and the Arawaks had fled the village, believing the Spanish were their deadly enemy. On 22 November, the flotilla crossed the Mona Passage, making landfall in eastern Hispaniola. Columbus continued along the northern shoreline, and five days later anchored at Caracol Bay, where he had left his outpost with thirty-nine men eleven months earlier. As the vessels lay in the bay, they were approached by a canoe with several Indians sent by chief Guacanagari. When questioned about the fate of the settlers, Columbus was told they had become aggressive while searching for gold and women to enslave, and were massacred by natives from the mountain tribe of chief Caonabo. The Spaniards guarding the fort were then attacked and killed, while the settlement was destroyed.

After the murder of his men, it became increasingly important for Columbus to choose a secure site for his new settlement. He took his fleet along the coast searching for a protected location. On 2 January 1494, he anchored his seventeen ships in a sheltered bay and began preparations to build his permanent trading colony on a flat plain with little water, naming it after Queen Isabella. The colonists were landed and the town laid-out with a square plaza at the centre of a grid of streets. The settlers cleared the land, cut trees, dug a canal to channel freshwater to Isabella and fashioned stones from coral, while building temporary huts. During January construction on the outpost slowed when many workers became ill from malaria and malnutrition. While the work on Isabella continued, the admiral sent two armed parties to explore the fertile Cibao region in the current-day central Dominican Republic, searching for gold and spices. As the Spaniards reconnoitered the Vega Real Valley of the island, they found large nuggets of gold in the streams and rivers.

With several hundred of his settlers sick and provisions running low, Columbus was forced to send twelve of his ships back to Spain for new supplies. He chose Antonio de Torres to command the returning fleet, giving him a letter for the two sovereigns requesting additional men, farm animals, Spanish food and wine, tools, seeds, plants and clothing. In his report he discussed the construction of the settlement and recent island discoveries, while exaggerating the presence of spices for trading and the amount of gold found. He also suggested that additional money could be generated by exporting Indian slaves to Spain.

While Torres was in Spain, Columbus personally led a large force of 500 soldiers and adventurers into the interior in search of gold in mid-April. The men were dressed in head and chest armour and marched in military formation to the beat of drums. They soon came upon a vast rich green valley, which they named the Royal Plain. With friendly Indians as their guides, the explorers pushed on through the dense forest and heavy underbrush, discovering a plateau overlooking the Rio Janico River. Fifty soldiers were detached from the expedition with orders to construct an earthen fort and continue looking for gold in the area. The admiral moved deeper inland, hunting for the precious metal in the stream and river beds but finding none. The only gold brought back to camp after twenty-nine days of reconnoitering was acquired through trading with the natives.

Before leaving on his expedition into the interior of Hispaniola, Columbus appointed his brother, Diego, as interim governor for Isabella. As the colonists struggled at the unhealthy site with hot weather, harsh conditions, bad food and no opportunity to search for gold, dissent spread throughout the camp. Diego was unable to control the men and mutiny threatened to erupt. When Columbus returned to the settlement, he ordered several troublemakers placed in irons and all weapons seized to enforce order. He attempted to raise morale by organizing another expedition to hunt for gold in the interior under the command of Alonso de Ojeda, a court favourite of Queen Isabella.

As Ojeda's soldiers and gentlemen adventurers moved inland, initiating a ruthless campaign of stealing gold from the Indians and enslaving them, Columbus sailed from the settlement on 24 April to renew his exploration of Cuba. He still believed the island was part of the Chinese mainland and was eager to find the Great Khan. Four days later, the small fleet of three vessels crossed the Windward Passage, landing on the eastern cape of Cuba. He was rowed ashore with the flag of Spain blowing in the wind, claiming the land for the crown of Isabella and Ferdinand II. He steered along the southern coast for 50 miles, discovering several large sheltered harbours. The seamen continued to explore along the shore, finding friendly natives but no gold. In early May, the flotilla left Cuba, changing course to the south-west and encountering strong winds. The sailors ploughed on through the pounding sea, discovering the island of Jamaica. The Spaniards anchored their three ships at present-day St Ann's Bay, where they were soon attacked by seventy natives from their dugout canoes. As their arrows threatened the Spanish crews, Columbus fired a cannon shot at the Indians, scattering them in a wild fury of paddling back to shore. After continuing west and still finding hostile natives but no gold, Columbus returned to Cuba.

The Spanish resumed their exploration of the southern Cuban coastal region, while Columbus continued to look for signs of the Chinese and their great cities of gold. As the sailors moved along the shoreline, marvelling at the beautiful mountain ranges with their rugged hills and peaks and the white beaches with their mangrove trees, marshes and great flocks of bright red flamingoes, the natives welcomed the strange visitors in their great white ships. The fleet navigated west, searching for gold and the Chinese, but with provisions nearly gone, the vessels leaking and the crewmen increasingly discontent, on 3 June Columbus ordered his men to return to the settlement on Hispaniola.

As the three caravels sailed east, they struggled against the prevailing westerly winds and strong currents. Columbus could make little headway and changed course to the south, heading to Jamaica. He sailed around the western tip of the island, exploring the southern coastline. The natives, dressed in lavish multi-coloured headdresses of parrot-feathers and little else, were friendly, providing provisions and water. On 19 August, the flotilla rounded the eastern cape, crossing the Windward Passage toward Hispaniola. At Saona Island, Columbus anchored his three ships to ride out an approaching hurricane. After the storm passed, the fleet continued along the southern coast. As Columbus entered the Mona Passage, he became ill from exhaustion, overexertion and inadequate food. Unable to command the

24

expedition, the three captains took the vessels to Isabella, anchoring on 29 September. The admiral was so weak that he had to be carried ashore by the flagship's officers.

When Columbus reached the settlement, he found his brother, Bartholomew, who had been sent by the Spanish crown with a relief fleet of three ships. While Columbus was regaining his health, he had to intervene against the reoccurring dissatisfaction of the settlers. During the admiral's absence, Diego had been unable to quell the escalating uprising of the colonists and a rebellious faction seized several of Bartholomew's caravels, returning to Spain. Reaching home, the malcontents spread derogatory stories about the Columbus brothers at court and around the country. Later in the year, Antonio de Torres was sent to Hispaniola by the monarchy with four caravels carrying provisions and supplies for the settlers and a private letter for Columbus. The queen and king had become aware of the ongoing misadministration in the town and urged Columbus to return to court.

The admiral refused to accept the invitation, becoming determined to regain control of the settlement and establish a profitable export trading outpost. Unable to find enough gold to make his colony lucrative, he ordered his soldiers to collect and enslave large numbers of Indians for sale in Spain. As Torres prepared to return home at the end of February 1495, Columbus' troops had captured 1,500 Tainos; over 500 were loaded on the ships, while those remaining were given to the settlers or set free. During the voyage to Spain, over 200 of the Indians died, while some 300 were sold in Seville as slaves.

The Indians on Hispaniola reacted to the aggression of the Spanish by uniting several tribes under chief Gumtiguana. He assembled a large force in the Vega Real, moving against the settlement. As the Arawaks approached the colony, Columbus met them at Puerto de los Hidalgos with over 200 soldiers and a unit of twenty cavalrymen. Some of the Spaniards were armed with arquebuses, and the loud sound of their firing frightened many of the Native Americans away, while the charge of the cavalry completely overwhelmed the remaining Indians.

The admiral intensified the war against the Arawaks, and by early 1496 had conquered the entire island. To collect more gold, he built several forts in the interior and the Spanish soldiers were ordered to force the Indians to search for the precious metal and deliver it in specified amounts. A system of grants was initiated, giving the colonists the right to settle the land and enslave the natives. As the Spaniards expanded their reign of escalating genocide, settlers returning to Spain began to complain to Isabella and

Ferdinand II. In response, the royal court sent Juan Aguade with a commission to investigate the reports. The commission arrived in late 1495, finding the number of settlers had been greatly reduced by desertion and disease, while the Indians had suffered a high death rate under Spanish occupation. As Aguade continued his inquiries, on 10 March 1496, Columbus took two ships, the *Nina* and *India*, returning to Spain to defend his administration of the settlement. He sailed on a more southerly route, fighting strong headwinds most of the way home. Following a long and difficult voyage, the two vessels made landfall on 8 June at Saint Vincent Cape in Portugal, and three days later Columbus' flotilla dropped anchor at Cadiz, ending the two-year and nine-month second expedition.

As Columbus remained in Cadiz, he wrote to the monarchs notifying them of his return from Hispaniola and informing them of his eagerness to discuss his second voyage. Unlike his arrival from the first expedition, he was not greeted with great acclaim and adulation by the regime or the Spanish people. The disillusionment of the settlers and failure to find Asia energized his critics and alarmed the crown. While waiting for his summons to court, he travelled to the Franciscan monastery of La Mejorada, spending part of the summer with the priests. On 12 July, he received a letter inviting him to the royal residence at Burgos.

In late October, the admiral set-out northward toward Burgos, travelling with several Indians and servants. Reaching the court, he was courteously received by Isabella and Ferdinand II, presenting them with an array of gifts from his Indies expedition. He gave the queen and king several beautiful birds, previously unknown animals and plants, Indian masks decorated with gold and large nuggets of the precious metal. They discussed his explorations of the newly discovered islands and conditions at the Isabella settlement. During their talks, Columbus made a request for a third voyage, outfitted with three ships to renew his search for China and five vessels with provisions and supplies for Hispaniola. After two unprofitable expeditions, Isabella and Ferdinand held out little hope of a successful third undertaking. However, with the Portuguese preparing a large, well-equipped voyage under the command of Vasco da Gama, and rumours that Henry VII of England was sending John Cabot by a northern route to the Indies, the sovereigns gave their approval to the new project.

Due to rapidly changing political events in Europe, Columbus was compelled to remain at Burgos with the royal court. While he waited at Burgos, preparations for the third voyage were delayed by the marriage of Princess Juana to Philip of Habsburg and war with France. Finally, by April

1497, the royal wedding had been held and the French conflict resolved, allowing arrangements for the new expedition to begin. Columbus was authorized to employ over 300 skilled workers to transform Hispaniola into a self-sustaining agrarian settlement. He was also to include in his colonists enough priests for the conversion and spiritual needs of the Indians. The land grant system previously initiated by Columbus was approved by the Spanish crown to ensure the steady flow of gold to the monarchy. Unlike the recruitment of settlers for the second voyage, the admiral had difficulty finding enough men for his outpost and was compelled to accept ten pardoned criminals. As he laboured to make all the necessary preparations, the unexpected death of the Spanish heir, Juan, further delayed his return to the Americas. Finally, in May 1498, the fleet was ready to sail and he began his third Indies expedition with six ships.

The fleet put to sea, heading to its first destination in the Canary Islands. After taking on fresh supplies and water, the three ships carrying the settlers and provisions sailed to Hispaniola, while Columbus took his remaining vessels to explore the region south of Hispaniola. He steered down the African coast to the Cape Verde Islands before swinging west with favourable strong breezes for the Atlantic passage. At mid-ocean, the winds died down and the ships drifted slowly in the current for eight days under the blistering hot equatorial sun. On 22 July, the trade winds finally picked up and the lifeless white sails billowed out, carrying the flotilla forward. On 31 July, after a voyage of twenty-four days, land was spotted, which Columbus called Trinidad. The Spaniards navigated along the southern coast, anchoring at modern-day Erin Bay. The sailors went ashore to refill the nearly empty water barrels and search the beaches for natives. On 2 August, the admiral continued exploring the shoreline of the island before manoeuvring north, attracted by the sight of lofty mountains. Crossing the Gulf of Paria, the crews spotted the northern coast of the South American continent, at present-day Venezuela, on 5 August. Travelling through the Paria Gulf, the Spanish viewed a land of beautiful mountain ranges where the rain forest vegetation stretched to the edges of the ridgelines. Two days later, the region was formally claimed for Spain by the ship's captain. As the flotilla remained anchored, local Indians in their canoes paddled out to the vessels and a lively barter ensued, with the Native Americans trading local fruits and beer for beads and hawks' bells. On 8 August, Columbus continued his exploration, discovering the islands of Grenada and Margarita before piloting north-west for Hispaniola and a reunion with his two brothers.

Before Columbus departed for Spain in March 1496, he had appointed his brother, Bartholomew, governor of Hispaniola. During the admiral's absence at the Spanish court, Bartholomew was again unable to control the growing rebellion among the settlers. When a new gold field was discovered in the southern part of the island, the governor transferred supplies and equipment from Isabella to the region to search for more gold. The Spaniards remaining at the settlement rose up in revolt at the loss of their equipment, which made it impossible for them to gather gold. During the time that Columbus was away, the insurgency spread throughout the island, as the administration of Bartholomew alienated the Spanish colonists and failed to protect the Indians. When Columbus returned in late August 1498, he found an escalating crisis in the colony. As he attempted to settle the uprising and restore order, in Spain the monarchs were besieged with loud complaints from disgruntled returning noblemen and settlers about conditions on the island. The Spanish regime appointed Francisco de Bobadilla as royal commissioner for Isabella, ordering him to Hispaniola with full powers to enforce crown policy.

When Bobadilla reached the colony and confirmed the reports of the discontented settlers, he arrested the Columbus brothers, sending them back to Spain for trial. In early October 1500, Christopher Columbus boarded a caravel in chains for the voyage back across the Atlantic. Near the end of the month he arrived in Cadiz and was taken to a monastery in Seville still in shackles. Six weeks later, the Columbus brothers were released from their chains and summoned to the royal court at the Alhambra in Granada, where they were promised justice by the monarchy.

While Christopher Columbus waited for the decision of the regime, he was occupied compiling two documents to justify his actions in the Indies and solidify his claims to the governorship of the new colony. He assembled in the *Book of Privileges* notarized copies of agreements, orders and letters relating to his grants of titles, offices and properties by the monarchy and papers dealing with his expeditions. A second collection, the *Book of Prophecies*, was filled with biblical passages and writings of church officials supporting the need to spread Christianity in alien lands. While Columbus remained in Granada, in September he finally received the ruling of the throne. Under the terms of the royal decree, he was allowed to retain his properties and titles of admiral and viceroy, but the office of governor for the Indies was withdrawn, while the decision for a fourth voyage was delayed.

Columbus was forced to languish without approval for a new expedition until March 1502. After receiving his licence from the royal government, he began preparations for the new voyage. A fleet of four caravels - *Capitana,*

Bermuda, Vizaina and *Gallega* (*Captain, Bermuda, Vizcazan and Galician*) - was assembled in Seville on 3 April, with a crew of 130 sailors. On 9 May, the ships departed from the harbour steering south-west toward the Canary Islands. Columbus anchored at the island of Gran Canarias, replenishing his provisions and drinking water before beginning the transatlantic passage on 25 May. The journey across the ocean was made with fair winds and little trouble, reaching Martinique three weeks later. The admiral remained on the island for three days, resting his crews and collecting water and food before sailing through the Antilles chain of islands and making his way to Hispaniola.

As part of Columbus' charter for the expedition, his fleet was prohibited from landing on Hispaniola; however, with an approaching hurricane, the ships were anchored on the southern coastline to ride out the storm. Once the hurricane blew past, he rested his men and repaired the damage to his vessels before putting to sea. The sailors navigated west across the Windward Passage and along the southern coast of Jamaica, before steering across the Caribbean Sea and making landfall on the Central American mainland in Honduras. Columbus was rowed ashore, claiming the land for Isabella and Ferdinand. He continued his voyage, manoeuvring slowly down the shoreline against the prevailing winds and exploring the coastal territory. While the flotilla struggled on, the weather became rainy, with thunder and lightning piercing the skies as sails became ripped and equipment and stores were lost overboard. After reaching Cape Gracas a Dios on 14 September, the winds changed direction and the seamen were steadily pushed forward by favourable breezes. After sailing over 100 miles, the vessels anchored at Rio Grande in current-day Nicaragua, taking on water and wood, while making repairs to the caravels. Columbus continued south, stopping at Puerto Limon in Costa Rica. A landing party was sent ashore and the men soon made contact with friendly natives from the Talamanca tribe. The explorers travelled inland with the Indians as guides, reporting substantial numbers of deer, pumas, monkeys and a large variety of birds, while finding a land with a dark and thick rain forest stretching to the edges of the grey sandy beaches.

On 5 October, Columbus resumed his voyage south, and after several days the expeditionary force paused in the Chiriqui Lagoon in modern-day Panama. The Spanish sailors remained in the lagoon for a few days, trading beads and hawks' bells for gold discs with Indians from the Guaymi tribe. Columbus continued along the coast during October, anchoring his flotilla several times to trade with the natives and make repairs to his leaking vessels, while marvelling at the gleaming white beaches in front of the hardwood rain forest that stretched inland to the base of a chain of rugged mountains. The weather now turned rainy again, with violent gales and strong winds pounding the fleet back and forth in the raging sea. The expedition was compelled to anchor in the harbour at Christobal to ride out the storm. During the last two weeks of December, the exhausted seamen suffered through the hardships of violent weather and shortages of food.

In early January 1503, the admiral reversed his course, sailing west in search of a site for his trading outpost. He anchored off the Belen River in Panama, making contact with the Ngabe tribe. Columbus decided to build his fortified settlement on a hill close to the river, naming it Santa Maria de Belen. While his men began construction, some of the Spaniards began stealing gold from the Ngabe Indians and taking their women. When the Ngabes became hostile, the admiral ordered the seizure of their chief, Quibian. However, Quibian escaped his captors, leading his warriors in an attack against the fort and forcing the Spanish to abandon their colony. On 16 April, the *Capitana, Bermuda* and *Vizaina* navigated from Belen, leaving the damaged and sinking *Gallega* behind.

As the Spanish seamen sailed east along the Panamanian coast searching for a passage to the mainland of China, their vessels began to severely leak from damage caused by shipworms. The crews had to bail water and work the pumps constantly to keep the ships afloat. Despite the efforts of the sailors, the *Vizaina* leaked so badly it was abandoned. Columbus managed to struggle down the shoreline toward the present-day Panama border with Colombia. While the expedition navigated along the coastline, the captains and navigators of the fleet calculated that Columbus had piloted too far east, exhorting him to change course to due north. On 10 May, the two remaining vessels passed Little Cayman Island west of Jamaica, and two days later landed on the Cuban island of Cayo Breton, where the flotilla was reprovisioned. Columbus resumed his voyage, manoeuvring his fleet east along the Cuban coast, but as the ships took on more water he was compelled to head into the open sea in a desperate attempt to catch a strong wind toward the colony in Hispaniola. However, the *Bermuda* and *Capitana* were now taking on so much seawater that the admiral was forced to steer for Jamaica. On 25 June, the sinking vessels entered St Ann's Bay, where they were beached in the sand, side by side.

With the two beached ships firmly secured to the shoreline, Columbus turned them into a fortress, constructing huts on the decks to shelter his 116 sailors. The Spaniards began trading with the Indians from a nearby village, bartering beads and hawks' bells for a steady supply of food. To maintain friendly relations with the Jamaicans, Columbus ordered his crewmen to remain at the settlement, sending only trusted men to deal with the Native Americans. There was virtually no chance of rescue by a vessel from Hispaniola, compelling Columbus to dispatch two dugout canoes to the island, fitted with masts and sails and manned by twelve sailors and twenty natives. In late July 1503, the two small boats, under the command of Diego Mendez, departed from Jamaica on the 180-mile journey. With a fair wind and the Indians paddling, the rescue party landed on the island of Navassa on the third day, only 30 miles from Hispaniola. The water containers were refilled, while the crews caught fish for food. The canoes put back to sea on the fourth day, reaching the coast of Hispaniola late in the day. The Spanish and natives continued along the shoreline before moving inland to search for the island's governor, Don Nicolas de Ovando. However, when Mendez located the governor, he was occupied with a military campaign to suppress the local Indians, and Columbus' seamen were forced to wait eight months before a ship was sent to Jamaica for them.

While Columbus waited for rescue, in early January 1504 a mutiny erupted among a faction of his men, led by Diego and Francisco Porras. The Porras brothers and nearly fifty mariners seized ten canoes and attempted to paddle to Hispaniola. As the mutineers reached open water, they were driven back by the strong easterly winds and compelled to return to Jamaica, living off the land and terrorizing the natives. While the Spanish remained stranded, the Indians stopped trading food to them when their surplus supplies became depleted. From his astronomical charts, Columbus knew an eclipse of the moon was soon to occur, telling the Jamaicans that his God was angry with them for not trading with the Christians and would send them a warning of his impending punishment. When the rising moon began to disappear during the eclipse, the natives became frightened, running frantically to the fort with food and promising to provide future provisions.

After waiting over eight months, in March 1504, a small caravel from Hispaniola arrived at St Ann's Bay. The ship had been sent by governor Ovando to report on the condition of Columbus and his men, but also brought a letter from Mendez stating that he was attempting to charter a relief vessel. The captain of the caravel had been ordered not to take any of Columbus' crew on board, sailing away and leaving the stranded expedition. With rescue now imminent, Columbus attempted to negotiate a reconciliation with the rebellious Porras' faction. However, the mutineers refused to discuss any resolution, unleashing an attack against the settlement. On 29 May, Columbus' men, armed with swords and knives, clashed with the rebels, driving them back in a spirited fight. Following the encounter with the Porras brothers, Columbus' mariners had to wait almost a month before Mendez's rescue ship finally arrived. On 29 June 1504, after a year at St Ann's, Columbus and his survivors boarded the small caravel steering north to Hispaniola.

Once Columbus reached Hispaniola, he chartered two ships and on 12 September sailed for Spain with twenty-four mariners from the fourth voyage. The long and difficult journey home took fifty-six days, but finally, on 7 November, the admiral reached the town of Sanlucar de Barrameda on the southern Spanish coast. He travelled up the Guadalquivir River, settling into a rented house in Seville. While resting from the ordeals of the thirty-month expedition, he wrote to the monarchy hoping for a summons to the royal court. However, Queen Isabella was seriously ill and Columbus was not called to meet with the sovereigns. The admiral felt abandoned by the crown, lobbying to have all his titles, offices and grants named in his licence restored. While Columbus had become wealthy from his share of the gold from his expeditions, he believed the regime had denied him his rightful privileges and franchises. Suffering from arthritis and deteriorating health, he was forced to send his two sons to court to defend his claims. Finally, in May 1505, Ferdinand II agreed to an audience and Columbus travelled north to the royal court at Segovia. He was graciously received by the king but was unable to negotiate a settlement to his rights. As his health continued to decline, he remained at court, following it to Salamanca and Valladolid, hoping to find justice. Christopher Columbus, admiral of the Ocean Sea, died on 20 May 1506, with his sons, brother Diego and a few faithful friends at his bedside.

SELECTED SOURCES:
Fernandez-Arrnesto, Felipe, *Columbus*.
Morison, Samuel Eliot, *Admiral of the Ocean Sea – A Life of Christopher Columbus*.
Morison, Samuel Eliot, *Christopher Columbus – Mariner*.
Morison, Samuel Eliot, *The Great Explorers – The European Discovery of America*.
Phillips, William D., and Phillips, Carla Rahn, *The Worlds of Christopher Columbus*.

John Cabot

In 1496, John Cabot received letters patent from King Henry VII of England for an expedition to discover a western trade route to the riches of Japan and China. With financial backing from Bristol merchants and London bankers, on 2 May 1497 he steered across the Bristol Channel, sailing west into the unknown waters of the Atlantic Ocean in the bark, *Matthew*, with a crew of eighteen seamen. Navigating the leaky wooden vessel in the northern latitudes of the ocean, the sailors made landfall at Newfoundland on 24 June after a voyage of fifty-four days. Cabot was rowed ashore holding the white English flag with the red cross of St George, claiming the territory for the throne of Henry VII and opening the regime's quest for a colonial empire. Back in England, he was hailed as the first European to reach the mainland of the North American continent since the Vikings landed on North America in the tenth century.

Cabot was born in 1450 in the independent Republic of Genoa, the son of a spice merchant. He spent his first ten years at the prosperous maritime city, helping his father in his business. In 1461, the Cabot family moved across the Italian peninsula to Venice, where they established a successful spice trading firm. Growing up in the two mercantile cities John Cabot was exposed to the constant flow of ships, sailors, travellers and goods from distant ports entering the harbours.

In the fifteenth century, Venice was a formidable sea power and commercial centre, strategically located on a trading route between East and West. Similar to Genoa, Venice was a prosperous republic governed by the Great Council, which was composed of over 200 members from the city's noble families. The daily administration of the government was handled by the Council of Ten, which elected the Doge as head of state. Venetian ships sailed the waters of the Mediterranean, dominating commerce with the East. While Venice expanded its territorial possessions in the Mediterranean, controlling a string of islands to Cyprus, the city's army began a campaign of conquest on the mainland of Italy. By 1428, Venice had extended its possessions south of the Alps in an unbroken stretch of land from the northern tip of the Adriatic Sea to the gates of Milan. John Cabot was present in Venice near the summit of its greatness, witnessing the constant flow of commerce at the harbour, with traders and goods from distant ports, thriving construction of vessels at the Arsenal and the rush of merchants through the canals and streets of the city. He viewed magnificent Renaissance palaces along the Grand Canal and ceremonies of great pageantry and ostentation at St Mark's Basilica and the Doge's Palace.

John Cabot continued to work in his father's business, learning the system of trading in Asian spices purchased from the eastern shores of the Mediterranean Sea, and through his many close relationships acquired a knowledge of several languages. Through his access and association with the city's merchants, seamen and tradesmen, he became skilled in navigation, geometry, astronomy, map-making and seamanship. By 1471, Cabot had become a respected and successful merchant and was accepted into the Society of St John the Evangelist, which was one of the city's most prestigious religious fraternities.

When Cabot was 26 years old, he applied for citizenship in Venice, and after satisfying the requirement for fifteen years of residency in the city, the Senate approved his petition by a unanimous vote, with the decree signed by the Doge, Nicolao Trono, on 28 March 1476. The resolution of the Venetian Senate read, 'That a privilege of citizenship both internal and external be made out for Ioani Caboto on account of fifteen years residence.' As a citizen of Venice, Cabot expanded his business interests, becoming involved in a variety of enterprises. He speculated in real estate, buying and selling houses, farmland and commercial properties, before serving as an agent for a Venetian mercantile firm. Several years later, Cabot was married to Mattea, and during their fourteen years of marriage they had three sons - Ludovico, Sebastian and Sancto.

Cabot now sailed extensively throughout the eastern Mediterranean and Middle East, visiting the spice markets in Alexandria, Egypt, ports on the Black Sea and travelling south to Mecca, trading luxury Asian goods. Travel for a European Christian to the holiest of Islam's shrines was dangerous, and it was likely that he was compelled to journey to Mecca dressed as a Muslim pilgrim. Mecca was a trading centre for the exchange of goods between the West and Asia, and Cabot was interested in learning the origins of eastern silks, spices, sugar and other Oriental luxury goods that were transported from China and Japan. During his many explorations in the Middle East, Cabot came into contact with Arab traders, discussing with them the source of their imports. He discovered from the merchants that their goods came great distances by ship and caravan from the East, causing him to consider that these far lands could be more easily reached from the western coast of Europe. By the second half of the 1480s, Cabot had become an experienced sailor and traveller, acquiring a broad education in navigation and seamanship, while developing into a skilled cartographer. He was familiar with the earlier travels of Marco Polo to the Far East and the recent discoveries of the Portuguese and Spanish explorers in new lands. From his extensive journeys, studies and discussions with seamen and traders, he concluded that the world was not flat and that the shortest route to the riches of the Orient was westward from Europe.

In 1490, Cabot, Mattea and their three sons left Venice, travelling to their new home in Valencia on the Spanish coast of the western Mediterranean. Cabot was eager to find financing for a voyage to the Indies by sailing west, and the Spanish and Portuguese were actively engaged in the exploration of new routes to Asia and its wealth. While in Valencia looking for an opportunity to meet with the regime's officials to promote his expedition to the west, he was hired by the town to design a new harbour, twice meeting with King Ferdinand II of Aragon to secure the crown's approval for the undertaking. In February 1493, the construction design was adopted by the government of Aragon, but as Cabot began preparations for the building of the port, the work was suddenly stopped for lack of funding. Following the loss of the harbour project, Cabot moved his family to Seville, where he was employed to build a stone bridge across the Guadalquivir River. He laboured on the bridge for several months before the town council also cancelled that construction.

In 1493, Christopher Columbus returned to Seville following his first transatlantic voyage, announcing his discovery of a new western route to the Indies. Cabot was in Seville at this time and likely witnessed Columbus' triumphant arrival. The stories of Columbus' expedition reinforced Cabot's desire to sail west, and he was granted an audience with King John II of Portugal. Since the patronage of Prince Henry in 1418, the Portuguese had been sending ships down the coast of western Africa in search of an eastern passage to Asia, and after Bartholomew Diaz rounded the tip of the continent in March 1488, the regime had no interest in financing Cabot's western venture.

Following his rejection by the Portuguese throne, Cabot met with Ferdinand II of Spain, discussing his plans to travel west to the Indies, but with Columbus' recent discoveries the crown had little enthusiasm for another project. While Cabot was in Spain, he had heard from local merchants that English explorers had made regular voyages in search of the island of Brasil, which was depicted on contemporary maps as located west of Ireland. Cabot believed that the new land might only be an island, but it could serve as an outpost on the journey to China, or could possibly be the northeastern coast of the Orient.

As the Spanish and Portuguese continued their voyages in search of a shorter passage to the wealth of China, Henry VII of England became attracted to sending vessels under his flag to claim a share of the rich Asian market. The city of Bristol was at the centre of the kingdom's Atlantic trading market, and to pursue his quest for an expedition Cabot decided to relocate his family there to take advantage of the growing interest of the regime. In early 1495, the Cabots arrived in Bristol in south-west England after sailing up the Avon River from the Bristol Channel. When Cabot reached the city, it had over 10,000 inhabitants and was surrounded by a fortified wall with reinforced gates and turrets. Bristol's survival depended on commercial trade, and the local merchants aggressively protected their businesses against outside interference. The medieval city was the kingdom's second most prosperous seaport after London, and being located on the west coast it served as the gateway to the Atlantic Ocean. It was built on hillsides that ran up from the river, and after arriving by sea Cabot and his family made their way along the narrow winding streets to the Genoese community. From his years of travel in the Mediterranean and the Middle East, Cabot had earned a reputation as a skilled and experienced seaman, and was welcomed by the Genoese. After consulting with the Italians, the Cabots settled with the immigrants in a rented house on St Nicholas Street. Bristol was home to England's most skilled Atlantic seamen, who had earlier made probing voyages into the northern waters of the Atlantic Ocean. From the early 1480s, English mariners from Bristol had made regular journeys into the higher latitudes in search of the island of Brasil, and during their explorations were reported to have found a new mainland. In Bristol, Cabot could hire sailors who had mastered the currents, winds and navigation necessary for a western passage.

The port of Bristol was ideally located as the headquarters for Cabot's planned expedition, with easy access to the sea, available ships and seamen experienced in making long voyages in the North Atlantic as far as Iceland. Through the local Genoese and English traders, sea captains and sailors, he learned about the difficulties and dangers of sailing and navigating in the cold northern Atlantic, with the threats of icebergs, strong storms and dense fog banks. To secure financial support for his venture from the English, Cabot travelled to London in early 1496, meeting with bankers and merchants from the Italian community. He found several backers interested in participating in the project, and through their intervention he was granted an audience with Henry VII. He arrived at court with his numerous maps, charts and exhibits, prepared to present his proposal for travel to the Indies by a shorter route to the west. When Cabot met the king, he discussed why Christopher Columbus had not reached Asia. He demonstrated on his maps that by sailing west along a more northerly latitude, his ships could reach the Orient more quickly and by a shorter course compared to the trade winds area in which Columbus had made his crossing. Cabot presented Henry with a draft of his requested charter, which petitioned the crown for permission to undertake an expedition, 'To seek out whatsoever isles, countries, regions or provinces of the heathen and infidels in whatever part of the world, which before this time have been unknown to all Christians.'

Henry had earlier received the brother of Christopher Columbus, Bartholomew, who made a similar proposal to sail west to China. The king showed little interest in financing Columbus' expedition, missing the opportunity to gain a share of the trade in the riches from Asia, and now considered Cabot's project very carefully. To gain access to commerce in the Orient, Henry agreed to sanction Cabot's expedition, but limited him to travelling west in the northern latitudes to avoid infringing on lands previously claimed by the crowns of the Portuguese and Spanish. On 5 March 1496, Cabot received his letters patent to navigate to the Indies by a western route under the flag of the English throne, which further stated, 'Authorizing Cabot, his sons, their heirs and their deputies to sail with five ships to the north, east and west.' Cabot was empowered to hold any newly discovered lands under the realm's name, and no other English subject was allowed to visit the region without his permission. The English king had given his approval for the voyage, but did not agree to fund it. Cabot was forced to seek financing from Bristol merchants and London bankers, and through the influence and contacts of his Bristol friends and traders, was able to secure enough money for one ship.

Cabot returned to Bristol from London and began making preparations for his Indies expedition. Lacking any prior knowledge of the dangerous waters of the North Atlantic, he talked to veteran seamen in the city and studied his charts and sailing instructions from pilot books to plan his course. The books provided useful navigational information on tides, currents, magnetic directions and astronomical data. A vessel in the bark class was chartered, and a crew of twenty men hired. As a foreigner with no prior experience in North Atlantic sailing and planning to explore the uncharted waters to China, when Cabot attempted to employ his mariners he was only able to recruit Englishmen of questionable skills. In the early summer of 1496, the sailors loaded equipment, supplies and provisions on the vessel and made ready to leave the harbour. As the summer sun rose over the horizon, Cabot's ship was towed down the Avon River into the Bristol Channel to wait for a favourable breeze from the east. After a short delay, the sails caught the winds, billowing out their white canvas and pushing the vessel into the Atlantic. The course was set to the west, passing south of Ireland into the open sea with a steady wind. Steering to the north and away from land, the weather became stormy as the white-capped waves battered the sides of the ship. As the storm grew steadily stronger, the seamen began talking about turning back, threatening to mutiny. The winds now blew harder, the sails were torn and tattered, and equipment was lost over the side. As the squall pounded the ship, Cabot was forced to return to Bristol. He managed to reverse his direction, steering back to Bristol harbour to end his disappointing first attempt to reach the Orient from the west.

Undeterred by the failure of his initial voyage to the Far East, Cabot spent the winter of 1497 preparing for a second expedition. While he still retained Henry VII's charter for the venture, he needed new financing. His first attempt had been met with only limited enthusiasm from the Bristol merchants and London bankers, and Cabot visited them again, trying to promote greater interest. Despite his repeated efforts through the winter months, he was able to raise enough money to fund an expedition with only one ship. In the early winter of 1497, he chartered the 50-ton *Matthew* from its Bristol owners for his undertaking. The *Matthew* was a relatively new bark, most likely constructed in Bristol and outfitted with a foremast, mainmast and rear mast rigged with square sails for navigating in trade winds against the prevailing breezes. The vessel was approximately 60 feet long and 20 feet wide, with a shallow draft for exploring shallow waters close to the shoreline. Sixteen Bristol seamen were recruited to man the *Matthew*. The crew included a ship's master, Genoese surgeon, navigator, carpenter, cook, cooper, steward and priest, along with the ordinary sailors. In April, the men began loading the *Matthew* with enough provisions for six or seven months at sea. Large quantities of dried fish, salted pork and beef, flour for baking bread, hardtack and many barrels of beer were stocked below the deck of the bark. Cabot planned to make an extended journey, carrying extra sails, riggings, ropes, timber and framing to replace broken or rotted pieces. The ship was equipped with the tools and materials needed to make any necessary repairs. During the western voyage, Cabot had no instruments for measuring the vessel's longitude or the east-west position, but was able to determine his latitude or north-south location from the equator by using an astrolabe to plot the stars and sun.

The loading of provisions, equipment and supplies took several weeks, and in early May the *Matthew* was ready for the voyage across the unknown dark green waters of the northern Atlantic to the Indies. The bark moved slowly down the Avon River to the Bristol Channel, and with an easterly breeze the sails unfurled as the vessel surged forward. As the ship caught the winds and ebbing tide, the *Matthew* began to pass westward through the Bristol Channel into the open sea. Once into the Atlantic, Cabot set his course north-west, steering through St George's Channel, stopping on the southern coast of Ireland at Dursey Head to refill his water barrels and provisions. After remaining in port for several days, on 22 May the ship sailed into the Atlantic Ocean, piloting up the Irish shoreline. Many sailors from Bristol had ventured into the North Atlantic as far as Iceland on earlier expeditions, discovering the direction of the winds and currents. By talking with these experienced mariners, Cabot had learned that the winds along the English coast blew predominately from the west, forcing him to first navigate to the north to pick up the easterly breezes.

The *Matthew* soon left the Irish coast behind as the fresh breezes filled the sails and Cabot steered into open waters. As the *Matthew* moved steadily to the northwest into the Atlantic, its progress was slowed by the constant westerly winds. While Cabot navigated through the tranquil ocean, the ship remained on a route familiar to the Bristol seamen sailing south of Iceland. At the more northerly latitudes, the direction of the winds changed from west to east, and the sails now pushed the *Matthew* forward at a faster speed. Despite the fair and mild weather, the lookout was warned to keep a sharp watch for floating icebergs as the moon hung low in the western skies in late May.

Sailing in the northern latitudes, the weather was cold, even during the summer months. Adding to the misery of the journey was the worm-infested food and cramped living spaces for the men. The flour and dried foods soon became riddled with numerous vermin and the water turned rancid. The men preferred sleeping on the deck under sails and tarps, but during inclement conditions were forced to stay below deck in the foul air. The seamen were occupied during the day cleaning the decks, making repairs, setting the sails and standing watch, while the navigator took compass readings, plotted the vessel's position by the sun and stars and estimated the ship's speed. During the night, the *Matthew* travelled in near total darkness, with only the light from a candle casting a dim, flickering glow over the deck by the helmsman's station. The crewmen were poor, with few possessions, working shoeless to gain a better grip on the wet deck and dressed in linen shirts and pants. Every crew member was Catholic, and with a priest onboard, Mass was held each day on the deck as the mariners asked for God's protection and guidance.

During early June, the *Matthew* continued to plough forward in a westerly direction with favourable winds. However, in the middle of the month the weather suddenly turned stormy, strong winds and waves battering the ship, while the sails were torn and ripped. The vessel rolled and pitched in the violent sea as Cabot and his crew rode out the gale. During the night, the storm began to diminish and in the morning the bright orange sun broke over the horizon, bringing an eastern breeze that drove the *Matthew* under full sails toward the expected coast of the Indies, as the mariners began to see the first signs of approaching land. After travelling for several more days, spotting birds in the air and floating branches in the ocean, in the early morning of 24 June, land was sighted ahead, rising out of the Atlantic. The first landmass the Englishmen saw was named St John's Island by Cabot in honour of St John the Baptist, the current-day Belle Isle near the coast of Labrador in Canada.

From St John's, the Englishmen could see a large landmass to the south, and as the ship steered closer, Cabot discovered the island of Newfoundland. He anchored the *Matthew* at Cape Bauld on the north-eastern tip of the island, while observing the Labrador mainland to the west. The captain assembled a small landing party and went ashore, claiming the land for Henry VII of England. Cabot was hailed as the first European to reach the North American mainland since the tenth century, when Viking ships reached there. The sailors erected a crucifix on the beach and raised the flags of England, Pope Alexander VI and Venice. Following the ceremony, the crewmen ventured inland on a trail for several hundred yards, locating a recently abandoned Indian campsite with remnants of a fire, wooden tools, snares for catching animals and needles for making fishnets. With only a handful of armed men, the Genoese captain felt unsafe in the strange country of dark, dense forest and, after filling his water barrels, returned to the *Matthew*, making no contact with the native inhabitants.

After returning to his ship, Cabot explored the northern coastline of Newfoundland, navigating offshore in an easterly direction. As the vessel sailed along the rocky shoreline down the eastern side of the island, Cabot with the aid of his son, Sebastian charted the land, noting the windswept mountain range to the west. The *Matthew* continued to the east and Cabot observed the many coves, protected bays, small inlets and forested islands found along the cliff-bound coast. He was particularly interested in the large quantities of fish, which would provide a new source of the product for the merchants of Bristol. Many contemporary writers told of the large quantities of cod found at Newfoundland, writing, 'The sea there is swarming with fish which can be taken not only with the net, but in baskets let down with a stone, so that it sinks in the water.' During the expedition, the lookouts sighted numerous icebergs and the seamen carefully steered around the dangerous obstacles, while struggling through numerous days of fog-covered seas. Cabot spent over a month reconnoitring the region, exploring and mapping the numerous harbours and bays as the ship sailed south-east. During the journey down the Newfoundland coast, the Englishmen were the first Europeans to investigate White Bay, Notre Dame Bay, Hamilton Sound and Bonavista Bay. As Cabot navigated further south, he explored the shoreline of current-day Trinity Bay and Conception Bay, making note of the temperate climate and forests of tall trees, writing in his logbook, 'Of the kind ships' masts are made'. After reaching Cape St Mary's at the bottom of Avalon Peninsula, he ended his expedition, ordering his men to sail north. As the Bristol sailors retraced their course, their captain surveyed several more harbours and coves bypassed on the outward passage. The Englishmen reached Cape Bauld in mid-July, refilling the water caskets and preparing the ship for the transatlantic journey home. On 20 July, Cabot began his return voyage to England, strongly convinced he had reached the outer islands of the Great Khan's realm.

As Cabot piloted toward England, the sails of the *Matthew* billowed out under the strong favourable breezes. Sailing away from Newfoundland, two new islands were discovered but were not explored. The ship steered a more direct course toward Europe, and with the predominately strong western winds of late July made landfall near the coast of Brittany in early August under the light of the moon's first quarter. During the return journey, the Bristol seamen became convinced that Cabot was navigating too far north, forcing him to change his route to the south and causing the vessel to sail past England. After landing at Ushant Island on the coast of France, John Cabot turned the *Matthew* to the north-west, navigating across the southern English Channel and arriving in Bristol on 6 August after an expedition of over two months.

Following his return to England, Cabot was hailed as a national hero for discovering a western route to China, and was greeted everywhere he travelled by large cheering crowds. The report of the voyage was recorded in the Bristol chronicle, stating, 'This year on St John the Baptist's Day the land of America was found by the merchants of Bristol in a ship called the *Matthew*; the said ship departed from the port of Bristol the second of May and came home again the sixth of August.'

Shortly after reaching Bristol, Cabot rode to London to report the discoveries of his expedition to the Tudor court. On 10 August, Cabot was granted an audience with Henry VII where he described his journey with maps, charts and a globe showing the course of the ship and locations of the newly-found lands. He related to the king that his ship had reached the kingdom of the Khan, and on his next voyage he intended to follow the coastline southward to Japan. The Duke of Milan's ambassador at the court of Henry VII wrote, 'He has the description of the world in a map, and also in a solid sphere, which he made and shows where he has been. He tells all this in such a way, and makes everything so plain, that I also feel compelled to believe him.' The Genoese captain was seeking the throne's funding and licence for a third expedition and greatly exaggerated the wealth of the island he visited, describing a region rich in tradeable goods. The king was greatly impressed with Cabot's presentation and seized the opportunity to expand the English presence and trading opportunities in the riches of the Indies, while challenging the Spanish in the West with an incursion into their claimed territory. The Spanish ambassador at the English court wrote to Queen Isabella and King Ferdinand II, 'Having seen the course they are steering and the length of the voyage, I find what they have discovered or are in search of is possessed by Your Highnesses. I told the king that I believed the islands claimed were those found by Your Highnesses.' To the Spanish monarchy, the purpose of Cabot's third journey was to return to the newly discovered lands and establish an English trading outpost with Cathay. Cabot was promised another expedition in the spring of 1498 with a fleet of ten vessels to explore new territory for England.

In December, the royal crown granted Cabot an annual pension of £20 in recognition of his accomplishment. He received numerous honours and was now called 'admiral' by the court. While he waited for his charter, Henry VII was distracted by a revolt in Cornwall led by Perkin Warbeck and the threat of invasion from Scotland by King James IV. By early October, Warbeck had surrendered and the Scots had been driven back across the border, allowing the king to address Cabot's request for a new expedition. On 3 February 1498, the Tudor throne issued letters patent to Cabot for a voyage to explore the Atlantic Ocean to the west and establish trading relations with Japan and China in the name of the English regime. The charter further authorized

JOHN CABOT

Cabot to 'Impress six English ships of 200 tons or smaller burden, to conduct them to the lands and Isles late found by said John, and to take with him out of the realm any of the king's subjects who would go on the voyage.'

After receiving his charter in early 1498, Cabot was occupied for the next several months with preparations for his third western journey into the Atlantic, which was much better funded than his first two transatlantic voyages. The Tudor crown agreed to deliver one fully provisioned vessel, and Cabot visited merchants in Bristol and London to arrange financing for several more. The admiral told his investors he planned to cross the Atlantic and, after arriving at his 1497 landfall, continue on a south-westerly course until his fleet reached the kingdom of the Great Khan, which was considered the source of all spices and jewels. After holding discussions with the admiral, the investors pledged to invest in the enterprise, providing funds for four ships. As part of their contract, Cabot agreed to take merchandise for trade with the Japanese and Chinese. With the money for the project secured, the admiral returned to Bristol to begin negotiations with local ship masters for his flotilla. He chartered four vessels from Bristol owners which were outfitted with provisions, equipment and supplies from London and local merchants. The king equipped the fifth bark, which was hired from London financiers. The vessel supplied by Henry II was the largest bark and Cabot made it his flagship.

While Cabot was making arrangements for his barks, he started hiring a crew of Bristol seamen. Preparing to undertake a voyage into the uncharted waters of the Atlantic to Japan and China and requiring a sizeable crew to man his five ships, he encountered resistance in recruiting experienced sailors from Bristol and the surrounding area. However, under the terms of his charter with King Henry II, paroled prisoners were available to meet the shortfall. By April, the five vessels were chartered and enough provisions for a year loaded in the holds. Trade merchandise to establish a trading centre on the coast of China was part of the expedition's cargo at the insistence of the English merchants, and their four small vessels were stocked with coarse cloth caps, lace and other trifles. As the English prepared to sail, the Milanese ambassador wrote to his patron, 'Cabot proposes to keep along the coast from the place at which he touched, more and more towards the east, until he reaches an island which he calls Cipango [Japan] situated in the equinoctial region, where he believes that all the spices of the world have their origin, as well as the jewels, and they will go to that country and form a colony. By means of this they hope to make London a more important market for spices than Alexandria.' In early May, the English fleet slipped its moorings in the

Bristol harbour to begin the expedition to the riches of the Orient by a new, faster western route compared to the longer eastern course explored by the Portuguese around the tip of Africa.

The five barks, manned by over 100 seamen, were towed down the Avon River, catching favourable winds and sailing into the St George Channel, as the motionless white sails suddenly swelled out and the fleet slowly increased its speed. The men made a brief stopover in southern Ireland to refill the water barrels and take on provisions before steering into the Atlantic, setting a course similar to the second expedition and navigating in a north-western direction toward the coast of southern Iceland. During the voyage in the open sea, the skies began to blacken with dark grey clouds and streaks of lightning pierced the darkness, as Cabot's flotilla was struck by a powerful storm. As the vessels rolled and pitched in the pounding waves, one of the ships became severely damaged, having to turn back to Ireland. The remaining four barks continued into the full fury of the squall as the fierce winds and pounding seas grew stronger and more dangerous. Cabot and his four crews fought to save their vessels but were never seen again, disappearing in mid-ocean.

The fate of the four ships and over 100 seamen has been the subject of much speculation, with historians generally agreeing on four possible scenarios. The majority of researchers believe the vessels continued to sail to the north-west into the gale, and were destroyed during the violent storm, with all hands lost. There are several contemporary letters supporting this option. An Italian ambassador wrote, 'They are on the very bottom of the ocean.' The second possibility suggests Cabot returned to England in 1499 in disgrace following the failure of his expedition, and his death was never reported. The king's pension continued to be paid until 1499, which indicated the Tudor crown considered him dead at that date. No historical records have been located on any of the four ships to support the alternative that any of them returned.

Evidence has been found that supports a third alternative, indicating that Cabot and his fleet survived the storm, landing in north-eastern Newfoundland and priests from the expedition establishing a religious community for the Augustinian Order of the Carbonara on the island at Carbonear. Further clues suggest the ships continued their voyage from Newfoundland, sailing down the North American continent and reaching the coast of South America in present-day western Venezuela.

Following Cabot's 1497 voyage to Newfoundland, King Manuel I of Portugal began financing expeditions to the North Atlantic in search of new lands. In May 1500, Gaspar Corte-Real was issued a charter for a voyage with one vessel to explore the northern latitude region. He set a course to the north-west, making landfall at Greenland in the vicinity of Cape Farewell. The following year he returned with three caravels, attempting to reach the territory sighted the prior year. However, the sea was still frozen, forcing the Portuguese to change direction to the south-west. The Portuguese flotilla crossed the Davis Strait, landing on the east coast of Newfoundland. Corte-Real led a search party ashore to reconnoitre the interior, and during his exploration was reported to have found Indians on the island with a broken sword and two silver Venetian earrings, implying the natives had earlier acquired the three items from Cabot's crew.

As Cabot and his crewmen supposedly built a settlement and remained on the coast of western Venezuela, the Spanish continued to explore the lands discovered and claimed by Columbus on his four expeditions. In 1499, Queen Isabella and King Ferdinand II sent Alonso de Ojeda with a small fleet to explore the northern shoreline of South America. He was issued letters patent from the crown for a voyage to map the coastline and end the exploration activities of the English in the region claimed by Spain, while renewing the quest for the North-west Passage. Ojeda departed from Spain with three caravels in May, sailing south along the coast of Africa before turning west and landing in eastern Venezuela. The Spanish steered along the continental shoreline in search of a route to China. The ships sailed west, anchoring at the islands of Curacao and Aruba before investigating the Gulf of Venezuela in August. The vessels' navigators made a detailed reconnaissance of the coastline, noting locations for future trading settlements. As the Spanish navigated the large gulf, they encountered Englishmen settled near the shore. Since there were no new transatlantic crossings from England prior to 1500, if the reports of Ojeda's expedition are true, the strangers can only be identified as members of John Cabot's crews.

Several secondary sources propose a fourth possibility, suggesting Cabot and his vessels weathered the storm and continued across the Atlantic. According to these letters, the English fleet reached the North American mainland before turning south and navigating down the coast, exploring the region as far as the current-day Carolinas before returning to England. This fourth alternative could have been drawn from the same information as the third option. However, no contemporary sources have been found supporting the scenario, and if Cabot had returned to England after such a triumphant voyage it would have been reported throughout the courts of Europe and in many official documents and letters. Despite the limited successes of Cabot's second voyage in 1497 and the following expedition in 1498, they laid the foundation for England's claims to Canada and his ventures proved the existence of a shorter route across the northern Atlantic Ocean, which would later facilitate the establishment of new colonies in the New World in the seventeenth century and the beginning of the British Empire.

SELECTED SOURCES:

Beazley, Raymond, *John and Sebastian Cabot – The Discovery of North America.*

Firstbrook, Peter, *The Voyage of the Matthew – John Cabot and the Discovery of North America.*

Harrisse, Henry, *John Cabot – The Discoverer of North America and Sebastian His Son.*

Morison, Samuel Eliot, *The European Discovery of America – The Southern Voyages.*

Morison, Samuel Eliot, *The Great Explorers – The European Discovery of America.*

Potter, Philip J., *Monarchs of the Renaissance.*

Hernan Cortes

In the wake of the discovery of silver and gold in Mexico by Spanish conquistadors, the governor of Cuba appointed Hernan Cortes captain-general for a military campaign to conquer the Aztec Empire ruled by Emperor Montezuma. In March 1519, Cortes sailed from Cuba with 600 soldiers, landing at the port of Veracruz on the eastern coast of Mexico. Cortes advanced inland with his small army to begin the subjugation of the Aztecs. To defeat the vast Aztec Empire, the Spanish negotiated a series of alliances with the enemies of Montezuma through warfare, bribery, threats and diplomacy. With the martial support of his native allies, by 1521 Cortes had defeated Montezuma and subdued Mexico for King Charles I of Spain.

Hernan Cortes was born in 1485 in the small town of Medellin in south-western Spain, the only child of an impoverished minor nobleman, Martin Cortes de Menroy, and Catalina Pizarro Altamirino. Growing up in the rugged foothills of interior Castile, he developed an early attraction for adventure, exploring the region's many streams and mountains. Cortes received a limited education in Medellin, taking little interest in his studies and preferring adventurous activities in the wilderness. At the insistence of his father, in 1499 the 14-year-old Hernan was sent to prepare for a career in government at the renowned Salamanca University. At the school he exhibited little desire to study his courses in Latin, grammar and law, and after two years returned to his family in Medellin.

After spending three restless and troubled years in the small provincial town, hunting, fishing and learning the skills of a soldier, Cortes sailed to the island of Hispaniola in the Spanish West Indies in 1504 in search of gold and adventure. The newly appointed governor for the island, Nicolas de Ovando, was a relative of Cortes' mother, and after discovering that a fleet bound for Santo Domingo was assembling at the port of Sanlucar de Barrameda in southern Spain, he decided to join him. The vessels sailed down the African coastline, following the earlier routes of the conquistadors to the Spanish Indies. During the transatlantic crossing to Hispaniola, the squadron was struck by a violent storm, which pounded the ships with fierce winds and waves. As the flotilla struggled against the powerful gales, Cortes' vessel became separated from the others and was driven off course, making its way to Santo Domingo alone.

Shortly after landing at Santo Domingo, Cortes went to the house of his relative, the governor. Ovando was away leading a raid against rebellious Taino Indians, but his secretary assured Cortes that the governor would grant him land and slaves for a farm. Cortes retorted, 'I came here for gold not to till the soil like a peasant.' The governor arrived several days later, and through his political influence Cortes was employed in the local Spanish government, serving the crown in several administrative positions. He later performed the duties of a notary, establishing useful relationships with many colonial authorities. To supplement his income, Ovando granted Cortes a plantation and Indian labourers to cultivate the land. He became involved with the supervision of his farm and the search for gold on his properties, but had little interest in pursuing a career as a planter or governmental official, preferring a life of adventure as a soldier. When the natives on Hispaniola rose up in rebellion against the harsh policies of the administration and abuses of the colonists, Cortes volunteered for service in the town's military unit sent to quell the revolt. During the campaign against the Taino tribe in south-western Hispaniola, Cortes joined the troops of Diego Velasquez, who were mustering at the town of Azua. The small force advanced against the natives, hunting them down and ending their uprising with ruthless attacks. The Spaniards unleashed their savage offensive without restraint, killing and enslaving the Indians with brutality and barbarity. Cortes took part in several skirmishes, learning the fighting skills of a soldier and tactics of the enemy. He fought with distinction during the battles against the Tainos, winning recognition for his leadership and gallantry.

During Christopher Columbus' first voyage to the Indies in 1492, the Spanish explorers discovered the large beautiful island of Cuba. In the following years, the conquistadors were involved with new expeditions, ignoring the peaceful Indians on the island. However, in 1509, Diego Columbus regained the inheritance rights to his father's lands and titles, and began preparations to colonize Cuba. He organized an armed expeditionary force to conquer the island, naming Diego Velasquez as captain-general. During the earlier campaigns against the Tainos on Hispaniola, Cortes had served in the captain-general's contingent of soldiers, becoming close friends with him and quickly volunteering for the new venture to search for gold and adventure.

Diego Velasquez recruited a force of 300 soldiers, sailing from Santo Domingo in four ships in 1511 to begin his conquest of Cuba. After landing on the eastern tip of the island, he built his first fortified settlement at Baracoa before sending his small army into the interior with orders to subdue the natives of the Taino tribe with a ruthless campaign. The Spaniards were well armed with swords, crossbows and arquebuses, while the Indians fought with crude clubs and bows and arrows. As Velasquez's men advanced against the Cubans, Chief Hatuey, who had earlier experienced Spanish brutality on Hispaniola, rallied a force of natives to resist their incursion. Reinforced with followers from Hispaniola, Hatuey's Tainos unleashed a series of hit-and-run attacks against the foreigners, keeping them pinned down at the Baracoa fort. The Indians fought valiantly but were overwhelmed by the firepower of their enemy's arquebuses and crossbows, as Cortes continued to participate in the fighting with his company of troops. During a skirmish, Hatuey was captured and cruelly burned to death on orders from Velasquez. Hatuey's warriors were terrified by the savage act, giving no further resistance to the Spanish occupation of their lands. Despite outnumbering the conquistadors, the Tainos in other regions of the island offered only sporadic opposition and the Spaniards quickly seized control of the once-peaceful Cuba.

Following the conquest of Cuba, Velasquez was appointed governor of the island and Cortes served in his administration as treasurer, ensuring that the government received its share of all gold discovered. The governor encouraged colonists and adventurers from other islands and Spain to settle in Cuba, as the population quickly expanded and additional towns were established. Velasquez rewarded Cortes for his services during the campaign against the Tainos with the grant of lands and native slaves. As his labourers cultivated the fields planting cash crops and worked in his gold mines, Cortes began raising herds of cattle to supplement his earnings. From the income of his properties in Hispaniola and Cuba, he became a wealthy and respected planter. In 1515, Velasquez established another settlement on the south-eastern end of the island, naming it Santiago de Cuba. To further compensate Cortes for his military and administrative skills, the governor appointed him mayor of the new colony.

When Diego Columbus returned to Santo Domingo in 1509 to assume the office of viceroy, his fleet brought many new colonists to the island. Among the arrivals was an impoverished nobleman with four daughters, who came to the Indies in search of rich husbands. While serving in the government on Hispaniola, Cortes met one of the daughters, Catalina Suarez Pecheco, developing a romantic relationship with her and proposing marriage. Velasquez also became involved with one of the daughters, and before leaving on his expedition to Cuba they were married. Despite becoming betrothed to Catalina, Cortes had departed from Santo Domingo without marrying her, and following the conquest of Cuba she followed him to the island. After reaching Cuba, she complained to her brother-in-law about Cortes' dishonourable conduct. Cortes had recently incurred the disfavour of Velasquez when he agreed to utilize his prior training and experience in law to represent several local settlers, who were protesting against the Cuban government's distribution of new Indian lands. To protect his family's honour and reassert his authority, Velasquez intervened, ordering Cortes to marry Catalina. Cortes had no desire to give up his care-free life, joining the local conspiracy to take his personal grievance directly to Columbus in Santo Domingo. The governor discovered the plot, ordering the arrest of Cortes and imprisoning him. He was quickly tried, found guilty of treason and sentenced to death. However, Cortes escaped from his chains, taking asylum in a church. He stayed in his sanctuary for several days before attempting to flee again. The governor had placed guards at the church and Cortes was quickly recaptured. He was sent to a ship in the harbour bound for Santo Domingo for his execution. Confronted with certain death, he managed to slip out of his chains and flee back to the church. Not willing to risk another arrest, he finally agreed to marry Catalina. Throughout their thirteen years of marriage, Cortes and Catalina had a stormy relationship that ended with her mysterious death in 1522 in Mexico City.

In the aftermath of the recent Cuban conquest, the conquistadors became occupied with the exploration of new areas across the present-day Yucatan Channel. While Cortes managed his farms and mining operations in Hispaniola and Cuba, Velasquez organized an expeditionary force of three ships and 100 soldiers under the command of Francisco de Cordova, sending it to search the unknown waters to the west. De Cordova set out from Santiago in early February 1517, steering toward the setting sun and making landfall at the island of Cozumel several days later. He continued to navigate to the west, discovering the north-eastern tip of the Yucatan Peninsula and claiming the region for the Spanish throne. The troops were rowed ashore to explore the interior, but were beaten back by fierce attacks from the local Mayan Indians. The fleet moved up the coast, attempting to land at several different locations. As the soldiers advanced beyond the beaches, reconnoitring inland, they were relentlessly assailed by the Mayans and after over half of his men were killed, de Cordova ordered his conquistadors to steer back to Cuba. As the Spaniards prepared to leave, they burned their smallest vessel, returning in the two remaining ships. During the fighting on the Yucatan Peninsula, Francisco de Cordova was seriously wounded, dying soon after reaching the harbour of Havana. After the death of their captain, several of his soldiers sent a report to the governor describing the expedition's discoveries of new lands with rich cities built of stone and the presence of large quantities of gold.

Shortly after Velasquez read the report of the discoveries by his first expedition to the Yucatan Peninsula, he began preparations for a second voyage to explore the region. He outfitted four ships and recruited 250 soldiers for the venture, largely at his own expense. On 5 April 1518, the fleet, under the command of Juan de Grijalva, raised anchor and steered from the port of Matanzas on the northern coast of Cuba. As the vessels entered open waters, the fresh winds drove the conquistadors steadily to the south-west. After eight days at sea, the Spaniards made landfall on the island of Cozumel off the eastern coast of the Yucatan Peninsula. Grijalva led a search party ashore, trying to trade with the local Mayans, but they fled in terror into the dense woods. The men returned to their ships and crossed over to the mainland, sailing up the shoreline and making frequent attempts to exchange their trade goods with the Indians. Despite their friendly overtures, they were attacked by the fierce Mayan warriors, armed with two-handed wooden swords, clubs and bows and arrows, and dressed in quilted cotton armour. Confronted by waves of arrows and outnumbered by the enemy forces, Grijalva's troops were compelled to withdraw to the flotilla. The captain continued along the coast, reaching current-day Campeche, where the Mayans were more friendly, agreeing to exchange gold for blue and green glass beads. From the natives, the conquistadors heard stories of the rich and powerful Aztec Empire far to the west, ruled by Emperor Montezuma.

Drawn by the prospects of acquiring great wealth and new lands to the west, Grijalva sent a ship to Cuba with a glowing account of the recently found empire, along with specimens of gold and a detailed description of the Yucatan's geography. The two remaining vessels resumed their voyage, navigating up the coastline as far north as Veracruz. The captain anchored his squadron in the harbour and sent several search parties ashore to trade Spanish goods with the natives for gold, food and water, before returning to Cuba. Following the five-month expedition, Grijalva landed his small flotilla in the bay of Havana eager to meet with governor Velasquez and discuss the discovery of the empire of the Aztecs, with its promise of great quantities of gold and silver.

While Velasquez's conquistadors were exploring the Yucatan Peninsula, Cortes remained on his lands in Cuba and Hispaniola, enjoying the life of a prosperous planter, but by 1518 his extravagances and excessive spending had depleted his riches. To regain his lost wealth and satisfy his desire for adventure, he volunteered to lead the next expedition to Mexico. To ensure his selection by the administration, he bribed friends of the governor, promising them a share of the plunder for their support. Velasquez was apprehensive about Cortes' independence, preferring a captain-general who would act only as his representative pursuing his personal gains. The governor delayed making a decision for several weeks, but under pressure from Cortes' allies finally named him captain-general for the expeditionary force.

Following the announcement of his appointment, Cortes began to plan his campaign against the Aztec Empire. He recruited veteran soldiers and sailors from Cuba and assembled his fleet at Santiago. As the expeditionary force gathered in the harbour, Velasquez became increasingly uneasy about Cortes' selection, attempting to revoke his commission. When Cortes learned of the governor's actions, he ordered his men to sail to the port of Trinidad on the southern coast of Cuba to renew their preparations. While remaining at the port, he was relieved of his command by Velasquez, but the order was ignored and the arrangements for the voyage continued. After spending ten days at Trinidad, he steered around the western end of the island to Havana, resuming his mobilization of troops and loading provisions on his ships. The governor again attempted to remove his captain-general; however, Cortes wrote to him politely, telling him that his vessels were sailing the next day.

Cortes completed his preparations for the conquest of the Aztec Empire, and by early February 1519 had assembled a fleet of twelve ships, comprising one carrack, three caravels and eight barks. The largest vessel was the 100 ton *Santa Maria de la Concepcion* (*Saint Maria of the Conception*), which Cortes chose as his flagship. His expeditionary force comprised 110 sailors and slightly over 550 soldiers. Included in his armed forces were sixteen horsemen, thirty-two crossbowmen and thirty arquebiers, along with numerous pikemen and several small pieces of artillery. All the infantrymen were armed with steel swords, while jackets thickly padded with cotton were issued as protection against the enemy's arrows and spears. Cortes adopted a black banner as his flag, and embroidered it with a gold cross and the words 'Let us follow the cross. Under this sign, with faith, we conquer.' On the eve of his departure to Mexico, he spoke to his assembled men telling them, 'You are to fight under the banner of the cross, onward then with eagerness. Gloriously terminate the work so promisingly begun. Be true to me and I will make you masters of wealth of which you have never dreamed.'

On 10 February, Cortes' vessels slipped their moorings in Havana harbour, setting a south-western course toward their first destination of the island of Cozumel. When Cortes entered the Yucatan Crossing, his fleet was struck by a violent storm, the ships slammed by fierce, white-topped waves and powerful winds. The fury of the gales scattered the squadron in every direction, with the ship captained by Pedro de Alvarado reaching Cozumel first. When he sent a trading party ashore to barter, the terrified local Mayans fled into the hills. Alvarado's men followed them inland, discovering an Indian enclave of thatched huts. As the troops searched the village, they found a Mayan temple with gold offerings on an altar, which the Spaniards quickly seized. After Cortes reached the island the following day and learned of the appropriation of the gold, he ordered the arrest of the guilty soldiers for disobeying his orders to respect the property and lives of the natives. He returned the stolen gold to the temple and reconnoitred the countryside for the Indians. His forces located three older Mayans, who were given glass beads as gifts and told that the foreigners had come as friends. The Indians were sent into the hills to bring the Mayans back to their village. They soon came out of hiding and began trading with the Spanish.

While the expeditionary force remained on Cozumel, the captain-general heard stories of two Spanish survivors from an earlier shipwreck, who were held on the Yucatan as slaves by the Indians. Cortes negotiated the ransom of the two men, but only Jeronimo de Aguilar agreed to join the Spaniards. During his eight years in captivity, he had learned the language, culture and customs of the Mayans, and he agreed to serve as interpreter for the expedition.

Shortly after making contact with the Mayans, Cortes sent soldiers to reconnoitre the interior of Cozumel. During their exploration, the Spaniards discovered numerous pyramid-shaped temples. The tops of the structures were covered with bones and bloodstains from the natives' sacrifices of animals and humans to their gods. As part of his commission from Velasquez, Cortes was ordered to convert the pagan Indians to the Christian faith. He gathered the island's chiefs together, telling them to destroy their gods' images and accept the religion of the one God. When the Mayans refused, fearing the wrath of their deities, Cortes issued instructions for his troops to smash the pagan idols. He constructed a new altar with a wooden cross, ordering the islanders to worship the all-powerful God of the Christians.

After spending two weeks exploring Cozumel, the Spanish fleet sailed on 4 March across the narrow channel to the coast of the Yucatan Peninsula. The ships navigated along a shoreline covered with dense tropical foliage for eight days before reaching the bay of Campeche. Cortes anchored his flotilla near a sand bar in the bay and rowed up the Grijalva River toward the village of Tabasco to barter with the Mayans. As his soldiers moved up the Grijalva, the riverbanks and mangrove swamps were filled with hostile Indians with their bodies painted black and white. When the Spanish were approached by canoes containing many warriors, Cortes ordered Aguilar to tell them that they came in peace and to trade, but their chief replied his men would attack if the strangers attempted to land. When Cortes had Aguilar repeat the message, the Indians replied with a volley of arrows.

As the Spanish rowed toward the village, they were assailed by enemy forces from their canoes and along the riverbanks. The Mayan warriors were armed with spears, large two-handed swords, darts and powerful bows and arrows, while carrying shields and wearing cotton quilted armour for protection. Cortes' soldiers fought their way upriver, breaking through the hastily built enemy barricades and attacking Tabasco. After gaining control of the village, the captain-general claimed the region for the king of Spain. The battle continued into the following day, but after artillery pieces and horses were brought from the ships anchored in the bay, the conquistadors gained the advantage, despite being greatly outnumbered. The Indians had never seen warhorses before, and as Cortes led his cavalry in a charge with his horse soldiers dressed in steel armour and with flashing swords, the warriors fled into the swamps and woods.

Despite defeating the Indians at Tabasco, the Spanish lacked the military power to pacify the Yucatan by force of arms. Following the battle, Cortes sent messages to the peninsula's tribal leaders, telling them he came in peace and wanted to meet with them. Over thirty chiefs came to the expedition's camp, and the captain-general told them their lands were now the property of the Spanish king. He blamed them for starting the battle at Tabasco, offering a pardon if they pledged peace and obedience to their new ruler. To demonstrate the invincibility of his army, he fired one of his cannons into the dense forest, tearing a huge hole through the trees. The Mayans, terrified by the noise and destruction, agreed to submit to the Spaniards.

The following day, chiefs from other parts of the Yucatan came to meet with Cortes, bringing gifts of gold, cotton cloth and women slaves. When the captain-general asked through Aguilar where the gold came from, the Indians pointed to the west and said Mexico, the land of the Aztecs. Among the women was Malinche, the daughter of a Mayan chief. She spoke the language of the Aztecs as well as Mayan, and Cortes decided to use her as his interpreter. Aguilar was only fluent in the local language, and when the

Spanish advanced into Mexico, Malinche translated the Aztec into Mayan for him. She soon became a Christian and was called Dona Marina.

Before the chieftains departed the Spanish encampment, Cortes ordered the Indians to abandon their gods and accept the Christian faith. He built a small church at Tabasco, placing a cross on the altar where the natives pledged their allegiance to the pope and king. After spending several more days at Tabasco, Cortes ordered his sailors and soldiers back to their vessels in the harbour, continuing his voyage north-west along the coast in search of the Aztec Empire. The fleet sailed over 400 miles up the shoreline in warm spring weather, with strong winds. On 21 April, the expedition reached the harbour at Veracruz, which spread out with narrow white beaches in a wide curve. Cortes ordered his ships' captains to anchor in the bay, which had first been seen by Grijalva the year before. While the conquistadors remained on their vessels, Indians from the beach paddled out in two canoes, announcing to the strangers that they represented the great emperor Montezuma and had been sent to learn their identity and intention. Cortes met with the envoys, led by Tendile, telling them he came in peace and to trade. After they exchanged gifts, the captain-general asked the Indians to take his presents to their chief, inviting him to meet with the Spaniards.

Shortly after the Indians left the flagship, Cortes established a strong fortified encampment on the beach to await the return of Tendile. Several days passed before the ambassadors arrived, bearing more gifts of gold, silver and cotton cloth. Tendile also brought painters with him, who were instructed to draw portraits of the Spanish, their ships, horses and weapons. Cortes presented the envoys with a finely carved wooden chair for their emperor. Before the emissaries left the camp, the captain-general demonstrated the military might of his army, leading a wild charge of his armour-clad cavalrymen, while his artillery pieces fired volleys of cannonballs.

While Cortes' soldiers remained on the beach, they were supplied with fresh food and water by the local Indians. After waiting for a week, Tendile returned with two noblemen from Montezuma's court to meet the captain-general. The two diplomats bowed deeply before Cortes, presenting him with numerous gold, silver and cotton cloth gifts from their overlord. Along with the gold and silver objects, the emperor sent a personal message welcoming the foreigners to his lands, but telling them he did not wish to meet with them and requesting they return to their kingdom. Cortes sent the ambassadors back to Montezuma expressing his desire to visit the Aztec capital.

While the conquistadors waited for the return of the Mexicans, dissent erupted among the expeditionary force after the Indians stopped delivering food and water, on orders from Tendile, and disease began spreading among the men. After the Spaniards spent another ten days on the beach, the ambassadors finally arrived at the encampment with a message from Montezuma, telling them not to enter his lands. During the night, the local natives deserted their village and in the morning the Spanish awoke all alone on the white beaches. Two opposing factions now quickly formed, with one group of soldiers favouring an immediate withdrawal to Cuba and the other demanding the continuation of the expedition. Cortes was fully committed to the conquest of the Aztec Empire, but to quell the threat of rebellion agreed to sail from Mexico to Cuba. While preparations for departure began, he rallied his supporters, sending them into the camp to raise an uprising against the abandonment of the campaign. His supporters forcefully persuaded most of the dissenters to join their faction with promises of glory and great wealth.

With the expedition reunited, Cortes resigned his commission issued by Velasquez, calling on his men to choose the captain-general of their choice. Without hesitation, the Spaniards unanimously elected Cortes to his former rank, but in the name of King Charles I. A new charter was issued, making Cortes responsible only to the Spanish court, while giving him undisputed control of the army. To further assert his independence from Velasquez, the troops were ordered to establish a new colony under the authority of Cortes. Legal documents were drawn up creating a government, with Cortes appointed governor and answerable for his actions only to the king.

As Cortes' men began construction of the permanent colony, several Indians from the Totonac tribe came to the camp asking to meet with the captain-general. They had been sent by the chief from the village of Cempoala, seeking an alliance with the Spanish against Montezuma. The kingdom of Totonac had been conquered by the Aztecs and annexed into their empire. Under the harsh rule of Montezuma, the Totonacs were oppressed by the Aztecs, their people enslaved and children taken for sacrifice to the gods. Cortes was greatly interested in forming a union with the tribe as a means to provoke civil war against the Mexican emperor, and agreed to visit their chief.

The selection of Veracruz as the site for the colony proved to be a poor choice due to its persistent inadequate food and water supplies and the presence of diseases from the surrounding wetlands. The decision was made to move the settlement near the town of Quiahuitztlan, 30 miles to the north and several miles from Cempoala. Cortes sent his fleet ahead to the new location, while marching his conquistadors overland. As the army travelled through lands rich in floral growth and dense forest, the soldiers soon reached the village of Cempoala. Cortes was welcomed by the chieftain with great pomp and ceremony. With Dona Marina and Aguilar acting as interpreters, he told the chief his army had come from a far distant land to aid the oppressed and punish the tyrants, offering to protect his tribe against Montezuma.

After spending the night at Cempoala, the expeditionary force resumed its advance to the site of the new colony, which Cortes again named Veracruz. The men began building fortifications around the settlement and erecting houses. The soldiers were soon joined by Indians from Cempoala and nearby Quiahuitztlan, and together they worked on the construction of a church, central square and arsenal. As the work on the capital of New Spain continued, five noblemen from Montezuma's court entered the town, ignoring the Spaniards as they walked by. The local Totonac chieftains were summoned to their presence and charged with aiding the foreigners in violation of instructions from their emperor. The Mexican envoys demanded a penalty of forty boys and girls for sacrifice to the gods. Cortes later met secretly with the chiefs, telling them to arrest the five Aztecs and accept his protection. The chieftains had already offended Montezuma beyond pardon by welcoming the Spaniards, and agreed to seize the emperor's lords.

Following the seizure of the five Aztec lords, Cortes told the Totonacs to place them in a hut, which his men would guard. During the night, Cortes had two of the Mexicans secretly brought before him, telling them he regretted their arrest and ordering their release. He requested they return to Montezuma, notifying him of the Spaniards' unrelenting friendship and desire for peace. Shortly after the seizure of the Aztec noblemen, the chiefs from Quiahuitztlan and Cempoala formed alliances with over twenty Totonac villages in defiance of their overlord. However, after learning of the escape of the two Aztecs, who would report their treachery to Montezuma, the Totonacs were now more strongly bound to the military support of Cortes' army. Through Cortes' deceitful acts, the expeditionary force gained a faithful ally. The chiefs now encouraged other communities to join their league, as the size and strength of Cortes' army continued to grow stronger.

With the Totonacs now dependent on the Spanish for protection against Montezuma, Cortes ordered them to abandon their gods and practice of human sacrifice to accept the Christian religion. The chieftains protested, believing their gods provided bountiful harvests, fair weather and kept them safe, and refused to destroy them. To show the power of his one God, Cortes instructed a contingent of his soldiers to demolish the pagan images. As the Spanish conquistadors smashed the idols, the chiefs and priests cried out in fear of reprisals from their deities. Cortes turned their temples into churches, ordering the priests to care for the symbols of their new religion. He assured the natives they were now Christian brothers with the Spanish, under the shield of the Holy Virgin and cross. The Totonacs were bewildered that their gods took no act of revenge, willingly accepting the Christian faith.

Cortes had spent three months on the coast exploring the region and establishing a colony at Veracruz, while forming alliances with the Indians for the conquest of Mexico. He had earlier appointed himself governor for the new lands, in defiance of Velasquez's commission, and before moving inland needed assurances from the royal court that the king would recognize his new authority. He wrote a letter to Charles I, asking him to ratify his actions and confirm his assumption of power over New Spain. To impress his sovereign with his accomplishments, he ordered his men to load all the treasures accumulated thus far onto two ships and sent them to Spain. Many of the sailors and soldiers loudly protested the loss of their gold and silver, but were promised greater riches in the Aztec Empire. On 26 July 1519, the two vessels sailed from Veracruz with orders to deliver the treasure and letters directly to Spain without stopping at Cuba.

Shortly after the departure of the ships, a plot was organized by a faction of men in opposition to remaining in New Spain and in protest against Cortes' decision to send the gold and silver to the king. In great secrecy, they planned to seize a vessel and return to Cuba. When Cortes was notified of the conspiracy by a defector, he ordered the arrest of the mutineers. The leaders of the uprising were quickly hanged and the others freed. Confronted with the constant threat of dissatisfied conquistadors again rising up in a new conspiracy and sailing to Cuba, Cortes ordered his fleet burned. He gathered trusted mariners, instructing them to take the sails, navigational equipment and supplies from the flotilla and then destroy all of the ships except one small bark. When the soldiers learned of the scuttling of the squadron, a wave of bitterness spread against the captain-general, but he told them, 'They must conquer or die.' The Spaniards quickly realized their destiny now depended on their loyalty to Cortes, shouting their allegiance with cries of 'To Mexico, to Mexico.'

Cortes ordered preparations made for the campaign against the Aztec capital, and on the morning of 16 August, after leaving a small garrison at Veracruz, began his march into Montezuma's empire with 400 soldiers, a small cavalry unit, several artillery pieces and his Totonac allies. The army advanced through lands with rich green foliage, dense forest, beautiful flowers and scattered native villages. Following a two-day journey, Cortes reached the town of Jalapa, located at the base of a vast mountain range. His men pushed on, climbing through the mountains onto a wide plain, which extended before them for many miles. After a week's trek, the expeditionary force reached the large town of Tlatlanquitepec, where they encountered an Aztec garrison. The troops of Montezuma offered no opposition, but their commander attempted to discourage the Spanish from moving farther inland with vivid descriptions of the military might of his overlord.

The captain-general stayed in the town for five days, resting his forces and gathering fresh supplies before continuing his advance to the west. The conquistadors soon entered the independent kingdom of the Tlaxcalan tribe. The Tlaxcalans, fierce warriors who had repeatedly repelled Montezuma's attempts to subjugate them, remained autonomous. The kingdom was formed by the union of four city-states, who united their armies to defeat their enemies. The state of Tizatlan, the dominant military power in the realm, was ruled by Xicotencatl II. Cortes' expeditionary force totalled less than 3,000 men, including his Totonac allies. To defeat the large Aztec Empire he needed additional soldiers, sending envoys to open alliance discussions with the Tlaxcalan chief. Despite the Spanish attempts to establish friendly relations, when Cortes advanced into their territory he was ambushed by Xicotencatl II. The small skirmish quickly turned into a pitched battle as more than 3,000 warriors slammed into Cortes' position. With Cortes leading his troops from the front, the Spaniards manoeuvred forward, with the firepower from their cannons and arquebuses driving the enemy off.

Following the first clash with Xicotencatl II, Cortes moved his army deeper into the Tlaxcalan kingdom, marching west for several days. As his soldiers advanced onto a wide spreading plateau, on 5 September they encountered the enemy forces drawn up in battle formation. The Tlaxcalan warriors were armed with spears, clubs, wooden swords and powerful bows and arrows, and numbered over 40,000. The warriors rushed forward, firing volleys of arrows and throwing spears into the ranks of Cortes' men. The captain-general deployed his soldiers and Totonac allies in a square formation, repelling wave after wave of Indian attacks. When he brought his artillery into position, the guns opened up with devastating effect. The fighting continued throughout the day as Cortes' troops stood firm against the fury of Xicotencatl's charges. As darkness began to sweep across the battlefield, the Tlaxcalans withdrew, leaving the Spanish to claim victory. The conquistadors sustained light casualties, as their steel armour gave them protection against the Indians' primitive weapons.

Xicotencatl II resumed the battle in the morning, but after four hours of fighting was compelled to retreat, with the bodies of his dead and wounded warriors covering the field. Several days later, envoys from the Tlaxcalan chief appeared at the Spanish encampment bringing gifts of food. Despite the peaceful appearance of the emissaries, the captain-general learned through Dona Marina that the men were spies sent to determine the strength and size of the foreigners' army. He ordered the arrest of the Tlaxcalans, cutting off their hands and sending them back to Xicotencatl II with the message that the Spaniards were ready for war or peace. The following day, the chief entered the camp with a large escort, submitting to Cortes and offering peace. Xicotencatl agreed to join his forces with the Spanish and their allies and serve in the invasion of the Aztec Empire. The campaign against the kingdom of Tlaxcala secured the expedition a well-trained and equipped army of many thousands, powerful enough to challenge Montezuma's military might.

After the victory over Xicotencatl's army, Cortes visited the Tlaxcalan capital of 30,000 residents at Tlascala, staying for three weeks while resting his men and preparing for the fight against Mexico. He held meetings in the city with the Indian chieftains, gathering intelligence on the size of the Aztec armies, their battle tactics and weapons. The Tlaxcalan chiefs were eager to take part in the campaign against their feared enemy, offering a force of 10,000 soldiers for Cortes' clash with Montezuma. While the Spaniards remained at Tlascala, Montezuma was increasingly concerned by the strength of Cortes' growing alliances, sending five of his noblemen with many rich gifts to their encampment to encourage the strangers not to enter his lands. If they agreed to leave Mexico, he pledged to pay a large yearly tribute and accept the authority of the Spanish king. The captain-general sent a message telling the emperor that he had been ordered by his overlord to visit the Aztec capital and must obey. After several days, Cortes received a reply from Montezuma, inviting him to travel to his city of Cholula to await his decision on whether or not to meet with him. Despite warnings of treachery from his Indian allies, Cortes issued instructions for his conquistadors to march to Cholula.

As the Spanish advanced toward Cholula, they were greeted by representatives from Montezuma, who escorted them into the city. While Cortes and his troops rested from the journey, envoys from Montezuma secretly entered the city, meeting with the local chieftains and ordering them to assail the foreigners. Cortes was soon informed of the plot by Dona Marina, who had learned the Cholulans' plans from the wife of a chief. To thwart Montezuma's conspiracy, Cortes placed his soldiers around the central square near the massive temple of Quetzalcoatl and asked the Cholulan warriors to assemble near the shrine. When the Indians gathered in the square, Cortes ordered his conquistadors to open fire with their cannons, crossbows and arquebuses. With all the exits blocked by Cortes' troops, the Cholulans were massacred by the firepower of the Spanish weapons. When the Indian allies of Cortes joined the battle, the city was ravaged as the Spaniards and Tlaxcalans roamed the streets, killing every man, woman and child they found. Following two days of savage slaughter, the captain-general ordered his men to end their attacks, with over 6,000 dead. Shortly after the end of the fighting, he sent messengers to Montezuma blaming the Cholulans for plotting the ambush and requesting a meeting with him as his friend. When the Aztec emperor was notified of another Spanish victory against overwhelming numbers, he finally invited Cortes to meet with him in his capital at Tenochtitlan.

Cortes remained at Cholula for three weeks before beginning the advance to the Mexican capital on 1 November. The Spanish marched through arid and mountainous country, gaining additional native allies as they trudged west. The captain-general reached Tenochtitlan on 8 November, discovering a large and beautiful city built on an island on Lake Texcoco. The city's lofty palaces, temples and buildings seemed to float over the water, surrounded by fragrant orchards and flowering gardens. Clad in armour and on horseback, Cortes was welcomed at the capital's gate by Mexican nobles and escorted over a drawbridge to meet Montezuma. The Aztec emperor arrived, carried on a litter extravagantly decorated with precious metals and jewels, covered by a canopy of green feathers. In an elaborate ceremony, Montezuma, dressed in magnificent robes, made a speech welcoming the Spaniards and presenting them with rich gifts of gold and silver. The conquistadors were housed in a grand palace and invited to discover the many wonders of Tenochtitlan.

The Spanish spent the following week exploring the Aztec capital, while Cortes held several private meetings with Montezuma. During their discussions at the high temple of the war god, Huitzilopochtli, Cortes called the deities of the Aztecs' devils, greatly offending the emperor and straining their relationship. As part of his charter for the Mexican campaign, Cortes had been instructed to convert the pagan natives to Christianity, and as he pressed his attacks against the Mexican gods and their practice of human sacrifices, relations with the Aztecs deteriorated rapidly. When Cortes learned that Montezuma had ordered his governor on the east coast of Mexico to assail his Veracruz settlement, he moved to seize the emperor as a guarantee against an attack at Tenochtitlan on his soldiers. He assembled a contingent of troops and met the Aztec emperor at his palace. During their talks, the captain-general accused Montezuma of ordering the assault at Veracruz and planning to kill the Spanish in the capital. He ordered the emperor to return with him to his palace as his prisoner.

While Montezuma remained under Spanish control, he was treated courteously, continued to hold meetings with his nobles and ambassadors, and was attended by his many servants. Under pressure from Cortes, the emperor acknowledged that the Spanish king now ruled over his empire and instructed his noblemen to accept the power of their new overlord and his local representative. After the Aztecs pledged to obey their overlord, Cortes ordered his men to seize the emperor's treasury of gold, silver and jewels, placing it under his guards. With control of the city, he moved to compel the Mexicans to abandon their gods and accept the Christian faith. Accompanied by an armed force, the captain-general went to the main temple, and with the priest watching began destroying their idols. He instructed the natives to construct a church at the temple and end their practice of human sacrifices. The Aztecs were outraged at the desecration of their gods and began planning an attack against the Spaniards. Dona Marina soon learned of the plot, warning Cortes of the danger.

As Cortes made preparations to escape from Tenochtitlan after learning of the Aztecs' plans, information reached him that Diego Velazquez had sent a fleet of eighteen ships with over 800 men under the command of Panfilo de Narvaez to seize Veracruz. Velazquez had been informed of the Spanish victories in Mexico, and ordered his soldiers to capture Cortes and take over his campaign. Threatened by the large force of Spaniards from Cuba, Cortes sent messengers to de Narvaez with offers to unite with him. When the proposal was rejected, the captain-general prepared to attack de Narvaez's encampment. Cortes placed Pedro de Alvarado in charge of Montezuma and Tenochtitlan with nearly 300 troops, ordering him to hold the city, while he advanced with the remainder of his forces against Velasquez's soldiers. After marching his army to the east, in late May 1520, he unleashed a night assault during a rainstorm, catching the enemy by surprise. The veteran forces of Cortes quickly overran de Narvaez's men, forcing their surrender. De Narvaez was sent in chains to Veracruz, while his troops agreed to join Cortes' army.

While Cortes was defeating Velazquez's men, de Alvarado was assailed by the Aztecs in the capital. He sent urgent messages notifying the captain-general of the danger. Cortes quickly ordered his reinforced army to return to Tenochtitlan, arriving on 24 June. After reaching the capital, he joined his soldiers with de Alvarado and began organizing the defences at his palace.

On the following day, the Aztec warriors attacked the Spanish, wave after wave of them crashing against Cortes' parapets. Cortes' troops managed to repel the Mexican assaults, driving them from the palace walls with their cannons, crossbows and arquebuses. After pushing back the Aztecs, the Spanish commander attempted to negotiate a settlement with the newly elected emperor, Cuitlahuac. He refused to talk with the Spaniards, compelling the captain-general to use Montezuma as his spokesman. When the emperor tried to speak from the palace balcony, he was assailed by a storm of stones and arrows and struck numerous times, dying several days later.

With most of their escape routes destroyed, ammunition supplies nearly depleted and facing an overwhelming army of fierce warriors, Cortes' only option was to force a breakout. He was compelled to abandon most of the gold and prepared his men to leave after midnight on 1 July, trying to catch the Aztecs unprepared. The conquistadors moved silently out of the palace and through the dark and deserted streets during a heavy rainstorm. They reached the last remaining bridge, and as they started across the alarm was sounded. Out of the night the Indian warriors charged forward, ploughing into the Spanish rearguard with swords and spears flashing in the night. A violent fight broke out as the troops and their allies struggled to safety. Encumbered by the weight of the gold they had taken from the treasury, many of de Narvaez's soldiers were killed or captured. When the surviving Spaniards reached the mainland, the Mexican forces abandoned their pursuit to celebrate the recapture of their city and to sacrifice their captives, allowing Cortes and nearly half of his army to escape.

The conquistadors now moved north toward their camp at Tlascala, fending off enemy reconnaissance parties as they marched. On 8 July, Cortes received a report from his scouts that a large Mexican force had assembled on the plain close by at Otumba. The field was covered by the Aztec army advancing toward the Spaniards, armed with spears, swords and bows and arrows. The warriors soon attacked Cortes' hastily deployed rectangular formation as both forces fought fiercely. When Cortes spotted the Aztec commander, he charged forward, knocking him to the ground, while one of his soldiers killed him with his lance. Without the leadership of their commanding general, the Mexican attacks became disorganized and they soon began to fall back.

As the Aztec troops abandoned the battlefield, the Spanish renewed their march to Tlascala. When Cortes and his surviving men arrived at the town, they were welcomed by their friends. After resting his troops the captain-general soon began planning his return to Tenochtitlan. He reorganized his shattered forces, pressing his allies for reinforcements. While the Spanish prepared for the campaign, Velazquez sent additional soldiers in two ships to reinforce de Narvaez's army, while three ships from the governor of Jamaica landed on the coast with settlers to establish a new colony. After learning of the arrival of the new conquistadors, Cortes departed from Tlascala, travelling east to gain their allegiance. He met with the soldiers, and through his stories of adventure and great riches convinced them to join his expedition. With these reinforcements and additional warriors from his Indian allies the Spanish army grew to nearly 75,000, and by late December the captain-general was ready to attack the Aztec capital.

Cortes moved his army south, establishing his fortified encampment at the town of Texcoco near the eastern end of Lake Texcoco. The Spanish commander planned a three-pronged offensive against Tenochtitlan, sending one force to attack from the west and another from the south, while he led a contingent of soldiers across the lake by boat from the east. In the early summer of 1521, the conquistadors reinforced with their Indian allies unleashed their campaign, slamming into the Aztecs in hit-and-run assaults in the city. The thirteen boats that Cortes had built were used to transport the Spaniards across Lake Texcoco to assail the enemy and destroy the city's aqueduct and bridges, blocking their food and water supplies. The Aztecs soon began to suffer the effects of thirst and hunger from the blockade, and with smallpox ravaging the population, Cortes' men slowly began to gain the advantage with more tribes joining his expeditionary force to free themselves from the tyranny of the emperor. Cuitlahuac had been killed by the smallpox epidemic, and the newly elected emperor, Cuauhtemoc, refused to negotiate, leading his warriors in a fierce fight. The battle raged for two months, but by mid-August the Aztec survivors began to flee their destroyed capital. When Cuauhtemoc was captured attempting to escape, the Mexicans ended their resistance and the once powerful and wealthy Aztec Empire was destroyed.

In the aftermath of his victory, Cortes restored order in New Spain and began to rebuild Tenochtitlan. Cuahtemoc was reinstated as figurehead emperor and ordered by Cortes to instruct his subjects to bury the rotting bodies and begin construction of a new Spanish style city, renamed Mexico City. A Christian church was built on the site of the former sun god's temple, and Cortes' rebuilt palace replaced the ruined one of the emperor. The captain-general unofficially administered New Spain in the name of King Charles I, and on 15 October 1522 was officially appointed royal governor of the land by the Spanish crown.

Cortes remained as governor of New Spain for the next five years, rebuilding the capital and colonizing the region. He was occupied expanding the economy by importing and raising herds of horses, sheep and cattle, while introducing new crops. He awarded grants of land to his men as rewards for their service and to gain their continued loyalty to his rule. The governor promoted the acceptance of the Christian faith and destruction of the pagan idols among the Aztec people. Under the governor's administration, the search for gold and silver was renewed and the mines reopened, while the natives were encouraged to grow corn, cotton and vegetables.

While Cortes continued to govern New Spain, in July 1522 his wife, Catalina, arrived from Cuba with her large family. Surrounded in the palace by his wife's demanding relatives, Cortes and Catalina began to openly argue. Several months after her arrival, she was found dead in her room following a party. Cortes was accused by many of his enemies of murdering her when suspicious marks were discovered on her neck, but the official doctor's report claimed death was by natural causes.

Shortly after the Spanish occupied New Spain, Cristobal de Olid was sent by Cortes to establish a new colony in Honduras, but under the influence of Diego Velazquez he claimed the land for himself. In 1524, the governor sailed to Honduras with a small army to suppress Olid's revolt. Cortes remained in the region for nearly two years, crushing the rebels and establishing his authority. During the prolonged campaign, Cortes' health suffered, and he returned to Mexico City in ill-health.

Following the defeat of the Aztecs, Cortes had sent a steady stream of silver, gold and precious stones to the Spanish court. However, Charles I was involved in costly wars with France and in need of more money to finance them. He dispatched several auditors to Mexico City to ensure the crown received its correct fifth share of all wealth. When Cortes returned from Honduras, he was charged with misappropriation of funds and plotting to gain personal control of New Spain. To repudiate the accusations, he decided to return to Spain and defend himself before the king.

In 1528, Cortes sailed to Spain with two ships filled with gold, silver and precious objects. He made a grand entrance into the royal city of Madrid with exotic birds and animals, and Indian slaves dressed with brightly decorated Aztec featherworks. The captain-general was greeted by Charles I, receiving a gracious welcome. However, when Cortes asked the king to reappoint him governor for New Spain, the request was denied. Instead, he was ennobled, named marquis of Oaxaca and granted an extensive estate in New Spain. While in Spain, Cortes was married to Dona Juana de Zuniga, who was from a wealthy and influential noble family. Unlike his first marriage, Cortes had a happy family life with Dona Juana and their four children during their eighteen years together.

In the early summer of 1530, Cortes returned with his wife to New Spain and his properties. He was occupied with the management of his large plantations, mills and gold and silver mines. The captain-general cultivated corn, cotton and sugar on his estates, while raising herds of horses and cattle. From his estates he sent numerous expeditions at his personal expense to search for new lands. In 1532, he outfitted two ships to explore the Mexican Pacific coastline, but when the crews mutinied the project was cancelled. Additional expeditionary forces were dispatched along the Pacific shore, and in 1536 Cortes personally led a voyage to reconnoitre the western Mexican coast, discovering the Baja of California and claiming it for the king. As Cortes planned new and larger ventures, disputes developed with the royal governor over his rights to search the region, forcing him to return to Spain to resolve his injustices.

In the spring of 1540, Hernan Cortes sailed to Spain to again present his grievances to the royal court. Despite his earlier conquests in the New World, the king largely ignored him and Cortes spent the next six years waging legal battles to secure his rights of exploration. Hoping to regain his lost privileges and influence, he joined Charles I's campaign against the Moslem governor of Algiers, Hassan Agha. He served in the army of the Duke of Alba, Fernando Alvarez de Toledo, taking part in the unsuccessful attack against Islamic forces at Algiers in October 1541. However, following his return to Spain he gained little response from the crown and his petitions continued to be rejected. Cortes spent his remaining years in Seville, lobbying the throne to resolve his injustices. He died on 2 December 1547 at the age of 62, still embittered at his loss of recognition and prestige.

SELECTED SOURCES:
Abbott, John S.C., *Hernando Cortez.*
Horgan, Paul, *Conquistadors in North American History.*
Levy, Buddy, *Hernan Cortes, King Montezuma, and the Last Stand of the Aztecs.*
Marks, Richard Lee, *Cortes The Great Adventurer and the Fate of Aztec Mexico.*
Wagner, Heather Lehr, *Hernan Cortes.*
Wepman, Dennis, *Hernan Cortes.*

Jacques Cartier

While the Spanish, Portuguese and English monarchies were sending expeditions to explore the Western Hemisphere, France was occupied in Europe with a series of wars against the Holy Roman Empire and England, and attempting to seize new princedoms in Italy. However, in 1532, during a truce in the war, King Francis I issued a commission to Jacques Cartier for a voyage of discovery to the New World. In mid-1534, Cartier sailed from Saint-Malo with two ships and sixty-one men, and following a transatlantic crossing of twenty days explored the Gulf of St Lawrence, discovering a large river flowing from the interior, the modern-day St Lawrence River. He claimed the land for the king, laying the foundation for the future settlement of New France and the vast French Empire in North America.

Jacques Cartier was born in France in the Breton seaport of Saint-Malo in late 1491, the third son of Jamet Cartier and Geseline Jansgrt. Jamet Cartier was a sailor and pilot, employed on commercial ships travelling from Saint-Malo. Through the influence of his father and the stories of the town's many sailors and fishermen, Jacques developed his interest in going to sea. At a young age he began sailing on his father's vessels as a cabin boy, learning the duties of navigator, astronomer and map-maker. He later attended the naval academy at Dieppe, receiving training as a mariner, while mastering the skills of seamanship. Soon after leaving the school, Cartier began his career at sea, serving as an apprentice seaman and rising rapidly through the ranks to ship's captain.

In 1520, Jacques Cartier was married in Saint-Malo to Marie Catherine des Granches. She was from a prominent Breton family and her father served the monarchy as Constable for Saint-Malo. The marriage into an eminent local family gave Cartier access to influential officials in the French court and church, resulting in his meeting with King Francis I in 1532.

While sailing from Saint-Malo, Cartier made multiple voyages to European ports and several extended expeditions to the New World, visiting the territory of present-day Canada and Newfoundland. In the spring of 1528, he took part in Giovanni da Verrazzano's third journey to the New World, navigating from Dieppe in three ships to search for a new passageway through the Americas to the Pacific Ocean, while gathering a cargo of valuable brazilwood and Indian slaves in Brazil for the journey's investors.

In 1528, with financial backing from two merchants, Verrazzano made another Atlantic passage, sailing to Brazil to harvest a cargo of brazilwood for his sponsors. Serving as master-pilot on one of the three ships in Verrazzano's expeditionary force, Cartier crossed the Atlantic, first making landfall on the coast of Florida. The French vessels steered south down the Florida shoreline into the Gulf of Mexico to the Bahama Islands. Cartier continued to navigate the ships south-east, passing north of Hispaniola and Puerto Rico. He reached the present-day Virgin Islands and began following the Leeward Islands south. When the fleet reached the island of Guadeloupe, Verrazzano ordered his vessels to drop anchor. He assembled a small landing party and was rowed to the shore. As the longboat approached the beach, Verrazzano waded ashore alone and was suddenly attacked by a band of cannibal warriors from the Carib tribe. He was quickly overpowered and killed by the Carbs. While Cartier and the sailors watched from their ships' decks, their captain was cut up and eaten by the Caribs. Cartier assumed command of Verrazzano's flagship and resumed the voyage, sailing south-eastward to Brazil and still searching for the passageway to the Orient. While in Brazil, the crew collected a shipload of brazilwood to defray the cost of the expedition for the investors before returning to Dieppe.

By the early sixteenth century, Spain had become the dominant European power in the New World. The discoveries in the new lands brought vast quantities of gold, silver and precious stones to the Spanish court, and Francis I was eager to gain a share of the wealth. In 1506 and 1508, he chartered expeditions to look for gold and silver in the West, but they ended in failure. Later, Verrazzano sailed under the French flag in 1524, searching the region between present-day South Carolina and Newfoundland for the North-west Passage and precious metals, but his voyage was also unsuccessful.

The French king was undeterred by the failures, and during a truce in the war against Spain began planning a new voyage. The Bishop of Saint-Malo, Jean Le Veneur, was a trusted and influential adviser to Francis I and supported his venture to the New World. He was also well acquainted with Cartier and recommended him to the royal court as the captain of the expeditionary force. Cartier also received the endorsement of the Count of Charni, Philippe de Chabot, who was a close friend of Francis I and an admiral in the French navy. After discussing the expedition with Veneur and Chabot, the monarch agreed to appoint Cartier as captain and issue a charter authorizing the venture. He further pledged to provide funding for two ships of 60 tons each. Under the royal licence, Cartier was ordered to search for a western passage to Asia north of Newfoundland and discover new sources of gold and silver. By April 1534, he had assembled his two vessels at Saint-Malo and recruited a crew of sixty-one sailors. Before sailing, Cartier and his men gathered in Saint-Malo church to receive the priest's blessings and take an oath administered by Admiral Charles de Mouy to serve their sovereign truly and faithfully.

On 20 April, Cartier's fleet departed from Saint-Malo in calm waters under clear skies. He crossed the English Channel and rounded southern England into the Atlantic Ocean, following the familiar route of French fishermen toward Greenland. Strong winds from the east pushed the Frenchmen forward. Cartier's flotilla made the transatlantic passage in twenty days, sighting land at Cape Bonavista on the northern coast of Newfoundland on 10 May. As the vessels continued sailing northward along the shoreline, they encountered dangerous icebergs and Cartier was compelled to take refuge in a sheltered bay. While the sailors waited for the ice to clear, they made repairs to the ships' rigging and tackle. By 21 May, the floating ice had disappeared and the captain resumed his expedition up the shoreline. When the flotilla approached the small island off the Newfoundland coast called Isle of Birds, Cartier ordered them to drop anchor. The island was the nesting ground for many thousands of birds, and a landing party was rowed ashore to replenish the crews' food stocks of meat. The seamen spent less than an hour killing a large supply of birds for fresh food.

Cartier piloted his ships northward and around the tip of Newfoundland into the Strait of Belle Isle. He changed his course, sailing south and skirting the coast of Canada's mainland. As the French moved through the passageway, Cartier mapped the bays and landscape, claiming the region for Francis I by planting a large cross with images of the fleur-de-lys on the land. He continued along the coastline of Labrador, anchoring in the bay at Old Fort to resupply his firewood and water. The French captain left his vessels in the bay and rowed south-westward in his longboats to explore the modern-day Gulf of St Lawrence. He discovered many small islands and the outlet of a large river flowing from the interior. While the sailors remained in the gulf, a French fishing ship came into view. The crew was searching for the harbour at Old Fort, and from his recently drawn maps Cartier was able to direct the vessel's captain to the bay. Cartier resumed his expedition, pressing on to the west, but bad weather soon forced him to return to his fleet.

The Frenchmen remained at anchor at Old Fort for the weather to improve before resuming their exploration. Cartier then headed south, following the western coastline of Newfoundland to Point Rich before changing course to the west into the Gulf of St Lawrence. In late June, the seamen reached the Magdalen Islands. This small group of islands was unlike the rocky and barren lands Cartier had earlier observed in Newfoundland, being rich in pine, cedar, ash and elm trees, with abundant growth of underbrush. The fleet continued to the south, sighting present-day Prince Edward Island before turning to the west and following the coast of modern-day New Brunswick, exploring the many bays for possible passages to Asia. Cartier was pleased with the terrain, calling it, 'The fairest land that may possibly be seen, full of goodly meadows and trees.'

The French fleet reached the southern entrance to Chaleur Bay in early July, when the sailors made their first contact with local Indians. On 4 July, Cartier anchored his two ships in a small harbour he called Saint Martin and spent the next eight days exploring the large bay located between New Brunswick and the Gaspe Peninsula. As the Frenchmen rowed their longboats in the bay, looking for the waterway to China, they had their first encounter with natives from the Micmac tribe of the Algonquin Nation. While in a cove, their boats were approached by nearly fifty canoes filled with yelling and boisterous warriors. When the Micmacs surrounded the longboats, the mariners became frightened, firing their small cannon to scare off the natives. The following day, the seamen met ten canoes with Indians displaying animal pelts for trade. Cartier sent two men ashore with beads, knives and hatchets, and a lively barter quickly developed. On 8 July, the French captain resumed his exploration, rowing to the end of the bay without finding the strait to the Orient. As they turned back to the flotilla, the explorers met over 300 Micmac men, women and children carrying gifts of cooked seal meat, and the sailors gave them presents of knives, tin bells and glass beads as the Indians danced and sang for the foreigners. By 12 July, Cartier had rejoined his vessels, renewing his search for the route to China to the north.

From Chaleur Bay, Cartier navigated his fleet along the coastline, exploring the Gaspe Peninsula. While the French were reconnoitring for the channel to the Orient, they encountered Indians from the Iroquois tribe led by Chief Donnacona. As the sailors were trading with the warriors, Cartier developed a friendship with Donnacona. However, when he raised a large wooden cross decorated with the fleur-de-lys and the words 'Long Live the King of France', Donnacona became angry, telling the French mariners in sign language that the land belonged to him. Cartier tried to convince the chief that the cross was a navigation beacon, but had little success. He later met the chief and two of his sons on his flagship, giving them food and drink. He explained again in sign language that the cross was a landmark for other ships, and that he would be soon sailing back to his kingdom. Cartier asked the chief to allow two of his sons to return with the expedition to France, promising they would be treated well and returned the next year. After considering the request, Donnacona finally agreed.

In late July, Cartier ordered the crews of his ships to sail north-east into the Gulf of St Lawrence. He piloted the fleet across the Gaspe Passage, discovering a large island he named Assumption, now known as Anticosti. The French navigated eastward along the island's coast before changing course to the west. When the expedition reached the present-day Jacques Cartier Passage, the vessels encountered strong headwinds and dangerous currents. It was now early autumn, and with the threat of strong storms growing, the French captain decided to end his expedition before the men were forced to spend the winter in the uncharted wilderness.

Cartier set sail to the north, and with a strong westward wind pushing his fleet entered the Strait of Belle Isle on 8 August. He put in to a bay on the Canadian mainland, staying for seven days while preparing his vessels for the open sea passage to France. On 15 August, they raised anchor and, after crossing the northern coast of Newfoundland, steered into the Atlantic Ocean. The French seamen encountered fair weather and favourable western winds for the first half of the voyage, but after reaching the mid-point of the Atlantic they were struck by a fierce storm. The ships were pounded by powerful winds and waves as they pitched and rolled in the violent sea. The dangerous tempest lasted for three days before calm weather returned. Under the seamanship and navigational skills of Cartier, the flotilla survived the storm without the loss of a single sailor, and on 5 September he guided his two ships back into Saint-Malo harbour.

While the French expedition had failed to discover the western route to the riches of the Orient or return with quantities of gold or precious stones, Francis I was pleased with Cartier's accomplishments. The voyage had claimed new lands for the Valois crown and made contact with local native tribes. The captain had also begun talks for an alliance with the powerful Iroquois Indians, and brought back reports and samples of valuable natural resources. He had found rich fisheries, herds of seals and walruses and large forests of pines and numerous varieties of hardwood trees. The Indians had been friendly and offered an opportunity for missionaries to spread the Christian religion. From the natives, the French had heard stories of three powerful kingdoms in the interior that contained large amounts of gold, while vast regions remained to be explored where passageways to Asia might still be located.

The 1534 voyage enhanced Jacques Cartier's status and reputation as a mariner and explorer with the French court and church. The first expedition to Canada served as a reconnaissance of the coastline, and Cartier quickly began planning a larger and more extensive venture. Through the influence of his patron, Philippe Chabot, in late October 1535 he received a royal commission and the funds necessary to return to the New World to renew the exploration for the route to Cathay beyond Newfoundland. With a royal warrant, the master-pilot obtained three ships from the French navy and recruited crews from the experienced sailors of Saint-Malo. The flagship was a 100-ton carrack named *La Grande Hermine* (*The Great Ermine*) with twelve guns, while the second vessel, *La Petite Hermine* (*The Small Ermine*), was a caravel of 60 tons and four guns. The last ship, *La Emerillon* (*Sparrowhawk*), was a small bark of 40 tons and was designed to explore shallow coastal waters with sails and oars. The fleet was manned by 112 seamen, including several gentlemen volunteers, twelve relatives of Cartier and the two sons of Donnacona, Domagaya and Taignogny. In late April, supplies and equipment were loaded on the vessels and the men made ready to depart. On 16 May, the captain and his mariners gathered in Saint-Malo church to receive Holy Communion and the blessings of the bishop. Three days later, they boarded their ships and Cartier sailed out of Saint-Malo harbour under fair weather with bright blue skies and favourable seas.

The master-pilot followed the course of his first voyage, sailing past southern England and steering into the Atlantic Ocean under bright sunny skies during the day and the light of a full moon at night. The weather remained fair for a week before turning hazardous, with strong storms and contrary winds. The French fleet struggled across the North Atlantic as powerful gales battered the ships for five weeks. During a fierce squall on 25 June, the three vessels became separated and were compelled to sail to the rendezvous point alone. *La Grande Hermine*, piloted by Cartier, reached Blanc Sablon on the coast of Labrador on 15 July, and had to wait eleven days before the two smaller vessels arrived. The French remained on the Labrador mainland for three days, repairing damage from the crossing, collecting firewood and refilling their water barrels. At daybreak on 19 July, the sailors resumed their expedition, navigating down the Labrador shoreline.

Cartier continued to follow the course of his first voyage, piloting through the Belle Isle Strait and along the mainland coast of Canada, passing to the west of Anticosti Island with an eastern wind pushing the vessels forward.

During their nearly nine months at Saint-Malo, the two sons of Donnacona had learned to speak French, and they told the captain that the large body of land was an island and not part of the mainland as he had earlier believed. As the crews steered in a south-westward direction, Cartier erected a cross in a harbour west of Natashquan to mark his route before sailing through the Jacques Cartier Passage to the mouth of a large river that Cartier named the Grand River, later renamed the St Lawrence River. The ships anchored in a large bay that the master-pilot called St Lawrence, present-day Saint-Genevieve. From the two Iroquois brothers, he learned that the country to the west belonged to the kingdoms of Saguenay and Canada, while the river continued for many miles into the interior. Cartier now believed he had at last discovered the passageway to the Orient.

On 1 September, Cartier renewed his quest for Cathay, piloting his fleet up the St Lawrence River. The vessels moved slowly through the waterway, fearful of running aground in the uncharted river. The voyage was slowed further by periods of dense fog and contrary winds. While the French pushed forward, they observed an abundance of wildlife and animals never seen before, including beluga whales. The ships' officers made maps of the area, measured the depth of the river and noted the terrain features as they advanced upriver. Cartier soon noticed that the further his flotilla sailed from the Gulf of St Lawrence, the waterway gradually turned from saltwater to fresh. When the expeditionary force passed the outlet of a rapid and deep river, Domagaya and Taignogny told the Frenchmen that the waterway was the route to the Saguenay Kingdom. The sailors anchored the vessels and search parties were sent to reconnoitre the banks of both rivers. As the men investigated the region, they encountered a band of Iroquois, who had paddled their canoes from the kingdom of Canada to fish and hunt seals. They were frightened by the strangers, but Donnacona's sons were able to reassure the Indians that no harm would come to them and they agreed to board the flagship, greeting the French in friendship.

After the seamen had travelled over 60 miles from the St Lawrence Gulf up the river, on 7 September they encountered a series of small islands in the waterway that Donnacona's sons said marked the beginning of Canada. The largest of the fourteen islands was over 20 miles long and 7 miles wide, and was named Ile d' Orleans after Charles, Duke of Orleans, the third son of Francis I. When Cartier spotted a group of Indians on the island, he went ashore in his longboat with Domagaya and Taignogny to talk to them. The warriors were from Donnacona's tribe, and as Cartier and the two Iroquois brothers approached the shore, the natives became frightened and began to flee. However, when their chief's sons spoke to them, they returned, welcoming the two brothers and the foreigners. The Indians began dancing and singing, while more Iroquois brought gifts of eels, maze and several large melons for the Frenchmen. Cartier presented the Indians with presents of beads, knives and small bells. After the expeditionary force rowed back to the fleet, many canoes filled with members of Donnacona's tribe came to the ships to welcome the return of their chief's sons.

The following day, the Frenchmen renewed their voyage, navigating slowly and carefully up the river, as Cartier continued to map the territory and log the terrain features. As the fleet neared the Iroquois village of Stadacona, near current-day Quebec City, Donnacona, accompanied by twelve canoes of warriors, paddled out to meet the ships. The chief made a speech welcoming the sailors and his sons. When the Indians boarded the flagship, Donnacona was reunited with his two sons, who began describing to him their experiences and the favourable treatment they had received from the French. The chief was overjoyed at the stories his sons told him, and thanked Cartier with a kiss to the cheek. Cartier had food and wine brought on deck for his friends, and after a brief celebration they travelled upriver to Donnacona's village of Stadacona. During the journey, the captain noted the large cultivated fields of recently harvested beans, corn, squash, melons and tobacco.

While the ships steered toward the settlement, Cartier told the chief that he planned to sail further upriver to the kingdom of Canada, looking for a passageway to Cathay. When Donnacona heard this, he quickly became irritated, telling the Frenchmen there was little of value to the west. The chief and his sons attempted to convince the sailors to remain with their tribe near Stadacona. Cartier replied that he had been ordered by his king to travel up the waterway as far as possible, and must obey. Unknown to Cartier, the village of Hochelaga was located further upriver in the kingdom of Canada and was inhabited by Indians from the Huron tribe, who were not part of the Iroquois Nation. The Huron Indians were enemies of Donnacona, who wanted to remain the only trading partner of the French. He was determined to prevent Cartier from establishing a trading alliance with his rivals.

Despite the protests of the chief, Cartier began preparations to leave in the *La Emerillon*. Donnacona became more insistent, telling Cartier that his two French-speaking sons would not go on the voyage. When the captain insisted that he had to obey his king, Donnacona offered him two boys and a young girl as slaves if he would stay with his people, but the master-pilot refused to halt his exploration. While the French sailors were preparing the bark for the upriver expedition, Donnacona ordered three of his warriors to dress as devils with long horns and black faces and paddle their canoe by the French ships, shouting and making gestures. After the three devils passed Cartier's fleet, Taignogny and Domagaya told Cartier that their god, Cudouagny, had sent the spirits to warn the Frenchmen they would perish in the cold and snow at Hochelaga. Cartier replied that his God would protect his men from the dangers of the harsh weather.

On 19 September, Cartier sailed to the west in the *La Emerillon* with fifty seamen, leaving the remainder of his crews to guard the two larger ships. The bark moved slowly through the water, as the master-pilot recorded the terrain features and large numbers of birds in the area, listing swans, geese, ducks, pheasants and many other varieties in his logbook. The land on both sides of the St Lawrence River was covered with pine and hardwood trees, and the banks with ripe grapevines. He wrote in his log that, 'The sailors came back on board with their arms full of grapes.' During the voyage to Hochelaga, the explorers made contact with many Indians, who were mostly friendly and eager to trade for French goods. In mid-September, the *La Emerillon* reached the small village of Hochelay, some 30 miles west of Stadacona. The Frenchmen dropped anchor near the settlement of huts as the chief arrived to greet them. The Hochelay chief was welcomed aboard the ship and given several presents. During the chief's discussions with Cartier, he warned him through sign language that the river ahead was dangerous to navigate, with waterfalls, rapids and strong currents. When the captain renewed his journey, he soon encountered narrow channels and a series of cascades that slowed his progress.

The French sailed slowly forward, but in late September, with the approach of winter, Cartier decided to leave the bark and continue the voyage in two longboats to travel more quickly. The men loaded supplies and equipment in the boats, and taking half of the crew he resumed the search for Hochelaga. The two boats moved through the waterway in fair autumn weather, with three oarsmen on each side propelling the mariners west. Three days later, they reached the village of Hochelaga, modern-day Montreal. As Cartier's longboats approached the large village, the sailors were greeted by over 1,000 friendly natives on the river's edge. The Indians brought gifts of cornbread to the strangers, and spent the night dancing and singing in celebration.

On 3 October, Cartier with his gentlemen adventurers and twenty seamen armed with pikes and swords left their longboats and were escorted to Hochelaga by a sub-chief. As the French crossed an open field, they saw the village protected by a circular wooden wall with a single fortified gate and two redoubts. When the French sailors walked through the gate, they noticed over fifty wooden longhouses, with a large open space in the middle for a fire and divided into individual rooms. Cartier and his sailors were led to a central plaza, surrounded by men, women and children, who beseeched the foreigners to touch them as if they were gods. When the Frenchmen were seated at the centre of the plaza, ten Huron warriors carried their partially paralyzed chief to them on a deerskin litter in a ceremony of great pomp. Through sign language, Cartier was asked to rub the arms and legs of the chief. After he touched the Indian with his hands, the chief gave him his symbol of power, a red headband of porcupine quills. Numerous blind and crippled Hurons now came forward to be touched by the god-like strangers, as Cartier read passages from the Bible and said prayers in Latin. The ceremony ended when the French captain ordered his trumpeters and drummers to play their instruments, as the Indians danced and sang.

Following the ceremony in the central square, Cartier set out to explore a nearby mountain that he had earlier seen from the river. The reconnaissance party was guided to the peak by warriors from Hochelaga; from the summit, the Frenchmen saw a landscape of magnificent trees and thick underbrush blazing with early autumn colours of yellows, browns and reds, sweeping across the valleys and mountain ranges to the north and south for many miles. Cartier could follow the course of the St Lawrence River, noting a chain of powerful rapids upriver from the village that blocked any further travel to the west. He was disappointed that China could not be reached by the St Lawrence River, but learned from his Huron guides that another waterway to the north also flowed from the west, which was later named the Ottawa River. Cartier speculated that this river might be the route to the gold and silver of the kingdom of Saguenay. However, it was too late in the year to survey the region, and the Frenchmen departed from Hochelaga, beginning the journey back to the anchored *La Emerillon*. They reached the ship in mid-October, setting sail to Stadacona, and following a week of uneventful travel the expeditionary force arrived at its two waiting ships.

While Cartier and his explorers were away, relations between the French and Donnacona's Indians at Stadacona had rapidly deteriorated. Threatened with an attack by the Iroquois, the seamen had constructed a protective stockade near the ships. The structure was made from cut logs planted upright and joined together. For additional security, cannons from the vessels were positioned at strategic locations along the walls of the fort. It was too late in the year to return to France, and with winter fast approaching, Cartier was compelled to remain with the Indians at Stadacona. He ordered his men to stockpile food and firewood, and reinforce the defences of the compound.

Following his return from Hochelaga, Cartier was invited by Donnacona to meet with him in Stadacona. When the captain, accompanied by fifty sailors armed with pikes and swords, walked into the village, they observed that the natives lived in 25 feet longhouses built in semi-circles and covered with tree bark for warmth. The Frenchmen received a cheerful greeting from the Iroquois, with singing and dancing. In return for their friendly welcome, Cartier gave small presents to the Indians. Relations between the explorers and Iroquois had remained strained, and during the visit Donnacona gave Cartier a demonstration of his warriors' military might, showing him scalps taken by his men during battle in the summer as a warning. When the French returned to the fortification, the captain ordered his seamen to strengthen the defences, adding night guards and constructing a moat around the walls.

The French spent a pleasant October at Stadacona, as the early autumn foliage in the forest on both sides of the St Lawrence River broke out in magnificent colours of brilliant yellows, reds and golds against the background of evergreens. By mid-November, the river began to freeze, and the fleet remained frozen until April. The ice on the St Lawrence grew to 12 feet thick, and snow on the shoreline was over 4 feet high. Cartier had expected wintry conditions similar to northern Europe, but was surprised by the frigid temperatures and deep snow.

Conditions along the St Lawrence River quickly grew worse when scurvy broke out among the Frenchmen, who suffered from swollen limbs, rotting gums and acute pain. By February, twenty-five seamen had died and Cartier had only a few healthy men. He was concerned that the Iroquois chief would learn of his vulnerability and mount an attack, so ordered his able-bodied sailors to create noise behind the fort's wall as if the entire fleet's crew was working. As his mariners continued to suffer from the effects of scurvy, Cartier vowed to make a personal pilgrimage to Rocomadour and pray to the Holy Virgin if a treatment was discovered. Several days later, during a visit to the village, the captain learned of a native remedy for the disease from Domagaya. Donnacona's son told him that the boiled ground-up pulp from the white cedar tree's branches provided a cure. When the potion was made, many of the French explorers refused to drink the mixture at first, but after a few quickly recovered their health the objections disappeared.

During the winter months at Stadacona, Cartier compiled the first narrative of the culture, religion, society and customs of the Indians along the St Lawrence Valley. He held frequent discussions with Donnacona and other warriors, who provided additional information on the geography of the region. They confirmed the earlier Huron stories about the eastward course of the Ottawa River, reinforcing Cartier's hopes that the waterway was the North-west Passage. He also heard about the current-day Richelieu River, which flowed from the south into the St Lawrence River. From the description of the terrain in the area, Cartier assumed the land to the south was Florida. He listened to Donnacona's reports of the kingdom of Saguenay, which was accessible from the Ottawa River. The kingdom had large quantities of gold, silver and precious stones, and was inhabited by white men and women, according to the chief. Cartier was eager to launch a new expedition the next year to this rich kingdom, and decided to kidnap Donnacona and have him relate the wonders of Saguenay to Francis I at court to gain the crown's support for another voyage.

Cartier planned the kidnapping of Donnacona carefully, and trained his sailors in secret to carry out their parts. On 3 May 1536, he invited Donnacona, his sons and several others to witness the raising of a huge wooden cross decorated with French fleur-de-lys and a Latin inscription. When the Indians attended the ceremony, they were seized and hurried to the *La Hermine.* The next morning, a large crowd of angry Stadaconans gathered at the shore, threatening to attack the ship. To quell the rancour of the natives, the captain assured the chief that he and the others would return the following summer. The Indians were appeased when Donnacona spoke to them, promising to be back within a year. During the scurvy outbreak, the French had lost over twenty-five men, so lacking enough seamen for three ships, Cartier was forced to abandon *La Petite Hermine.* On 6 May, Cartier, his crew of eighty-five and ten Iroquois prisoners set sail for France in two vessels.

As the explorers began their journey home, the St Lawrence River became swift and deep from the spring floods, and the captain was compelled to anchor in a safe harbour until 16 May. The small flotilla was delayed again when the winds shifted from the east and the vessels were unable to travel downstream. Five days later, the winds finally changed direction and the men steered down the St Lawrence into the gulf. Cartier navigated through the Gaspe Passage into the strait that now bears his name. He sighted Newfoundland on 4 June, landing at Port aux Basques on the southern tip of the island. Two days later, the French seamen resumed their voyage, sailing east across open waters to the island of St Pierre, where they encountered fishing vessels from France. After exchanging news with the fishermen,

Cartier made a brief stop at Renewse harbour to replenish his supply of firewood and water before piloting across the North Atlantic. The fleet departed the harbour on 19 June, and with favourable western breezes made the transatlantic crossing to Saint-Malo in less than four weeks, ending the fourteen-month expedition.

The French ships docked at Saint-Malo on 16 July, and shortly after Cartier sent his report of the expedition to Francis I. He described his voyage across the Atlantic to the Gulf of St Lawrence and discovery of the St Lawrence River, by which his vessels had travelled deep into the new continent. During the venture, the Saint-Malo seamen had found a southern route to the St Lawrence Gulf from the Atlantic Ocean and made accurate maps of the river's valley. Cartier told the king he had met Indians from numerous tribes, establishing friendly relations with most of them, and had catalogued the region's abundant natural resources. The captain also wrote about his discussions with chief Donnacona and his stories of the vast wealth of the Saguenay Kingdom.

The French king was pleased with the results of the second expedition, rewarding Cartier with the gift of his flagship. However, Francis I was on the verge of war with Spain and was distracted by the ongoing diplomatic search for allies and preparations for the conflict. He finally met with Cartier and Donnacona the following year at his chateau of Fontainebleau. During the audience, the Iroquois chief told the king about the mines of gold and silver in the realm of Saguenay, describing the fabulous wealth in great detail. He discussed the kingdom's agricultural products, telling the monarch the local natives grew exotic crops of various spices, oranges, pomegranates and other mysterious fruits. The chief reported that he had personally visited the kingdom, and the region was inhabited by a white race, who flew with wings like bats. He further supported Cartier's belief that the Ottawa River flowed from the Orient. Francis I was delighted with Cartier's report and anxious to launch a third voyage to the riches of Canada. However, when war broke out with Charles I of Spain, the Saint-Malo captain was forced to wait before receiving his third charter for the expedition to the St Lawrence Valley.

While Cartier waited for the war with Spain to end, he received a commission from the French court, authorizing him to plunder Portuguese and Spanish treasure ships returning from the West Indies with cargoes of gold and silver. He further aided the king's war effort by supporting the rebels in Ireland in their war against Spain's ally, England. During the scurvy epidemic at Stadacona, Cartier had pledged to make a pilgrimage to Rocamadour, and following his return home he made the journey to the pious shrine in south-west France. When Cartier was not at sea, he managed his farm at Limoilou and renewed his relationship with the town's bishop and other influential officials from his small house in Saint-Malo.

Finally, after four years of delays, on 7 October 1540, Francis I issued a royal charter for a new voyage of exploration to the land of Canada. The expeditionary force was authorized to search for the kingdom of Saguenay and establish a permanent colony to enforce France's claim to the territory. The commission named Cartier as captain-general and master-pilot for the fleet of five ships and governor of the settlement. While he began making arrangements for the venture, in January 1541, Francis I placed Jean-François de La Rocque de Roberval in charge of the expedition as lieutenant-general. To Cartier's dismay, he was now under the command of Roberval. The lieutenant-general was from a noble family, a favourite of the king and former soldier. He had no prior experience as a mariner and left the preparations for the enterprise to Cartier, who spent the next four months enlisting the crews and settlers, collecting plant seeds and livestock for the farms and loading tons of supplies and equipment on the vessels. He had problems recruiting enough men for the settlement, and was compelled to supplement his colonists with fifty prisoners. The expedition was provisioned for two years, and in early May 400 sailors, 300 soldiers and several women began boarding the ships. By the time the French were ready to return to Stadacona, Donnacona and all but one of the Indians brought to France had died. In mid-May 1541, the flotilla was prepared to leave, but Roberval informed Cartier that his artillery and ammunition had not arrived, ordering him to sail without him. On 23 May, the five ships steered out of Saint-Malo harbour, following the course of the earlier voyages across the English Channel and around southern England into the Atlantic.

Several days after Cartier navigated into the Atlantic, his fleet was struck by a succession of violent storms, and for most of the journey to Canada his ships encountered strong winds and pounding waves. During a fierce gale, all but one vessel became separated from *La Grande Hermine*. The flagship took over a month to make landfall on the northern coast of Newfoundland. While the French waited at Belle Isle for the missing ships to arrive, the captain-general ordered his sailors to make repairs to their vessels and prepare to resume the voyage. Finally, in mid-July, his flotilla was reunited and the explorers renewed their passage up the St Lawrence River to Stadacona. The fleet anchored close to the Iroquois village on 23 August, the Frenchmen receiving a joyous reception from the natives. When the captain-general told the Stadaconans of Donnacona's death, they were surprised and agitated, but when he lied and told them the others were well and living in luxury in France, the Indians became pacified.

Cartier had originally planned to establish the colony near Stadacona, but with the mutual distrust between the French and natives intensifying, the location of the settlement was moved several miles away. He left his fleet at the village and was rowed upriver in a longboat, searching for a place to erect the town. He chose a site to build the colony past the entrance to the Choudiere River at Cape Rouge, naming it Charlesbourg-Royal after the king's son, Charles, Duke of Orleans. The five vessels were brought upriver and the settlers, livestock and supplies unloaded. The captain-general ordered the construction of temporary shelters and supervised the planting of cabbage, turnip and other vegetable crops, while some of his men were instructed to mine newly discovered fields of gold and diamonds. After samples of the gold and diamonds were gathered, the *Saint-Brieux* and *Saint George* were sent back to France with the precious metals and stones for the king. During the summer months, the French fortified the settlement with walls, while a second stockade was placed on a cliff overlooking Charlesbourg-Royal for added protection against an attack by the Iroquois.

While the construction of the colony continued, on 7 September the captain-general took two longboats, and with his gentlemen adventurers and fourteen crewmen set out to search for Saguenay. The reconnaissance party rowed in a westerly direction, passing Hochelay to the small village of Tutqnagy, where the local chief gave Cartier two guides to direct him upstream to the rapids. When the French reached the La Chine Rapids, the current-day Lachine Rapids, Cartier realized there was no way to sail a ship past the massive and powerful waterfalls, ending his exploration for Saguenay, and returning to the new settlement.

Following Cartier's return to Charlesbourg-Royal, relations with the Iroquois continued to deteriorate and he issued instructions to his mariners to prepare for a long and harsh winter season without assistance from the Stadaconans. The defences of the fort were shored-up and firewood and food supplies stockpiled, while men continued to hunt for gold and silver. Winter came early as the river froze and deep snow piled up. The Indians became more hostile, unleashing regular raids against the French in the settlement. All during the winter, the Stadacona warriors kept the French confined to the fortification with their relentless attacks. As the cold weather dragged on, an outbreak of scurvy erupted among the men, but was successfully treated by the drink made from the branches of the white cedar tree. When the snow and ice began to melt in the spring, Cartier decided it was impossible for the settlers to defend themselves against the bellicose natives, forcing him to abandon the colony and sail back to France.

In early June 1542, the captain-general and the French mariners left Charlesbourg-Royal in three ships, sailing down the St Lawrence River into the gulf and landing in the harbour at St John's, Newfoundland. Anchored in the bay he found Roberval with 300 men and three vessels, the *Vallentyne, Saint Anne* and *Leahefraye* (*Valentino, Saint Anna* and *Leah*). The lieutenant-general had been delayed for nearly a year before his expeditionary force departed from France on 16 April 1542. When Cartier met with Roberval, he warned him about the ongoing threat of Indian attacks at Charlesbourg-Royal. The French nobleman ignored the warning, ordering Cartier to return to the settlement with him. Cartier was convinced that the colonists could not defend themselves against the Canadian natives, and after carrying several chests of gold and diamonds on board his ships he disobeyed Roberval's orders, slipping out to sea during the night. He arrived at Saint-Malo in mid-October after a voyage in fair weather and favourable winds from the west.

Cartier received a hero's welcome from the population of Saint-Malo, where he became a permanent resident. When he sent the treasure chests to the French court, the king's assayers quickly determined that the 'gold' was worthless iron pyrite and the 'diamonds' quartz crystal. While Cartier remained at Saint-Malo, Roberval crossed the St Lawrence Gulf, travelling up the St Lawrence River with maps previously prepared by Cartier. He re-established the French colony at Charlesbourg-Royal, renaming it France-Roy. The French settlers were able to stay in Canada for less than two years due to the severe winters, outbreaks of scurvy and continued belligerence of the Indians. In mid-summer 1543, Roberval's expeditionary force abandoned the settlement, sailing back to France. Despite the many failures of the third voyage, Francis I rewarded Cartier with the gift of two ships from the expedition. He put the vessels into service as commercial transports, moving cargo to the ports of Europe. During his three expeditions to eastern Canada, Cartier was the first mariner to map the coast of the St Lawrence Gulf, record the culture, customs, religion, clothing and food of the native Indians, while describing the terrain features of the St Lawrence River Valley, establish the initial French colony in the New World and discover the St Lawrence River, which became the nucleus of a vast empire in the New World for the kings of France. The third venture to Canada was Cartier's last, and he spent his remaining years in Brittany, where he managed his farm at Limoilou and was treated as a nobleman by the residents of Saint-Malo. Jacques Cartier died at Saint-Malo on 1 September 1557, aged 66, and was interred at the local St Vincent of Saragossa Cathedral.

SELECTED SOURCES:
Brebner, John Bartlet, *The Explorers of North America 1492-1806.*
Coulter, Tony, *Jacques Cartier, Samuel de Champlain and the Explorers of Canada.*
Greene, Meg, *Jacques Cartier – Navigating the St Lawrence River.*
Morison, Samuel Eliot, *The Great Explorers – The European Discovery of America.*
Woog, Adam, *Jacques Cartier.*

Hernando de Soto

In May 1539, Spanish conquistador Hernando de Soto landed his army of 600 soldiers on the western coast of Florida near Tampa in search of gold and silver. Over the next three years, de Soto's men travelled more than 3,000 miles over unexplored territory in their quest for precious metals, fighting numerous battles with native Indians, while suffering from disease, starvation and exhaustion. During their expedition, the Spaniards explored the lands of modern-day America's deep southern states, becoming the first Europeans to cross the Appalachian Mountains. As the army struggled out of a dense wilderness in western Mississippi in early May 1541, de Soto stood on a low bluff overlooking a broad, swift river flowing from the north. He named the nearly mile-wide waterway the Great River, the present-day Mississippi River. Hernando de Soto's expedition opened the future American south to Spanish colonization from South Carolina in the east on the Atlantic coast to Missouri in the west.

Hernando de Soto was born in 1500 at the village of Jerez de los Caballeros in south-western Spain, the second son of Francisco Mendez de Soto and Dona Leonor Arias Tinoco. Hernando de Soto was from an impoverished noble family with a heritage extending back to Mendez Sorrel, who served King Alfonso IV of Leon as a squire and knight in the tenth century. Hernando was raised in the desolate province of Extremadura, receiving little formal education. His mother encouraged her second son to pursue a career in the church, sending him to school to study reading, grammar, Latin, mathematics and religion, taught by the local priest. However, Hernando was not a serious student, preferring to roam the rugged countryside and train as a soldier among the ruins of an abandoned castle with his many friends. De Soto spent his days drilling as a warrior, mastering the skills of fencing, equestrianship and archery, while engaging in mock battles with other boys from the town. As the second son, Hernando would not inherit the family's meagre possessions, and growing up hearing stories of conquistadors from Extremadura finding adventure and great riches in the New World, he was drawn to a career in the army.

In late 1513, Hernando de Soto left Jerez de los Caballeros, travelling to the port city of Seville, lured by the opportunity for adventure and gold in the New World. When he reached Seville, Pedrarias Davila, a conquistador and newly appointed governor for the town of Santa Maria del Darien, was recruiting a large expeditionary force for the colonization of Panama. De Soto volunteered for the campaign and was hired as a squire. In early January 1514, tons of equipment and supplies were loaded on the expedition's vessels, including weapons, ammunition and armour for the soldiers and seeds, tools, livestock and young fruit trees for the farmers. Late in the month, the armada of twenty-one ships and over 2,000 men was ready to leave port. After they attended Mass at the cathedral and marched in a grand parade through the narrow streets of Seville, the colonists and troops boarded the vessels. On 26 February, the adventurers departed from the harbour, navigating down the Guadalquivir River to the coast of Iberia before they were struck by a fierce late winter storm, forcing Davila to anchor his flotilla off-shore. The strong winds and waves pounded the fleet for two days, damaging most of the vessels. The expedition was compelled to spend six weeks in the small port of Sanlucar before repairs were completed. Finally, on 11 April, Davila's squadron set out for the island of Gomera in the Canary Islands to replenish its water, wine and food supplies before the transatlantic crossing. The Spaniards departed for the open sea on 9 May, steering on a south-western course and making landfall in the New World at the island of Dominica in the Lesser Antilles chain following a passage of twenty-six days. During the voyage, de Soto performed his daily duties as a squire, attending to the weapons, armour, equipment and horses of the knights, while taking care of their personal needs and continuing his training as a soldier.

The Spaniards remained on the coast of Dominica for four days, taking on fresh water and firewood and making repairs to the ships, before steering south to the Gulf of Santa Marta on the north coast of Colombia. Davila anchored his fleet off-shore and ordered a landing party of sixty soldiers to reconnoitre inland. After reaching the beach by longboats, the Spanish troops soon encountered a band of over 100 warriors with their bodies painted red, making threatening gestures and shouting. The commander of the conquistadors attempted to communicate with the Indians through sign language, but they began shooting arrows at the strangers. The soldiers then fired their arquebuses into the air, frightening the natives away.

The next day, Davila sent another contingent of troops ashore to continue reconnoitring inland. De Soto volunteered for the search party, taking part in the advance into the dense woods and discovering three recently abandoned villages. As the Spanish looted the huts and seized pieces of gold, they were suddenly assailed by the Indians. When the warriors fired a salvo of arrows, the Spaniards answered with shots from their arquebuses and crossbows, driving the hostiles away. The brief skirmish with the natives was de Soto's first encounter with belligerent forces. While the conquistadors renewed their exploration, Davila arrived with over 1,000 men, unleashing a brutal attack against the Indians. For three days, de Soto and the Spaniards burned villages, massacred the natives and enslaved the survivors of their savage assaults, while looting the huts and stealing nuggets of gold. After remaining on the Gulf of Santa Marta for several more days, the fleet sailed west to Darien in eastern Panama.

In late June, the Spanish ships reached the coast of Panama, steering up the San Juan River for 6 miles to the settlement at Santa Maria del Darien. Soon after the fleet anchored, Davila sent one of his lieutenants ashore to meet with the acting governor of Darien, Vasco Nunez de Balboa, to arrange his grand entrance into the colony. As the fully armed troops of the new governor led the procession into Darien on 26 June 1514, Davila walked in the tropical heat and humidity into the weather-beaten town, followed by the gentlemen adventurers and colonists, and was greeted by Balboa at the central plaza. Following their initial talks, the governor confiscated Balboa's house, establishing his headquarters and family in the small rooms. The next day, Balboa was summoned by Davila and the two met for several hours, discussing conditions in the settlement and surrounding area, the locations of the gold mines, relations with the Indians and recent expeditions to search for precious metals and a passage to the Orient. While Davila established his administration, de Soto remained with the troops, setting up his temporary living quarters in a tent on a dusty street. Staying in the town, de Soto renewed his training as a soldier, practising fencing, shooting with a crossbow and fighting with a halberd.

Santa Maria del Darien was unprepared for the arrival of over 2,000 new settlers and troops, and food supplies quickly became depleted. As the crisis escalated and colonists began dying from starvation, the governor ordered his soldiers to search the countryside for provisions. The poorly trained and ill-disciplined conquistadors raided the Indian villages, unleashing a fierce campaign of murder, looting, enslavement and torture. The Spanish seized the natives' gold and food, while forcing them to mine for more nuggets. The Spaniards' reign of terror continued over the next several years as the troops decimated the Panamanian native population. As one of the army's squires, de Soto took part in many of the bloody raids, pillaging and fighting alongside the knights and infantrymen.

While de Soto continued to train as a soldier and participate in raids against the natives, relations between the governor and Balboa became increasingly hostile. Late in 1515, the king appointed Balboa governor of Panama, while confirming Davila as viceroy for all the colonies in the region. Davila was already jealous of Balboa's exploits and discovery of the Pacific Ocean, and now felt threatened by the royal decree. He issued instructions for the arrest of the new governor and placed him in a cage. However, when the settlers threatened to revolt in support of Balboa, he was forced to order his release and forge a reconciliation with him. During the animosity between the two officials, de Soto learned to shift his support to the individual who best advanced his position in the army.

De Soto remained at Santa Maria del Darien with Davila's army until autumn 1517, when he joined Juan de Tavira's expedition to explore for gold in present-day western Colombia. Davila had heard stories from the Indians that large quantities of gold were located in the kingdom of Dabaibe, and appointed Tavira to lead an expeditionary force into the area. In September, the small fleet of three barks and seven large canoes departed from the beach, travelling south. After navigating over 30 miles, the Spanish reached the Atrate River and paddled upstream over 60 miles in several days to the border of the Dabaibe territory. The banks of the waterway were bordered with thick marshlands and dense forests. As the Spaniards slowly manoeuvred upriver during the rainy season, they were attacked by a band of Dabaibe warriors firing volleys of arrows from several canoes. During the skirmish, one Spanish soldier was killed before de Soto and the others drove the Indians away with their crossbows, swords and lances. The conquistadors continued to cautiously push on in their barks and canoes, when their small flotilla was struck by the flooding river as waves of water uprooted trees and pounded the boats. Tavira's canoe was overturned during the surge and he drowned in the raging waters. The rain-swollen river killed many of the Spaniards, and with most of their supplies and equipment lost, the soldiers were forced to return to Santa Maria del Darien.

Shortly after returning from the Dabaibe disaster, de Soto took part in Balboa's South Sea expedition to establish a new colony on the Pacific coast of Panama. In late November 1517, he joined Balboa's forces at the recently built staging area at Acla, 80 miles west of Santa Maria del Darien on the Caribbean Sea. The governor planned to use several thousand Indian slaves to transport pre-cut timber and equipment overland to a location on the Chucunaque River, and construct four barks to sail down the waterway to the Pacific. Once a base camp was erected, Balboa intended to search for a site on the Gulf of San Miguel coastline for his settlement. De Soto joined the Spanish as they slowly made their way to the river, guarding the enslaved native labourers and pushing them forward through the rugged, mountainous terrain. When Balboa reached the Chucunaque, he ordered his men to establish a camp and begin assembling the vessels. As the crews worked on the barks, the Chucunaque River suddenly flooded, washing away the expedition's supplies and partially assembled ships. Once the raging waters subsided, the encampment was rebuilt and troops sent into the wilderness to raid Panamanian settlements for food. While the soldiers were collecting provisions, new timber was cut and construction on the barks begun. In the late summer of 1518, two vessels were launched, sailing down the river with over 100 men, including de Soto, to the San Miguel Gulf. After building a camp on the Pacific coast, Balboa began exploring the gulf for a permanent settlement site. He chose the Pearl Islands, conquering the local inhabitants and seizing their land. De Soto was part of the expeditionary force, serving as a soldier raiding the native villages and ravaging the Indians.

As the Spaniards built the new colony in the Pearl Islands, Charles I of Spain issued a decree replacing Davila as viceroy for the Panama region with Balboa. When Davila learned of the king's decision, he was enraged that Balboa would take his offices, ordering the Panamanian governor to meet him at Acla. When Balboa arrived at the settlement, he was immediately arrested and charged with treason. Following a short trial he was found guilty and executed before a revolt erupted. After the death of their captain-general, de Soto and the soldiers remained isolated in the Pearl Islands, exploring the Gulf of Panama and searching for gold and slaves. Finally, in late spring 1519, they were ordered to abandon the colony and relocate to Davila's new capital at Panama City on the Pacific coast of Panama.

Following the execution of the Panamanian governor, de Soto continued to serve in Davila's army as it unleashed new campaigns of destruction and plunder against the natives in western Panama and Nicaragua. He again participated in raids against the Indians, while learning to organize pillaging forces, deploy his troops into battle line, gather intelligence, equip an expedition and lead men into combat. De Soto relentlessly devastated the Panamanians' lands, searching for gold and natives to enslave, developing into a brutal conquistador who ravaged and tortured the Indians without remorse in his quest for riches.

Hernando de Soto remained in Panama City for a few months before joining the expeditionary forces of Gaspar de Espinosa to search for new food supplies and gold in western Panama. In late July, Espinosa's fleet of two barks and 150 solders sailed south-west from Panama City to the village of Pocri on the Azuero Peninsula. The Spanish advanced north into the territory controlled by the Coiban, seizing food and slaves while searching for gold. The troops pillaged the first village they found, enslaving hundreds of Indians and plundering gold from their grave sites. As Espinosa's men marched deeper into the interior, they attacked the village of Asiento Viejo, easily overpowering the Coiban warriors. Espinosa met with the defeated chief and gave him the option of accepting Spanish rule and becoming Christian or suffering the wrath of his army. The chief agreed to become a vassal of the invaders, providing them with food and labour. During the campaign in western Panama, de Soto was appointed a captain and commanded a unit of cavalry, protecting the infantry from a surprise attack. In October, Espinosa ended his expedition and returned to the capital after gaining the fealty of the chiefs in the area.

De Soto remained in Panama City until 1520, when he joined Espinosa's new campaign to extend Spanish rule in the area around the village of Nata and search for a rumoured large cache of hidden gold. Before leaving the capital, Espinosa divided his small army into two forces. The main body of men led by the captain-general sailed west to the Parita region, while the remaining troops with Francisco Pizarro in command advanced overland. During the march, de Soto led Pizarro's vanguard of thirty horse soldiers. As captain de Soto travelled across the foothills of the Tabasara Mountains at the head of Pizarro's mounted conquistadors, he heard the sound of fighting, rushing his men forward to reconnoitre. When the captain rode over a hilltop he saw Espinosa's and Pizarro's reunited army surrounded and under attack from a large force of warriors. He ordered his troops forward, and as the cavalry charged down a ridge the Coiban Indians panicked at the unexpected assault, withdrawing and allowing Espinosa to escape to his ships. Espinosa reformed his scattered troops, sailing down the coast to the village of Nata.

Shortly after reaching Nata, the captain-general ordered Francisco Companon, along with de Soto and fifty men, to fortify the settlement, while the army transported shipments of plundered food to the capital. Following the Spanish departure from Nata, the Coiban warriors launched an attack against the settlement, driving Companon and his defenders back into their fortifications. With the troops greatly outnumbered, de Soto and one other horseman were ordered by Companion to break out and ride to Panama City for reinforcements. The two cavalrymen charged through the Indians' camp, riding overland to the capital in two days. After reporting the attack to Davila, de Soto was sent back to Nata with forty soldiers, while the viceroy assembled a larger relief force. De Soto returned by ship, reaching the colony in time to bolster Companon's resistance until Davila arrived with additional conquistadors to break the siege. Soon after the warriors withdrew into the hills, the viceroy dividing the territory around Nata and rewarding de Soto with the grant of a farm and Panamanian slaves to work the land.

For the next three years, de Soto remained in the foothills of the Tabasara Mountains near Nata, raising crops on his land. He took part in expeditions into the mountainous region of Parita, plundering native villages for gold and enslaving the Indians, while hunting for escaped slaves. As de Soto's wealth escalated and his reputation as a ruthless and skilled soldier grew, he developed a close relationship with Companon and the two conquistadors frequently campaigned together.

In early June 1523, Gil Gonzalez Davila arrived in Panama City, spreading stories about the abundance of gold deposits in an area to the north-west he called Nicaragua. When Pedrarias Davila heard the reports, the viceroy formed a partnership with several investors, raising an army to explore Nicaragua and plunder the gold. Late in the year, Hernando de Cordoba was given command of the expedition by Davila, sailing to present-day northern Costa Rica with over 200 soldiers before launching his campaign into southern Nicaragua. When de Cordoba assembled his troops, de Soto joined his forces and, after reaching Nicaragua, led the Spanish vanguard of infantrymen as the army advanced into a wide region of fertile lands stretching over 200 miles to the north and inhabited by several hostile tribes. As the expeditionary force marched up the valley, the Spaniards passed through expansive fields planted with various fruits and vegetables, while entering cities with narrow streets lined with white adobe houses and a central square surrounded by religious temples and pyramids for human sacrifices to the gods. Cordoba's men were attacked repeatedly by the native warriors, but the conquistadors with superior armament and firepower from their steel swords, lances, arquebuses, cannons and crossbows quickly overwhelmed them. The powerful 2,000-strong armies of the Nicoya and Diriangen city-states fell to the fury of the Spaniards' onslaught. By the spring of 1524, most of Nicaragua was under Spanish control and Cordoba began to build a permanent settlement by establishing the towns of Leon, Granada and Segovia on the Pacific coastline. He located his capital at Leon, installing a colonial government under his authority.

As Cordoba's settlers and Indian slaves built the new settlements, de Soto and several other captains were sent to reconnoitre the area to the north, where rival Spanish conquistadors had been discovered exploring and plundering the Indians. The search parties returned to Leon, reporting that Gil Gonzalez Davila was advancing south with a large army from Honduras and Pedro de Alvarado was heading into northern Nicaragua from modern-day El Salvador. With his authority and presence in his newly established settlements challenged, Cordoba ordered de Soto to take eighty soldiers and enforce his supremacy. In the summer, he led his men up the western region of the colony, locating Alvarado's forces in southern El Salvador. A confrontation was avoided when Alvarado began withdrawing his troops after receiving the governorship of present-day Guatemala.

With the threat of hostilities from Alvarado ended, de Soto marched his conquistadors 200 miles to the east, locating Davila near the Indian village of Toreba in Honduras. Davila soon learned of the presence of de Soto's men, and launched a surprise night attack as they slept. De Soto's forces were initially thrown back in disarray by the charging enemy, but the captain rallied his troops and drove off Davila. As his soldiers retreated, Davila asked for a truce, which de Soto granted, despite the protests of his lieutenants. While the two forces maintained an uneasy peace, Gil Gonzalez Davila sent for additional men. When his reinforcements arrived, he unleashed a second night assault, overwhelming the Spaniards from Leon and capturing de Soto. When Davila learned that Cordoba was assembling an army for the relief of de Soto, he agreed to free the prisoners and end his campaign in Nicaragua, withdrawing to his base in northern Honduras. After successfully completing his mission to defend Cordoba's government, de Soto returned to the capital and was rewarded by the captain-general with appointment to the office of mayor for Leon and granted a large share of the plundered gold.

While de Soto managed his extensive plantations and gold mines, Cordoba began to plot the overthrow of Pedrarias Davila's rule in Nicaragua, forming an alliance with Hernan Cortes in Mexico, who had recently come to Honduras to quell the revolt of his local governor. When de Soto learned of Cordoba's plans, he spoke out forcefully against the conspiracy. Confronted with strong opposition from de Soto, the captain-general ordered his arrest. He was imprisoned at the fortress in Granada, but was quickly rescued by Companon and several other conquistadors, who fled overland to Pedrarias Davila in Panama with the news of the rebellion. After travelling for nearly two months through wilderness and swamps, avoiding Indian attacks, the men reached the capital, reporting Cordoba's revolt to the viceroy. In March 1526, Davila and de Soto returned to Leon with a small army, forcing Cordoba to surrender.

Davila remained in Leon to personally administer the colony. However, in late 1526 he was forced out of office by Diego Lopez de Salcedo, who assumed the governorship by force of arms. De Soto enthusiastically supported the new governor, and when the Indians in the north rebelled he was sent with an army to reimpose Spanish authority. In the spring of 1527, he unleashed a campaign of savage attacks against the native villages, killing and torturing the Indians and forcing them to accept the king's rule. De Soto was richly rewarded for his support and battlefield victories, receiving grants of more land and Nicaraguan slaves, along with the appointment to the captaincy of the Governor's Guard.

Salcedo's governorship was short-lived when Charles I sent a royal decree confirming Pedrarias Davila as the crown's viceroy. However, when Salcedo refused to relinquish his office, de Soto again switched his allegiance, forming a faction in opposition, arresting and imprisoning him. In March 1528, Davila reached Leon and assumed the governorship for Nicaragua. De Soto spent the next four years in Leon, continuing to expand his land holdings and Indian labourers, excavating his many gold mines, selling captive natives in the slave markets and operating a profitable commercial shipping company. He again led raids into the mountains and tropical forests, hunting down the Nicaraguans and enslaving them. By the end of the decade, de Soto through the force of his personality and military skills had become a ruthless conquistador and wealthy landowner and investor, while developing into a respected and feared politician contending for governmental powers.

While Hernando de Soto was occupied with the subjugation of Nicaragua for the Spanish crown, Francisco Pizarro received a charter from Charles I giving him the authority to organize and command an expeditionary force for the conquest of the Inca Empire in Peru. Serving as a conquistador in the Spanish Indies, Pizarro had heard widespread rumours of a rich empire extending over 2,500 miles down the Pacific coast, from modern-day Ecuador in the north of South America to Chile in the south. The land of seven million people had been ruled since the early thirteenth century by a hereditary emperor, and despite the absence of a system of writing and the wheel, it had achieved a high level of civilization. The Incas had developed elaborate irrigation networks, intricate systems of roads and aqueducts, magnificent stone and adobe fortifications and buildings, extensive agriculture centres and mines with vast quantities of gold and silver. Motivated by the wealth seized by the conquistadors in Mexico and Central America, Pizarro was eager to pillage the gold and silver of Peru in the name of the Spanish king.

While in Leon, de Soto learned of Pizarro's expedition to Peru, and with the profits from the Indian slave trade diminishing and his gold mines producing less, decided to leave Nicaragua and join the mustering army. He negotiated an agreement with the brother of Francisco Pizarro, who was in Panama City enlisting soldiers for the venture, and was offered the lieutenant governorship of the largest Peruvian city, a vast tract of land and the appointment as lieutenant general for the army. After accepting the contract, he began recruiting troops, collecting supplies and preparing his ships for the voyage to Peru. The expeditionary force was largely financed by de Soto and his two partners, Hernan Ponce, a conquistador lieutenant, and Francisco de Castaneda, an investor partner, and in the autumn of 1531 their fleet of two vessels and 100 men set sail south for the coast of Peru.

After sailing for two weeks, de Soto's men joined the Spanish army in modern-day southern Ecuador on 1 December. The governor-general of the Peruvian expedition, Francisco Pizarro, had earlier reached the South American coast, establishing his base of operations on the island of Puna following several months of searching for the Incas. The new soldiers from Nicaragua were dismayed at the physical condition of Pizarro's troops, who were suffering from disease and starvation after struggling through the jungles and crossing arid lands, while under relentless attacks from the Indians. Far more distressing to de Soto was the discovery that the governor-general's brother had been given the rank of lieutenant general, which had earlier been promised to him. He was greatly disappointed at the decision and began scheming to enhance his own position and weaken Pizarro's standing and loyalty with the conquistadors.

In early 1532, Pizarro ordered his army of less than 200 infantrymen and 100 horse soldiers to advance against the Inca Indians. De Soto was named captain of the vanguard and led the cavalrymen on rafts across the Gulf of Santa Clara south of Puna to the village of Tumbez. Nearing the shore, the Spaniards were ambushed by the Tumbez warriors, with several conquistadors killed. Once Pizarro landed his entire force, the Spanish unleashed a fierce attack against the natives, hunting them down and killing them while destroying their villages and crops. The troops remained at Tumbez for a month, as Pizarro rested his soldiers and de Soto led reconnaissance patrols to collect intelligence about the location and strength of the Incas.

On 16 May, the expeditionary force left Tumbez, marching down the Peruvian coastline searching for a suitable port to establish a base for reinforcements and supplies to land. Following several days of reconnoitring the area, the governor-general chose the small village of Paita on the Pacific shoreline as his base of operations. The conquistadors remained along the coast for over three months, recovering from the journey, fortifying the Indian town against attack and preparing for the campaign against the Inca Empire. In September, after leaving fifty soldiers to hold Paita, the army of 200 men-at-arms began the advance inland toward the Andes Mountains.

While the Spanish were struggling through Peru, the Inca Empire was embroiled in a civil war that decimated the population, divided the Indians' loyalties and weakened the military power of the emperor. Atahualpa, the younger son of the recently deceased emperor, had just deposed his half-brother, Huascar, by force of arms and was attempting to reunite the northern and southern regions of the empire under his rule. As the Spanish expeditionary force advanced toward the mountains, with de Soto commanding the vanguard, Pizarro learned of the civil war and ordered his army to move to the town of Cajamarca, where Atahualpa was resting and holding court at his palace on the outskirts of town. De Soto and several mounted soldiers were sent ahead to arrange a meeting between the governor-general and the Inca emperor, inviting him to a celebration honouring his assumption to the throne. In mid-November, de Soto was received by the emperor, who agreed to attend the festival. The night before the meeting, Pizarro hid his troops in several abandoned buildings at Cajamarca and placed over thirty men with crossbows and arquebuses, along with several pieces of artillery, in a stone structure in the middle of the square to ambush Atahualpa the next day.

Shortly after noon, Atahualpa was carried into the plaza on a litter in a grand procession of dancers, singers, Inca noblemen and 5,000 unarmed soldiers. He was first met by the Spanish priest, Vicente de Valverde, who speaking through an interpreter urged the emperor to accept Charles I as king and convert to Christianity. When Atahualpa angrily refused, the priest signalled for the conquistadors to attack. The Spaniards unleashed a furious assault as their cannons, arquebuses and crossbows opened fire, while the troops charged from the buildings into the unarmed Indians. Crammed into the small square and narrow streets, with no escape, the Incas were slaughtered in the fury of the Spanish onslaught. The massacre continued for several hours as the invaders killed most of the emperor's men and forced the rest to flee in panic.

During the melee, Atahualpa was captured and taken to the governor-general. Realizing that by keeping the emperor alive the Spaniards were protected from assault, Pizarro ordered him held prisoner. On 17 November, the conquistadors pillaged the Inca camp and palace, taking large quantities of gold, silver and precious stones. Atahualpa noticed the Spaniards' lust for precious metals, offering them one room filled with gold and twice that amount in silver for his release. Pizarro accepted the emperor's proposal, and allowed him to continue ruling his empire while the payment was collected. It took eight months for the Inca Indians to gather the required amount of gold and silver ornaments and decorations for the ransom, and when it arrived at Cajamarca it was quickly melted down into small bars for ease of transportation. De Soto received a large share of the gold and silver, and while waiting for the treasure to be collected had developed a friendship with the emperor. When Pizarro ordered Atahualpa to be killed, de Soto argued against his slaying. The governor-general waited until his vanguard captain was searching for a reported Inca army, rumoured to be advancing against the Spanish from the north, to arrange the execution of the emperor. While de Soto was away, Atahualpa was tried for plotting a revolt and sentenced to death by burning. However, when he agreed to accept the Christian faith to avoid being burned, Pizarro had him strangled on 26 July 1533.

Without the emperor as a hostage, the Spanish were now vulnerable to attack by Atahualpa's army in Quito, located in current-day northern Ecuador. Pizarro moved quickly to influence the election of a new emperor who would be friendly to the invaders. He ordered the Inca chiefs to gather in Cajamarca for the selection of Atahualpa's successor. Pizarro's choice was Tupac Huallpa, the younger brother of the murdered Huascar, and when the chiefs assembled in the central square he was elected emperor. The governor-general later met with the Incas, convincing them to accept Christianity, submit to Charles I as their overlord and become allies of the Spaniards against the northern Quito army.

In mid-August 1533, the Spanish left Cajamarca, heading nearly 800 miles south to the Inca capital at Cuzco, with de Soto again leading the vanguard. The expeditionary force advanced down the royal road built by the Incas through the Andes Mountains, and with the support of Tupac Huallpa was greeted as liberators from the harsh rule of the Quitoans by the local natives. Under constant threat of ambush through the mountainous terrain, Pizarro divided his forces and personally led de Soto with most of the cavalry in the search for the Incas ahead of the army. After riding for two days, they found part of the Inca army in the valley of Jauja. As the horsemen rode down into the valley from the Andes, they were joined by the local Indians, who had suffered under the occupation of the Quito army. Reaching the valley floor, the Spanish charged into the Quito warriors, their steel swords and lances overrunning the enemy's first line of defence. Most of the fighting took place in fields of corn, where the Incas could not use their large numbers to overwhelm the Spaniards. Unable to defeat the invaders and their native allies, the Quito Indians withdrew to the south as de Soto and his horse soldiers continued to harass their rearguard.

Pizarro's men remained at Jauja for two weeks, resting and preparing for the push to Cuzco. Before leaving the village, he sent de Soto with a force of cavalrymen to scout ahead of the army. When de Soto returned to the advancing conquistadors, he reported that the Quito forces were destroying the bridges and food supplies on the road to the capital. In late October, the captain was ordered to take seventy horsemen and manoeuvre ahead of the enemy to secure the bridges and food stocks. Over a period of less than a week, the mounted soldiers dashed south through rugged terrain of steep ridges and deep canyons, seizing the bridges and holding them until Pizarro arrived with the army and heavy baggage. While scouting ahead, de Soto located troops from the Peruvian army on 28 October near the village of Vilcas. After reporting the information to Pizarro, the Spaniards launched a surprise attack early the following day. The Spanish and their native allies battled the force of 25,000 soldiers for two days before being compelled to fall back. As they withdrew, the Incas broke-off their pursuit, prompting de Soto to unleash a fierce counter-attack. However, as the Spaniards and their allies surged down a ravine, they were ambushed by several thousand Quitoans. De Soto and his men fought their way out of the trap, retreating to a strong defensive position. The enemy closely pursued the conquistadors but were driven off by a charge of the cavalrymen.

De Soto stayed at Vilcas for a short time before renewing his dash for Cuzco. From the village, he moved his fifty exhausted cavalrymen out of the mountains, advancing across parts of the Pampas Rivera Valley before turning east, riding through deep canyons and crossing several large rivers. In early November, the conquistadors reached the Vilcacongo River, and as the sun broke through the morning mist began to climb the eastern slope of the nearby canyon. As de Soto's men neared the summit, they were ambushed by thousands of Quitoans, who hurled rocks and spears and fired arrows at them. The weary Spanish tried to charge up the hillside, but were driven back. De Soto re-formed his troops on a flat area and waited for the Indians to attack. The warriors, dressed in vividly coloured uniforms and painted wooden helmets, surged forward but were struck by the cavalrymen on their charging horses and beaten back. The fighting continued until after dark, when the Spaniards and Peruvians broke off hostilities. During the night, de

Soto repositioned his soldiers to a nearby hill and posted his sentries. Shortly after midnight, the conquistadors heard the faint echoes of a trumpet from the valley below. As the calls grew louder, the captain ordered his trumpeter to answer. A relief party of fifty men had been sent by Pizarro and followed the sounds of de Soto's trumpet to join him. Early the next morning, de Soto's reinforced troops unleashed a surprise assault, charging up the slopes and pushing the unprepared Quito warriors back toward the crest of the hill. As the Spaniards pressed their attack, the battlefield was suddenly blanketed in a thick fog rising from the valley below, forcing both sides to end the fighting. The Incas retreated into the mountains to rejoin the forces of general Quitquit at Cuzco, while de Soto waited for Pizarro to arrive with the remainder of the army.

The united Spanish army continued its advance to Cuzco, and by mid-November was on the outskirts of the Inca capital. Quitquit had earlier positioned his forces in the hills, blocking the entrances to the city. Pizarro sent his troops and native allies charging into the Quitoan defensive line, steadily forcing them to withdraw. After his last position was breached, the Inca general ordered his soldiers to abandon Cuzco and retreat. The following day, the conquistadors slowly entered the city, expecting an ambush, but were greeted by the cheers of the population, who had suffered under the harsh rule of the Quitoans from the north of Peru. As Pizarro rode at the head of his army, he was accompanied by the new emperor, Manco, who had been elected as successor to his recently assassinated older brother. When the Spaniards reached the centre of Cuzco, they found street after street of stately homes built by the Inca nobility, magnificent palaces of the emperors, temples richly decorated with gold and silver and grand plazas. The Spanish camped in the central square and posted guards to warn of the expected Quito counter-attack.

While the Spaniards waited at Cuzco for the Quito army to return, the conquistadors began pillaging the city's public buildings, palaces and temples, seizing large quantities of gold, silver and precious stones. They stored the religious idols, plates, statues, armour, vessels and personal effects of the emperors in several large storehouses, under heavy guard. The soldiers spent much of November and December looting the riches of the Inca capital, while engaging in numerous parties, games, festivals and hunting expeditions in celebration of their victory. In late December, Pizarro received word that Quitquit was advancing against the Spanish outpost at Jauja. With the town in jeopardy, de Soto was sent with fifty conquistadors and 7,000 Indian soldiers from Manco to reinforce the garrison. De Soto's men had a difficult time moving through the mountains in the rainy season, arriving too late to take part in the fighting against the Quitoans. However, while de Soto's forces marched to the town, the local chief had rallied to the Spaniards' support, supplying several hundred troops to bolster the defences of Jauja and compelling the enemy to retreat.

After de Soto arrived at Jauja, he spent several months organizing a large army to drive Quitquit out of Peru. He received reinforcements from Cuzco, and Manco dispatched over 20,000 soldiers to the mustering force. The conquistadors began their campaign in March, marching north in pursuit of Quitquit. When the Incas learned of the strength of de Soto's army, Quitquit abandoned his quest for Cuzco, returning to his empire in the north. The Spaniards and their Indian allies followed the retreating enemy for over 200 miles before finally ending their chase and travelling back to Jauja in June.

While de Soto was forcing Quitquit north, the Spanish troops in Cuzco disregarded Pizarro's orders not to pillage and harass the population after he left the city to build a new capital on the coast at Lima. De Soto met Pizarro in Jauja and was appointed lieutenant governor for Cuzco to quell the rising disorder. He reached the Inca capital in early August 1534, establishing his headquarters and residence in a magnificent palace and moving quickly to end the plundering and violence against the inhabitants. He spent the next year creating a permanent governing council, installing a system of courts and police force and overseeing city services, while secretly pillaging the public buildings and palaces.

Relations between Pizarro and de Soto had remained strained during the Peruvian campaign. Following the defeat of the Quitoans, the governor-general became convinced that Diego de Almagro was more loyal and willing to follow orders than de Soto, appointing him as the new lieutenant general for Cuzco. As Almagro rode to take his office in March 1535, he received reports that the king had appointed him governor of Chile and Cuzco. When Almagro reached the capital, he attempted to take control of the city in place of Pizarro. However, his claim was disputed by a faction of Pizarro supporters, and hostilities quickly threatened to erupt. De Soto supported Almagro to gain his favour for another office in his administration. The crisis was finally resolved when Francisco Pizarro arrived in Cuzco with the king's charter, showing the appointment had not been awarded to Almagro. When Almagro read the document, he agreed to abandon his claim to the city. De Soto had openly sided with Almagro and was now deserted by Pizarro. With no further opportunities in Peru, he decided to return to Spain and petition the king for a new expeditionary force in the New World. In late 1535, he sailed from the port of Lima with his share of the pillaged gold, Inca treasures and slaves.

De Soto reached Spain in the *Santa Maria del Campo* (*Saint Maria of the Country*) in early spring 1536, sailing up the Guadalquivir River to Seville, after twenty-two years in the Spanish Indies. Leaving his ship, de Soto was greeted as a hero by the large cheering crowds as he made his way to the cathedral to offer prayers and gifts in thanks for his safe return. He stayed at the home of a friend while making arrangements to purchase a palace. After de Soto paid the taxes on his gold, he bought a large mansion and hired a household staff appropriate for a nobleman. During the summer months, he was occupied attending parties, martial tournaments and gambling events.

Shortly after reaching Seville, de Soto began planning for his expedition to the New World, petitioning the regime for approval to conquer present-day Colombia and Ecuador or explore the Pacific Ocean area. De Soto built a large network of courtiers and nobles at court to present his application to the crown, and from the widow of his former patron, Pedrarias Davila, he gained a high-placed supporter with great influence with the throne. Through her, the captain was reintroduced to her daughter, Isabel, whom he had previously met in Panama. To enhance his standing with the nobility by marrying into a powerful family, de Soto agreed to the marital contract arranged by Isabel's mother. The wedding took place in November 1536 in a grand ceremony attended by nobles, courtiers and soldiers. In late March of the following year, de Soto was finally summoned to court and met Charles I, promoting his commission for a new conquest. He later received his charter for an expedition to Florida in the West Indies. The contract was signed on 20 April 1537 and gave de Soto permission to seize and settle the territory from northern Mexico eastwards to Florida, while naming him governor of Cuba. The Spanish regime had earlier sent several expeditions to Florida, and in 1525 had sailed up the present-day coast of Georgia searching for gold. In mid-July 1526, three Spanish ships under the command of Lucas Vasquez de Aylion navigated from Hispaniola, with 600 settlers coming ashore near the mouth of the Savannah River and founding the colony of San Miguel de Gualdape on Sapelo Island. The outpost was the first European attempt to establish a permanent settlement in the future United States. After struggling through outbreaks of disease, food shortages and Indian attacks for three months, the less than 200 survivors abandoned San Miguel and returned to Hispaniola. With his exploration licence, de Soto was eager to renew the quest for the reported riches in the region.

De Soto spent the next year purchasing the ships for his fleet, recruiting gentlemen adventurers, sailors, soldiers and settlers, while collecting supplies and equipment for the Florida expedition. He assembled his flotilla of seven carracks and three caravels in Seville, making the 800-ton *San Cristobal* (*Saint Christopher*) his flagship. In early April 1538, the expeditionary force of 700 men and several women gathered at the port of Sanlucar de Barrameda on the southern coast of Spain. On 7 April, the Spaniards heard Mass in the cathedral, and after a last meal of fresh food boarded their vessels to sounds of blaring trumpets and booming cannons as the armada slowly moved out to sea. De Soto made a stopover in the Canary Islands to replenish his food supplies, wine and water before sailing for the Spanish colony of Santiago in Cuba.

The Florida expeditionary force made landfall in early June 1538 at Santiago in south-eastern Cuba, with de Soto quickly assuming his office of governor at Government House. He was occupied for the next four months purchasing additional supplies, food and livestock, while training his troops and governing the island. He chose the port of Havana in the north-west of the island as his base of operations for the invasion, and in the early summer assembled his cavalry to ride to the city. During the long overland journey, he visited the towns on his route to monitor his local officials, while continuing to drill his cavalrymen, recruit additional soldiers and buy horses and mules. After reaching Havana, de Soto began finalizing his plans and preparations for the Florida venture. He sent one of his trusted captains with two ships to explore the western coastline of Florida and locate a safe harbour for his army to land. Before departing, he named his wife acting governor, establishing her in a spacious mansion in Havana. On 18 May 1539, the Spanish fleet of five carracks and four smaller vessels with 600 soldiers and seamen sailed out of Havana harbour for the short voyage to the western coast of Florida.

In late May, the expeditionary force landed in present-day Tampa harbour, with de Soto and his army soon leaving their ships to clear a campsite on the beach, while scouting patrols were sent to reconnoitre inland for gold and Indians. After the equipment, supplies and animals were unloaded, de Soto led his men north, with the vanguard of horsemen leading the way, as hostile Florida natives delayed the Spanish with ambushes and sporadic attacks. As the Spaniards marched up the peninsula in the hot and humid weather, they discovered many villages that had recently been deserted by the Indians. The conquistadors pillaged the natives' huts, looting food and everything of value. De Soto kept pushing his troops forward, while sending his scouts ahead to search for gold and food.

Despite the repeated hit and run attacks of the Floridians, the conquistadors reached the hastily abandoned native settlement of Ocale in late July, where they found a large supply of corn, beans, plums and several other fruits, but no gold. The Spaniards remained at Ocale for a few days, resting from their journey through the heat and swamplands. As they resumed their march north, the explorers were ambushed by the natives at a river crossing. The Indians unleashed volleys of arrows from their 7 feet longbows but de Soto's soldiers, dressed in armour, charged forward with their slashing swords, thrusting lances and thundering arquebuses, forcing the enemy warriors to fall back.

After crossing the river and advancing toward present-day Gainesville, a Spanish scouting party captured seventeen natives, including the daughter of chief Aluacaleyquen from the Timucuan tribe. The following day, the chief surrendered to de Soto, offering to exchange himself for his daughter but the Spaniards ignored his proposal and also held him prisoner. As the invaders marched on, they were followed by a large band of warriors, who harassed the conquistadors with repeated attacks and calls for the release of the captives. On 15 September, de Soto's expedition reached the Timucuan village of Napuituca, where the Indians planned to ambush the foreigners by luring de Soto into a meeting with their chief. However, he discovered the plan and prepared his men to attack. When the governor approached the chief, the signal was sounded and the conquistadors surged out of the woods into the unsuspecting Timucuans. A fierce fight erupted on a flat clearing, where the cavalrymen charged into the warriors, running them down and killing them with their swords and lances. The Floridians were crushed by the fury of the Spanish charge and forced to retreat.

The expeditionary force stayed at Napuituca for over a week before continuing west and crossing the Suwannee River in northern Florida. The Spanish army found several Timucuan villages, but they had been deserted by the fleeing natives after hearing of the defeat at Napuituca. While at the settlement of Uzachile, one of de Soto's reconnaissance patrols captured over 100 Timucuans, who were enslaved and used as porters and servants. By the end of September, de Soto's troops were entering the lands of the fierce Apalachee tribe, which had earlier driven off several Spanish expeditions in search of gold and slaves.

The Apalachee warriors had been monitoring the Spanish army's march, and as de Soto moved into western Florida near the Aucilla River on 1 October, his men were attacked. The warriors surged out of the woods into the vanguard as it entered a marshy area, while de Soto rushed his forces forward in support. The fighting raged throughout the day, but after the Spaniards manoeuvred the Indians onto a flat clearing, de Soto's horsemen beat the enemy troops back with many casualties. As the Apalachees withdrew, the conquistadors continued their advance, reaching the settlement of Ivitachuco. As they approached the abandoned native village, the Indians set the huts and storehouses on fire. However, de Soto arrived in time to save most of the crops. His army spent the day in the village, harvesting the corn, beans, squash and other vegetables before trudging north to the Apalachee capital at Anhanica.

During the trek north, the conquistadors were struck by sporadic raids by the Indians, who assailed their vanguard, flanks and rearguard. The Spanish continued to push forward, finally reaching the native capital on 6 October. De Soto's troops cautiously entered the quiet settlement, wary of an ambush, but Anhanica was deserted. With the winter season fast approaching, the Cuban governor decided to stay in the village until spring. He ordered his men to fortify the capital, turning it into a fortress. While the Spaniards remained in the settlement, the Apalachee warriors continued their sorties against the stronghold, while ambushing reconnaissance patrols. De Soto sent envoys to the Apalachee chief asking to negotiate a peace, but the Indians responded by intensifying their forays, firing flaming arrows and throwing torches over the walls. During the long winter nights, de Soto and his conquistadors were entertained by the tales of a captured native boy, who described in great detail a rich land to the west called Cofitachequi, ruled by a woman, who regularly collected tributes of gold and silver from her chiefs. The stories inflamed the soldiers' desire to resume the expedition, despite the danger and hardships.

While remaining at Anhanica, the governor sent one of his trusted captains, Francisco Maldonado, south to search for a harbour to land his supply ships. After exploring the coastline, Maldonado returned to the fort reporting the discovery of a sheltered deep-water bay he named Achuse, present-day Pensacola. Shortly after his arrival, he was ordered back to Cuba with authority to organize a fleet of relief ships to rendezvous with the army in the autumn at Achuse.

After spending five months in the abandoned Apalachee capital, on 3 March 1540 the conquistadors resumed their quest for gold and silver, marching north. During the hard winter, many of the Indian porters had died from starvation and exposure, forcing the troops to carry much of their own equipment and supplies. The advance was soon delayed by the rain-flooded Capacheguy River, compelling the men to build barges to safely ford to the opposite bank. After several weeks of trudging through the wilderness, the army entered modern-day southern Georgia, where the local Creek tribe was more friendly and accommodating than the Floridians. The Creeks willingly provided food to the Spanish and served as guides as they passed through their lands. As the soldiers reached the northern boundary of the Georgia Indian kingdoms, de Soto was told by a captured native that the realm of Cofitachequi was only a short distance to the north-east. The Spanish struggled on in search of the rich kingdom through uninhabited lands of pine forests and valleys as food supplies became depleted.

In early May, the Spanish army reached a large village of the Cofitachequi ruler located on the Wateree River in present-day central South Carolina. Soon after the arrival of the Spaniards, a delegation of the realm's nobles met with de Soto to find out the motives for his expedition. The governor told them he came in peace and requested a meeting with their sovereign. A short time later, a woman arrived in a canoe covered with a white cloth canopy. The queen welcomed de Soto and gave him gifts of freshwater pearls and painted animal skins. When he questioned her about the gold and silver that were to be found in Cofitachequi, she commanded the town's population to give the Spanish troops all they had. The natives brought freshwater pearls and worthless nuggets of mica. The disappointed conquistadors had expected to find substantial quantities of the precious metals and began plundering the settlement's temples and gravesites, seizing large amounts of pearls but no gold. Once the town had been looted of its riches, the Spaniards attacked the nearby village of Talimeco, pillaging its temple and coffins. De Soto's men stayed in Cofitachequi for nearly two weeks, continuing to search for gold and food. When the kingdom's warriors began to threaten an attack, de Soto took the queen hostage and on 13 May marched his army north-west toward the chiefdom of Chiaha, where he had heard large supplies of gold and silver could be found. During the journey, the queen managed to escape and returned to her people.

The Spanish expeditionary force trudged through the foothills of the Appalachian Mountains into modern-day western North Carolina, where de Soto entered the territory of the Cherokee Indians. The Cherokees welcomed the Spaniards, sharing their food with them, carrying some of the expedition's baggage and serving as guides on the difficult advance along the Hiwassee River below present-day Murphy, North Carolina. With the assistance of the Cherokees, de Soto's troops were the first Europeans to cross the Appalachian Mountains, and on 31 May they entered the chiefdom of Chiaha, 25 miles east of Knoxville, Tennessee. The Cherokees were initially friendly, but when de Soto demanded thirty women for his soldiers, they smuggled them out of the village into the woods. In retaliation, the Cuban governor unleashed a brutal pillaging raid on the natives, destroying their crops and huts. A compromise was finally reached when the Cherokees offered 500 men to serve as porters for the journey.

In mid-August 1540, the conquistadors broke camp, and with the Cherokees carrying the baggage began the march south into present-day Alabama. The expedition followed the Alabama River into the lands of the Choctaws. As the Spanish trudged on, they were met by a delegation of nobles sent by a powerful chief, Tascaluza, who welcomed the soldiers to their territory and invited them to visit their capital. With the nobles guiding the explorers, they reached the town on 10 October. As de Soto entered the settlement, he was presented to Tascaluza, who was seated on a platform surrounded by his nobility. De Soto was greeted with contempt by the chief, and when he demanded food and porters for the continuation of the journey, Tascaluza replied that they would be provided at the village of Mauvilla, north of present-day Mobile.

As the Spaniards advanced to Mauvilla, de Soto's reconnaissance patrols warned him of an ambush in the village. The governor ignored the danger, and on the morning of 18 October rode into the heavily fortified settlement with his vanguard's cavalry in a show of force. The village was encircled by wooden palisades with strategically placed towers for the Choctaw archers. He was greeted by flute players and dancers, who escorted him to the central open space, where the Spanish met the chief. The horse soldiers were at first received in friendship, but when Tascaluza disappeared and the Spaniards noticed the houses were full of armed warriors, they drew their swords and attacked the Choctaws. Several thousand natives stormed out of the huts and other buildings with clubs, spears and bows, attacking the horsemen. De Soto mounted his horse, and with several cavalrymen charged into the Indians, clearing an opening for his soldiers. The conquistadors rode through the open gate to safety. As the main body of Spanish troops began arriving, de Soto deployed his army into four detachments, launching an assault against the sides of the fortification, while under fire from Tascaluza's bowmen positioned in the fort's towers. After making repeated unsuccessful attacks against the defensive walls, in the late afternoon the Spanish broke into the settlement and began burning the houses, huts and storehouses. Hundreds of Choctaw warriors became trapped in the fort and were killed by the fire. The Indians who escaped from the town were slaughtered by de Soto's waiting forces as they entered the open field beyond the stronghold. During the fighting at Mauvilla, the governor's men sustained over twenty killed and nearly 200 wounded, with many later dying from their wounds, while Tascaluza lost close to 3,000 warriors. The troops also suffered the loss of their supplies, equipment, food and pillaged pearls in the raging fire.

De Soto and his army spent nearly a month at Mauvilla, resting, tending to the wounded and searching for food. Before leaving the settlement, the governor learned from captured Indians that Maldonado's ships from Cuba were at anchor in Achuse Bay. However, after the loss in the fire of his only treasure, and with his men in battered and emaciated condition, de Soto knew if he returned his reputation as a successful conquistador would be ruined and he would never receive a charter for a second expedition in the Spanish Indies. To keep alive his quest for riches similar to those found in Mexico and Peru, in mid-November he decided to leave Mauvilla and resume his march in a north-western direction in search of a winter camp. After crossing the Black Warrior and Tombigbee rivers, the Spanish army entered the lands of the Chickasaw Nation in north-eastern Mississippi. In the region around present-day Tupelo, the soldiers located an abandoned village and established their winter quarters, building new huts of wood and straw and erecting fortifications. The natives had quickly deserted their settlement after learning of the approach of the Spaniards, leaving their crops, and de Soto's men found enough corn, beans and squash to survive the winter.

In January 1541, the conquistadors' camp was visited by the local Chickasaw chief with several warriors, bringing gifts of food and animal furs. For the next few weeks, the Indians continued to visit the troops, establishing friendly relations. Despite their perceived attempts to gain the Spaniards' trust, in the early morning of 4 March several hundred Chickasaws launched a surprise assault against the sleeping soldiers, setting their huts on fire. The Spanish were caught completely by surprise and struggled to beat back the enemy forces. However, when their horses panicked and broke loose from their halters, running into the warriors, they withdrew into the woods. During the battle, de Soto lost fifteen men and much of his supplies. He relocated his camp several miles away, caring for his wounded and preparing for a second assault. When the Chickasaws attacked again, the Spaniards were prepared, driving them off.

De Soto's battered and ragged army stayed at their encampment until April 1541, when they headed west. During the march, the soldiers continued to raid Indian villages for food, fending off their counter-attacks. After trekking through the dense wilderness of western Mississippi, in mid-May de Soto standing on a cliff looked down on a broad muddy river, calling it the Grand River, now known as the Mississippi. The outlet of the river had earlier been explored by the Spanish, but de Soto was the first to discover and reconnoitre the waterway inland. The expeditionary force was now blocked by the river, forcing de Soto to build four large barges to ferry his men, animals and supplies to the opposite bank. It took nearly a month to cut down trees and assemble the rafts. As they worked on the barges, the Indians drifted down the river, firing volleys of arrows at the work parties from their canoes. Despite the relentless attacks of the natives and strong river currents, on 18 June the Spaniards boarded the rafts with their horses and baggage, fording the river without incident.

On the Arkansas side of the river, the Spanish army travelled to the west, noting the many fortified settlements of the local Indians. At the village of Pacacha, the conquistadors traded with the natives for food and animal skins to replace their threadbare clothes. They remained in the village, resting and collecting food, while scouting the region for information on gold or other treasures. De Soto led his troops further west, discovering the Arkansas River near present-day Little Rock, but again found no gold. The expedition marched to the Ouachita Mountains before turning south-westward to Camden, where the Spaniards spent the winter. The soldiers survived the heavy snows and freezing temperatures in their wood and straw huts, while stealing food from the natives and hunting the bountiful deer. During the winter, de Soto decided to return to the Great River and, after constructing two ships, sent a party of men to Cuba for more supplies and reinforcements.

In March 1542, de Soto and his 300 survivors began the trek back east to the Mississippi River. They struggled through snow and forded the swollen Ouachita River, while fending off repeated assaults by the Ais and Asinai Indians. By early May, the remnants of the army neared the Mississippi River, close to present-day Ferriday, Louisiana. During the march to the river, de Soto became seriously ill with a high fever from typhoid or malaria, dying at the age of 42 on 21 May 1542. Before his death, he named Luis Moscoso de Alvarado as the new leader of the army. To conceal the death of de Soto from the Indians, who had been made to believe that all Christians were immortal, Alvarado and several men placed the corpse in a large hollow log and rowed it out into the Mississippi River. After reaching the middle of the river, they heaved the rotting body into the swirling muddy water, where it quickly sank to the bottom.

After Moscoso de Alvarado assumed command of the tattered and battered Spanish army, he first attempted to return to Cuba by advancing overland to Mexico, but was soon forced to return to the Mississippi River.

Near the banks of the river, the Spaniards built seven small ships, sailing south in early July 1542 into the Gulf of Mexico, and then along the coast, finally reaching the mouth of the Panuco River near Tampico, Mexico. The 311 surviving conquistadors were found by local Indians, who took them to the nearby Spanish colony, ending their 3,000-mile overland journey that had taken over three years. While Hernando de Soto failed to find deposits of gold or silver, his expedition opened the future American south to Spanish colonization from present-day South Carolina on the eastern Atlantic coast to Missouri in the west.

SELECTED SOURCES:
Albornoz, Miguel, *Hernando de Soto – Knight of the Americas.*
Duncan, David Ewing, *Hernando de Soto – A Savage Quest in the Americas.*
Whitman, Sylvia, *Hernando de Soto and the Explorers of the American South.*
Young, Jeff C., *Spanish Conquistador in the Americas.*

Francisco Coronado

In the autumn of 1542, Francisco Coronado and his battered and torn Spanish army returned to Mexico City after spending over two years searching for the fabled Seven Golden Cities of Cibola. During the expedition, his conquistadors trudged into the interior of the current-day American southwest, travelling through parts of New Mexico, Arizona, western Texas and north through the Oklahoma Panhandle to central Kansas. While reconnoitring for the Seven Cities of Gold, the expeditionary force discovered the Grand Canyon, explored the Colorado River and investigated the Rio Grande Valley near modern-day Santa Fe, New Mexico. After the exploration parties returned to their basecamp without finding any treasure, Coronado moved east into the Palo Duro Canyon region of Texas in the spring of 1541, still looking for the Seven Golden Cities. In the valley, the Spaniards heard stories of a golden city to the north and Coronado led a small force of soldiers into Kansas to be disappointed once again, finding only another native settlement. Finally realizing that the Seven Golden Cities were only Zuni, Hopi and Wichita Indian villages, in early 1542 Coronado ended his failed two-year 6,000-mile quest for riches and fame, returning to Mexico.

Francisco Vasquez de Coronado was born in 1510 in the town of Salamanca in west central Spain, the second son of Don Juan Vasquez de Coronado and Isabel de Luxan. Francisco was born into a wealthy noble family with a large estate and influential friends at the Spanish court. As a nobleman, he was educated in the local schools, receiving instruction in reading, writing, mathematics, religion, science and Latin. Following local tradition, the family's estate was inherited by the older brother following the death of his father, and with little prospects in Salamanca, Francisco chose to pursue a career in the royal government. Through friends of the family, he secured an administrative position with the crown. While serving at court, he met and became friends with Antonio de Mendoza, a relative and favourite of King Charles I. With Mendoza's support and influence, Coronado rose quickly through the ranks of the government to hold offices of responsibility. While working for the king, Coronado was employed by Mendoza as his personal assistant, further strengthening the bonds between the two. Despite his success at court, Coronado had only a limited future in Spain and was increasingly drawn to the stories of great riches and fame in the Spanish Indies. His dreams of adventure and wealth in the New World were realized when Mendoza was appointed to the office of viceroy for New Spain and Coronado became part of the new administration in Mexico City.

In 1535, the 25-year-old Francisco Coronado arrived in Mexico City with Mendoza's government to the sound of welcoming trumpets. Retaining the favour of the viceroy, he was named to a position of importance in the administration, and with his natural abilities, leadership and charisma, rose quickly to a high office. As Coronado oversaw the king's policies in the capital, he became a power in the political circles of New Spain. Through his relationship with the viceroy and position in the government, Coronado was introduced to Beatriz Estrada, the daughter and heiress of Don Alonso de Estrada, the Mexican royal treasurer and illegitimate son of King Ferdinand II. The wealthy Estrada family owned several large estates in New Spain and was highly influential at court in Spain and in Mexican affairs. In late 1536 or early the next year, Coronado and Beatriz were married in Mexico City. Beatriz was described by contemporaries as a woman of beauty and piety. During their seventeen years of marriage, they had five children – one son and four daughters. The union with the Estrada family gave Coronado a link to Spanish nobility, while bringing him a large plantation south of Mexico City and a mansion in the capital. More importantly for Coronado, the marriage gave him greater influence with the regime and Antonio de Mendoza.

Shortly after his marriage, Coronado was ordered by the viceroy to take a detachment of soldiers and suppress the ongoing rebellion in the town of Taxco, 45 miles south-west of Mexico City. The Indians and African slaves had seized control of the local silver mines and refused to surrender to the town's officials. Coronado marched his men into the town, and with overwhelming military power quickly restored order with few casualties. Following Coronado's return to the capital, Mendoza rewarded him with an appointment to Mexico City's governing council.

When Nuno de Guzman, the Spanish governor for the Mexican province of New Galicia, was arrested in August 1538 for his harsh policies and cruelty against the Indians, Coronado was named as his replacement through the intervention of the viceroy. He and his wife soon moved to the province's capital at Compostela, where he assumed his duties as governor. During his governorship, Coronado was occupied building roads and improving the defences of the region against Indian attacks. He continued to expand his network of politically powerful supporters and friends with the prominent men of New Galicia. As governor, he initiated measures to protect the natives from abuse by the settlers and investigated rumours of the discovery of gold near Culiacan in western Mexico for the viceroy.

In December 1538, Coronado received messengers from the mayor of Culiacan, Melchior Diaz, that his town was under attack by Indians led by chief Ayapin. The governor quickly assembled a small force of soldiers, marching west to the relief of the town. The Spaniards trudged through the dense jungles, reaching Culiacan late in the month. With the military support of Diaz and his settlers, Coronado easily quelled the uprising, driving Ayapin and his warriors into the hills. The Spanish pursued the fleeing natives, capturing their chief and later executing him.

As the governor was mustering his army for the defence of Culiacan, he was joined by Friar Marcos de Niza, who had been sent by viceroy Antonio de Mendoza to explore and investigate the country to the north, where survivors of an earlier expedition had reported finding large quantities of gold and silver. Eight years before Coronado arrived in New Spain, Panfilo de Narvaez led an army of Spanish settlers in 1527 to establish a new colony in Florida, while searching for gold. After the Spaniards were repeatedly attacked by Indians, and facing starvation, Narvaez was forced to abandon his settlement and return to Mexico. The explorers built several small ships, sailing from the coast of Florida into the Gulf of Mexico to the west. The small flotilla was struck by a fierce storm, with powerful winds and waves pounding it and sinking most of the vessels, while driving one ship to an island near modern-day Galveston, Texas, where the survivors were rescued and cared for by the local natives. The men stayed with the Indians for several years before four soldiers from the expedition, led by Cabeza de Vaca, left south-eastern Texas and began walking south toward New Spain. They were later found by slave traders and taken to Mexico City, where de Vaca described his journeys to viceroy Mendoza. Vaca told the viceroy about the magnificent and rich cities to the north that he had heard about from the Indians.

After the uprising at Culiacan was subdued, in March 1539 Friar Marcos and his search party travelled to the north to investigate de Vaca's accounts of riches, making inquiries at each Indian village they passed, showing the natives samples of gold, silver and pearls. As de Niza continued to move north looking for gold, near the end of the month he began hearing tales from the Mexicans of the Seven Golden Cities of Cibola located to the north-east. Friar Marcos and his men trudged on in search of the golden cities through the wilderness, finally reaching the village of Hawikuh in present-day western New Mexico. However, when he sent one of his men ahead to announce his arrival, the Indians attacked and killed him. With his life in danger, Marcos de Niza only viewed the settlement from a distant hilltop before departing, and later described it to Coronado as 'shining like gold and silver in the sunlight'. Friar Marcos decided to end his expedition, returning to Culiacan in late June. He stayed in the small Spanish colony for a few days before travelling back to Compostela to report his discoveries to the New Galician governor.

In the governor's house at the New Galicia capital, Friar Marcos told Coronado of his expedition's discoveries and his sighting of the first golden city of Cibola. After listening to the friar's description of his journey, the governor wrote a report to Mendoza, and on 15 July set out for Mexico City with the priest to personally relay the stories to the viceroy. The news of the friar's reported discoveries spread rapidly throughout New Spain, and was linked to the old Spanish legend of the seven golden cities founded by seven Portuguese bishops, who had fled to the New World to escape a Muslim invasion. As the rumours circulated, wild speculation swept the colony, while the stories became more exaggerated and magnificent with the telling. Many Spaniards believed that Cibola was the golden city of El Dorado, which had propelled conquistadors to the Indies in search of riches since the voyages of Christopher Columbus. Mendoza readily accepted the priest's narratives and began preparations for a large expeditionary force into the interior to reconnoitre for quantities of gold and silver to rival the findings of Cortes in Mexico and Pizarro in Peru. He planned to take possession of the kingdom of Cibola in the name of King Charles I, adding it to the lands of the Spanish Empire.

The expeditionary force was organized in Mexico City under Antonio de Mendoza's direction and financed largely by him and Coronado. When the public announcement for enlistment was issued, numerous volunteers eagerly responded with dreams of acquiring great wealth. The ranks of the mustering army were quickly filled with many young adventurers. Over 300 men were recruited and Francisco Coronado appointed captain-general of the provinces of Cibola, the Seven Cities and any new kingdom discovered. Under Mendoza's guidance, his soldiers were armed, equipped, clothed and provided with horses, while cattle, sheep and goats were collected to provide fresh meat. A force of approximately 1,000 Tlaxcalan warriors joined the army as auxiliary troops, while several hundred Indians served as servants and scouts. The viceroy issued instructions for the conquistadors to maintain peaceful relations with the natives they encountered, and the expedition carried trade goods to barter with the Indians for provisions and supplies to prevent looting.

At the end of 1539, the volunteers began to move to the final assembly point along the Pacific coast near Compostela. A final muster was held in the town square on 22 February 1540, with 225 mounted soldiers and sixty-two infantrymen reporting for duty, along with several priests to spread the Holy Faith. The conquistadors were armed with swords, lances, knives, crossbows and arquebuses. Before leaving Compostela, the army was organized into six companies of cavalry, one of infantry and one artillery unit of six bronze cannons. A final review of the army was held as the troops marched past Mendoza and Coronado, who wore a full suit of armour overlaid with gold and a plumed gilded helmet. Following the review, the officers and men heard Mass and pledged to serve God and the king to the best of their abilities. Finally, on 23 February, with colorful banners blowing in the breeze, the expeditionary force departed from the New Galician capital, advancing to the north toward the town of Culiacan, with Friar Marcos serving as guide, while two ships under the command of Hernando de Alarcon sailed up the coast of the present-day Gulf of California with supplies for Coronado's forces. Alarcon was to rendezvous with the Spanish at various locations along their route. Two friars walked ahead of the procession, announcing the coming of the Spaniards and spreading the word of the cross to the natives.

From Compostela, the Spanish army moved up the Pacific coast toward the village of Tepic, following a frequently travelled trail. The dense tropical jungles made the journey difficult and the inexperienced soldiers struggled as they cut their way through the harsh terrain. While the Spaniards trudged forward, Coronado sent Melchior Diaz and a search party ahead to look for the golden cities. When Coronado's men reached the coastal foothills, the expedition was compelled to delay its advance to build rafts to cross the alligator-teeming Santiago River. After the troops and animals forded the river, the trek was renewed as the Spanish marched into the interior, passing through several deserted and weather-beaten villages. When the conquistadors reached the Chiametla River, Coronado ordered them to halt for a period of rest. While the expeditionary force remained along the river, captain Melchior Diaz and his reconnaissance party arrived at the encampment after searching the region ahead. To Coronado's disappointment, Diaz reported that Friar Marcos' glowing descriptions of the country and towns were greatly exaggerated, and he was sceptical about the presence of gold or silver. While the scouting patrol had not reached the first city of

Cibola at Hawikuh, Diaz learned from the Indians on his route that the Zuni warriors in the pueblo were unfriendly and would not welcome foreigners. Driven by the quest for great wealth and fame, Coronado decided to continue his journey, despite the risks.

When the expeditionary force reached Culiacan in northern Mexico, Coronado divided his forces, leaving the main army with the slow-moving animals and baggage, while forming an advance party of approximately 100 horsemen and several hundred Indians. He left Culiacan on 22 April with his vanguard, passing over rivers, mountains and through difficult terrain that Friar Marcos had described as beautiful green valleys and open trails. When the Spaniards finally reached the village of the Opata tribe at Corazones, they were welcomed by the friendly natives. Coronado spent nearly a month at the settlement waiting for the remainder of his army to arrive. In late May, he resumed his journey, crossing through the Sonoran region into the present-day United States in south-eastern Arizona. The Spanish followed the San Pedro River into the Gila Valley, trekking through the Winchester Mountains to the abandoned ruins of Chichilticale, where they rested after their gruelling march. The conquistadors had expected to find a magnificent settlement, but were distraught by the deserted red earth huts. After a few days, the vanguard continued to explore to the north-east, travelling across the Sonora Desert, where many horses and mules died from dehydration and exhaustion and the soldiers suffered greatly from the heat and lack of food and water. During the march through the Sonora, the troops were confronted by dangerous wildcats, rattlesnakes, armadillos and other animals they had never seen before.

Following the punishing 150-mile trek across the desert, the troops finally left the Sonora and entered the Mogollon Mountains in western New Mexico, where they found water and grass for the animals but little food. The expedition continued to push onward, crossing mountains, open country and rivers. As Coronado neared his first destination at Hawikuh, he sent Captain Lopez de Cardenas and several horsemen to scout ahead of the army. Several days later, Cardenas encountered a small band of warriors from the Cibolan tribe. He gave a cross to the Indians and told them that the Spaniards came in the name of their king and in peace. Two of the Cibolans were sent back to their village to announce the coming of the soldiers, while several others remained with Cardenas' patrol. As he continued to the east, following the Zuni River in present-day western New Mexico, his men were ambushed at night by the natives, who stormed out of the darkness into the conquistadors' camp with wild shouts. With their steel swords and lances and thundering arquebuses, the Spanish drove off the Indians. In the morning the scouting party moved on, crossing open grassy plains, when Hawikuh was finally sighted. When Cardenas dispatched messengers to the captain-general with the news, Coronado ordered his army to quickly march forward. While the advance party waited, Coronado finally rejoined Cardenas and the Spanish advanced toward the treasures of the golden city.

As the united Spanish forces approached Hawikuh in early July, following a seventy-seven-day march, the conquistadors had expected to find a golden city, but were greatly disappointed by the adobe dwellings. The Zuni warriors were prepared for the arrival of the soldiers, running out of the pueblo ready to defend their village. In defiance of the Spaniards, they shouted, waved their weapons and sounded their war horns. A Zuni priest drew a line in the ground with cornmeal, warning the enemy not to cross.

While the two forces faced off against each other, Coronado sent Captain Cardenas, two friars and an armed escort forward to speak to the natives. The Catholic priest demanded the Zunis acknowledge King Charles I as their ruler and accept the pope as their spiritual leader. He told them that if they refused, the Spanish would attack and enslave them. After listening for several minutes, the warriors unleashed several volleys of arrows. With his army under attack, and after receiving the official sanction of the church from the priests, the captain-general rode to the front of his men, his gilded armour shining in the sun, shouting, 'For St James and at them' as he led the charge against the Zunis.

The conquistadors quickly overran the Indians' first line of defence, the cavalrymen riding down and killing many Zunis from their warhorses with slashing swords and lances. The remaining warriors withdrew into the pueblo's protective walls and put up a fierce fight, throwing stones and shooting arrows at the Spaniards. The captain-general ordered his bronze field guns hauled into position, while the arquebusiers and crossbowmen opened fire. As the troops fought their way into the settlement, Coronado led a charge against the Indians and was struck twice by flying rocks, knocking him to the ground unconscious. He was carried from the battlefield as his soldiers entered the pueblo, killing the Zunis and forcing the survivors to flee, completing the conquest of the first golden city of Cibola. However, when the troops searched the interior of the village for gold, silver and precious stones, they were disgruntled to find no riches. The angry men threatened to cut off the head of Friar Marcos for his repeated lies, but the recovered captain-general quickly quelled their wrath. While the Spanish failed to discover any gold or treasure, they did find a large stock of much-needed corn, beans and various fowl. Following his victory, Coronado claimed the land for the kingdom of Spain.

Before Coronado had departed Culiacan in northern Mexico in April for Hawikuh, he had ordered Captain Tristan de Lunay Arellano to remain with a small force of soldiers to establish a basecamp. After collecting supplies from the local harvest, Arellano moved his encampment forward to the village of Corazones, and following the defeat of the Zunis the captain-general directed him to join the rest of the Spaniards at Hawikuh. He dispatched Captain Melchior Diaz to deliver his instructions to Arellano, while sending several couriers with messages for Antonio de Mendoza in Mexico City. The discredited Friar Marcos had been repeatedly threatened by the conquistadors in Hawikuh, and was ordered back to the capital with the messengers for his protection. In his letters to the viceroy, the captain-general reported that Friar Marcos' accounts of the countryside and Hawikuh had been completely inaccurate. He told Mendoza that the great Seven Cities of Gold were only seven small settlements, and Cibola was the name for all of them. Coronado added that he judged there was little chance of finding any gold or silver, but assured the viceroy that his men would aggressively pursue the search for them. He described the Zuni people in his letters, detailing their appearance, dwellings, religion, agricultural products and animals.

After completing his mission, Diaz was to lead an expeditionary force of fifty soldiers to the north toward the Pacific Ocean to search for Alarcon's supply ships. Diaz reached Corazones in mid-September, spending several weeks helping Arellano prepare for the journey to the Zuni village. At the end of the month, Arellano began his march with reinforcements and provisions for Coronado, while eighty men stayed to guard the encampment.

In October, Diaz began his search for the supply ships of Alarcon, travelling to the north-west through harsh desert lands before reaching the lower Colorado River near current-day Yuma, Arizona. The conquistadors continued their advance, crossing over flat fertile lands spotted with many small Indian villages from the Yuma tribe. As the Spanish marched down the Colorado, Diaz was told by the natives that ships had been seen anchored downriver. When the soldiers reached the mouth of the Colorado River, Diaz found a message beneath a marked tree saying Alarcon had sailed upriver as far as possible, but after waiting for Coronado had finally returned to New Spain. During his voyage, Alarcon explored the Gulf of California, discovering that the Baja California was not a large island but a peninsula.

After failing to find the supply ships, Diaz led his small party upriver, but with provisions nearly exhausted and the local Yuma Indians becoming less friendly, decided to cross the river and explore the region to the west. As his troops were building rafts from reeds and trees, they were attacked by a band of Yuma warriors. The Spaniards, led by Diaz, fended off the Indians with their steel swords and lances, forcing them to retreat into the mountains. The men soon completed construction of the rafts, crossing to the opposite bank with little trouble. The troops resumed their advance until they neared the Mojave Mountains, becoming the first Europeans to enter modern-day California. Shortly after reaching the mountains, Diaz was accidentally killed when he impaled himself with his lance while riding his horse. Following the death of their captain, the conquistadors abandoned their expedition, returning to Corazones.

While Diaz and his expeditionary force were searching for Alarcon, the conquistadors from Culiacan made their way north-east toward Hawikuh. The Spaniards marched over the earlier trail of Coronado and had little trouble with the Indians, who remained friendly. The soldiers passed through the ruins of Chichilticale and continued to press onward. During their trek they encountered a herd of buffalo, another animal the Europeans had never seen before. As the Spanish neared the Zuni pueblo, they were struck by fierce winds followed by a heavy snow storm. The men were forced to seek shelter in caves until the weather improved, before ending their journey in Hawikuh.

By the middle of July 1540, Coronado had recovered from his wounds suffered during the fighting at Hawikuh and was now ready to explore the settlements and countryside of Cibola. Soon after conquering Hawikuh, he sent messengers with gifts and promises of peace to the Zuni chiefs and elders in the neighbouring pueblos. However, the Indians remained distrustful of the Spaniards with their thundering weapons and fierce animals. The captain-general visited the nearby village of Matsaki, with its massive five- and seven-storey dwellings of stone and fortified walls with tall defensive towers. He rode throughout the Cibola province, telling the Zunis at each pueblo to acknowledge the Spanish king and accept the Christian god in return for peace. With Cibola now under his control, Coronado decided to send several small parties of conquistadors beyond the province to search the towns and countryside for gold and silver.

During his talks with the Zuni chiefs and elders, Coronado had heard stories of a powerful and rich kingdom called Tusayan located to the north-west of Hawikuh. In mid-July, he sent Captain Pedro de Tovar, Friar Juan de Padilla and seventeen horsemen to explore Tusayan. The search party was guided by several Zuni warriors and travelled through the desolate and uninhabited area of eastern Arizona. The Spaniards advanced past Navajo Springs and the Petrified Forest before entering the Jeddita Valley. As they pressed onward, the conquistadors saw the Hopi village of Awatowi. The men made camp for the night before pushing on to the settlement, but in the morning they were discovered by Hopi warriors armed for battle with bows and arrows, wooden clubs and spears. Tovar attempted to speak with the Hopis through an interpreter, telling them to accept Christianity and acknowledge the Spanish king as overlord. The natives responded by drawing a line in the soil with cornmeal, warning the soldiers to go no further, while warriors shouted and danced in defiance of the troops. When the Indians moved closer, Tovar yelled 'Saint James' to his army, leading his cavalrymen in a fierce charge with slashing swords and thrusting lances. As they slammed into the Hopis' defensive line, killing several natives, the survivors fled to their village and soon offered gifts to Captain Tovar for peace.

Word of the thundering Spanish attack spread quickly through Tusayan, and chiefs from neighbouring pueblos came to Awatowi to offer their submission to Tovar. With the Indians' pledge of peace, the conquistadors explored the province, visiting several large villages and travelling through the region searching for gold and silver. Despite riding from pueblo to pueblo and talking to the natives, the captain found little of value in the lands of the usually peaceful Hopis. During his discussions with the Indians, Tovar heard stories about a great river to the west where giants lived. Following his reconnaissance, the captain abandoned his search returning to Hawikuh in mid-August.

Following his return to the Spanish army, Tovar discussed his expeditionary force's findings with Coronado, who was interested in learning more about the great river to the west. The captain-general began preparations for a new expedition to search for the waterway, naming Don Garcia Lopez de Cardenas as captain. On 25 August, the reconnaissance patrol of twenty-five horse soldiers left the Zuni pueblo, retracing Tovar's route to Tusayan before continuing to the west. During the journey to Tusayan, the local Indians welcomed the Spaniards and provided them with food and guides. With Hopi escorts leading the way from Tusayan, the conquistadors travelled through a desolate and uninhabited desert country, finally reaching the Coconino Plateau in north central Arizona in September. As the exhausted and dehydrated men moved across a high plateau, they suddenly reached a deep canyon with a great river flowing through the bottom of it. The horsemen slowly approached the rim of the gorge, becoming the first

Europeans to view the Grand Canyon. The explorers were amazed at the size and beauty of the mile-deep chasm with its walls of reds and browns. The soldiers reconnoitred the southern rim of the canyon for three days looking for a trail to the river below. Three men located a pathway that took them approximately a third of the way to the bottom of the canyon before they were forced to climb back to the top. Unable to cross the canyon and with supplies of food and water running low, Captain Cardenas ordered his troops to return to Hawikuh.

While the Spanish were reconnoitring the area to the west, word of the conquistadors' arrival and conquest of Hawikuh spread quickly through the Indian lands. In the summer of 1540, a band of natives from the village of Cicuye, 300 miles to the east on the Pecos River, travelled to Cibola to invite the men to visit their kingdom. The Indians were led by chief Bigotes and an elder named Cacique. They met with Coronado, giving him gifts of animal hides and head pieces as tokens of their friendship and offering to guide the Spaniards to their pueblo. The captain-general was interested in exploring the territory to the east, questioning the natives about the inhabitants, settlements, crops and animals in the region. When Cacique told Coronado about the giant cows that roamed the plains, he decided to send a scouting party to investigate the area. Captain Hernando de Alvarado was appointed to lead the expeditionary force of twenty soldiers, and on 20 August the explorers struck out eastward across New Mexico, with Cacique and Bigotes serving as guides. As the men trudged through dry and barren territory, they encountered a chain of abandoned fortifications and a large destroyed city. After travelling for five days, the Spaniards reached the town of Acoma, built at the summit of a high mesa. The village was only accessible by a single set of stairs, which was closely guarded by the Indians. When the villagers saw the conquistadors approach, they quickly climbed down the stairs to confront the Spanish, drawing the traditional line of cornmeal on the ground as a warning. Through the intervention of chief Bigotes, the troops were invited to visit Acoma. After struggling to the top of the plateau, Alvarado and his soldiers were welcomed and given gifts of fowl, cornmeal, deerskins and pieces of turquoise.

Leaving Acoma, the captain and his soldiers advanced north-east, reaching the Rio Grande River on 7 September. Cacique and Bigotes continued to act as guides, leading the Spaniards through the Rio Grande Valley and past the many agricultural villages of the Tiwa Indians. The conquistadors named the territory Tiguex. After travelling from Acoma for three days, the Spanish entered an area with irrigated fields of corn, melons, beans and other crops situated on both sides of the river. The local Tiwas were friendly, greeting the troops in peace. The men established their camp near the upper Rio Grande and spent several days recovering from the gruelling trek across the desert. While they remained at their encampment, chiefs from twelve pueblos visited the Spaniards, the sounds of flutes announcing their arrival. The warriors welcomed Alvarado's troops, offering gifts of food, animal skins and cotton clothing as a sign of their friendship. The captain learned from the Indians that there were over seventy villages extending to the north and south along the river. The people of Tiguex were farmers living in pueblos of two- and three-storey dwellings made of dried mud. The region offered the soldiers a ready supply of food and water, and with little sign of hostility from the Tiwas, Alvarado sent a map and message to Coronado recommending that the army relocate to the pueblos of Tiguex for the coming winter season.

While waiting for Coronado and his forces to arrive in Tiguex, Alvarado resumed his exploration, advancing to the east. After travelling for several days, the conquistadors reached the fortified pueblo of Cicuye near the Pecos River. Similar to Acoma, Cicuye was heavily protected with strong walls and soaring five-storey terraces. The village was the home of Bigotes and Cacique, and the native Tano population celebrated their return with dancing and drums. The Spaniards were welcomed and presented with gifts of cloth and turquoise. With the winter season fast approaching, Alvarado was anxious to continue his search for the buffalo herds and Bigotes gave him several slaves to guide his reconnaissance.

The captain and his soldiers rode to the south-east from Cicuye, and after several days reached a large open flat plain in current-day eastern New Mexico. As they continued to press onward, the Spaniards encountered the thundering herds of buffalo that the Indians had earlier described as large shaggy creatures. While riding on the plains hunting the buffalo, Alvarado and his men heard accounts from one of the guides of a wealthy kingdom to the north-west called Quivira that was rich in gold and silver. The guide, named the Turk by the Spanish, told the soldiers that he had a gold bracelet in Cicuye as proof of the kingdom's great prosperity. The conquistadors had been searching for precious metals for nearly a year and had been continually disappointed, but the Turk's claims created a wave of renewed enthusiasm for the quest for gold and silver and the captain quickly abandoned his expedition, ordering his troops back to Cicuye.

After returning to Cicuye, the Spanish captain asked both chief Bigotes and Cacique about the gold bracelet. When they repeatedly denied any knowledge of it, Alvarado had them and the four guides put in chains. As the soldiers departed for Tiguex from Cicuye, with Bigotes, Cacique, the Turk and the three guides still in irons, the Indians became angry, losing all trust in the promises of the Spaniards. After the natives pleaded in vain with Alvarado for the release of the prisoners, the Tanos unleashed volleys of arrows at his men as they fled the pueblo.

While Alvarado was searching the eastern plains of New Mexico, Coronado was relocating his army to the Tiguex pueblos near present-day Albuquerque, New Mexico. By late November 1540 he had completed his journey from Hawikuh, establishing a new basecamp. Shortly after the army's arrival, Alvarado rejoined Coronado with his six captives. The captain-general met with the Turk, who repeated his stories about Quivira. The prisoner told Coronado that he was from the marvellous city located near a large river to the east, where the fish were as big as the Spaniards' horses. The realm was ruled by King Tatarrax, who frequently travelled on the river in a large canoe driven by sails and forty oarsmen, with a golden eagle on the mast. Gold was so plentiful in the king's palace that the servants ate from bowls of the precious metal. When Bigotes was questioned about the golden bracelet, he again denied knowing anything about it. After his repeated denials, the conquistadors took the chief to a field, turning the war dogs loose on him to make him talk. The local Tiwa natives watched the dogs attack Bigotes, becoming more fearful and withdrawn from the Spanish.

By December the weather turned bitterly cold, with deep snows. The Spanish soldiers were unprepared for the harsh winter, lacking adequate clothing, housing and food supplies. They made frequent demands on the Tiwas for provisions and shelter. The troops forced the Indians to leave the pueblo of Alcanfor, so they could occupy the dwellings. While the winter wore on, food and clothing were stolen from the natives, and the Tiwa warriors grew increasingly hostile. When a Tiwa woman was raped by a Spaniard, the Indians prepared to assail the soldiers in retaliation. They raided the foreigners' corral during the night, killing numerous horses and stampeding the rest. The captain-general responded by ordering an assault against the pueblo of Arenal. The conquistadors and their Indian allies stormed into the fortified village, driving the natives from their defensive walls into the dwellings. A fierce house-to-house fight ensued, with Coronado's men climbing onto the rooftops to fire their crossbows and arquebuses, as the infantrymen attacked the Tiwas from room to room. When the troops began to burn the pueblo, the Indians sought safety in the open, where they were quickly cut down by the thundering cavalry. The soldiers left Arenal a smoking ruin with hundreds of dead Tiwas.

Coronado quickly ordered his men to renew their rampage, assailing other villages. Unable to withstand the enemy's onslaught, the Tiwas withdrew from their scattered settlements to the fortified pueblo of Moho, preparing to repel the conquistadors' assault. Coronado sent his forces against Moho's defensive walls, but despite repeated attacks was unable to break through the barricades, compelling the Spanish to besiege the stronghold. The Indians held out for nearly two months, but in March 1541, facing starvation, they were forced to try to fight their way through the siege lines. The warriors ran out of the pueblo, fleeing toward the river. In the open country, the Spanish cavalrymen quickly rode them down, cutting them to pieces with their slashing swords and thrusting lances. Coronado continued his offensive, crushing all resistance in Tiguex by the end of the month and destroying twelve pueblos.

In the aftermath of the conquest of Tiguex, Coronado began preparations to explore Quivira. On 23 April, the army began its quest for the elusive gold that had thus far eluded it. With colourful banners flying from their lances, the soldiers moved to the east toward the hoped-for El Dorado. When the expeditionary force reached Cicuye, the captain-general released Bigotes and Cacique from their chains, allowing them to rejoin their tribe. With the Turk now serving as guide, the Spanish set out on 1 May, following the course of the Pecos River south for several days before fording the rain-swollen waterway to the east bank on a hastily built bridge. After crossing the river, the troops and their 1,500 Indian allies entered a treeless flatland that stretched unbroken into the eastern horizon. Eight days after reaching the Great Plains, the troops encountered their first herd of buffalo grazing on the grass fields of the north-western Texas Panhandle. The Great Plains seemed endless to the Spaniards, and with no landmarks to indicate a trail they easily became disoriented. When men were sent ahead to reconnoitre or hunt, they frequently lost their way, the conquistadors firing their arquebuses and blowing trumpets to guide them back to the camp.

Several days after the Spanish first saw the buffalo, they discovered the camp of the Querecho tribe, which lived on the vast prairie hunting buffalo. The nomadic Indians followed the great herds, using trained dogs harnessed with two long poles to transport their tents, food and baggage. They lived in portable tepees made of buffalo skins stretched over poles. The Querechos hunted buffalo on foot with their bows and arrows, and were dependent on the animals for their survival. The natives were peaceful, greeting the

Spaniards as friends. Using sign language, Coronado asked the natives about the great kingdom of Quivira and was told about a large river with numerous cities along its banks that stretched for many miles. The next day, the captain-general resumed his journey, moving to the north-east in search of the first city of Quivira, called Haxa. Two days later he again encountered a large buffalo herd and more Querecho hunters. From the Indians, Coronado reconfirmed the Turk's information of a great city in the direction of the rising sun.

The small army continued to travel through the huge featureless prairie of grass, pressing on to the north-east. Several days later, the Turk told Coronado that Haxa was only a short distance away. Hoping to quickly locate Quivira, Diego Lopez was sent ahead with ten cavalrymen to scout for the city, but returned having found only more buffalo and open grassland. The troops of the expeditionary force trudged onward through endless flatlands, spotting bands of Querechos in the distance and various wild animals, including antelope, wolves and prairie dogs. As Coronado led his soldiers forward into the treeless land, Captain Rodrigo Maldonado rode ahead with several men to reconnoitre for Haxa, and after four days of searching his patrol found a settlement of the Teya tribe at the bottom of a large canyon. Several of his horsemen were sent back to guide Coronado's army to the Indian pueblo. Like the Querechos, the Teya natives hunted buffalo but they also cultivated fields of beans, corn, grapes and other fruits and vegetables. They lived in clusters of tepees and frequently followed the buffalo herds. The Teya settlements extended along a stream for several miles. The faces and bodies of the Teyas were covered with tattoos, and they were less friendly to the Spaniards than the Querechos. After Coronado joined Maldonado's troops along the creek and began exploring the area, in late May they were struck by a powerful thunderstorm with high winds and large hailstones. Caught in the open, the men and horses were pelted by swirling hailstones, which injured many of the animals, damaged equipment, ruined tents and dented the soldiers' armour.

Coronado's men had been trudging through the endless prairie lands for thirty-seven days, suffering from the lack of water, with many ill from a diet of buffalo meat and no grain, while others were becoming demoralized. Suspicions of the Turk's accounts of gold and rich cities had steadily increased, while the local Teyas claimed that Quivira was not a kingdom of great wealth but an area where the natives were farmers living in grass huts. They also said that Quivira was located far to the north and the Turk was guiding the Spaniards in the wrong direction into a barren plain. In late May,

122

the captain-general held a meeting with his captains to determine whether to return to Tiguex or continue the search for the Golden Cities. After listening to the opinions of his officers, Coronado decided to take thirty cavalrymen with six foot-soldiers and travel north to find the kingdom, while Captain Tristan de Arellano was ordered to return to the Rio Grande with the remainder of the army.

In early June, Coronado and his soldiers began their journey to Quivira, travelling northern with seven Teyas acting as guides. They advanced for nearly thirty days over the boundless barren country of northern Texas, crossing the Oklahoma Panhandle into current-day central Kansas. After fording the Arkansas River, the Spaniards followed the north bank of the waterway downstream. As they continued to advance along the side of the river, the conquistadors encountered a small party of Quivira warriors from the Wichita tribe, who were hunting buffalo. The Indians gave the Spanish troops directions to their village, and in late July Coronado led his men on the final leg of the journey to El Dorado. Further down the Arkansas, the men found six or seven settlements of thatched grass huts spread out along the river. The explorers were greatly disappointed at the sight of the straw villages, with their lack of soaring stone buildings, magnificent palaces or wealthy inhabitants. In his later letter to King Charles I, the captain-general reported that the Wichitas ate raw buffalo meat, were dressed in animal skins and worshipped the sun god, while living in round huts made of straw. He noted that the soil in Quivira was black and fertile, while nuts, grapes, oats and melons grew wild. The troops searched the villages for gold and silver but found nothing of value. Still unwilling to return to Mexico City without discovering his El Dorado, Coronado sent several small expeditionary parties inland from the river, looking for the precious metals. The captain-general's horsemen located over twenty additional settlements and were welcomed by the peaceful natives. They reconnoitred the area but only found poor farmers, who cultivated crops of corn and beans while hunting buffalo and harvesting wild grapes and nuts. While his men were looking for gold, Coronado claimed Quivira for the Spanish kingdom and convinced the Wichitas to acknowledge the pope as their spiritual leader. After his patrols returned without finding any gold, he finally accepted that further exploration was useless. Before leaving present-day Kansas, he erected a large cross on which he carved 'Francisco Vasquez de Coronado, general of an expedition, reached here.'

While the Spaniards remained in Quivira searching for gold, the Turk began to conspire against them, encouraging the Indians to assail and kill the small party of conquistadors. When the plot was discovered by Coronado, he ordered the Turk placed in irons. The captain-general now realized that the Turk was an enemy, had repeatedly lied about the presence of gold and had deliberately guided the expedition in the wrong direction. He confronted the slave, who finally admitted to his lies, telling the Spanish general that the Cicuye Indians had convinced him to lead the Spaniards into the Great Plains, so they would become lost and perish from thirst and starvation in revenge for the imprisonment of Bigotes and Cicuye. After listening to the Turk's confession, Coronado ordered his execution and he was strangled to death.

After spending twenty-five days in Quivira, Coronado and his small army began the long ride back to Tiguex in August, leaving behind all hopes of discovering their El Dorado. Shortly after advancing south, the conquistadors stopped at a Quivira settlement in the south-west of the kingdom to collect supplies of food and guides for the journey. After crossing the Arkansas River with the new escorts leading the way, the expeditionary force travelled through modern-day north-western Oklahoma and Texas into New Mexico, reaching the Rio Grande River in the middle of September and reoccupying the pueblo of Alcanfor. When the men at Tiguex learned that the captain-general had brought back no gold or treasure, they still believed that the precious metals were to be found further to the north. Despite the lack of gold, a feeling of optimism continued to linger with the troops as they prepared for the coming cold and dangerous winter season.

As the winter wore on along the banks of the Rio Grande River, the Spaniards suffered from the lack of adequate provisions and clothing. To survive the cold, the soldiers frequently raided the Indians' pueblos, stealing their food and clothes. During the stay at Alcanfor, the horsemen were kept busy looking for firewood and supplies, keeping watch on the natives and periodically exercising the horses. While Coronado and Captain Rodrigo Maldonado were exercising their horses in late December 1541, the two conquistadors broke into a gallop. As the captain-general thundered ahead, the cinch on his saddle suddenly broke, throwing him from his mount into the path of Maldonado. The hooves of the captain's horse struck Coronado in the head, seriously injuring him. He was unconscious and lay near death for several days before slowly beginning to recover. However, the riding accident badly impaired his physical and mental health. Coronado had earlier promised his men that in the spring the expeditionary force would renew its search for gold in the area north of Quivira, but his injury forced him to abandon such plans. Throughout the winter months he remained weak, but gradually regained some of his strength. However, unable to lead his troops in person, Coronado lost their respect and confidence as their leader.

By early April 1542, the harsh winter was finally over in Tiguex and the Spanish began preparations to return to New Spain. Coronado was still unable to ride his horse, travelling most of the way on a litter drawn by two mules. As the conquistadors trudged toward Mexico in their tattered clothing, they were harassed by Indians, who fired poisoned arrows at them and at night approached their encampments shouting insults and attacking the horses. The army remained at Cibola for several days, resting before continuing their advance. At Corazones, Coronado and his troops were welcomed by the natives and provided with much-needed food and supplies. However, the Indians to the south were hostile and the troops were repeatedly assailed and harassed. From the beginning of the journey back to New Spain, Coronado's men had frequently deserted from the army, and when he reached Mexico City there were less than 100 tired, starving and disillusioned soldiers in the ranks.

Shortly after arriving at the capital of New Spain, the captain-general met with viceroy Mendoza, reporting the failure of the expedition to find the Seven Cities of Gold. The viceroy had largely financed the project and was displeased at the loss of his investment, but maintained his confidence and trust in his friend. Soon after his return, Coronado was reinstated to the governorship of New Galicia by Mendoza and retained his seat on the municipal council of Mexico City. He returned to New Galicia with his wife and children, governing the province from the city of Guadalajara.

As Coronado administered the Spanish crown's laws and policies and kept the peace in New Galicia, in the summer of 1544 he was compelled to answer charges of mismanagement, theft, corruption and cruelty to the Indians during his expedition. A royal inquiry was held by a representative of the king, dragging on for fifty days. Witnesses were ordered to testify and evidence of the crimes was gathered. After the hearings, the governor was absolved of some of the charges but found guilty of several crimes and required to pay a large fine.

While Coronado was searching for the Seven Cities of Gold, in the spring of 1540 the Caxcan Indians and their allies in the province of New Galicia in north-western Mexico rose up in revolt against Spanish rule. After two failed attempts to quell the rebellion in New Galicia, and concerned that the insurrection was spreading, viceroy Mendoza personally commanded an army of nearly 500 Spaniards and over 30,000 Aztec and Tlaxcalan warriors against the Caxcans. With overwhelming military might, he destroyed the enemy's strongholds one-by-one, and in late 1541 captured the rebel fortress at Mixton, ending the fighting. After regaining control of the province, the viceroy initiated a ruthless campaign of suppression, ordering thousands of Indians to labour in the silver mines, while many more were executed or sent to work on Spanish plantations as slaves. Francisco Coronado was later implicated in the brutal suppression of the native uprising in New Galicia and placed under house arrest. However, through the intervention of Antonio de Mendoza the captain-general was found innocent but compelled to resign his governorship. Coronado later appealed the loss of his New Galicia office to the Council of the Indies, but the decision was sustained.

After surviving the ordeal of the royal investigation, Coronado returned to Mexico City with his family. He lived in a large comfortable stone house built by his wife's parents at the south end of the Municipal Plaza. He continued to serve on the city council, administering the municipal affairs of Mexico City and supporting the policies of Mendoza. In January 1547, Coronado appeared before a royal board of inquiry as a witness supporting the viceroy's administration. When asked about the expedition to Cibola, the former captain-general defended his actions as having brought a large new region under the king's rule. In the following year, he received an increase in his allotment of Indian slaves in recognition of his service to the Spanish crown. In addition to his duties in Mexico City, he was also occupied with the management of his large plantation in the country, supervising the planting of crops and raising of sheep and cattle herds. Coronado never fully recovered from the rigours of the expedition, continuing to suffer from declining health. By the summer of 1554 he was seriously ill, dying aged 44 on 22 September and was buried beneath the high altar of the Church of Santo Domingo in Mexico City. While Francisco Coronado had failed to find the Seven Cities of Cibola, his exploration had expanded the boundaries of New Spain's northern frontier, leading to the Spanish settlement of the current-day American south-west.

SELECTED SOURCES:
Bolton, Herbert E., *Coronado – Knight of Pueblos and Plains.*
Day, A. Grove, *Coronado's Quest.*
Favor, Lesli J., *Francisco Vasquez de Coronado.*
Horgan, Paul, *Conquistadors in North American History.*
Morris, John Miller, *From Coronado to Escalante: The Explorers of the Spanish Southwest.*
Mountjoy, Shane, *Francisco Coronado and the Seven Cities of Gold.*

Samuel de Champlain

In the spring of 1615, Samuel de Champlain returned to New France to resume his exploration of present-day Canada. During his previous expeditions in the St Lawrence Valley, he had built a bond of friendship with the local Huron, Algonquin and Montagnais tribes, and after reaching Montreal in July agreed to join their raid against their long-standing Iroquois enemy to renew his investigation of the Canadian interior and reinforce his military alliance with the Indians. Travelling in canoes up the Ottawa River and its tributaries, Champlain began his boldest and most significant journey with two Frenchmen and ten Huron guides. As he paddled through the region, he made illustrations of the local natives and their villages, while drawing detailed maps and writing descriptions of the geography, wild animals, vegetation and landscape. Throughout his nine-month expedition into the interior of New France, Champlain explored two of the Great Lakes, expanded the strength of the French regime's presence in the country and reinforced his coalition with the northern Indian tribes, while his travels through Huronia made significant contributions to the Europeans' knowledge of inland New France.

Samuel de Champlain was born around 1570 in the largely Protestant town of Brouage on the Bay of Biscay in south-western France, the only son of Antoine de Champlain and Marguerite Le Roy, the daughter of a local fisherman. Samuel's father had gone to sea as a sailor, rising through the ranks to pilot, master and captain in the king's navy. He later owned his own ship and was an investor in numerous trading ventures, earning a substantial income. Antoine de Champlain was a man of property, owning three houses in the small town, and was well-respected by the inhabitants. Samuel likely attended the local academy, receiving a basic education in reading, writing, mathematics and religion, while becoming skilled in equestrianship, fencing and firing the arquebus. Raised in the prosperous port of Brouage and near the Atlantic Ocean, the young Samuel was exposed to tales from sea captains and sailors of their expeditions to the cod banks of Newfoundland, the St Lawrence Gulf and other unexplored regions, enhancing his desire to go to sea. From any early age, Samuel began sailing with his father on his voyages along the coast of France and into the Atlantic Ocean, studying the tides, weather, currents, winds and navigational instruments. During his many journeys with his father, Samuel learned the skills of navigation, seamanship, astronomy and piloting. Antoine exposed him to the world of commerce, business and money, and the art of negotiations. Through his years in Brouage, Samuel de Champlain acquired an education that prepared him well for his life as an explorer and colonial governor.

France had been involved in a series of bloody and devastating religious wars for nearly thirty years, and in 1589 when Cardinal Charles of Bourbon was recognized as monarch by the Catholic League, the War of the League erupted between the ultra-Papists and the regime of King Henry IV. In 1594, a formidable Spanish army invaded Brittany in support of the League, seizing many of the major seaports. The moderate Papal faction and Protestants rallied to the king's cause, and although a Catholic, Samuel de Champlain joined the royal forces in Brittany. He first served as a sergeant with the quartermasters and was responsible for providing the soldiers with food, clothing, equipment and living quarters. The army in Brittany was mainly resupplied by sea, and Champlain's experiences and skills as a sailor were well-suited to delivering provisions and materials to the troops. Within a year, he was promoted to the officer ranks in the quartermasters, serving on the staffs of several marshals.

After landing in Brittany, the Spanish built a massive fortress manned by 5,000 soldiers on the Crozon Peninsula, commanding the entrance to the port of Brest. In late 1594, the French Protestants with support from Elizabeth I of England launched a combined offensive to capture the stronghold. After a failed attempt to storm the walls, a tunnel was dug under the fortification, and on 7 November a large mine was exploded. A breach was opened and the allied troops rushed in, with Champlain taking part in the fighting and winning recognition for his gallantry. Following the victory at Crozon, he continued to serve in the French army for the next thirty months, rising to the rank of captain in an infantry company. From his service in the king's army he learned the skills of leadership, obedience to orders and command of subordinates, which were later employed in his conflicts with the Indians in New France.

When Henry IV and the Spanish ended the War of the League in May 1598, the French army was disbanded and Champlain was unemployed. He had earlier heard stories from the sailors at Brouage and during his numerous voyages with his father about the riches in the New World, and with Henry IV now expanding his interest in America he decided to visit the Spanish

Indies to learn from their experiences before embarking on an expedition to New France. After the Spanish troops in France were repatriated, the 500-ton *Santa Julian*, (*Saint Julian*) commanded by Champlain's uncle, Guillaume Allene, was chartered to take them home. As the ship prepared to sail, Champlain was invited by his uncle to join his crew as his assistant, and on 28 August he steered for the port of Cadiz. After a journey beset with late summer storms, the *Santa Julian* reached Cadiz, where it remained for the next four months. Champlain took the opportunity to visit the town, drawing sketches and studying the fortifications while learning about the Spanish Empire from the local sailors and merchants. He later travelled to Seville, making drawings and maps of the city's walls, defensive towers and gates.

While Samuel de Champlain continued to visit local towns and learn the Spanish language, in late 1598 naval officials began assembling the treasure fleet for its return to the West Indies, and the *Santa Julian* along with its tender, *Sandoval*, were chartered for the expedition. Captain Allene did not take part in the voyage but his nephew was allowed to serve onboard the ship as his representative. On 3 February 1599, the large flotilla sailed from Spain for the Canary Islands before steering due west to begin the transatlantic passage. Strong winds swept the vessels to the West Indies, making landfall in six weeks at a small island near Guadeloupe. The *Saint Julian* was leaking badly and its captain was forced to stop at Guadeloupe to make repairs. As the men worked on the ship, Champlain went ashore with the crew to refill the water caskets and gather fresh fruits. He took the opportunity to explore the island and talk with the Indians, but was disappointed when they disappeared into the forest. After the repairs were completed, Champlain continued his journey to Puerto Rico to rejoin the flotilla, as the ship and its tender rolled and pitched through the Caribbean Sea. When the Spaniards reached the Virgin Islands, the captain of the *Sandoval* was ordered to sail south alone to the Isla de Margarita off the coast of Venezuela to pick up a cargo of pearls for the homeward-bound treasure fleet. Champlain was permitted to make the voyage in the tender, visiting the Spanish Empire's centre for pearl harvesting. After reaching the settlement, he drew detailed maps of the island and wrote vivid descriptions of pearl fishing. When the cargo of pearls was loaded onto the tender, the crewmen piloted across the Caribbean to rejoin the *Santa Julian* in San Juan, Puerto Rico. Remaining on the island, Champlain explored many areas of the countryside, sketching maps, writing about the dense forests of towering trees and large varieties of flowering flora and drawing pictures of the plants and animals, while talking to the Spaniards about their trading activities. Before leaving the island, the Spanish fleet was divided into three squadrons and Champlain joined the vessels going to Mexico.

Champlain's squadron of three ships was commanded by Joannes de Urdayre, and after departing from the port he navigated westward to Hispaniola, following the earlier route of Columbus across the northern coastline and circumnavigating the island, searching for English raiders and pirates, as the treasure fleet prepared to sail for Spain. During the journey to Mexico, the squadron made a stopover at Santo Domingo, where Champlain visited the city, continuing to make maps and write narratives of the terrain, wild animals, plants and appearance and customs of the Indians. From the island's capital, Urdayre steered his ships westward, making stops in Cuba and the Cayman Islands before sailing on to Campeche, New Spain. Champlain spent several days exploring the countryside around the port before the flotilla travelled up the coast to Veracruz. While staying in the town, Urdayre sent two officers to Mexico City with orders to arrange the shipment of silver to the fleet, with Champlain allowed to accompany them. He spent over a month trudging through the country and visiting the capital. As Champlain trekked north, he marvelled at the rich flora, soaring trees, exotic and strange wild animals and great plains of fertile land. Exploring Mexico City, he was surprised by the magnificence of its splendid temples, palaces, mansions and beautiful streets.

Soon after his return to the coast, Champlain sailed south-west across the Caribbean in a pinnace to Porto Bello on the Isthmus of Panama. He wrote about the town in his *Brief Discours* (*Brief Narrative of the Most Remarkable Things that Samuel de Champlain of Brouage Observed in the West Indies*) describing it as 'The most evil and unhealthy residence in the world with constant rain and extreme heat.' Champlain remained in the town for a month, investigating parts of the isthmus and observing that if a transcontinental canal was built it would greatly aid trade by shortening the distance to the Pacific Ocean. Following his stay in Porto Bello, he travelled in the pinnace back to Mexico to rejoin the squadron, remaining fifteen days as the ships were made ready to return to Spain.

In July the fleet departed from the Mexican coast, and as the sailors steered across the Gulf of Mexico they were struck by a violent hurricane. The *Santa Julian* began to leak badly again, and Champlain wrote in his *Brief Discours* that 'We thought we could not escape the peril.' During the storm, his vessel became separated from the squadron, finally struggling alone into Havana in early August. While in Havana, he made frequent visits to the city, studying the harbour and sketching the Indians, buildings and fortifications. He later made a voyage to Cartagena in Colombia, remaining over a month, scouting the countryside and observing the people, animals and varied vegetation. He expanded his knowledge of the West Indies further by navigating north in a Spanish vessel, crossing the Florida Strait and investigating the peninsula and Spanish settlement at St Augustine, writing about the area's resources, terrain and its advantages as a future French colony. After returning to Cuba, he stayed in Havana for a short period as the treasure ships gathered in the harbour. When the fleet, loaded with gold and silver, departed for Spain in the summer of 1600, Champlain sailed home with it. After piloting north, the Spaniards rode the prevailing strong winds east to the Azores, where they evaded prowling English privateers and pirates, arriving at Cadiz in mid-August.

During his absence in the Spanish Indies, Champlain's uncle, Guillaume Allene, had died and his nephew was occupied for nearly a year resolving the will. Under the terms of the document he was named the sole heir, inheriting a large estate near La Rochelle, Spanish properties, investments and a ship, making him a wealthy man. While he worked on the settlement, he wrote his account of the twenty-month expedition to the West Indies for King Henry IV. Before departing on the voyage in 1598, he had met with the king and was commissioned to gather information on the Spanish-occupied lands where no other Frenchman had visited. The *Brief Discours* contained narratives and sixty-two drawings of the terrain and Spanish settlements, enhancing the crown's knowledge for a planned French colony in Canada. Following the completion of the report, Champlain travelled from Spain to Paris. He was quickly granted an audience with Henry IV and presented him the book. The monarch was pleased, granting Champlain a pension and raising him to the lesser nobility as sieur de Champlain.

Samuel de Champlain remained at the Paris court during the winter of 1603, serving the king as a geographer. He had an office in the Louvre and began studying the geography of New France. He frequently visited the seaports, gathering information from sailors and fishermen on Canada while studying the logs of previous failed French expeditions to Florida and along the St Lawrence River. While Champlain was at court, the king appointed Aymar de Chaste as commander for an expeditionary force chartered to establish a trading company and permanent colony in New France. When Champlain learned of the expeditionary force, he arranged to meet with Chaste and was asked to join the expedition. A formal order from the king was issued by the crown's secretary, Louis Potier of Gesvres, instructing

Champlain to serve in the venture and prepare a report of his journeys for the throne.

By mid-winter 1603, Chaste had raised enough money from the merchants and investors of Saint-Malo and Rouen to fund an expeditionary force with three ships. Champlain joined the fleet under the command of Francois Gravé Du Pont at Honfleur. After supplies and trading goods were loaded, on 15 March the Frenchmen hoisted their anchors and steered into the English Channel. Champlain travelled south, passing the Channel Islands and French coastline into the Atlantic Ocean. After a week of fair weather, the mariners were struck by a fierce western gale, Champlain's ship rolled and tossed for seventeen days before skies began to clear. Gravé Du Pont continued west for two weeks, arriving off the Grand Banks near Newfoundland on 2 May. As the seamen kept a close watch for icebergs high atop the riggings, the flotilla navigated through Cabot Strait, reaching the St Lawrence Gulf several days later. After sailing by the Gaspe Peninsula, the sailors moved up the St Lawrence River to the French seasonal fur trading centre at Tadoussac, arriving near the end of May.

The Frenchmen were received as friends by the local Montagnais natives, who were ready to trade their furs for European goods. Their chief held a celebration in honour of his guests, and the mariners ate moose, beaver, fish and vegetables as the Indians danced, sang and beat drums. During the banquet, the chief told Gravé Du Pont and Champlain they were welcome to settle in his country. While Champlain waited for a small pinnace brought onboard the *Bonne Renommee* (*Great Renown*) to be reassembled, he reconnoitred the Saguenay River, travelling 40 miles upstream but finding the region unsuitable for a permanent colony. Following his return to Tadoussac, Champlain renewed his exploration and on 18 June, guided by several Montagnais, sailed up the St Lawrence River in the pinnace. When they reached the site of Jacques Cartier's fort at Quebec, Champlain visited the ruins, noting that its location satisfied all the requirements for a trading centre and future settlement. The scouting party continued upriver, reaching Montreal before encountering the La Chine Rapids, which blocked their passage. During the expedition, Champlain talked to the local Indians he encountered while gathering detailed descriptions of the lands surrounding the Ottawa and Richelieu rivers. He heard stories from the natives of the territory beyond La Chine as far as Lake Ontario. He was told about Niagara Falls and Lake Erie, which was described by the guides as a vast saltwater sea. This reignited the hope of finding the North-west Passage to the Orient. After two weeks of exploring the St Lawrence and talking with the Indians,

Champlain had found the site for the French colony and on 4 July began the journey downriver to Tadoussac.

As Champlain was exploring the St Lawrence River, the French at Tadoussac were bartering with the Indians for their fur pelts and cod fish. When he reached the outpost, the men had completed their trading with the Montagnais and the cargo of fish and furs was loaded on the ships. The fleet sailed down the St Lawrence in mid-August, spending nearly a month surveying the Atlantic coast of the Gaspe Peninsula. While Champlain was scouting the peninsula, he met a French trader who told him about several mountains in Acadia, modern-day New Brunswick, Nova Scotia and eastern Maine, which were rich in deposits of copper, iron and silver. The trader's stories confirmed earlier accounts he had heard from the Indians.

On 5 September, Gravé Du Pont's vessels left New France for home, as the blazing red, yellow and brown shades of the early autumn foliage flashed across the Canadian mountains and valleys. With prevailing steady winds and the Gulf Stream pushing the Frenchmen eastward, they reached the harbour at Le Havre in only fifteen days.

During the return to France, Champlain began writing his account of the expedition for the king, naming it *The Savages, or The Voyage of Samuel de Champlain of Brouage*. The manuscript was published in Paris on 15 November, and described the terrain features of the St Lawrence River Valley, with its networks of deep rivers, thunderous rapids and vast forests, and his travels through Acadia. Champlain repeated the Indians' claims of the great saltwater seas to the west, Niagara Falls, and silver and copper deposits in Acadia. He devoted large parts of the book to the Indians, describing their appearances, customs, religion, food and villages. Champlain believed that, 'They would speedily be brought to be good Christians if their country were colonized.'

Following his return to France, Champlain was invited to an audience with Henry IV, giving him a copy of his manuscript and discussing his explorations, while promoting a permanent colony in Canada along the St Lawrence River. After his interview with the king, he began holding regular meetings with Pierre Dugua de Mons, who had replaced Chaste as head of the expeditionary force following his death. During their many discussions, Champlain continued to support establishing a French settlement in the St Lawrence Valley, but de Mons favoured a site further south in Acadia because of its more favourable weather, presence of friendly Indians and possible deposits of silver and copper. When de Mons presented his proposal to the court with the promise to fund it entirely with investor subscriptions, the king gave his approval in November 1603, naming him lieutenant general. As de Mons began organizing his expedition, Champlain was asked to serve as the chronicler for the crown.

Under his charter, de Mons was commissioned by the French regime to establish a permanent settlement in Canada. He recruited an expeditionary force of over 100 sailors, soldiers, skilled artisans, general labourers and two miners, while several gentlemen adventurers, two Catholic priests and one Protestant minister also joined the venture. During March 1604, tons of provisions, equipment, animals, building supplies for houses and replacement sails and riggings were loaded on the two vessels in the harbour at Le Havre. On 7 April, the seamen on the flagship, *Don de Dieu*, (*Gift of God*) raised the anchor, sailing into the Atlantic to begin their passage to Canada. Three days later, the second ship, *Bonne Renommee* (*Good Renown*), left port, following the route of the flagship. Champlain was aboard the flagship, and with favourable eastern winds the *Don de Dieu* was driven across the Atlantic, reaching Cap de la Heve on the coast of Acadia in a month. After surveying the harbour, the mariners steered further down the coast, looking for a suitable location for the colony. After reconnoitring for nearly two months, de Mons found a site for the settlement on a small wooded island that Champlain named Sainte Croix (Holy Cross Island). The island was easily defendable, with fertile lands for farming and freshwater.

After the colonists, animals and supplies were unloaded, the Frenchmen fortified the island with barricades and palisades while construction of the small town began. A storehouse, covered gallery, two blocks of houses for the officers and barracks for the labourers and soldiers were built around a central square. As the work on the settlement continued, Champlain was sent by de Mons to reconnoitre the coast of the Bay of Fundy in a small pinnace, searching for silver and copper deposits. He returned to the island a few weeks later with some samples of suspected copper, but analysis by the miners was inconclusive. During the exploration he met several times with local Micmac Indians, gaining their friendship and trust.

While Champlain was in the north, de Mons increasingly realized that Sainte Croix island could not support a colony of over 100 men. The soil was too sandy to grow vegetables and the freshwater supply soon dried up. Shortly after his return, Champlain was ordered by the lieutenant general to explore the coast of Acadia looking for a new settlement location. Sailing in the pinnace with twelve mariners and two Indian guides, he departed from Sainte Croix in early September, steering down Fundy Bay and observing many islands, inlets and harbours. During the journey he made maps of the coastal terrain, while keeping a record of his meetings with the different native tribes. Champlain surveyed along the shore of present-day Maine as far as Bangor before the weather turned increasingly foul, forcing the search party to return to Sainte Croix on 23 September.

When Champlain returned to the colony, he found the buildings finished and the settlers preparing for the winter. The freezing weather set in early, with snow starting to fall during the first week of October as bitter winds howled across the island. By December, the waters surrounding the island had frozen, while the colonists suffered from shortages of firewood and provisions. Scurvy soon broke out, raging through the settlement during the winter with terrible effect, killing nearly half of the men before spring. The Frenchmen with scurvy endured exhaustion, swelling of body limbs and ulcerations of the gums. In March, a band of Indians visited the colony, bartering fresh meat for trade goods, which helped to limit the effects of the disease. De Mons expected a relief ship from France to arrive in the early spring, but it was the middle of June before the *Bonne Renommee* finally reached the island.

On 18 June 1605, Pierre Dugua de Mons and Champlain led a search party down Fundy Bay, exploring the coastline of Maine for a new settlement site. During the summer, the Frenchmen sailed south as far as Cape Cod, anchoring frequently to search inland, while Champlain sketched maps of the coast and talked to the Indians about the local geographic features. Near modern-day Boston, he encountered the first natives with cultivated fields of corn, beans, pumpkins and tobacco, indicating that the local weather and soil were conducive to growing crops. The sailors were greeted by the Indians as friends during the voyage, with gifts of food and welcoming dances and songs. In mid-July, the Frenchmen visited Boston harbour, surveying the Charles River and the bay. After a stopover to reconnoitre the land around Plymouth, de Mons and Champlain steered on, reaching Cape Cod on 19 July. They spent several days searching the sandy peninsula before returning to Sainte Croix in early August after an exploration of nearly fifty days.

While the scouting expedition to the south had found many suitable sites for the colony, de Mons decided to relocate the settlement to the western coast of Nova Scotia at Port Royal, which had been discovered in 1604. The buildings on Sainte Croix were dismantled and transferred across the bay to Port Royal, where they were reassembled into a single rectangular structure 60 feet long and 48 feet wide, with separate sections for officers, labourers and sailors, while defensive fortifications were built along the waterfront.

When the construction was completed, de Mons returned to Paris to report to Henry IV, carrying many gifts, including a large red birchbark canoe and baby moose to encourage the continued support of the crown. Following his audience with the king, de Mons remained in France, appointing Gravé Du Pont as lieutenant for the expedition, with Champlain serving as his second in command. While the settlers cleared land for planting, hunted the plentiful wild game and fished in the streams, Champlain made friends with the local Micmac Indian chief, Memberton, who wanted to form an alliance with the French against his enemies and establish a close trading relationship. The colonists' first winter at Port Royal was not as severe as the previous year at Sainte Croix. As the cold weather set in with the ground covered in deep snow, scurvy reappeared, twelve of the forty-seven men dying before spring. Memberton and his people proved to be true friends, frequently providing the Frenchmen with wild game and fowl.

When the first signs of spring appeared, Gravé Du Pont and Champlain left Port Royal in the pinnace in late March 1606 to search for a warmer site for the colony. They made several attempts to sail south down Fundy Bay, but were beaten back by foul weather. During the last voyage, the pinnace sank after hitting a submerged rock and the sailors were forced to build a replacement. However, by the time the new craft was finished, it was beyond the expected arrival date of the relief ship and Gravé Du Pont decided to abandon the settlement and take the colonists to Cape Breton in the hope of intercepting a fishing vessel for the return voyage to France. As the mariners steered around the bottom of Nova Scotia, they met a French shallop and were told by the crew that the *Jonas* was on its way to the colony. When Gravé Du Pont and Champlain returned to Port Royal, they found the vessel at anchor with a new governor, Jean de Poutrincourt.

With the colony now resupplied for the coming winter, Poutrincourt and Champlain prepared the pinnace to search for a new site to relocate the settlement. The expedition finally sailed on 9 September, steering a course down the Bay of Fundy and surveying the southern coastline of Acadia. After anchoring and surveying present-day Gloucester Harbour on Cape Ann in northern Massachusetts, the French party continued down the shoreline, crossing Boston harbour and reaching Cape Cod. They navigated along the outer shore of the cape, slowly making their way south after encountering dangerous waters with shoals and breakers. During the voyage, Champlain met frequently with the local natives, finding them friendly and willing to provide information on the terrain. He wrote about their customs, clothing, cultivated fields and villages in great detail in his narrative, while describing the Cape Cod wigwam dwellings as circular, lofty and covered with matted grass or corn husks. Champlain noted the dramatic change in the landscape features, from the rugged Maine shoreline to the beauty of Cape Cod's coves, meadows, ponds and salt marshes. In late September, the Frenchmen reached Stage Harbour near modern-day Chatham, Massachusetts, spending two weeks exploring the region and finding it suitable for a colony. By mid-October, the behaviour of the local Indians changed as they became more hostile, fearing the strangers intended to take their land. Suspecting an attack when the natives sent their women and children into the forest, Poutrincourt ordered the sailors to return to the ship. However, four men remained to finish making bread, and in the late afternoon they were assailed and killed by a large band of warriors. After erecting a cross and burying the dead seamen, the expeditionary force departed from the harbour, piloting about Nantucket Sound for several days before returning north to Port Royal, reaching the settlement on 14 November.

The winter months of 1607 were milder than the two previous years, and with the help of the Micmacs the Frenchmen had ample provisions, consuming supplies of fowl, otter, beaver, fish and dried vegetables. The settlers had built an oven, and with wheat from France they had bread to go with the wine brought by the relief ship. Despite the milder weather, there still was some sickness, with five men dying. As the daylight hours grew longer and the sun warmer, the colonists prepared the fields for planting and began fishing in the many local streams for trout and smelt.

While Champlain and the settlers remained at Port Royal, a pinnace from the fishing town of Canso on the north-eastern coast of Nova Scotia arrived in late May 1607 with supplies and news that de Mons' monopoly had been revoked by the king due to pressure from fur trading consortiums. With the loss of the crown's support, Poutrincourt was forced to abandon the colony and return to France. When the pinnace returned to Canso with the settlers, Champlain and eight men stayed at Port Royal for a month, harvesting the crop of early wheat as proof of the area's fertility. After collecting the wheat, the Frenchmen rejoined the colonists at Canso and on 3 September set sail in the *Jonas* for France, making the transatlantic passage with fair weather in twenty-three days.

Shortly after his return to Paris, Champlain arranged to meet with Pierre Dugua de Mons in October 1607, convincing him to reorganize his syndicate of investors and concentrate on establishing a colony at Quebec on the St Lawrence River. They petitioned the crown to restore their fur trading monopoly, and after Henry IV agreed, de Mons equipped three ships and recruited seamen and settlers for the expedition to Canada, appointing

Champlain as commander with the rank of captain of the seas. On 13 April 1608, the fleet put to sea with colonists, supplies, weapons and trade goods. After passing Newfoundland and piloting through Cabot Strait, Champlain steered up the St Lawrence, reaching the French trading centre at Tadoussac on 3 June. At the outpost he was reunited with Gravé Du Pont, who had earlier arrived in the *Le Levrier* (*The Greyhound*). While Champlain was sailing to French Canada, a group of Basque traders began bartering with the Indians for their pelts in violation of the king's charter. Gravé Du Pont ordered the Basques to leave, but they refused, attacking and wounding him. After taking command at Tadoussac, Champlain met with the illegal traders and negotiated a resolution.

After spending nearly a month at Tadoussac, Champlain sailed up the St Lawrence River in a pinnace on 30 June with craftsmen, soldiers and building supplies, reaching Quebec three days later. He chose a site for the new colony near the point where the river narrowed, and put his men to work cutting trees for the fort, digging a cellar and constructing several buildings that were joined together with a gallery. The fortification was surrounded by a wall and moat, with drawbridge and wooden palisade by the entrance.

While Champlain continued strengthening his stockade, several Frenchmen began plotting to murder him and surrender the colony to the Basques. The conspiracy was soon exposed to Champlain and he ordered the arrest of the plotters. The leader of the group was executed and the others sent back to France as prisoners. The captain spent the autumn preparing the fort for the coming winter and meeting with the local Montagnais Indians, buttressing his friendly relationship with them. The winter of 1609 set in early, with the temperatures dropping quickly and the river freezing, while snowstorms with howling, freezing winds blew across the land. The Frenchmen continued to be ill from the effects of scurvy, with over half of the twenty-eight colonists dying from the disease. The Montagnais in the region also suffered greatly during the severe winter, with little food, and Champlain provided them with bread and beans to strengthen his friendship and trading association.

By April, the warmer weather began to break up the ice on the St Lawrence, allowing Champlain to journey upriver to meet with the chiefs of the Montagnais, Huron and Algonquin Indians to form a trading alliance. On 28 June 1609, he sailed in two shallops with twenty men about 45 miles above Quebec to the present-day Richelieu River, where they encountered a large native encampment. Champlain held meetings with the chiefs, agreeing to join their coalition against their long-standing Iroquois enemy and participate in raiding parties to gain the tribes' trust and reinforce the new trading agreement. Following the talks, a great ceremonial banquet was held lasting for several days. When it was over, most of the warriors went home, 'With their wives and wares they had bartered from the French', as Champlain wrote in his 1613 book *Voyages*.

In mid-July, the remaining Indians and their French allies set out on their raid against the Iroquois, the war party of twenty Frenchmen armed with arquebuses and sixty native warriors paddling down the Richelieu River in twenty-four canoes. After a journey of 75 miles, they arrived at a large lake, which became known as Lake Champlain. The canoe fleet manoeuvred along the lake, with the snowcapped Adirondack Mountains visible in the distance, and after reaching its southern tip late on 29 July, came across 200 Iroquois at their fortified encampment. After spending the night on the beach, the French and their allies advanced at dawn against the Iroquois, who came running out of their camp to assail the raiders. Champlain, dressed in a breast plate and wearing a steel helmet with white plume, fired his arquebus at the chiefs, killing three of them. When the Iroquois warriors panicked, the Hurons and Algonquins charged after them, killing several and capturing fifteen. The victory secured Champlain's friendship and trading relationship with the northern Indian tribes.

Following the skirmish, Champlain left the Indians and paddled down the St Lawrence to the French settlement. He departed for France on 5 September to report the results of the venture to Henry IV and offer support for the extension of the trading monopoly to de Mons. After reaching Paris in early October, he travelled to Fontainebleau, giving the king his account of the expedition and arguing for a renewal of the charter, but the request was denied. Despite the loss of the monopoly, de Mons and Champlain decided to proceed with the colonization, and with additional financial backing from Rouen merchants, on 8 April 1610 he set off back to Quebec in two ships with fresh supplies and additional settlers. He arrived at the colony in early May, finding the garrison had suffered little during the mild winter. Champlain planned to explore the territory to the north, but the Indians wanted to resume their war against the Iroquois by assailing a war party camped near the mouth of the Richelieu River. When Champlain and the Montagnais warriors reached the enemy's improvised fort of logs on 19 June, they joined the local Algonquin and Huron warriors and unleashed an assault, with the Frenchmen firing their arquebuses. During the fighting, Champlain, dressed in his armour, suffered a minor ear wound. After the coalition's first attack failed to capture the fort, the captain persuaded his allies to storm it, and with firepower from the French arquebusiers they broke through the walls, killing most of the Iroquois.

In the aftermath of the clash on the Richelieu, Champlain returned to Quebec, where he learned that Henry IV had been assassinated and without his continued support, the Quebec colony was in danger of failing. The new regency government of Marie de Medici cared little for Canada, and the captain was forced to return to France to find new patrons. He left seventeen men to maintain the settlement, and on 8 August steered down the St Lawrence and headed for Honfleur.

Soon after his return to Paris, Champlain signed a contract agreeing to marry 12-year-old Helene Boulle, daughter of the king's secretary. The agreement contained a provision restricting the consummation of the union for at least two years due to Helene's age. The marriage took place in late December 1610, bringing Champlain a large dowry. He invested part of the money in the fur trading syndicate, and after de Mons and his partners agreed to fund another year in Canada, he began assembling a new expedition. Establishing his wife in a Paris residence, he sailed from Honfleur on 1 March 1611, reaching Quebec on 13 May after the voyage was repeatedly delayed by dense fog and icebergs.

Shortly after arriving back at Quebec, Champlain travelled up the St Lawrence to the rapids above Montreal to barter with the Indians for furs and establish a new trading outpost, to ensure a steady supply of pelts from the Hurons and Algonquins for his investors. While waiting for the Indians, he explored the area for a site to locate the second colony. The native hunters finally arrived on 13 June, and the Frenchmen traded with them for their fur pelts of beaver, moose, wolf, fox, bear and otter. The captain had repeatedly pressed the Indians to guide a French expeditionary force of fifty men to explore the region north of the St Lawrence, and now they finally agreed. In order to secure the funds to outfit the expedition, Champlain was forced to return to Paris, and after reaching Tadoussac he found a ship bound for France, leaving on 11 August.

While Champlain was in Canada, de Mons sold his business and the new partners no longer planned to support the overseas colony without a fur trading monopoly. De Mons and Champlain decided to form a new syndicate to colonize and explore the St Lawrence Valley. To generate enthusiasm and financial patronage for the project, de Mons proposed appointing a prominent nobleman as figurehead for the enterprise. Following discussions with their friends at court, Henry de Bourbon, Prince of Condé, agreed to join their company. He used his influence with the king to receive a royal appointment as viceroy for New France, and on 12 November 1612 named Champlain as his lieutenant. With the prestige of the prince behind the firm, another syndicate of merchants was formed with a recently granted fur trading monopoly from the regime. While Champlain was involved with the formation of the new consortium, he published another book, *Le Voyages of Sieur de Champlain* (*The Voyages of Sir de Champlain*). The publication included many maps, charts and drawings of the native Indians, along with descriptions of his adventures, battles against the Iroquois and expeditions.

On 6 March 1613, Champlain sailed from Honfleur for New France again, reaching Tadoussac in late April. At the fur trading centre he posted warnings to all poachers that his company was now under royal protection. He continued up the St Lawrence in a shallop, arriving at Montreal in mid-May. He soon met with a small party of Algonquins who had been sent to guide him up the Ottawa River to explore the region beyond the waterway, searching for the great salt lake. On 27 May, he began his journey with four Frenchmen and an Indian guide in two canoes. After bypassing the La Chine Rapids, they trekked through the rugged land and reached the Ottawa River. The reconnoitring party paddled north-east, battling strong currents, numerous waterfalls and dangerous white water rapids. Continuing upriver, they travelled past the site of the present-day city of Ottawa and the spectacular Chaudière Waterfalls, the sound of its thundering water heard for miles around. After struggling through the wild terrain, Champlain and his men left the Ottawa and canoed across several lakes that were reached with difficult portages through dense forests of hardwood trees and thick underbrush, through thick underbrush where little sunlight filtered through the dense green branches. At the southern end of Muskrat Lake, the French encountered a friendly chief who lent them two canoes and guides to escort them back to the Ottawa River. With the help of the new escorts, the exploration party reached the Ottawa near modern-day Lower Allumette Lake in the domain of the Algonquin chief, Tessouat. The men were invited by the chief to his village and welcomed with a lavish banquet, after which Champlain asked him for canoes and guides to take them to the country of the Nipissing tribe and beyond to the North-west Passage. Tessouat was being paid a tribute by the Hurons travelling through his lands to trade furs with the French, and had no interest in encouraging the merchants to relocate beyond the St Lawrence. To deter the explorers, he told them that the Nipissing warriors were hostile to strangers and the route was very far and difficult. With opposition from the chief, Champlain decided to return to Montreal, arriving in late June. Through Champlain's later writings, the journey into northern Canada added greatly to Europe's knowledge of the vast, largely unknown territory of New France.

At Montreal, Champlain boarded a pinnace and, after a brief stopover at Quebec visiting the small garrison, sailed for France, arriving on 26 September. While Champlain was attempting to forge a larger French presence on the North American continent, the Spanish, English and Dutch were exploring and establishing colonies along the Atlantic coast, threatening the survival of the small Quebec settlement. To broaden the financial base of the company and better enable it to make additional Canadian voyages and settlements, in late November he convinced prominent merchants from Saint-Malo, Rouen and La Rochelle to join a new syndicate named *La Compagnie de Canada* (The Company of Canada). Champlain attempted to expand the French area of influence in New France by convincing the Order of Franciscans to send four missionaries to convert the Indians to the Catholic Church, while recruiting six additional families to settle in Quebec to enlarge the colony.

On 24 April 1615, Champlain set sail for New France in two ships, completing the transatlantic passage in a month. He piloted his small fleet through the Cabot Strait and up the St Lawrence River to Tadoussac. From the small outpost the French navigated upriver in several shallops to Quebec, where the new settlers and supplies were unloaded. After several days, Champlain continued up the St Lawrence to Montreal, where he met his northern Indian allies. The Huron, Montagnais and Algonquin tribes were planning another attack against the Iroquois, and to retain their loyalty and friendship Champlain agreed to join the raid. On 9 July he set out for the homeland of the Hurons to recruit warriors for the foray, with two Frenchmen and ten Indians paddling in two canoes up the Ottawa River. Following a difficult journey, their progress repeatedly slowed by portages around rapids and waterfalls, on 26 July they reached Lake Nipissing. The area around the lake was described by Champlain as 'Scattered with pretty islands and bordered by fair meadows'. At the lake he encountered the Nipissing Indians, who welcomed his party with two days of feasting, dancing and singing. On 29 July, the explorers crossed to the west bank of the lake, following the French River to Lake Huron, which Champlain named Freshwater Sea. The French and their guides went down the eastern shore, and four days later entered the domain of the Hurons.

They reached the Huron village of Otouacha on 1 August, where Champlain began recruiting warriors for the war party. He travelled from village to village, gathering men for the campaign. Champlain assembled the

Huron warriors at the large fortified village of Cahiague, and following a ceremony of feasting and dancing, the allies set out on 1 September. The raiding party of several hundred Hurons, augmented with Nipissings and heavily armed Frenchmen, paddled south, up several lakes and rivers to Lake Ontario. On 5 October, Champlain crossed the lake, landing at Stoney Point, where the raiders hid their canoes in the forest and advanced overland for four days, reaching the Iroquois fort near Lake Oneida. The stockade was a 30 feet-high six-sided structure, surrounded by a moat and with a platform circling the top. The Indians lived inside the stronghold in longhouses that were about 70 feet long and 16 feet wide, holding up to twenty families. The longhouses were framed with bent saplings and covered with bark.

Shortly after reaching the Iroquois settlement, the Hurons assailed the fortification but were beaten back by a hail of arrows and stones thrown from the palisades. After the failed attack, Champlain persuaded his allies to build a tower high enough for his arquebusiers to fire into the fort. Then on 11 October, the Huron and Nipissing warriors assaulted the stockade, as the platform holding four French arquebusiers was dragged forward, while Champlain, dressed in armour, fired his arquebus at the enemy manning the defensive walls. The Frenchmen and their allies fought the Iroquois for over four hours, but were repeatedly pushed back and finally forced to withdraw into the forest. During the clash, Champlain was wounded twice in the leg by arrows, and carried in a basket in great pain for six days to Stony Point. He was now able to walk with help from the Hurons, he travelled to Lake Ontario, from where the French planned to return to Quebec. However, the Indians wanted to keep the Frenchmen with them as protection against an attack by the Iroquois warriors, refusing to provide guides for the journey. With winter setting in, the war party was forced to trudge overland back to Cahiague, arriving on 23 December, where Champlain spent the next five months with the Hurons.

As Champlain's wound slowly healed, he was occupied during the winter exploring the Huron homeland and visiting neighbouring tribes. During his journeys he kept an account of the various tribes' culture, food, dress, dwellings, religion, laws and physical appearances, while making maps and drawing sketches of their villages and dwellings, with full-body illustrations of the men and women. On 20 May 1616, after the spring thaw, Champlain – guided by Hurons – returned to the St Lawrence River over the same route he had taken the prior year, reaching Quebec in early July. While the raid against the Iroquois had ended in failure and had emboldened them to return to their former homeland in the St Lawrence Valley, after having earlier been driven out, Champlain's expedition had reinforced the tribal alliance, made significant contributions to Europe's knowledge of new lands and Indian tribes, explored two of the five Great Lakes and strengthened the presence of France in Canada.

Champlain remained at Quebec until early August, constructing several buildings for new colonists and reinforcing his friendship with the northern tribes. Despite the unwillingness of the Canada Company to cede land to the settlers for the cultivation of crops, and the continued reliance on undependable relief ships from France, Champlain was determined to establish a permanent colony. He ordered his men to reinforce the defences and repair the interior and exterior of the older buildings. The company had earlier granted land to the apothecary Louis Hebert as an inducement to locate to Quebec, and Champlain encouraged him to grow more peas, beans and cabbages to supplement the colony's food supply. On 3 August, he once more set off for France, arriving at Honfleur thirty-seven days later, his voyage aided by strong winds from the west.

Shortly following his return to Paris, Champlain published an updated map of New France, which was later expanded to show the regions around Boston, Virginia and Hudson Bay, which became highly popular throughout Europe. While remaining in France for two years, Champlain completed a history of his service to the French crown during the past sixteen years. In the memoir, he warned the king that France was now in danger of losing its foothold in the New World, with its valuable resources of timber, arable lands, wild animals and possible access to China by the North-west Passage. With French settlements at Port Royal and Fort Caroline in Florida founded by Jean Ribault already destroyed by the kingdom's enemies, the colony at Quebec was key to securing New France, and he urged that it be fortified with new settlers.

In May 1618, Champlain sailed from Honfleur for New France, reaching Quebec in mid-June. He stayed in Canada for only a month, inspecting the colony and visiting his Indian allies to secure their continued friendship and trading relationship. On 30 July he departed down the St Lawrence River for France again, reaching Honfleur at the end of August. Champlain returned to Paris and quickly became involved in plans to gain support for the expansion of the settlement at Quebec. However, the royal court of Louis XIII was indifferent to overseas development and the merchants at Rouen and La Rochelle had lost their interest in Canadian ventures, becoming increasingly disinterested in funding new explorations. Champlain remained determined to make France's colony in the New World a success, and continued to press the regime for its patronage. He finally received a letter from the king confirming his appointment as vice-regal lieutenant for Canada, and ordering the merchants to cooperate with him and end their opposition. While struggling to gain patrons for New France, Champlain finished his third book, *Voyages and Discoveries Made in New France Between 1615 and 1618*, which was published in 1619. The volume was a description of his explorations in the New World and was written to promote his grand design for Canada with the court of Louis XIII, while highlighting the dangers caused by the lack of stable financial backing from the investor-merchants.

After remaining in France for two years, in May 1620 Champlain with his wife Helene returned to Quebec, where they received a joyous welcome from the sixty colonists and several hundred Indians. They moved into the settlement's only large building, staying for the next four years. Champlain now served as the royal administrator for the colony, labouring to ensure its survival. In January 1621, the Company of Canada was sold to Guillaume de Caen and Champlain struggled to maintain peaceful relations with the new viceroy of Canada. During his stay along the St Lawrence, he continually defended the company's fur trading monopoly against illegal traders, who repeatedly violated the king's charter. He frequently visited his Indian allies and managed to negotiate a peace treaty with the Iroquois. Quebec's defences were strengthened by Champlain, who ordered the construction of Fort Saint Louis near the river and had the first road in Canada built. While Champlain was in Quebec, the colony suffered from food shortages, the relief shipments from France being constantly delayed. He petitioned the company to give the settlers land to plant crops, but his pleas were ignored and the survival of the settlement remained precarious. By 1624, Champlain had become disillusioned with the company's lack of support, despite making huge profits from the fur trade. In the summer he decided to return to France, leaving in August with Helene, who had spent four miserable years in the hostile wilds of Canada.

Champlain and his wife were soon in Paris, where he purchased a house in the fashionable Temple district. Soon after his return, the trading company was sold again, and in February 1625 the new viceroy appointed Champlain his lieutenant with full powers in Canada. Champlain returned to New France in late April onboard the *Catherine*, reaching Quebec on 5 July. During the previous winter the settlers had struggled through severe weather, and were close to starvation by the time the relief ships arrived. Champlain quickly put the men to work repairing the buildings and constructing a large fort, but the colonists were still not granted land for cultivation by the new viceroy, despite Champlain's repeated requests. The winter of 1627 arrived early and lasted until April, with snow drifts over 8 feet high. As usual, the provisions from France ran short, but through Champlain's good relations with the Indians the garrison was furnished with food. During the year he continued to work to maintain peace with the tribes, frequently visiting their villages. Despite his pleas for more support, the Canada Company repeatedly ignored the plight of the colonists.

As the fifty settlers laboured to survive at New France, in mid-June 1628 an English war fleet sailed up the St Lawrence, occupying Tadoussac and threatening Quebec. While Champlain began preparations to reinforce the defences of the stockade, he received a messenger from the English on 10 July, demanding his surrender. He decided to defend his settlement, despite not receiving the yearly supply of provisions from France. The daily rations were decreased to only 9 ounces of barley, corn and peas, and were later reduced further. The enemy soldiers stayed below Quebec, blockading French access to the river and compelling Champlain and his men to remain in the fort. The garrison struggled through another hard winter as food supplies dwindled. By the end of May 1629, the Frenchmen faced famine and were forced to eat nuts and roots. On 19 July, an English vessel steered upriver to the colony with another demand for surrender. With the French now defenceless and starving, Champlain was forced to accept the terms. Three days later, the fleur-de-lys was lowered from the fortress and the royal English ensign raised, as the colonists abandoned the stockade. Following the surrender, he boarded the enemy's flagship and, after a brief stopover at Tadoussac crossed the Atlantic to England, arriving at Plymouth on 20 October. While he was sailing to England, an armistice was arranged between the warring kingdoms, and after reaching Plymouth, Champlain travelled on to London, staying with the French ambassador. He remained with him for five weeks, arranging the transfer of Canada back to France, before returning to Paris in late November.

While Champlain was in New France, Cardinal Armand-Jean de Richelieu had been appointed the king's first minister, and under his guidance the Canadian fur trading monopoly for Guillaume de Caen's consortium was cancelled, and the Hundred Associates organized as its replacement. Under the new company, Champlain was appointed the crown's lieutenant in New France. While waiting for the implementation of the peace treaty with England, Champlain published his longest and most ambitious manuscript, *The Voyages for New France in the West.* The book was a history of France's early explorations in the New World, and included his voyages up to 1619 along with a *Treatise on Seamanship*. He remained in Paris for the next three years, living with Helene in their Temple district house, albeit in separate rooms and mostly apart. Champlain continued to petition Louis XIII and the Hundred Associates, promoting the expansion of France's colonies in Canada. Finally, in early 1633, he was given command of a new expeditionary force. On 23 March 1633, as the white clouds streaked across the orange morning sky, he departed from France for the final time as the king's lieutenant and admiral of three ships outfitted by the Hundred Associates. Onboard the 100-ton *Saint Pierre*, Champlain set sail from Dieppe with his fleet, and despite encountering contrary winds and banks of dense fog, reached Tadoussac on 17 May.

At the trading centre, the king's lieutenant found English vessels still trading with the Indians for cod and pelts, in violation of the peace treaty. He ordered the Englishmen to leave, and after prolonged negotiations they finally raised their anchors, sailing down the river with their holds full of fish and furs. After a few days at the outpost, he steered up the St Lawrence, reaching Quebec on 23 May. Before abandoning the stockade, the English had burned it and Champlain found only charred ruins. He quickly put his men to work clearing the rubble and constructing a new storehouse for the supplies and provisions, while rebuilding the fortress and houses for the colonists. While the French laboured on the settlement, the Iroquois began raiding farther east, threatening to assail the Hurons and Algonquins as they travelled to trade their pelts with the French. To protect the Indians, the king's lieutenant built several armed trading outposts at strategic points along the riverbank, manned with soldiers and cannons.

As Champlain bolstered Louis XIII's presence in New France, Cardinal Richelieu issued a decree instituting the *seigneur* system to induce new farmers to relocate to Canada. Under the new edict, large estates were granted to nobles who agreed to recruit colonists with their families to cultivate the land. The system became highly successful in Canada, attracting large numbers of settlers and remaining in effect until 1842. During Champlain's last years, the fur trading company prospered, while under the cardinal's direction the supply ships from France arrived more frequently and the colonists usually had adequate provisions to last through the winter into spring.

In the autumn of 1635, Samuel de Champlain suffered a stroke and was confined to his bed. As his condition worsened, in early December he relinquished his governorship for New France to Francois Derre de Gand.

During the month the weather turned bitterly cold, with snow covering the ground as the black-robed Jesuits kept a close vigil on Champlain. By late December he was near death, and after receiving last rites from the Jesuit priests, the father of New France died on Christmas Day, aged about 65. He was buried in the church of Notre Dame de la Recouvrance in Quebec.

SELECTED SOURCES:
Armstrong, Joe C.W., *Champlain.*
Coulter, Tony, *Jacques Cartier, Samuel de Champlain, and the Explorers of Canada.*
Fischer, David Hackett, *Champlain's Dream.*
Legare, Francine, *Samuel de Champlain.*
Morison, Samuel Eliot, *Samuel de Champlain.*
Sedgewick, Jr, H.D., *Samuel de Champlain.*

Captain John Smith

After serving as a mercenary soldier in eastern Europe for nearly ten years, Captain John Smith joined the newly formed Virginia Company of London in 1606, sailing in December with its expeditionary force to establish England's first permanent colony in North America. When the three ships reached the Chesapeake Bay area, the settlers were landed on a peninsula of the James River and began clearing the land and constructing Jamestown, with Smith appointed to the governing council. During the first year at Jamestown, the colonists were beset with repeated shortages of food, bad water, disease, severe wintery weather and raids by Chesapeake Indians. As the men struggled to survive, in September 1608 the captain was elected governor of Jamestown, and under his orders a new set of regulations was issued to ensure the continued survival of the settlers. Under the captain's direction, additional land was cleared and crops planted, a military force was trained, a well dug for freshwater and attempts made to form alliances and trading relationships with the Indians. As governor, Smith was responsible for the continued existence of the settlement, and his later journeys exploring and mapping the coast of New England led directly to the voyages of the Pilgrim Fathers to Plymouth, Massachusetts. Through his writings about his many adventures and maps drawn of North America, Captain Smith became one of the primary forces in the founding of the New England colonies.

John Smith was born in 1580 in Lincolnshire, England, the eldest son of George and Alice Rickard Smith. George Smith was a yeoman in rank and owned a farm at Great Carlton, while leasing additional properties from the local lord. John grew up on his father's farm, planting, tending and harvesting the crops, while acquiring a basic education from the schools at Alford and Louth, studying Latin, Greek and mathematics and learning to read and write. At the age of 15, he was sent to King's Lynn, 60 miles to the south, becoming an apprentice to a prominent merchant. John Smith was ill-suited to the monotony of a countinghouse career, and was increasingly drawn to a life of adventure through the exciting stories of the voyages and explorations of Sir Francis Drake, Martin Frobisher and John Davis.

While John Smith struggled with the tedious daily routine as an apprentice merchant, in April 1596 his father died. Under the terms of the will, he inherited the farm along with pasture lands and orchards, while becoming a ward of Lord Thomas Willoughby. John Smith had no interest in farming, and persuaded Lord Willoughby to allow him to go to France. After crossing the English Channel and visiting Orleans and Paris for a few weeks, he decided to join a company of English mercenaries serving in the French royal army of King Henry IV. After several weeks of boredom in the army's encampment near the seaport of La Havre, with no money and only one meal a day, Smith and the English forces were ordered to besiege the Spanish troops encamped near Amiens. The mercenary companies marched for twelve days through the French countryside before finding the Spaniards at the fortified village of Grandviliers. As the English soldiers began manoeuvring to besiege Grandviliers, the captain of Smith's unit ordered his men to search for the abandoned manor house of the mayor. After locating the house, the mercenaries sacked the rooms, stealing everything of value. During the raid, Smith acquired a saddle, horse, woollen cloak and a sword, solidifying his position as a professional soldier in the company.

As the English companies remained in the service of Henry IV in northern France, Spanish troops captured Amiens in the early spring of 1597, in violation of the ongoing truce. The royal army marched to retake the city, and after beginning siege operations the English mercenaries were sent to guard the heavily wooded forest to the north. Smith took part in many patrols, fending off sorties and preventing supply trains from reaching the stronghold. As the investment wore on into the heat of summer, the Spanish dispatched a heavily guarded supply train to relieve Amiens. When the English and royal troops were outmanoeuvred by the advancing enemy forces, Smith's company managed to unleash several attacks against the rearguard, and for his actions during the fighting he was promoted to sergeant. With the city now resupplied, Henry IV summoned reinforcements to completely seal off Amiens, and on 25 September the Spaniards were compelled to surrender. Shortly after the fall of Amiens, a peace treaty was negotiated between France and Spain and the mercenary army disbanded.

After the loss of their employment in France, Smith's mercenary company travelled to Amsterdam, joining the Dutch Protestant army of stadtholder Maurice of Nassau. As Maurice held off the army of Spain, sergeant Smith participated in several attacks against enemy forces. In July, the Dutch assailed the Spanish troops at Nieuport on the English Channel, with Smith winning special recognition from Maurice in his report to the government, stating, 'The paid horsemen rode in the vanguard and were inspired by the example of an English sergeant, one John Smith, who laid about him with such rapid strokes that he left a path of Spanish dead in his wake.' During the encounter with the enemy, sergeant Smith was seriously wounded by a pistol shot and spent the next six months recovering at the home of a Nieuport merchant. When Smith rejoined his company, he discovered that the captain had promoted him to third in command of the soldiers with the rank of lieutenant.

When Maurice of Nassau negotiated a peace treaty with the Spaniards in late 1600, the English mercenary forces were discharged and Smith decided to leave his company of soldiers to return to England. Before leaving for his farm, Smith stayed in Amsterdam for a few weeks, and through friends in the army was introduced to the renowned geographer, Peter Plancius. He met Plancius numerous times, studying his many maps of the world and discussing geography. During his last visit, he received a letter of introduction from Plancius to the eminent English geographer, Richard Hakluyt, and after arriving back in England met with him, talking about his ideas on geographics and the discovery of the New World. Smith finally reached his farm in late December 1600, spending the Christmas season with his mother and family. He stayed at Great Carlton for the following six months, devoting himself to the study of geography, astronomy and seamanship, borrowing many books from Lord Willoughby's large library.

Smith remained in England until the summer of 1601, when he returned to France looking for employment as a mercenary soldier. He travelled to the coast of Brittany, joining the crew of a French privateer and spending the next several months sailing in Mediterranean waters, plundering rich merchant ships. By the winter of 1602, he had moved on to Rome to obtain a letter of introduction to the Catholic nobles at Graz, Austria, who were defending their realm against the invasion of the Ottoman Empire. When Smith met with a Jesuit English priest, he secured a letter recommending him for employment as a mercenary. Before leaving Rome, he witnessed a mass held by Pope Clement VIII at the cathedral of Saint John in the Lateran. Departing from Rome, he journeyed through central Italy before taking a ship from Venice across the Gulf of Venice to modern-day western Croatia. He travelled overland to Graz, where with help from the English priest's friends he was introduced to the Count of Meldritch. The count was recruiting a regiment of troops and in need of Smith's military skills, hiring him as a lieutenant for his staff.

After joining the Habsburg army, Smith was sent with an imperial force to relieve the Turkish siege against the town of Lower Limbach. When the

Austrians reached the surrounded garrison, Smith used his prior experiences with ordnances to send a message to the besieged men at night with three brightly lit torches, signalling that the relief soldiers would charge from the east and ordering the garrison to simultaneously sally out of the fortress. When the imperialists made their combined attack, the Ottoman troops were overrun and more than 2,000 Habsburgs rushed into Limbach with provisions. With the town now reinforced, the Turks abandoned their siege in the morning. For his services during the siege, Smith was promoted to captain and given command of 250 horsemen under Count Meldritch.

In the wake of the clash with the Ottomans at Lower Limbach, Captain Smith was sent with Meldritch's regiment to Komarno in present-day southern Slovenia, joining the imperial army of the Duke of Mercoeur, Philip Emmanuel. In early September, the duke was instructed to advance his forces and recapture the historic capital of the kings of Hungary at Szekesfehervar, located 40 miles south-west of Budapest. Following his rapid march into Hungary, Philip Emmanuel ordered a feint attack against Esztergom, while his main army moved to the capital, catching the Turks unprepared. The imperialists encamped to the north-west of the city, beginning a relentless bombardment. The besieged garrison responded with frequent sorties, sending the elite Janissary cavalrymen to assail the Habsburgs, with Smith engaged in the fierce hostilities. The Janissaries were a ruthless fighting unit composed of former Christian slaves. As the cannonade continued, Captain Smith was ordered to hurl burning bombs into the city to support the planned assault against the eastern defences. He fashioned the explosives out of pots packed with gunpowder and pieces of flammable hemp, and during the night his men lit the missiles, launching them over the walls with slings. While the Turks were distracted by Smith's flaming bombs, 1,000 imperialists trudged through the swamplands to the east, seizing the lightly guarded outer defensive fortifications, as the duke charged from the front, forcing the enemy to abandon its peripheral lines. On 20 September, the Habsburg army broke into the city after violent hand-to-hand fighting, with the Ottoman troops steadily driven back and compelled to surrender.

While the Christians occupied Szekesfehervar, the pasha of Buda ordered a large army to recapture the city. As the Turkish forces approached the Austrian encampment, Captain Smith was involved in numerous skirmishes with the enemy. On 15 October, the two armies clashed on a wide plain, the Habsburgs driving the Turks back and forcing them to retreat. With winter approaching, the imperial army was divided into three divisions, Smith's forces being sent with Meldritch to Transylvania in modern-day north-western Romania to dethrone the Ottoman-supported Prince Zsigmond. When the imperial army occupied northern Transylvania by force of arms, the prince dispatched envoys to negotiate a truce. After the agreement was signed, the Habsburgs began to withdraw. However, Count Meldritch owned large estates in Transylvania and had witnessed the brutal slaughter of his family by the Moslems, persuading his soldiers to remain with him to fight the Turks and plunder their camps.

Meldritch soon assailed the Ottoman-occupied town of Orastie along the Mares River. After his first attack failed, siege operations were initiated, with Smith occupied patrolling the countryside with his horsemen to scout for enemy reinforcements. As the siege wore on, a Turkish captain challenged any Christian of like rank to a duel to the death. Many of Meldritch's men accepted the call, but when lots were drawn John Smith was chosen. The Christians met with the Turks and a truce was quickly arranged. The clash was fought on horseback, with Smith charging at the Turk and killing him with his lance on the first pass, to the thundering cheers of the Christians across the battlefield. However, a friend of the dead Ottoman issued a challenge to fight the victor, and the next day a second duel took place, Smith killing the Turkish captain with his pistol. Emboldened by his victories, Smith issued a summons to any Turk to reclaim the severed heads of his comrades by winning them in a duel. After the offer was accepted, a third duel was fought mounted on horseback with battleaxes. As the two men charged at each other, Smith's heavy and unwieldy battleaxe was knocked from his hand. As the Ottoman charged again, Smith drew his broadsword, piercing the Turk under his armour and killing him. Smith was rewarded with the gift of a horse and elaborately decorated sword by the army's commander.

Shortly after the duels, the Habsburgs unleashed a relentless cannonade on the Turkish defensive walls, finally forcing a breach. The Christian soldiers stormed forward but were beaten back by the defenders on the ramparts. Reinforcements were thrown into the fray, eventually pushing the enemy troops back into the keep. As the imperial troops ploughed ahead with flashing swords and piercing lances, the Turks surrendered Orastie to the Habsburgs. Following the battle, the captured Ottoman forces were put to the sword and their severed heads strung on poles around the fortress. A religious service followed, with the imperialists giving thanks to their God for the victory. After the mass, Smith attended an audience with the prince of Transylvania, receiving authorization to place three severed Turkish heads on his shield as a symbol of his military skills.

Following the surrender of the Turks at Orastie, Smith and his men joined the forces of Count Modrusch, who was part of the army of General Giorgio Basta. The Christian troops were ordered to advance against the Ottoman-supported overlord of Wallachia, Jeremy Mogila. While they marched to confront the enemy soldiers, Basta's ally, the Habsburg sponsored warlord of Wallachia, Radu Serbun, defeated the forces of Mogila and the princedom came under imperial control. As the crushed remnants of Mogila's army retreated to the east, contingents of Tatar stragglers began ravaging the countryside, and Modrusch and his 11,000 troops were sent to restore order. During the advance, Captain Smith served in the vanguard, pushing his cavalrymen forward against the Tatars. As the Christians travelled to the east, the enemy forces united and 40,000 men-at-arms lay in ambush for Modrusch. Imperialist scouts soon discovered the waiting Tatars, and the Habsburgs were directed to withdraw toward the Red Tower Pass on the Wallachia and Transylvania border. When the Habsburgs approached the pass in early November 1602, they encountered the Ottoman troops and quickly threw up defensive works of sharp stakes and trenches, with Smith leading his horsemen in the fierce clashes. The Tatars unleashed their assault with trumpets blasting, drums beating and deadly flights of arrows striking Modrusch's first line of barriers. The Christians delayed the enemy for over an hour but were beaten back when Tatar reinforcements were rushed into the fray. The Ottoman forces stormed ahead, running into the unseen barrier of stakes, and were thrown into disarray as the artillery opened fire with devastating effect. As the Moslem attack faltered, reserve units were pushed forward and Modrusch's position began to crumble. When Janissaries charged into the defences, the Christians were overrun, withdrawing in disorder and abandoning the dead and dying on the bloody battlefield. Many thousands were killed and wounded during the brutal and savage fighting, while Smith was captured and held for ransom.

The surviving Christians were taken to the slave market at Axiopolis, east of Bucharest. At the auction, Smith was purchased by Bashaw Bogall for his young mistress and sent to Istanbul. His new owner had little use for Smith, sending him to her brother, who served as governor for a military district in present-day southern Russia. He was soon on his way to the north-east, reaching her brother near Nalbrits. Under the control of the governor, Smith was treated cruelly, with an iron ring placed around his neck, while suffering routine beatings. He learned from his fellow Christian slaves there was little chance of fleeing into the surrounding desert and mountains. However, when the opportunity unexpectedly occurred for him to attempt an escape, Smith quickly seized it. As he was working in the fields, he was approached alone by the governor, who began kicking and beating him. Enraged, Smith grabbed a farming tool, striking and killing him. He took the governor's horse and clothes, escaping into the wilderness. After spending several days wandering through the wasteland, Smith located a marker for a caravan route, following the signs north for Moscow and finally reaching an outpost after several days. The commander of the small fort took him in, providing food and shelter, while later placing Smith in a convoy to Habsburg lands with a safe conduct pass.

Entering imperial territory, Smith made his way through eastern Europe to the Protestant haven at Leipzig in current-day eastern Germany. He was reunited there in December 1603 with Modrusch, who used his influence to obtain a document signed by Prince Zsigmond describing his military service to the Habsburgs and requesting safe passage for him through all lands, while giving him 1,500 ducats in gold. He journeyed for several months before reaching France, making his way to Nantes in Brittany, where he boarded a ship for Bilbos in Spain on the Bay of Biscay. He rode through the Spanish countryside, visiting several large cities before sailing into the Mediterranean to Tangier and later travelling inland to the ancient Moroccan capital of Marrakesh.

While Smith was in Morocco, he became friends with a French naval captain named Merham, accepting his invitation to sail on his warship. He departed from the port of Safi, navigating into the Atlantic toward the Spanish-controlled Canary Islands searching for rich merchant ships to plunder. During the following weeks the privateers captured three vessels, seizing their cargoes. The French captain steered his ship to the east, and off the coast of western Africa encountered two Spanish warships, which were looking for raiders. When the Spaniards fired a salvo from their cannons, the Frenchmen attempted to escape but were closely followed through the day and into the night. In the early daylight, the Spanish renewed their attack and after an hour's bombardment ordered Merham to surrender. When he refused, the enemy ships manoeuvred closer, boarding the raider as hand-to-hand fighting erupted, with Smith taking part in the action. When a loud explosion rocked the deck and flames began to spread, the Spaniards fled back to their warships, but the French crew managed to put out the blaze. Merham fired his guns again at the fleeing Spanish before sailing away to escape, returning to Safi. Smith then left the French, travelling to El Araish, finding passage to Cadiz in southern Spain and finally boarding a vessel from there to England, arriving in early October 1605.

Captain John Smith spent several weeks in London visiting his many friends, who were delighted with his stories of his travels and adventures against the Turks. In late autumn he returned to Lincolnshire, spending time with his brother, sister and local acquaintances, while visiting his mother's grave. Smith now had little in common with his rural community relatives and friends, soon returning to London where he was idolized by the public.

While Smith was fighting against the Ottoman Empire, the Spanish and French kingdoms had sponsored voyages of discovery to the New World, beginning the formation of overseas empires. Earlier English attempts at colonization had failed, but now a wave of popular enthusiasm for new expeditions spread through the realm, and on 10 April 1606, King James I issued letters patent authorizing the organization of the Virginia Company of London. The company was chartered to establish a permanent English settlement between current-day Cape Fear, North Carolina, and Long Island Sound, New York. Since his return to England, Captain Smith had become increasingly attracted to the adventure of a voyage to the New World, and in 1605 joined the expedition to explore the Oyapock River in northern Brazil. However, when the project was cancelled he was forced to seek employment in another expedition, and through friends was recommended to Bartholomew Gosnold, an investor in the Virginia Company.

The Virginia Company began to carefully prepare for the voyage to Chesapeake Bay, hiring the experienced seaman captain Christopher Newport as commander and appointing Bartholomew Gosnold as his deputy. As Newport assembled his expeditionary force, Smith was recruited by Gosnold as a member of the expedition. Under Newport's direction, three ships were purchased, the square-rigged 100-ton *Susan Constant*, 40-ton *Godspeed* and 20-ton *Discovery*. During December, Smith was occupied assisting with the purchase and loading of supplies and equipment on the three vessels. Following a communion service at Westminster Abbey, in mid-December the sailors and 104 settlers boarded the ships. The fleet set sail from Blackwall, London, down the Thames, making its way to the east coast of England, as strong contrary winds delayed the transatlantic passage for many weeks. Finally, in February 1607, the wind changed direction and the squadron steered south to the Canary Islands, taking on fresh water and provisions before navigating across the Atlantic making landfall at Hispaniola in the Caribbean Sea. During the crossing, the colonists in the flotilla had endured cramped quarters and foul air, subsisting on salted meat and fish, stale biscuits and bad water. Soon after the beginning of the journey, dissension broke out between Smith and several gentlemen adventurers over the leadership of the colony. After reaching the island, they held a mock trial sentencing the captain to death by hanging. When they attempted to carry out the sentence, no one was willing to arrest Smith, fearful of his martial skills, and after Newport intervened they abandoned the planned execution.

On 27 March, the fleet put back to sea, making a brief stopover at Guadeloupe before anchoring at Nevis Island, remaining for six days as the men rested and recovered from the long voyage. When the expedition renewed its journey, the mariners sailed to the north-west stopping at several islands for fresh water and food before crossing the Florida Strait. As the seamen neared the North American coastline, a fierce gale blew the ships out to sea and Newport was forced to pilot westward for several days, finally reaching Chesapeake Bay at the southern edge of the outlet for the James River in late April.

After the arrival of the expeditionary force in Virginia, Captain Newport opened his sealed instructions from the London Company's directors, naming the seven governors of the colony. The list included John Smith, but a majority of the other governors voted to exclude him from the board. Rather than inflame the hostilities of the gentlemen adventurers further, Smith accepted the decision, albeit only temporarily.

Shortly after sailing into Chesapeake Bay, Newport led a landing party ashore to explore inland, and was pleased with the beautiful meadows, abundant water and dense forest he found. He decided to resume the reconnaissance in the morning and ordered his men to spend the night at their hastily built encampment. During the night, they were attacked by the local Indians, but when Newport fired his pistol the terrified Chesapeake natives scattered. After the clash with the Indians, Newport decided to scout other areas for the site of the colony, ordering construction of a shallop to search around Chesapeake Bay. Several days later he began looking for an easily defended location for the settlement, with Smith and twenty gentlemen adventurers travelling with him in the shallop, reconnoitring the numerous inlets and rivers. During the journey, Smith began making drawings of the large bay and its many islands, coves, streams and harbours.

As the English continued to explore for a favourable colony location, on 30 April they sighted a band of Indians on the shore. Newport ordered the crew to sail to the shoreline, and after reaching land Smith jumped ashore, giving the natives gifts of beads to gain their friendship. The Indians responded by inviting the strangers to eat with them and smoke tobacco, establishing the beginnings of a peaceful relationship with the tribe. Several days after his first meeting with the Indians, Smith left Captain Newport and took a search party in the shallop up the James River, locating a large native village called Paspahegh. He soon discovered that the settlement was the home of Powhatan, chief of the Chickahominy Confederation. Along with another Englishman, he stayed with Powhatan during the night and was invited to a grand feast celebrating the arrival of the explorers. Smith and his friend returned to the shallop on 5 May, piloting further upriver and visiting several villages where they were welcomed as friends.

In mid-May, the expedition returned to the ships and Smith gave his report of the journey to Newport. After considering his explorations and Smith's recent reconnaissance upriver, Newport decided to build the colony on the James River close to Powhatan's village. The location was nearly 60 miles up the James River, and the narrow peninsula provided protection against Indian raids and Spanish and French privateers, while the deep water port allowed vessels to easily anchor close to the shore. On 14 May, the colonists reached the site and went ashore with supplies to begin the construction of Jamestown. Land was cleared and the men started building the fort, storehouse and cabins, as trees were cut and sassafras roots gathered for shipment back to England to help the investors defray some of the voyage's cost.

As the Englishmen worked on the settlement, the ruling council was torn by internal hostilities among the directors. The head of the council, Edward Wingfield, was inexperienced and poorly qualified to lead the colonists as two opposing groups formed, battling each other for control of Jamestown. Most of the settlers supported Smith, who in defiance of the council, began military training for the men, teaching them to fire their muskets and defend themselves. Smith encouraged the Englishmen to clear more land and plant crops of corn, peas and beans to survive the winter, but was continually opposed by Wingfield. In late May, Newport led a voyage up the James River to explore inland, naming Smith to command the landing party. The English made frequent stops, visiting Indian villages, while Smith continued to establish friendly contacts with the natives of the Chickahominy tribes. Newport piloted the shallop about 70 miles upriver, as Captain Smith drew sketches of the river and interior territory encircled with dense green pines, hardwood trees and foliage. The expeditionary force travelled upcountry as far as present-day Richmond, Virginia, where Newport claimed the area for the English regime.

While the expedition was upriver, Jamestown was assaulted by Chesapeake Indians, who killed two of the unprepared colonists. After Smith's return to the fort, he took charge of the defences, completing construction of the barricades and stationing armed sentries. When the

Chesapeakes attacked again, the men were prepared, throwing them back with volleys from their muskets. Despite Smith's defeat of the Indians, Wingfield was displeased with his assumption of leadership. As the dissent between Smith and Wingfield intensified, the settlers rebelled in the captain's support, forcing the governor to place him on the council.

In accordance with instructions from the Virginia Company, Captain Newport put to sea for England with the *Susan Constant* and *Godspeed* in late June, leaving the *Discovery* with the colonists. Before leaving, he was given a petition from the council for the directors in London, asking for a shipment of provisions for the winter. Soon after the departure of Newport, an unknown illness spread rapidly among the settlers, brought on by foul swamp water, the summer heat and a limited diet of only wheat and barley. By mid-September, nearly half of the Englishmen had died, and Smith was ill for a short time. After Newport left in June, Wingfield ordered the colonists to end military drills, stop work on the defences and during the sickness prohibited anyone ill from receiving food. When the settlers threatened to execute Wingfield, the council voted to depose him, naming John Ratcliffe as president. Smith was appointed deputy president, quickly putting the men to work tending the crops and strengthening the fortifications. To stockpile additional provisions for the coming winter, Smith took the shallop up the James River, trading English goods with the Indians for food and returning to Jamestown with a large supply of corn, wheat, fish and meat. In the autumn, the colonists harvested their crops and stored them in the warehouse. Captain Smith made frequent trips upriver, bartering with the Native Americans for food, while continuing to draw maps and write descriptions of the Indians, land, animals and forest.

In early October, Wingfield and his supporter George Kendal persuaded the crew of the *Discovery* to abandon Jamestown and return to England. As they prepared to set sail, Smith ordered them to leave the ship. When they refused, the colonists on the shore opened fire with their pistols and muskets, forcing the deserters to surrender. The two conspirators were quickly tried for mutiny, with Kendal sentenced to death as the main plotter and Wingfield held as prisoner, to be returned to England for trial.

In the autumn of 1607, Captain John Smith made numerous journeys up the James and other rivers, trading with the Indians for food and exploring the interior. As Smith later wrote in his first book, *A True Relation*, during an expedition up the Chickahominy River in December by barge and canoe, he was captured by a band of Chesapeake warriors after putting up a fierce fight. The Indians paraded their prize captive from tribe to tribe, displaying him to the natives. They eventually reached Powhatan's village, where the chief demanded to know what the Englishman was doing in his land. Smith's reply was unacceptable and the chief ordered him killed. As the warriors prepared to execute him, Powhatan's young daughter, Pocahontas, dashed forward, begging her father to spare the stranger. Unable to deny his favourite daughter's request, Smith was set free. The highly romanticized account of Smith's rescue does not appear in the book's first edition, but was added only after Pocahontas' arrival in London, to the wild acclaims of the population. The story about his release was written in 1617 after the popular daughter of Powhatan came to England, and was likely included to capture the attention of the English audience. In relating the account, he failed to explain why Powhatan could have been surprised by Smith's presence in his land, after the settlers had been at his camp many previous times, and why his enemy the Chesapeakes would turn over a valuable prisoner to him.

As the colonists struggled through the long hard winter months, in early January 1608 Captain Newport sailed up the James River in the *Susan Constant*, bringing a cargo of provisions and supplies along with eighty volunteers for the settlement. Newport took charge of Jamestown, as Captain Smith sent the men to build houses for the new settlers. While construction of the cabins proceeded, a fire erupted, burning many houses, the storehouse and parts of the fortification before it was extinguished. Under the captain's direction, work on rebuilding the lost structures quickly began.

Newport remained at Jamestown until the spring, visiting Indian villages with Smith and trading for food, while reinforcing peaceful relations with the Chesapeake Bay chiefs. When he departed for England in April, Wingfield was put aboard the ship for his return to England for trial at the insistence of the council. The *Susan Constance* also carried a cargo of lumber for the investors. Shortly after Newport left, governor Ratcliffe accidently shot himself in the hand cleaning his musket, and weak from the wound, Smith assumed responsibility for the government, ordering the men to work in the fields clearing additional land and planting crops, while previously burned buildings were rebuilt. While he governed Jamestown, some of the new colonists from Newport's ship decided to search for gold. As they prepared to leave, Smith told the newcomers 'they would be denied the fort's protection and food if they departed'. Without support from the colony, the settlers decided to forget about the gold and go back to work.

In the early morning of 20 April, a strange ship appeared on the horizon, slowly making its way to Jamestown's harbour. The men rushed to the ramparts, armed with pistols and muskets, only to find that the vessel was the *Phoenix*, which had left England with Newport in the late autumn. During an Atlantic storm the crew became lost and were forced to spend the winter in the West Indies before heading to the colony. The ship carried a cargo of provisions and more settlers. Smith quickly put the new Englishmen to work tending crops, enlarging the farmlands, building houses and cutting trees for the London Company, while he taught them to fire their muskets. During the night, he spent long hours writing *A True Relation,* describing the New World and giving a history of the colony's development. Many of his maps and charts were included in the book. When the manuscript was completed, he gave it to a settler, who was returning to London on the *Phoenix*, to have it published.

Shortly after the departure of the relief ship, Smith left the settlement under the command of the recovered Ratcliffe on 2 June and took the shallop with thirteen men to explore and map the northern region of Chesapeake Bay. During the journey he carefully plotted and mapped the bay's shoreline, noting the locations of coves, inlets, rivers and islands, while describing the different tribes, richness of the soil and abundance of large hardwood trees, wild animals and fish in his logbook. On 16 June, they discovered the Potomac River, sailing up the waterway and scouting the banks. They continued upriver until one of the crewmen suffered a broken leg and the expeditionary force was compelled to return to Jamestown. When the explorers reached the colony on 21 July, they were met by a party of settlers demanding that governor Ratcliffe be forced to resign due to his poor leadership and be replaced with Smith. The captain hesitated, but after Ratcliffe agreed to peacefully yield he accepted the post, appointing his friend and trusted supporter Matthew Scrivener as his deputy.

With the colony under Scrivener's capable leadership, Smith felt safe to resume his exploration, and three days later departed in the shallop for another voyage to the north. He returned to Chesapeake Bay, exploring its northern area, discovering the mouth of the Susquehanna River and encountering warriors from the Susquehannack tribe who lived in the surrounding region. Smith talked with the friendly Indians, persuading them to guide him further up the river searching for the North-west Passage. He travelled with the Native Americans for three days, reaching present-day eastern Pennsylvania before determining the river's course was not the water passage between the two oceans. The expedition concluded its venture turning south down Chesapeake Bay, reconnoitring the Patuxent and Elizabeth rivers before returning to Jamestown with an enormous amount of new information on the geography, Indians, animals and vegetation of the region.

By early September 1608, Smith was back in Jamestown governing the colony. He continued to build houses and storehouses for the expected new settlers, while a grid of streets was laid out and the stockade enlarged into a five-sided fortification for greater security. Military training was renewed in the cooler weather, with routine musket practice and skirmish drills. In the autumn, the abundant crops were harvested and the corn, peas, grain and beans stored in the warehouses. During the nights he returned to his writing, beginning a second book, *A Map of Virginia, With a Description of the Country*, an account of his explorations and lands reconnoitred, along with maps and charts. In mid-October, Captain Newport arrived with provisions, supplies and seventy additional colonists. Among the arrivals were the first two women to settle at Jamestown, quickly resulting in a more civilized community.

Captain Christopher Newport brought with him a letter from the Virginia Company directors, ordering Smith to find the gold and jewels that they were convinced were in the region around Chesapeake Bay. To comply with the demand, the governor and a small scouting party sailed up the James River in the shallop, exploring the interior for 40 miles looking for the precious metal, but after several days they found nothing. When the ship returned to Jamestown, Newport and Smith fabricated an exaggerated report of the expedition, describing the search for gold by a large force of men over many miles.

With winter approaching, Smith prepared for the hostile weather by sending Scrivener to trade for corn and fur pelts from the Indians, continuing to build houses for the new colonists, drilling the men, cutting lumber and gathering sassafras roots for the London investors. In early November, the *Susan Constant* was loaded with lumber, furs and sassafras but no gold or gems for the return voyage to England. Before Newport departed, Smith gave him a letter for the directors describing the colony's ongoing struggle to survive in the wilderness, but highlighting the country's potential with its abundant natural resources and opportunity to establish a permanent English settlement in the New World. To ensure the survival of Jamestown, he encouraged the investors to dispatch at least three relief ships to sustain the nearly 200 settlers.

The Englishmen at Jamestown depended on trade with Powhatan's tribe for food to survive the winter, but in late 1608 the Indians became less friendly. With the storage houses rapidly emptying, Smith was forced to visit the chief to negotiate for more corn. Powhatan agreed to provide a larger supply if the English constructed a house for him like the ones at Jamestown. The offer was accepted and Smith set forty men to work building the dwelling. The labourers and carpenters toiled long hours in the cold weather, some of the new settlers becoming increasingly disgruntled at the strenuous work. A group of recent arrivals began plotting the murder of the governor by bribing several Indians to kill him. Smith was told about the plan but ignored it. Late one morning, as he and a friend, John Russell, walked back to the English camp from the worksite, they were attacked by twelve of Powhatan's warriors. Smith and Russell drew their pistols, killing three natives and fending off the others with their swords. When Smith charged into the warriors with his sword, they abandoned the fight and ran off into the forest. Following the skirmish, Smith returned to the construction site, ordering his men to attack the village and sack Powhatan's storehouse, seizing corn and meat to take back to Jamestown. Four of the English plotters were tried and found guilty, with a sentence of fifty lashes to serve as a deterrent against future mutinies. Shortly after the pillaging of the village, small bands of Indians started coming to Jamestown, trading food and pelts for English knives, axes and other goods, allowing the colonists to survive the winter with adequate provisions.

To keep the men occupied during the cold and snowy winter months, Captain Smith ordered them to dig new wells to provide fresh drinking water, instead of the brackish liquid from the swampy land. Additional houses were constructed and the fort strengthened, while military training continued. When the colonists complained about the work in the cold weather, Smith issued a new regulation stating, 'He that will not work shall not eat.'

In spring 1609, Smith attempted to buttress his friendly relations with the Indians, inviting chiefs from the Chesapeake region to a large feast in their honour. Powhatan refused to come, but his son and sub-chiefs attended the elaborate ceremony. The goodwill generated from the banquet resulted in expanded trading relationships with the natives, who freely brought corn, meat and animal pelts to barter for English goods. During the spring, the health of the English improved as they hunted the abundant deer and fowl, fished the streams and ponds and collected wild berries. Smith continued to govern the settlement, making improvements in the defences and housing while enlarging the land for cultivation and maintaining good relations with the Indians. In mid-July, a ship arrived from the London Company with provisions, supplies and a letter for Smith from the directors. The board criticized the governor, accusing him of mismanagement and maltreatment of the Indians. The investors were unhappy with the small shipments of lumber and furs, and showed no understanding of the colony's problems. The letter ended with the news that the settlement now had King James I's support and sponsorship, and nine ships with over 500 men and women were to be sent to Jamestown. The colony's government was dramatically revised, with a newly appointed royal governor and a large administrative staff. Smith was ordered to remain in office until the governor arrived, and then turn over the post to him.

During the voyage to Jamestown, the fleet sent by the Virginia Company was struck by a hurricane in the Gulf of Mexico, with numerous vessels damaged and supplies and passengers lost at sea, while many more died from an unknown sickness. On 3 August, the first ship from the flotilla struggled into Jamestown, with several others following within a few days. However, none of the vessels carried members of the new colonial government, and Smith was forced to remain as governor. Among the passengers who arrived were two gentlemen adventurers, John Ratcliffe and Gabriel Archer, who had earlier been returned to England by the council for their disruptive actions and rebellion. They immediately made trouble for Smith, plotting to have him removed from office. Smith acted quickly to quell the two troublemakers, placing them under house arrest.

The new immigrants created a housing shortage and the acting governor put the colonists to work building more dwellings, dispatching others to clear land and plant crops to supply provisions for the onrush of men and women. Settlers were sent to trade with the Indians for additional corn, meat and vegetables, while others hunted, fished or gathered wild berries to increase the stock of food in the warehouses.

While Smith was travelling up the James River in the shallop, visiting Indian villages and making arrangements for more food, he was badly injured when his gunpowder pouch was accidentally ignited by one of his men while lighting his tobacco pipe. Smith leaped from the ship into the river to put out the flames, but was seriously burned. The governor was taken back to Jamestown, where he was treated by the doctor, but for several days his recovery was in doubt. He slowly recovered, but received only limited treatment and was forced to agree to return to England with the next ship. On 4 October, he was carried onboard the *Unity* and, as the vessel sailed out of the harbour, the exhausted governor fell asleep. He would never again see Virginia, where he had toiled tirelessly to create England's first permanent colony.

Smith's transatlantic crossing lasted eight weeks before the *Unity* finally sailed up the Thames, dropping anchor near London. During the voyage, beset with autumn gales and pounding seas, the captain continued to suffer from his burns as his wounds slowly healed. Reaching London, he was too weak to walk and forced to hire porters to carry him to his new lodgings. Smith spent the next three months secluded in his room, seeing only the doctor as his still painful burns gradually healed. He finally contacted his mistress, Frances, Duchess of Richmond, with whom he had begun a romatic relationship in 1606. She found Smith a better house, supplying it with some of her furniture. He learned from Frances that his first book, *A True Relation*, was a huge success; the popular work had already earned him over £1,000.

Through the intervention of the Duchess of Richmond, Smith met several times with Richard Hakluyt, who served on the board of the Virginia Company, describing conditions at Jamestown and discussing the region's geographic features with him. He later contacted three other shareholders, including the king's eldest son, Prince Henry, relating the problems of survival at the settlement and the frequent plotting intrigues of the gentleman adventurers. As the result of his discussions with the prince, Smith was summoned to court for an audience with King James. He spent less than an hour answering the king's questions. After the audience, he met with several more of the London Company's board members, repeating his stories of the colony's needs and the difficulties of living in the wilderness. In May 1610, he was invited to a board meeting of the company, where he stressed the need to concentrate the efforts of the Jamestown settlers on Virginia's natural resources of timber and furs, while urging the investors to send more farmers and skilled labourers to the colony. After his meetings with the board, he left London, spending the next year continuing to recover from his burns and working on his second book.

In the summer of 1611, Smith returned to London in better health, visiting his publisher to inform him that his manuscript for *A Map of Virginia* was nearly completed. He returned to his residence and within several weeks finished the book. When Smith took the finalized manuscript to the printer, he was told the work could not be published. Suspecting intervention from the Virginia Company, he undertook a detailed investigation, finding that one of the company's shareholders with high political connections had stopped the production to protect his large investment. However, in the spring of 1612, *A Map of Virginia* was printed by Oxford University through the intervention of Richard Hakluyt, who had close relations with the seat of learning. The publication was an immediate sensation and prompted renewed interest in the first book, which was reprinted. The success of the two works propelled Smith to national prominence, and his advice on investing in the New World was eagerly sought by wealthy financiers willing to pay.

While Smith was in Jamestown, English investors had financed several voyages of discovery to the coast of North America between present-day Maryland and New England, but had failed to establish a permanent colony. Following his return to London, Smith had not lost his desire to explore the New World, and in 1613 wrote to the Earl of Southampton, Henry Wriothesley, proposing an expedition to map the shoreline of New England and explore inland. He had been introduced to the earl by the Duchess of Richmond, and was encouraged by him to make the necessary plans for the venture. The captain collected information from previous journeys and made careful preparations, reading logbooks and studying charts and maps, while spending time questioning two Indians who had been brought back to England from the region. Finance for the undertaking was provided by Frances' husband, the Duke of Richmond, and two London Company directors, Southampton and Sir Ferdinando George. They gave Smith full authority to outfit, staff and direct the project.

Captain Smith hired two veteran sea captains to command his ships and recruited experienced crews. He purchased two vessels, the 100-ton *Frances* and the 82-ton *Queen Anne*. Provisions, supplies and equipment were bought, with Smith personally inspecting everything to ensure inferior products were not delivered by the merchants. The small fleet was outfitted in Southampton, and in early February 1614 the forty-five seamen began boarding the ships. After a month's delay due to bad weather, Smith departed from Southampton on the morning of 3 March, sailing out into the English Channel. The mariners reached the Grand Banks off the shores of Greenland without incident, and continued south-west to Nova Scotia.

Once in the waters of the North American continent, Smith ordered his fleet to briefly anchor, as six small boats were unloaded and sent to fish for cod and tuna, while he mapped the coastline. The sailors had little trouble catching a large number of fish, filling the barrels in the ships' holds to sell in London for the investors. Following the stopover, he steered down the shore, continuing to make detailed charts of the region and write descriptions of the changing terrain features all the way to modern-day Rhode Island. He made several short layovers, trading beads, mirrors and other English goods to the local natives for fur pelts, while scouting inland. The Englishmen spent two days near Boston, bartering with the Indians for more pelts. Smith navigated south down the coast, stopping at Narragansett Bay in Rhode Island to reconnoitre the territory, which he believed could be the beginning of the

North-west Passage. After three months of exploring and mapping the shoreline of the country that Smith named New England on his charts, and with his cargo holds filled with salted and dried fish and bales of furs, Captain Smith ordered his seamen to return to England.

On 18 July, the two ships set sail for home, making the transatlantic crossing with few problems. Near the end of August, the flotilla docked in London and very quickly the whole cargo was sold to local merchants. From the proceeds the investors paid their expenses, and after giving Smith £1,500 still made a profit of nearly £10,000. The expedition demonstrated to potential English investors that a profit could be made from the natural resources of North America, not just gold or silver.

Soon after his return to London, Smith began planning his next expedition. He wanted to establish the first permanent English colony in New England sustained by the profits from the sale of the region's lumber, fur pelts and fish. The Earl of Southampton, Sir Ferdinando George, several other noblemen and Plymouth merchants agreed to finance the undertaking. In early 1615, Smith purchased two vessels and recruited forty-four settlers for the venture. At the beginning of summer, the small fleet was outfitted at Plymouth and the sailors began boarding the ships as supplies and equipment were loaded. After the preparations were completed, Smith and his colonists went aboard and the ships raised their anchors, sailing into the English Channel. When the flotilla reached the Atlantic, the smaller and faster vessel disappeared over the horizon, while Smith's flagship lumbered behind. After steering over 300 miles the older vessel began to leak badly and the main mast snapped, forcing the crew to return to England.

Smith refused to give up his quest for a new colony in New England, and began raising money for another ship, selling the wreckage of the flagship along with the equipment. With the funds he purchased a small 60-ton merchantman. Smith hired twenty-three seamen and set sail in late June. During the transatlantic crossing he was intercepted by an English pirate vessel. The slow merchantman was outmanoeuvred and outgunned, compelling captain Smith to surrender. When the pirates came aboard Smith's ship, he was astonished to see that some of the men were from his old regiment in Transylvania. The Captain convinced them to join his expedition, and the two vessels continued westward towards the New World.

In less than a week they were confronted by four French warships. When the Frenchmen closed on the two vessels, they fired a salvo, forcing Smith to raise the white flag. The English crews became prisoners of the French privateers and their ships were taken over by the enemy, while Smith was transferred to the French flagship. The six vessels now steered south toward Portugal, searching for a Spanish treasure fleet returning from the West Indies. After the French pirate captain captured three Spanish merchantmen, he replaced the crews with his men, reducing his seamen on the two English vessels. During the night, Smith's mariners overwhelmed their guards, retaking control of their ships and piloting away, leaving their captain with the French corsairs.

Captain Smith was forced to remain on the privateer's flagship until October, and during his idle hours began writing his third book, *A Description of New England*. When the French sailors finally returned to port at La Rochelle, Smith managed to escape at night, making his way into the city, where the residents treated him kindly. He was interrogated by French Admiralty officials, and after explaining his plight with the pirates, who had recently been seized after a storm wrecked their fleet, was given a share of the prize money. He remained in France until December before returning to Plymouth.

After establishing himself at Plymouth, Smith continued to pursue his quest for the creation of an English colony in New England. While he had not lost his passion for the expedition, his investors became increasingly disillusioned. Unable to find backers, he returned to London and became occupied finishing his manuscript for *A Description of New England*, hoping that regenerated enthusiasm for an overseas venture would be created with its publication. The book was published in June 1616 and was an immediate success with the English public, but the financiers and merchants remained uninterested. While Smith struggled to find new financial support, he fended off his many creditors with promises of a large share of his earnings from the book. His financial problems increased when he was ostracized from the aristocracy for openly living with a notorious courtesan, Barbara Courtenay. However, when Pocahontas and her husband, John Rolfe, arrived in London, drawing large and excited crowds wherever they travelled, Smith rewrote his first book, *A True Relation,* adding a section on his fictionalized experiences with the Indian princess. The revised book was well received by the public, increasing interest in New England while aiding Smith's financial condition. By the autumn of 1616, he had ended his affair with Courtenay and was slowly accepted again by the nobility.

When Smith again attempted to raise funds for an expedition, several investors and merchants agreed to finance the new venture. After finalizing his plans, he purchased three ships and began recruiting colonists. However, he had difficulty finding men willing to settle in the wilderness, so decided to earn the shareholders a quick profit by sending his fleet to gather fish off the coast of Newfoundland. The seamen departed from Plymouth in March 1617, returning five months later with a rich cargo of cod and tuna that earned the financiers a healthy profit.

After the success of his 1617 voyage, Captain Smith had little trouble obtaining funds for the New England colony. He raised enough money to send twenty vessels and over 1,000 men and women to North America, while receiving the title Admiral of New England. However, the venture quickly fell apart when the investors began disagreeing among themselves, and Smith was forced to cancel it. Shortly after the collapse of the expedition, Smith attempted to interest Francis Bacon, James I's Lord Chancellor, in a settlement in New England. He wrote a book promoting the potential and advantages of the colony, calling it *New England's Trials*. A copy was sent to Bacon to generate his enthusiasm in the project, but the chancellor politely declined. Smith refused to give up, contacting numerous potential financiers and merchants, but found no sponsors.

While Smith failed to find financial backing from the nobles or traders, the Separatists religious community living in exile in Holland made contact with him, enquiring about a settlement in New England as a safe haven for their sect. A secular colony had no appeal to the Separatists or Pilgrims, but they offered Smith command of their planned settlement's military force. He continued to negotiate with the Pilgrims until 1619, before finally declining the offer. Captain Smith remained driven by the New England colonial venture, continuing to seek investors during the next few years. To generate income for himself, he reissued two of his books, earning enough money to live comfortably. As Smith grew older and was beset with chronic illnesses, he slowly gave up on the project. He became reconciled with Frances, Duchess of Richmond, and under her influence began writing a history of English colonization in the New World. He spent over three years researching and working on the manuscript. The work, entitled *The General History of Virginia, New England and the Summer Islands*, was written in six volumes and published in July 1624. The book was an immediate triumph, with the first edition selling out, followed by two more.

The success of the publication swept Smith back to national fame, being regarded as the authority on the New World. In 1626, he wrote another book describing life at sea, giving advice and instruction to prospective mariners. The book, *The Seaman's Grammar*, became his bestselling work and was reissued many times. As a result of his widespread prominence, interest in Smith's earlier ventures in eastern Europe against the Turks spread in

England, and he wrote an autobiographical account of the experiences, but by greatly exaggerating his encounters destroyed his reputation and credibility as a historian. While the publication sold well, Smith was no longer considered an expert on North America, and the loss of esteem and social standing depressed him, causing his health to weaken further. In 1631, he began writing a new work describing all the sea voyages of discovery to the New World, but was soon forced to stop his research due to failing health. As his condition grew worse, Captain John Smith died on 21 June 1631, alone in his London room. Only a few friends attended his funeral at St Sepulcher Church, where he was buried under the choir vault with a small marker. The church was totally destroyed during the 1666 Great Fire of London.

SELECTED SOURCES:
Barbour, Philip L., *The Three Worlds of Captain John Smith.*
Gerson, Noel B., *The Glorious Scoundrel – A Biography of Captain John Smith.*
Vaughan, Alden T., *American Genesis – Captain John Smith and the Founding of Virginia.*

Henry Hudson

By 1600, Captain Henry Hudson had become a renowned navigator and explorer in Western European courts. He was a leading authority on the quest for the shortest route to Cathay, and in early 1610 was offered a contract by the newly organized Company of Gentlemen to search for the North-west Passage to the Orient. When he put to sea in April as captain of the *Discovery*, the voyage would end in disaster with the mutiny of the crew and the disappearance of Henry Hudson in the unknown waters of Canada's Hudson Bay.

Henry Hudson was probably born a few miles north of London in Hertfordshire around 1570, one of five sons born to Henry Hudson and an unknown mother. Henry was educated in local schools, studying mathematics, Latin and religion, while learning to read and write. He was raised in a family with close ties to the Muscovy Company and English commercial trading activities. His grandfather was a founding investor in the Muscovy Company and his father was involved in international commerce. Two of Henry's older brothers were employed by the Muscovy Company as agents and ships' captains. Through the influence of his family, Henry was attracted to a career at sea from a young age. He began serving as a cabin boy and later a common sailor on vessels from his father's businesses and the Muscovy Company, learning the skills of seamanship, navigation, map-making and astronomy.

In 1587, the 17-year-old Henry Hudson joined the crew of John Davis' expedition to search for the North-west Passage, exploring the north-eastern coastline of present-day Canada. On 19 May, the expeditionary force of three ships, led by the *Ellen*, put to sea from the port of Dartmouth, a fair north-easterly breeze driving the fleet into the English Channel and past the Isle of Scilly into the Atlantic Ocean. Hudson served as a seaman and was occupied during the day setting the sails, standing watch, cleaning the decks, pumping water from the leaking vessel and repairing the rigging and equipment. Sailing with favourable weather, the flotilla steered north-west, first sighting Greenland on 14 June. Following a brief stopover at Godthaak, the Englishmen navigated north along the western shore of Greenland, crossing the Arctic Circle and reaching a latitude of 72° North near modern-day Upernavik. Hudson and his fellow mariners now turned west, but were soon forced to change course to the south by a massive field of ice. On 18 July, the sailors spotted the mountains of Baffin Island and spent the next six days reconnoitring the region for the North-west Passage before manoeuvring south to Cumberland Sound. Davis and his crew onboard the *Ellen* continued down the coastline past Labrador with the other two vessels, anchoring along the Strait of Belle Isle. After exploring the waters off Newfoundland for several days, Davis was forced to give up his quest for the North-west Passage, and on 15 August set a course for England, arriving at Dartmouth in mid-September. During the voyage to Canada, Hudson was exposed to the hazards of sailing in Arctic waters, learning to pilot through dangerous ice floes, erratic winds, frigid temperatures and powerful currents.

While Hudson was exploring the coast of Canada, King Philip II of Spain began assembling his Grand Armada for the invasion of England and the overthrow of Queen Elizabeth I. Soon after his return to England, Hudson likely renewed his association with John Davis, volunteering to serve with his crew on the 20-ton warship *Black Dog* to oppose the Spanish seaborne attack. After Captain Davis and his ten mariners joined the fleet at Plymouth Sound in Devon, they were appointed as the escort vessel for the Lord Admiral, Charles Howard. Davis was ordered to support Howard's flagship, *Ark Royal,* by fending off approaching enemy galleons, scouting ahead of the queen's flotilla and serving as dispatch and resupply vessel. When the Spaniards, led by Alonzo Perez Guzman, were sighted by the English off Lizard Point on 19 July, Howard's ship, with the *Black Dog* close by, put to sea to harass the approaching enemy. While Howard's flagship sailed against the Spanish carrack *La Rata S. M. Encuerada* (*Torn Lord*), Davis and his men supported the attack, manoeuvring close to the Spanish and firing their guns to distract Guzman's mariners. As the battle raged into the afternoon, Hudson and the *Black Dog*'s sailors were sent to port for ammunition and supplies. When Guzman continued to steer up the English Channel, making for Calais and his rendezvous with Philip II's invasion army, Davis' vessel, along with other escorts, led the English fleet in pursuit, taking part in numerous actions. During lull periods, Davis and his seamen were occupied ferrying fresh provisions, stores and ammunition to Elizabeth I's warships. When the Lord Admiral sent eight fire ships packed with explosives into Guzman's anchored flotilla during the night of 7 August, the Spanish galleons and carracks were forced to cut their cables and flee in disorder. The English pursued Guzman's vessels, attacking them near Gravelines, with Hudson and the crew of the

Black Dog engaged in the fierce fighting. With his Armada now in disarray, the Spanish admiral abandoned the invasion and attempted to return to Spain. Hudson continued to serve with Davis, protecting the Channel ports against the return of the Spaniards, but most of the enemy's remaining ships were destroyed by storms off the coast of Ireland.

In the aftermath of the Spanish Armada's defeat, Hudson continued his maritime career serving as a seaman on English merchant vessels, sailing to ports along the English Channel and in the Mediterranean. While advancing through the ranks, rising from apprentice sailor to ship's officer, in the early 1590s he was married in London, and with his wife, Katherine, resided on a narrow street near the Tower of London in a three-storey brick house. They had three sons, living a comfortable life from his income as a mariner. Through over twenty years of marriage, they developed a close, loving and happy relationship, despite his frequent absences at sea.

By 1600, Henry Hudson had become an experienced ship's captain and was recognized as a skilled mapmaker, navigator and pilot. He was friends with many explorers and geographers, including Captain John Smith and Richard Hakluyt, and through his family's connections with the Muscovy Company, knew numerous merchant adventurers. While continuing to serve as a ship's captain, sailing for various merchant companies, Hudson held frequent discussions with his friends debating the Earth's geography, routes to the Far East, colonization of the New World and exploration of unknown parts of the world. Through his many conversations and studies of maps and documents, Hudson developed an obsession with finding an unobstructed waterway to the riches of Cathay, which he believed was located across the largely undiscovered North American continent. In 1607, Hudson finally secured his opportunity to search for the sea route to the East Indies through Hakluyt's recommendation to the Muscovy Company. However, he was commissioned to sail a course to the east through polar waters, and not by the fabled North-western Passage.

In late 1606, the directors of the Muscovy Company began planning for a voyage to search for a waterway to the wealth of the East Indies by sailing over the North Pole to China. In the late sixteenth and early seventeenth centuries, there was widespread belief among many English businessmen that an open route across the top of the Earth existed during the summer months, and the investors of the Muscovy Company were anxious to be the first to begin trading with the Chinese by a shorter and less expensive passageway. As the preparations for the venture advanced, the board of directors sent a delegation to Bristol to ask Richard Hakluyt his opinion of

Henry Hudson's qualifications to command the expeditionary force. He met with the delegates in his study, and when asked his opinion of Hudson replied, 'Henry Hudson is the most qualified man in England to lead a northern voyage of discovery.' Shortly after their return to London, the principals invited Hudson to their headquarters to offer him command of the expedition, which he immediately accepted.

During the early months of 1607, Captain Hudson was occupied planning for his voyage across the North Pole. He spent time at Bristol with Hakluyt discussing the expedition and studying his many charts and documents on the geography, ice floes, climate and currents in the northern seas. The Muscovy Company assigned the 40-ton bark *Hopewell* to Hudson, and after returning to London he began preparing to sail. He had the seasoned English oak planks on the three-year-old vessel recaulked with gum, while supplies and equipment for the hazardous journey were acquired. Hudson hired a crew of eleven seamen, including his fourteen-year-old son, John, as cabin boy. In March, provisions were purchased and the salted beef, fish and pork, dried peas and biscuits were loaded on the ship, along with kegs of beer and water. After a religious service for the safe return of the men was held at St Ethelburga's Church in London on 10 April, attended by members of the crew, their families and the Muscovy Company's directors, the sailors returned to the *Hopewell* to put to sea. However, after steering slowly down the Thames in a dense fog, Hudson was forced to wait at Gravesend for nearly two weeks for the weather to clear.

The bark finally departed the English coast on 1 May, navigating up the Channel against the wind and reaching the Shetland Islands twenty-six days later. As the mariners sailed to the north-west, they sighted eastern Greenland on 13 June and Hudson followed the shoreline northward, crossing the Arctic Circle. A cold thick fog set in, and the men were forced to climb the dangerous ice-clad rigging to make adjustments to the sails. Piloting into the Arctic Ocean, the seamen encountered whales, polar bears and walruses and a large variety of seabirds. When a grampus dolphin was spotted by a crewman, the superstitious sailors believed the mammal's appearance was an evil omen, pressing Hudson to return to England, but their pleas were ignored despite growing dissent. The weather continued to deteriorate, with freezing temperatures, fierce winds and strong currents as the *Hopewell* tossed and pitched in white-capped seas, struggling towards the North Pole. Hudson navigated up Greenland's eastern side until a barrier of solid ice forced him to alter his course and sail to the north-east. As the *Hopewell* steered toward the 80° North latitude, the periods of daylight increased and the air became marginally warmer, convincing the captain that the theories of navigable waters at the North Pole were correct. Encouraged by the desire to be the first explorer to reach Cathay via the polar cap, he pressed his men to push harder to the north.

As the Muscovy Company's ship navigated to the north-east, encountering icebergs and periods of dense fog, the men spotted the islands of the Spitsbergen Archipelago on 27 June, which had been previously discovered by the Dutch explorer William Barents. Captain Hudson steered his bark between jagged rocks and snow-covered shorelines, while cautiously avoiding the ice floes and exploring and mapping many of the archipelago's islands, hoping this was the route to the warm seas of the North Pole.

While Hudson and his seamen piloted through the polar waters of the Spitsbergen Archipelago, during the evening of 29 June they were struck by a violent storm from the north, threatening to drive the *Hopewell* onto the rocky shore and crush it. The crewmen took their posts as Hudson shouted orders to steer the ship into the partial protection of a cove. The men manned their stations on the deck and in the rigging, struggling through the night and into the morning to keep the vessel off the rugged rocks and away from the icebergs. When the weather improved, the Muscovy Company's captain resumed his journey to the north, spending the next two weeks making his way through the islands, constantly having to avoid the ice packs. In early July, he reached Northeast Island, the northernmost of the Spitsbergen Archipelago and 750 miles above the Arctic Circle. The English bark entered a large bay on the western coast of the island on 14 July, and Hudson was amazed by the hundreds of whales he found. The business of harvesting the large sea mammals was highly profitable, and he knew the Muscovy Company's directors would be greatly pleased with his discovery and the prospects of establishing a whaling station. Hudson sent a search party ashore to reconnoitre for a future base. When the sailors returned, they reported finding an area rich in wild game, with a supply of freshwater and enough resources for a station. The inlet was called Whale Bay by Hudson, and carefully marked on his maps as the site for the Muscovy's outpost.

In mid-July, the *Hopewell*'s seamen weighed anchor from Whale Bay, navigating to the north toward the polar cap. After reaching a latitude of over 80°, the Englishmen encountered a solid ice pack and were unable to find a way through it. Blocked by the ice Hudson, refused to give up his quest for the Orient and told his sailors they were going south around the Spitsbergen Archipelago, then up the eastern side of the islands to the North Pole. As Hudson steered down the western shoreline, his vessel was repeatedly battered by fierce storms, powerful polar seas and large ice floes. When the *Hopewell* was in danger of being crushed by a large mass of ice, Hudson used a rowboat to help tow it away from the hazard. Captain Hudson used all his skills of seamanship and navigation to keep his ship from crashing into the never-ending floes of icebergs. It was now late July, and with only a little safe time remaining for exploration, Hudson was forced to admit there was no open water route to the polar cap and it was impossible to sail over the North Pole to the Orient. He assembled his crew, announcing the end of the expedition and the return to England, which was greeted with loud cheers from the men.

Hudson began his return voyage to London, setting a course south down the western side of the Spitsbergen Archipelago and into the present-day Norwegian Sea. During the journey back to England, Hudson decided to delay the return home and steer west across the top of Greenland, then down the western shoreline through the Davis Strait before swinging east to London. After navigating over 400 miles to the west, the weather continued to deteriorate, forcing Hudson to turn back to the east and home. During the detour, he discovered a previously unknown volcanic island, naming it Hudson's Touches and marking its location on his charts. Today the island is known as Jan Mayen and serves as a Norwegian meteorological station. The *Hopewell* piloted to the south-east, making a brief stopover at the Faeroe Islands before sailing up the Thames and docking at Tilbury on 15 September after a three-and-a-half-month expedition. While Hudson's attempt to reach the Far East by crossing over the North Pole had failed, his voyage was highly profitable for the Muscovy Company, marking the beginning of the whaling industry.

Following his return to London, Henry Hudson presented his report of the voyage to the Muscovy Company's board of directors, and spent the winter with Katherine and his three sons. He again visited Richard Hakluyt in Bristol, continuing their discussions on the exploration of the New World and the location of the sea passageway to China. The two explorers talked extensively about the Novaya Zemlya Archipelago north of Russia. The archipelago marks the easternmost part of Europe, comprising two large islands and several smaller ones. Novaya Zemlya separates the Barents Sea from the Kara Sea, located to the east. Hakluyt had recently acquired journals and charts that suggested an ice-free sea existed to the east of the islands, which could be the North-east Passage to the Orient. After talking with Hakluyt, Hudson became interested in leading an expeditionary force to explore and map the islands, searching for the route to the Kara Sea and the Orient.

Hudson returned to London and made arrangements to meet with the Muscovy Company's board of directors. The captain presented his plans to sail to the east, suggesting he had secret information about a North-east Passage to the Orient. After the investors met privately to discuss Hudson's proposal, they pledged to finance the expedition, but only if he sailed with the *Hopewell* and accepted the same fee as paid for the 1607 voyage. The captain approved the offer, but with stipulations that the size of the crew was enlarged, the ship's planks were reinforced to better withstand the battering of the Arctic icebergs and a shallop boat replaced the vessel's current smaller rowboat. The directors hesitated at the extra cost, but finally agreed to his terms.

In mid-March 1608, the captain began purchasing provisions and supplies for his latest journey. Extra quantities of salted meats were bought, along with dried grains and vegetables. He recruited a crew of fifteen mariners, again including his son, John, while convincing the Muscovy Company to provide muskets for each man for protection against attacks by marauders. At the request of the board of directors, Robert Juet was hired as first mate. Juet was an experienced master pilot and navigator, but had a reputation for quarrelsome insubordination, and quickly clashed with the captain. On the morning of 22 April, a religious service was held on the deck of the *Hopewell*, an Anglican priest asking God's blessings on the crew and expedition. In the afternoon, the vessel put to sea from Katherine's Docks in London, following the Thames down to the English Channel and then up the North Sea, fighting fog and contrary winds into the Atlantic Ocean, then setting a course to the north-east.

The *Hopewell* sailed with favourable winds and weather off the coast of Norway, but as the seamen voyaged further to the north-east and approached the Lofoten Islands, dense fog and falling temperatures set in. On 7 June, snow fell and continued for several days, and the vessel was struck by a fierce storm. As the crew piloted north-east, the weather remained cold, with freezing fog covering the ship and strong Arctic seas battering the reinforced planks. Several of the sailors became ill and were forced to stay below deck in their hammocks. During the voyage, Hudson recorded in his logbook that two of his mariners claimed to have seen a mermaid swimming close to the *Hopewell*. The crewmen reported she had the features of a woman from the navel upward, with a fishtail body below the waist. The creature had long black hair down her back and her skin was very white. No more mermaid sightings were reported, but numerous whales and porpoises were seen by the men. The existence of mermaids was widely accepted in the early seventeenth century by people who believed that for every existing creature on land, a corresponding one lived in the oceans. Several days later, the weather finally improved, turning clear and warm with the Arctic rains ending.

When Hudson began preparing the shallop to explore the shoreline of northern Norway, he ordered Juet to supervise the work. Juet objected, claiming the task was not the duty of the first mate. When the captain threatened to replace him, Juet reluctantly obeyed the command, adding to the growing dissention between the ship's two officers. In mid-June, the *Hopewell* steered past the North Cape off Norway into the Barents Sea. As the bark ploughed on, Hudson encountered floes of ice and had to slowly make his way to the north-east in dropping temperatures. He was unable to break through an icepack and forced to change his course to the south-east. As the Englishmen continued to navigate toward Novaya Zemlya, they spotted great flocks of seabirds and large numbers of seals, while hearing sounds of polar bears thundering on the ice. Forward progress was slowed by contrary winds and ice packs, but finally, after over two months of slow progress in the Arctic Ocean, on 27 June the lookout sighted the Novaya Zemlya Archipelago, which formed an ice-covered barrier extending from the mainland of Russia to the frozen north-east.

As Captain Hudson mapped the coastline of the island group, he attempted to sail north, but the thick ice was impenetrable, forcing him to order the mariners to turn due south. When he located calmer waters, the vessel was anchored in a shallow cove off Novaya Zemlya and the search for a channel through the landmass was begun. Robert Juet and five seamen were sent ashore to explore the island and refill two water casks. They returned a few hours later, without locating a passageway but bringing back several whales' fins and deer horns and reporting identifying other animal tracks. The next day, a larger landing party was rowed to the beach, but returned after finding little of interest.

While the ship remained at anchor, Hudson and his crew spotted many walruses resting on the beach and rocks. Hoping to take back a cargo of walrus ivory tusks to the investors to defray some of the voyage's cost, on 30 June the captain ordered his sailors ashore with their muskets to hunt the sea animals. Lacking any experience as hunters, the men began running wildly and shouting toward the large herd after reaching the shore. As they approached, the walruses quickly slipped back into the water, escaping from the inexperienced Englishmen. When the seamen returned to the *Hopewell*, they brought back only one walrus tusk. Hudson was visibly displeased at the failure to bring back large amounts of ivory, venting his wrath on the crewmen.

After staying in the bay for two days, Hudson continued sailing south until 1 July, when he spotted a large inlet with an entrance to a river that could be the gateway across the island. The anchor was dropped and preparations made to send a search party ashore. Before the landing party departed for the beach, the *Hopewell* was driven out to sea when the anchor failed to hold the ship against the strong current from the river. The vessel was pushed back toward the island by the strong waves and winds until it ran aground on a shoal, coming to a sudden stop. The men quickly inspected the bark for damage, and Juet reported to Hudson that no serious problems were found. After making his report, the first mate shouted at the captain in front of the crew, criticizing him for placing the *Hopewell* in danger by anchoring in an unsafe location. Instead of admonishing Juet for his insubordination, Hudson ignored the outburst, ordering him to take the shallop and some seamen to pull the *Hopewell* free. Juet obeyed the command, and in several hours the ship was afloat. Hudson failed to enforce his position as captain and allowed Juet to question his competence in the presence of the sailors, increasing the hostility between them and diminishing the mariners' respect for their captain.

From his studies of maps and documents, Hudson was convinced there was a channel through the island to the Kara Sea. After sending a search party to survey the river's opening, on 5 July he ordered the crew to steer the ship into the waterway, but was forced back by the strong current and contrary winds. After the failed attempt, he instructed Juet to explore up the river with five seamen to determine if the water was deep enough for the *Hopewell*. While Juet was gone, another attempt to sail up the river was made, but again it failed. When the first mate returned, he reported finding the waterway's depth became increasingly shallow and there was no passageway for the *Hopewell*. Hudson refused to give up his pursuit of the North-east Passage, navigating up and down the coast for several days but finding no channel. As he continued to map Novaya Zemlya and search for the opening to the Kara Sea, the weather became colder, with dangerous ice floes in the sea. The captain was forced to admit his failure to find the strait to the east, and on 12 July ordered the crew to prepare for the homeward journey. Before departing from the island, Hudson sent a hunting party ashore to shoot sea birds. They came back with over 100 large geese, which were salted for the voyage back to London.

As the *Hopewell* sailed west into the Barents Sea, porpoises were again sighted in the warmer waters. Navigating south-west, by mid-July the *Hopewell* reached northern Norway, rounding the North Cape and heading back toward England. On 30 July, Hudson was off the Lofoten Islands heading south. However, without notifying the crew he now turned the ship to the west to once again search for the North-west Passage to Cathay, setting a course for Labrador. At first the change in direction was unquestioned, but in early August Juet and the sailors threatened to mutiny if the vessel was not taken back to England. Confronted by the hostile crewmen, the captain agreed to return home and signed a certificate admitting his change of direction and absolving the seamen of rebellion. A new course to the south-east was set, and the *Hopewell* arrived off Gravesend on the Thames on 26 August. No charges were brought against the mariners by the captain, but over the next few months rumours of the threatening mutiny spread through southern England, weakening Hudson's respect and perceived competence as a captain. The investors of the Muscovy Company were disappointed that Hudson had not found the North-east Passage, and considered the expedition an expensive failure. When he attempted to attract the directors with another venture to search for the North-west Passage, they were not interested. While Hudson's reputation was diminished in England following his unsuccessful voyage, two rival kingdoms were anxious to discuss a new undertaking with him.

Hudson returned to his family in London, and several months later was visited by a diplomat from the Netherlands. He talked with the envoy for several hours about the short route to the Far East, emphasizing his belief in the passageway to the north-west. A few days later he received an invitation from the Dutch to travel to Amsterdam and meet with directors of the Dutch East India Company. The company had been chartered by the government of the Netherlands with exclusive rights to all trade with the Orient. Before meeting with the directors, Hudson called on the eminent Dutch cartographer, Peter Plancius, who was a close friend of Richard Hakluyt. They shared a common interest in the mapping of the unknown world and possible conduits to the Orient. Studying many charts with Plancius, they were intrigued by the search for the shortest route through Arctic waters to China. During their conversations, Plancius advised Hudson of the Dutch company's preference for the north-eastern channel. When Hudson met with the investors of the company, they asked him about reaching Cathay from the north-east through the Kara Sea. Despite his strong belief in the north-western route, Hudson talked extensively about his recent voyage to Novaya Zemlya and the possibilities of finding the eastern passageway to the East Indies, using the maps he had drawn of the region.

Soon after his presentation to the Dutch East India Company, Hudson also received overtures from the French government of King Henry IV for an Arctic expedition to the Far East. He exchanged letters with French officials, but no offer was made. After waiting several months in London, Hudson was again called to Amsterdam in January 1609 and offered a contract to lead the voyage to China by the North-east Passage. He accepted the proposal and began preparing his ship, the three-masted, square-rigged, 60-ton *Half Moon*, for the journey back to the polar waters of Novaya Zemlya. The captain was unimpressed when he first saw his new vessel, writing to a friend, 'I fear that she will prove difficult to handle in rough weather.' Hudson was not happy with the size and draft of the *Half Moon*, petitioning the Dutch East India Company for a different ship. A few days later, he received a brief reply informing him that no other vessel was available, and if he did not want to command the expedition then another captain could be found. He compelled to accept the *Half Moon* and he began recruiting his crew of fifteen English and Dutch seamen, again hiring Robert Juet as his first mate, despite his recent insubordination and protests.

While the captain purchased provisions and supplies from Amsterdam merchants for the voyage, he was forced to intervene several times to resolve disputes between the English and Dutch sailors of his crew. They did not speak the same language and made little effort to develop friendships. Each group kept to itself and disliked the other, creating a hostile environment. The English crewmen objected to the Dutch cook and the diet of pickled fish, preferring salted beef and pork. Hudson was able to intercede, ordering supplies of pickled beef, to the dissatisfaction of the Dutch East India Company, which objected to the added cost. As Hudson prepared to weigh anchor, he was summoned to the offices of his Dutch backers. From their many spies, the directors had heard rumors that he planned to change course during the journey and sail to North America, looking instead for the North-west Passage. The captain had earlier told Juet and his second mate, John Colman, of his plans to navigate west, but denied the investors' accusation. When he was recalled to the company's headquarters two days later, Hudson was forced to place his right hand on a Bible and swear an oath to search for the North-east Passage.

On 6 April 1609, the brightly painted *Half Moon* put to sea from Amsterdam, with the letters GWC on the horizontal red, white and blue flag of the Dutch East India Company flying in the breeze. The mariners set a course to the north-east, sailing from the Dutch coast into the North Sea. As the ship travelled further north, the weather became colder with periods of freezing rain, and the Dutch sailors, accustomed to the tropical climate of the East Indies, avoided working on the deck and rigging, leaving the bulk of the tasks to the Englishmen, further inflaming the animosity between the two groups. Hudson's continued failure to intercede and compel the Dutch to man their stations weakened his respect among the officers and crew, jeopardizing his control of the vessel. By early May, he was off Norway's North Cape, making his way east. The Dutch ship reached the northern shoreline of Russia, where the crew encountered dense fog, freezing temperatures and large ice floes. As the vessel steered north-east, the seamen struggled against large ice fields, and when they approached Novaya Zemlya their passageway was blocked. Unable to navigate any further to the east, the sailors threatened to mutiny if the captain did not take the *Half Moon* out of the Arctic seas. Hudson now believed he had complied with the terms of his contract to look for the North-east Passage, offering his crewmen the option of returning to Amsterdam without finding any new passageway to the wealth of China, or piloting west to search for the north-western route. The men chose the second alternative, with its possibilities of gaining riches, while avoiding potential charges of mutiny from their captain.

In stormy cold weather, with strong contrary winds, the *Half Moon* reversed its direction, piloting back to North Cape. Despite repeated gales, the men sailed into the North Atlantic, making for the Faroe Islands, as the ship rolled and pitched in the turbulent waters. On 30 May, Hudson anchored his vessel at one of the Faroe Islands and was rowed ashore to acquire fresh vegetables and meat, while filling the water casks. They departed several days later, setting a course to the west. During the transatlantic crossing, the *Half Moon* was struck by frequent squalls followed by periods of clear blue skies and calm waters. A fierce storm battered the ship on 21 June, ripping the foresail and damaging the rigging. Hudson continued west with the mainsail, as the seamen hurriedly repaired the damage.

When Hudson reached the Grand Banks off Newfoundland, he decided to explore the North American coastline to the south, searching for the large river Captain John Smith had told him about as a possible passageway to Cathay. On 12 July, the crew passed by southern Nova Scotia, heading for present-day Penobscot Bay in central Maine. In mid-July, the vessel anchored in the inlet and the sailors had their first encounter with American Indians, who paddled out in their canoes to trade. Six natives were welcomed aboard the *Half Moon* and given small gifts to gain their friendship. The Native Americans were also provided with food and drink, while they talked using sign language about the presence of gold and silver mines close by. While the English and Dutch mariners remained on the bay, repairs were made to the ship, while some of the men were sent to fish for cod and Hudson taking a search party inland to explore. During the stay at Penobscot Bay, Juet and some of the crewmen began to keep watch on the Indians, fearing a surprise attack. When a sailor discovered the natives preparing an ambush, Juet and eleven seamen went ashore in the early morning of 25 July, raiding the Indians' village and brutalizing the natives.

Following the attack against the settlement, Hudson navigated south-west and reached Cape Cod on 3 August. He anchored in a cove, sending men ashore to search the interior. As the English and Dutch sailors reconnoitred the area, they encountered more Indian villages, taking note of their freshly cultivated fields of crops. The *Half Moon* was soon back at sea, steering down the shoreline, and on 18 August arrived at the English settlement at Jamestown. Sailing on a ship flying the Dutch flag, the captain feared a confrontation with the English settlers, ordering his mariners to continue south and reaching current-day Cape Hatteras six days later.

After reaching the cape without finding the river passage to the Orient, Hudson ordered his crew to return to the north, navigating past the coastline of modern-day Virginia and Maryland and anchoring in Delaware Bay in early September, becoming the first Europeans to explore the area. The large bay looked promising as John Smith's route to Asia, but after steering upriver the water became too shallow and Hudson directed his sailors to continue up the North American shoreline to resume the hunt for the channel to the East Indies. Several days later, off present-day Sandy Hook, New Jersey, he located a great outflow of water from the interior. He continued into the large harbour, passing the lower end of Manhattan Island and finding the opening to the river that now bears his name. He believed this must surely be the way to China, so long-sought. Hudson and some of his seamen went ashore on 4 September to explore, noting the size of the magnificent harbour and beautiful tree-covered hills. As the mariners searched the beach area, they were approached by a native group of men, women and children eager to trade tobacco and furs for beads and knives. Through sign language, the chief told Hudson that the river extended far inland, which increased his enthusiasm to travel up the waterway.

On 6 September, Captain Hudson sent second mate John Colman and several seamen in the gig boat to search further inland. They landed on Manhattan Island, reconnoitring for several hours, but as the sailors returned to the boat they were suddenly attacked by a band of warriors firing arrows from their canoes. During the clash, Colman was killed and two men wounded. The survivors made their way back to the *Half Moon* with Colman's body in the morning. On the morning of 9 September, with the *Half Moon* remaining anchored, it was attacked by two large canoes containing about forty armed warriors, shooting waves of arrows. At the approach of the hostile Indians, Hudson fired a warning shot from his pistol. One of the canoes retreated, and when he threatened the remaining natives with another pistol shot, they too fled in haste. While the English captain drew charts of the coastline, the ship's crew spent the following three days armed and ready to repel an assault. As they remained at anchor, several bands of Indians came to the vessel to trade, the crewmen cautiously bartering beads and trinkets for tobacco, corn and oysters, while Hudson finished drawing his maps of the large harbour.

In mid-September, Hudson began the journey up the river into the interior of the North American continent, stopping at night on the shore, with his crewmen on guard against attack. While the ship steered upstream, Hudson made note of the spectacular surrounding valley, with its abundance of wild animals, fish, trees and beautiful flowering plants, while continuing to chart the river's course. He was greatly impressed by the fertility of the soil, writing, 'Were our own industrious farmers to settle here, they would soon transfer this wilderness into a Paradise where no man need ever go hungry.' All along the waterway, peaceful natives in canoes paddled out to the vessel, eager to trade for European goods. Moving steadily to the north, the mariners explored the shoreline while taking depth readings of the Hudson River. During the voyage, the sailors continued to trade with the Indians but remained wary of an attack. On 22 September, the captain sent the gig upstream to check the depth of the waterway, and was greatly disappointed when the men reported that a few miles ahead it turned too shallow and narrow for the *Half Moon* to navigate. Hudson had travelled over 150 miles, reaching present-day Albany, before he was forced to turn back on 23 September.

As Hudson sailed back down the Hudson River toward the Atlantic, the *Half Moon* was driven aground several times by strong winds and refloated from the mud flats by high tides. Indians continued to paddle out to the ship to barter food and furs, while the crew remained on guard against belligerent natives. When an Indian quietly slipped aboard the vessel on 1 October, attempting to steal clothing and weapons, he was spotted by Juet and killed trying to escape. Several days later, two war canoes carrying bellicose warriors approached the ship, firing their bows and arrows and throwing spears. The European sailors fired their muskets, killing several of the hostiles. The remaining Native Americans dashed to the shore at Jeffrey's Hook, where they were joined by over 100 allies, shooting flights of arrows at the ship, hitting the timbers and sails. Hudson directed the mariners to fire the *Half Moon's* four cannons at the warriors, while other crewmen continued to shoot their muskets. The Indians made another attempt to storm the *Half Moon*, but were driven off when Juet fired a small cannon at them. The cannonball slammed into the canoe, tearing a large hole in it and killing two men. As the Indians retreated into the woodland, the captain ordered the anchor raised and the vessel resumed its voyage down the Hudson River into the magnificent harbour without further attacks. When the ship was off Hoboken in early October, Hudson was forced to drop anchor and wait for a dense fog to break up. Fearful of a surprise assault, Hudson posted armed guards on the *Half Moon* and sent patrols to reconnoitre the area.

After remaining in the harbour for a few days, Captain Hudson ordered the crewmen to raise the *Half Moon's* anchor and put to sea, departing the North American shores and ending the hunt for the North-west Passage. While the expedition had failed to find the passageway to the Far East, Hudson refused to abandon his quest, assembling the mariners and offering them two options to renew their pursuit for riches and renown. They could steer to Ireland to spend the winter, resuming the voyage in the spring of 1610, or wait close by on Newfoundland at a deserted fishing station. Fearing possible charges of mutiny from their earlier uprising, the men agreed to winter in Ireland. Despite his attempt to continue the search for China, during the transatlantic crossing many of the seamen changed their minds, threatening to mutiny again if Hudson did not return home. Without the support of the majority of the crew, he agreed to sail to Europe, anchoring on 7 November at Dartmouth in Devon.

Soon after reaching port, Hudson was directed by King James I's council to remain in England pending an inquiry for possible charges of treason for sailing for a foreign government. While staying in London, Hudson wrote to the Dutch East India Company detailing his voyage and asking for funds to outfit a new expedition to North America in the spring. The Dutch Company ordered him to Amsterdam with their ship, but he obeyed the royal order to stay in London. Hudson spent the next few months with Katherine and his sons at his London house, the king's spies watching his every move.

While he remained under house arrest, three wealthy and influential English investors became interested in the quest for the North-west Passage and had faith in Hudson's skills as a seaman and navigator. They met with Hudson at his London house, asking if he wanted to lead an expedition to find the short sea route to Asia. He was overwhelmed with joy at the unexpected offer, immediately agreeing to command the English venture. Through the influence of one of the patrons, a meeting was arranged with the heir to the English throne, Prince Henry, an avid enthusiast of geography and exploration. Several days after their discussions, the charges against the captain were dropped and a contract for the American voyage signed with the newly chartered Company of Gentlemen.

As Henry Hudson began preparations to sail to the North American continent, the investors from the Company of Gentlemen purchased the 55-ton *Discovery* for the expedition. The captain was pleased with the vessel, which had a specially reinforced hull for protection against Arctic ice and handled well in rough seas. He recruited a crew of twenty-three sailors, again including his son, John, as cabin boy. Juet was originally hired as second mate, but assumed his former duties after Hudson dismissed the investors' chosen first mate. A new crewman was Henry Greene, who was a personal friend of the captain and joined the venture as chronicler. In late March 1610, supplies and provisions were loaded in the ship's holds, and on 17 April Hudson was ready to put to sea. In the morning, a church service was held to ask God's blessings on the crew and voyage, and following a visit by Prince Henry and an investor, the *Discovery* steered out of St Katherine's Docks, navigating down the Thames. The captain turned the vessel to the north into the North Sea, passing the Orkney Islands on 2 May. He piloted to the north-west, anchoring in an inlet on the coast of Iceland several days later to wait for dense fog to clear. Staying in the cove, Hudson's men went ashore to hunt birds, while others fished for cod to replenish the food stocks. By early June, the weather had improved, and as the sailors departed from Iceland they witnessed an eruption of the 3-mile-long and 5,000 feet tall Mount Hekla Volcano, throwing hot lava and ash into the air. The *Discovery* renewed its journey to the west, arriving at the southern tip of Greenland on 9 June.

Hudson piloted the *Discovery* toward the North American coast, keeping clear of icebergs, while contending with periods of dense fog. The ship crossed the southern end of the Davis Strait and on 25 June the lookout in the rigging sighted Resolution Island. The captain swung south, entering the present-day Hudson Strait, struggling against strong currents, powerful tides and drifting ice floes, as the vessel moved along the rock-strewn shoreline of Baffin Island. Despite Hudson's efforts to steer west, the ferocious currents drove the *Discovery* into Ungava Bay, threatening to crash it onto the rocky coastline. For several days the captain fought against the powerful flow of water and drifting ice, finally breaking free and sailing into Hudson Bay.

While trapped in the bay, numerous crewmen began talking about seizing control of the ship and returning home. The mariners argued back and forth before deciding against mutiny. For his part in the mutiny talks, Juet was called to the captain's cabin on 10 September and demoted to common seaman, generating greater hostility between the two men.

As the crew struggled to navigate down the coastline searching for the North-west Passage, the ship was repeatedly struck by powerful Arctic winds, sending it on an erratic course and forcing Hudson to anchor for several days to await better weather. Once the skies cleared, the vessel continued down the shore, entering James Bay at the southern end of Hudson Bay. When the captain reached the bottom of the bay, the sea became shallower and the *Discovery* was grounded on rocks, remaining for twelve hours before it was freed by rising waters and stronger winds. As the captain spent weeks looking for the way out of the bay, discontent with the crewmen soared and their confidence in him sank to new lows. By now it was mid-November and Hudson decided to spend the winter at the south-western corner of James Bay, despite the pleas of the seamen to sail back the way they came. He beached the vessel, securing it to the rocky shore, and began preparations to remain in the frozen sub-Arctic location during the winter.

Hudson had departed from England with provisions for eight months, and estimated that six months of food still remained. To supplement the food stocks, the men were sent to fish and hunt. The waters in James Bay froze early and the vessel was soon trapped for the long Canadian winter. Tensions between captain and crew quickly flared again over the construction of a cabin on the shore, as Hudson continued to lose control of the sailors. The ship's carpenter, Philip Staffe, refused to work on the building, claiming it was too late in the year and the weather too icy and cold. Hudson was furious, cursing and striking Staffe, while threatening to hang him for insubordination. Staffe relented and built the cabin, but the crewmen supported him, adding to the growing discontent.

As the harsh winter months slowly passed, the seamen continued to hunt for ducks and geese, and fish through holes cut in the ice. By early spring, the flocks of birds had disappeared and the fish caught became less, while food supplies began to dwindle. The men were forced to eat frogs and boiled moss, and without a proper diet some of them became sick with scurvy. The ship's surgeon devised a concoction made from spruce buds which helped relieve the illness.

When the ice in the bay began to slowly melt, Hudson took the shallop with a few loyal men, sailing south to search for Indian villages to trade for food, while the remaining seamen began preparing the vessel to sail. He returned a week later without finding any natives, with provisions now diminished to dangerous levels. In the hope of replenishing the stocks of supplies, the captain sent the shallop with several sailors to fish, but they came back with only a small catch. As the *Discovery* was made ready to leave, Hudson replaced his first mate with John King, who could not read and had no experience as a navigator, while confiscating all course-plotting instruments. The men grew increasingly suspicious, fearing he planned to renew the search for the North-west Passage and not return to England.

After more than seven months at James Bay, on 12 June 1611 the *Discovery* set sail to the north through frigid polar waters. Before departing, the captain divided the remaining biscuits and cheese between the sailors. Most of the seamen soon ate their supply of rations, becoming increasingly hungry over the next few days. A rumour spread among the crew that Hudson had a secret supply of provisions and was sharing it with his few favorites. As the ship steered north out of James Bay, hostilities between the captain and crewmen escalated further when he ordered their personal belongings searched for food. By now the food stocks were nearly exhausted, and the mariners grew desperate. Talk of mutiny began to circulate on 21 June, led by Henry Greene and Robert Juet. In the morning, three seamen siezed Hudson in his cabin, dragging him bound to the deck. He was pushed into the shallop along with his son and seven of his loyal supporters. When the boat was cast adrift, the captain shouted at his crew, 'It is that villain Juet that has undone us.' As the shallop attempted to follow the *Discovery*, the Englishmen unfurled full sails, navigating north heading for England and soon losing sight of Henry Hudson, his son and seven mariners, who were never seen again. The vessel departed for England with thirteen crewmen, but when it reached port only seven had survived the voyage. Five men were killed in clashes with Indians, while Juet died of unknown causes during the transatlantic crossing.

SELECTED SOURCES:
Butts, Edward, *Henry Hudson – New World Voyager.*
Dalton, Anthony, *Henry Hudson – Doomed Navigator and Explorer.*
Hunter, Douglas, *Half Moon.*
Sherman, Josepha, *Henry Hudson – English Explorer of the Northwest Passage.*

Robert Cavelier de La Salle

In the early winter of 1682, Robert Cavelier de La Salle set out with twenty-seven Frenchmen and twenty-five Indians from the Great Lakes tribes to explore the Mississippi River. After making their way down Lake Michigan and the Illinois River by sleds over frozen land, the explorers reached the Mississippi River in early February. As the ice in the waterway melted, the trailbreakers lowered their canoes into the river, paddling downstream with the strong current. La Salle and his men navigated past the Missouri and Arkansas rivers, and in early April reached the Gulf of Mexico, becoming the first Europeans to travel nearly the entire length of the Mississippi. On 9 April 1682, La Salle erected a large wooden cross and claimed the river and the lands drained by its tributaries for Louis XIV of France. The newly appropriated country stretched from the current-day states of Montana to the north and northwest, Louisiana in the south and all the terrain west of the Appalachian Mountains. La Salle called the new territory Louisiana in honour of his king.

Robert Cavelier de La Salle was born in the French seaport city of Rouen in mid-November 1643, the second son of Jean Cavelier and Catherine Geest La Salle. His father was a highly successful cloth merchant and owned a large estate called La Salle. At a young age, La Salle was sent by his family to a Jesuit school, adapting well to the strict discipline and demanding teachings of the clergymen. In 1660, aged 17, he took his first vows toward becoming a Jesuit, entering a Society of Jesus college. Under the tutelage of the Jesuits the novice studied mathematics, literature, ancient and modern languages, geography, astronomy, cartography and theology. La Salle excelled at his studies, and was later sent to Paris to continue his education. Under the teachings of the priests, the novice was attracted to missionary work in China or the Americas, requesting an overseas appointment. His Jesuit superiors considered La Salle undisciplined with an independent spirit, refusing to grant his application. When his second petition was denied by the father-superior, La Salle chose to leave the Jesuit Order. Deprived of the adventure of a missionary's calling to a distant land, he decided to join his older brother, who was a priest in the Society of Saint Sulpice, in New France. From his readings of geography and talks with sea captains and seamen at Rouen, La Salle had developed an interest in searching for the North-west Passage to the great riches of China, and was now determined to explore the lands in Canada with the assistance of his brother, Jean.

In the spring of 1667, La Salle set out for Montreal to join Jean. After making the voyage across the North Atlantic in a small wooden ship, he reached Newfoundland and his first sight of the lands of New France. The French seamen steered the vessel down the eastern coast of the island into the Gulf of St Lawrence, as the lookout searched for dangerous icebergs and shoals. As the ship sailed closer to the shoreline, La Salle saw his first American Indians, while marvelling at the whales, porpoises and dolphins swimming near the vessel. The sailors navigated into the St Lawrence River, travelling up the northern bank and avoiding small, nearly hidden islands. As the French carefully made their way upriver, La Salle finally arrived at Quebec, the capital of Canada. The French-influenced designs of the church, stores and houses brought back images of their homeland to the passengers.

When the vessel dropped anchor, La Salle walked down the gangplank into the town, renting a room in a tavern, but soon left to make arrangements for his passage to Montreal. The St Lawrence River was full of riverboats travelling to and from Montreal with various cargoes, and the new immigrant quickly found a crew willing to take him upriver. The boat moved against the current, pushing slowly to the west, and he was soon with Jean at the Sulpician Seminary. He re-established contact with his brother, staying with him at the rectory. The region around Montreal was thinly populated by the French, and the Society of Saint Sulpice had a policy of ceding land to encourage new settlers. Through the influence of his brother, La Salle was given a grant of several thousand acres west of the town, with the stipulation that he settle immigrants on the land and cultivate crops.

After taking charge of his property, La Salle set aside 400 acres for his personal use and began offering the remainder for sale. He was successful in attracting new settlers, and within a year had turned his holdings into one of the most populated districts of Montreal. In the spring of 1668, La Salle began clearing his land for planting, removing large trees and rocks with the help of hired labourers, while building a small house fortified with log palisades. From his compound he hunted the abundant wildlife in the forest and fished the streams, salting the food for the coming long harsh winter months. As La Salle continued to explore the countryside, he met Indians from several tribes, studying their languages and customs. Leaving his men to work his property, he began exploring the area further away from Montreal, and was taught by the trappers and natives to survive in the wilderness, navigate through the dense woods, identify animals by their tracks and live in the bitter weather of frigid winter. During his first winter in Canada, La Salle was occupied roaming the woodlands, learning to travel on snowshoes, trap animals and fish through holes in the ice, while his endurance and strength steadily increased.

While making a steady income from his properties, La Salle still retained his interest in searching for the North-west Passage, and to accumulate enough money to finance an expedition he decided to organize a fur trading company. Beaver fur hats and coats were in great demand in Paris by the nobility, and with access to the St Lawrence and Ottawa rivers and Great Lakes, colonists in New France had ready supplies of animal pelts by bartering with the Indians. La Salle began travelling up the Ottawa in his canoe, trading firearms and alcohol to the natives and quickly earning a large profit. As the French trader paddled the rivers and lakes, he talked with the Indians about the area's geography, hearing numerous stories about a river to the south called Ohio, which followed a course to a great sea.

La Salle became convinced that the river was the waterway the Algonquins called the Mississippi, and was the route to the wealth of China and Japan. He sold his lands to acquire additional money for the expedition, and in the spring of 1669 set out for Quebec to petition the government for permission to search for the river. He met with governor Daniel de Remy de Courcelle and intendant Jean Talon, discussing his venture to the west. The two government officials were enthusiastic about the project, granting him letters patent to explore the lakes and rivers of North America. At the insistence of the governor, he was compelled to unite his expeditionary force with a group of Saint Sulpice missionaries led by Dollier de Casson, who had been authorized to minister to the Indians around Lake Ontario.

In early July 1669, the expeditionary force gathered in Montreal for final preparations to be completed. On 6 July, seven canoes with twenty-one Frenchmen and several Indian guides set out for the journey up the St Lawrence River, slowly making their way against the current, while forced to repeatedly carry their boats overland around cataracts, rapids and waterfalls. When the men stopped for the night, they camped on the damp beach cooking a meal of ground cornmeal mixed with fish or game, sleeping under an overturned canoe for protection from the abundant mosquitoes. They paddled day after day through the wilderness, finally reaching Lake Ontario on 3 August. La Salle and Father Casson then navigated south down the tranquil freshwater lake. By mid-August, the explorers had arrived at the mouth of the Seneca River, near present-day Rochester, New York, where they encountered friendly natives from the Seneca tribe of the Iroquois Nation.

While Casson and some of the men stayed at Lake Ontario with the canoes, La Salle took the remaining Frenchmen to visit the Indian village, with the Iroquois warriors leading the way. After travelling inland for several hours, they arrived at a large settlement of more than 1,000 natives. Soon after reaching the village, the explorers were invited to a feast in celebration of their arrival. Following the banquet, La Salle met with the elders and, after an exchange of gifts, questioned them about the location of the Ohio River, while asking for guides to lead the reconnaissance party. As the chiefs considered their decision, a band of Seneca warriors returned to their settlement in the morning after trading with the Dutch in current-day upper New York State. During their bartering for Dutch goods, the Indians traded their fur pelts for muskets and a cask of brandy. The explorers' prior experiences with the Native Americans had been cordial and peaceful, but under the influence of alcohol the Indians became violent and threatening, howling and waving their tomahawks. Several days of drunkenness followed as La Salle and his comrades found shelter and stayed out of the way. When calm finally returned, La Salle talked with the chiefs again, but they informed him his presence in the Ohio country would be dangerous and refused to provide guides. After spending several days with the Senecas, the French returned to the lake, rejoining Casson and his men.

The next day, the French explorers and missionaries set out along the south shore of Lake Ontario, reaching Niagara Falls. La Salle wanted to reconnoitre the area around the falls, but due to the lateness of the year was forced to move on. As his men canoed along the lake, they located another village, and following the usual exchanges of presents and discussions with the elders, the Indians agreed to provide two guides. One of the natives was a Shawnee named Nika, with whom La Salle soon formed a friendship. They travelled in the same canoe and walked together, while La Salle continued to learn the Indian languages with Nika as his tutor. The explorers and priests trudged on, frequently spending the night in the safety of Indian villages, with Nika making the arrangements. At one of their encampments the Frenchmen met Adrian Jolliet, the missing brother of fur trader Louis Jolliet. Adrian told the Saint Sulpice priests that the region around the southern shore of Lake Ontario was populated with many tribes, who had never been visited by missionaries. The two Sulpicians were enthusiastic about establishing their mission among the local Indians, deciding to abandon the expedition to the

Ohio River. La Salle and the strong-willed Casson were frequently at odds with each other, and after hearing Mass in the morning he was happy to leave the priests.

Due to the lateness of the autumn season, La Salle decided to spend the winter with the Great Lakes Indians. Following the advice of Nika, he moved his men several miles inland to establish his fortified camp for the winter. The French began preparing for the harsh weather, hunting, fishing, cutting firewood and preserving foods, while making friends with the neighbouring tribes. During the bitter cold weather, the trailblazers trapped wild game and traded with the Indians for cornmeal and other foods. The winter of 1670 was unusually mild, and in the spring the explorers were anxious to resume their search for the Ohio River. As the ice on Lake Ontario melted, La Salle and his Frenchmen prepared to renew the journey south. They paddled to the tip of Lake Ontario, where they were forced to transport their canoes, equipment and supplies over the portage to Lake Erie, which they navigated down to the point where the guides told them to move inland into current-day upper New York. The men with their Indian escorts paddled ashore and began hauling their canoes and supplies overland until reaching a small branch of the Ohio River. The tributary was clogged with masses of tree trunks, roots, rocks and debris, forcing the explorers to carry their equipment downstream day after day, with the water sometimes up to their shoulders. As the men trudged onward, the obstacles in the waterway began to clear and they could now use their canoes. With the current pushing them forward, the Frenchmen paddled through the dark murky waters for several days as they travelled south-west across the unmapped wilderness of western Pennsylvania, finally joining a large river that La Salle knew by its size was the Ohio, becoming the first Europeans to explore it. He followed the river downstream and westward across the present-day state of Ohio, reaching modern-day Louisville, Kentucky, in late August.

As La Salle prepared to renew the journey to the Mississippi River, during a late August night his men refused to go any further, deserting him and returning north before the onset of the winter snows. When the French left the camp, Nika remained with his friend and together they attempted to navigate downriver to the Mississippi. La Salle and the Shawnee guide quickly realized they were unable to push on alone, and were forced to travel back to Canada. With Nika leading the way, La Salle canoed back up the Ohio, making his way to Lake Erie as the snows began to fall. Despite the harsh weather, he continued north, and through the help of his Shawnee friend his encounters with the Indian tribes were peaceful, with many providing food and shelter. La Salle and Nika hunted, fished and trapped for additional provisions, and finally, in the dead of winter, they reached Montreal, emaciated and exhausted from their ordeal.

The failed journey to the Ohio River in search of the North-west Passage had ruined La Salle financially, and he needed to raise money to finance another expedition. After resting and recovering from his arduous trek, he went back to the highly profitable business of trading European goods to the Indians for fur pelts. The difficult trek down the Ohio had convinced him of the need to locate a shorter and less gruelling route to the Mississippi River, and after rebuilding his finances he set out for Quebec to meet with Talon. He discussed his latest venture and the new expedition with the intendent, who was always eager to expand France's presence to the west, quickly giving the crown's approval to the proposed project.

In August 1671, La Salle, his Shawnee guide and six men journeyed from Montreal up the St Lawrence River into Lake Ontario. The trailbreakers canoed across the lake to the Niagara portage, trekking overland to Lake Erie. The travellers crossed the lake, and at its western tip moved north through the St Clair River to Lake Huron. The French paddled their canoes up the western shoreline into Lake Michigan, exploring the waterway for possible routes to the Mississippi River. As La Salle navigated the two Great Lakes, he found it easier to travel on the deep, broad watercourses without the obstructions and delays encountered on rivers. He recorded in his journal that the network of lakes should be extensively utilized for future expansion and colonization of western Canada. He continued to reconnoitre the lake, but as temperatures dropped decided to return to Montreal with plans to resume his exploration of the Mississippi River by reaching it through the Great Lakes.

Soon after reaching Montreal, La Salle made arrangements through his friends in Quebec to meet the new governor-general, Louis de Buade, Comte de Frontenac. During the winter of 1673, La Salle held many meetings with Frontenac, becoming close friends with him and discussing his plans to expand France's overseas empire. The adventurer told the king's governor-general that he was convinced from his explorations that the Mississippi River flowed to the Gulf of Mexico, and if the French crown ruled the territory adjacent to the grand waterway, the regime could keep England isolated along the Atlantic coast and the Spanish to the south. They realized that to control such a vast area it was necessary to construct a network of strategic fortifications along the river's tributaries. Looking at a large map of the region, Frontenac proposed building a stockade at the eastern end of Lake Ontario, which would serve as a military base and commercial centre for trading with the Indians. A fort built at this location would be on the major trading route of the Native Americans, making it easier for them to barter their furs to the French rather than the English or Dutch merchants.

Frontenac quickly approved the plan and began issuing orders for its implementation. The governor-general planned a grand tour of the region to inspect it for himself, sending La Salle ahead to inform the Indians at Lake Ontario of his coming. By mid-June 1673, Frontenac had organized an inspection party of over 400 Frenchmen, setting out for Lake Ontario in 120 canoes. As the flotilla struggled up the St Lawrence River, battling summer rains and swarms of mosquitoes, Frontenac continually rallied the men's spirits and encouraged them to steadily push on. He planned a grand entrance onto the lake where the Indians from the Iroquois tribe were gathered to meet him. As the French entered the lake from the river, the governor-general put on a ceremony of court-like pomp to impress the Native Americans, arriving on a flatboat surrounded by his armed soldiers dressed in uniforms of blue and white, with the band playing and flags flying. When the French troops landed on the shore, great white tents were pitched and the king's flag of a gold fleur-de-lys on a white background was raised on a hastily erected pole. In the morning, the governor-general met with the elders, sitting before a council fire. Speaking through an interpreter as La Salle watched, he displayed an aura of authority and dignity, telling the gathered chiefs that they came in peace and goodwill, while stopping periodically to distribute gifts. At the conclusion of the meeting, Frontenac was convinced that the Indians considered the French friends and would not oppose the construction of the outpost.

Following the meeting with the Indians, the French began constructing the fort on 12 July, first clearing the land and sawing logs into planks, as other men dug trenches around the outside of the stockade. The fortress quickly took shape according to pre-arranged plans, and was completed in a week. As the fortification was being built, Frontenac continued to meet with the native elders, solidifying their loyalty to the French crown, while sending orders to Montreal to transport a year's supply of trading goods and food for the garrison. When the outpost neared completion, the governor-general assembled all the chiefs, telling them of the commercial and military advantages of an alliance with the Frenchmen, and after holding council meetings they agreed to a peace treaty. In late July, Frontenac and La Salle returned to Montreal.

Soon after reaching Montreal, La Salle and Frontenac formed a trading partnership, sending their agents to the fort to barter for the Iroquois' fur pelts. While La Salle was in the town, reports were received that Father Jacques Marquette and Louis Jolliet had travelled down the Mississippi River to its confluence with the Arkansas River, verifying that it flowed into the Gulf of Mexico. When Frontenac heard the news, he decided to send La Salle to Paris to ask Louis XIV to secure a royal charter for the continued exploration of the Mississippi River. La Salle left Quebec in 1674, sailing down the St Lawrence River and making the transatlantic crossing to France. He carried a letter of recommendation from Count Frontenac, and after paying several bribes to court officials he finally met with the king and his finance minister. He spoke to Louis XIV about the building of the fort to the east of Lake Ontario and the establishment of a trading alliance with the Indians. The king was pleased with La Salle's report, and on 13 May 1675 issued letters patent authorizing new expeditions on the Mississippi and its tributaries, while granting him the title of cavelier and confirming his appointment as governor for the newly constructed fort. Out of gratitude to the governor-general of New France, La Salle named the fortification Fort Frontenac.

La Salle had been forced to spend nearly a year in France before finally being granted permission to explore the region south-west of Montreal. He returned to Canada in the summer of 1675 and, after meeting with Frontenac, moved to the fort. As governor of Fort Frontenac, he enlarged and strengthened the fortification, rebuilding it as a stone structure, while constructing a mill, trading post and barracks, and clearing land for cultivation. After its completion, the fort was defended by a unit of soldiers, nine cannons and a strong rampart several hundred yards long. The cavelier maintained friendly relations with the Indians, encouraging them to trade their fur pelts with his agents. As he continued to expand his trade with the lake natives, the merchants in Montreal and Quebec began to suffer financially from the loss of their fur business from the Great Lakes. La Salle's presence also threatened the influence of the Jesuits, who had established a network of missions on the lakes. The religious order and merchants attempted to use their power to thwart La Salle's ambitions, but he countered their interventions through his strong relationship with the governor-general, as his trading post continued to grow.

The results of Father Marquette's and Jolliet's journey on the Mississippi River had given Frontenac reason to send another expeditionary force to reconnoitre the river to its end. He was enthusiastic about the opportunity to expand the French Empire in North America, sending La Salle back to Paris in 1677 to acquire a licence to search for the mouth of the Mississippi and build forts as required to protect the throne's interest. On 24 October, the cavelier embarked for France, carrying a detailed memorandum from the governor-general to the crown exhorting the advantages of claiming new territory along the route of the Mississippi. After arriving in Paris, La Salle made contact with several friends of Frontenac, and through them met the king's minister of finance, Jean-Baptiste Colbert. The adventurer presented his proposal to Colbert, promoting the expedition to expand French interests in North America. Soon after meeting the minister, La Salle was granted a licence to explore the Mississippi River, build as many forts as necessary and given a monopoly on trading buffalo hides. While royal approval for the venture had been bestowed, La Salle still had to find a way to finance it. He met with relatives and friends in Paris and Rouen, raising the estimated amount of money required. Before leaving France, La Salle was introduced to the Italian soldier and adventurer Henri de Tonty, and the two quickly became friends. Tonty agreed to travel with him when the cavelier returned to Canada, and they sailed together from the port of La Rochelle on 14 July 1678.

Prior to his return to Montreal, La Salle had decided to build a large sailing ship to transport men and cargo on the Great Lakes. Before leaving France, he hired carpenters, coopers, iron workers and pilots to help construct the vessel, also bringing naval goods that were not available in Canada. When the supplies and seamen reached Montreal, he sent them to the Niagara River on the western tip of Lake Ontario. A fortified camp was established just south of the falls, and the men began construction of a 40-ton cargo ship, which La Salle named the *Griffin* in honour of Count Frontenac. While work continued on the bark, La Salle was forced to return to Montreal in February 1679 to calm the financial concerns of his investors.

La Salle spent the winter in Montreal reassuring his creditors that they would be repaid and putting his finances on a solid footing, while Tonty supervised the building of the ship. He was forced to liquidate much of his accumulated property, but managed to relieve the worries of his investors. In the spring, La Salle returned to the construction site, bringing supplies and equipment. By August, the *Griffin* was completed and La Salle and his men sailed the vessel down the treacherous Niagara River into Lake Erie, becoming the first Europeans to pilot an ocean-going ship on the Great Lakes. With a crew of twenty-five and a cargo hold loaded with muskets, trade goods and provisions, the Frenchmen steered south-west across the lake in the twin-mast ship. When the bark reached the western end of the lake, La Salle cautiously guided the *Griffin* up the St Clair River into Lake Huron. Progress up the lake was slowed by strong contrary winds, as the clouds turned increasingly dark and ominous. While the sailors struggled on, the ship was struck by a violent storm that threatened to sink it, but suddenly the winds abated, allowing the Frenchmen to regain control of the vessel. A week later, the *Griffin* reached the Jesuit mission at St Ignace at the northern tip of Lake Huron.

The cavelier had dispatched an advance party to the Jesuit mission the previous year to trade with the Indians, expecting to find his employees with a cargo of fur pelts to help defray the cost of the expedition. However, after arriving at the mission, the Frenchmen began trapping for their personal profit, and when the traders saw La Salle they ran off to Sault Ste Marie. Before sailing from St Ignace, Tonty was sent by La Salle with twenty soldiers to capture the deserters and recover his stolen goods. After spending nearly a month at the mission, the explorers steered the ship through the Strait of Mackinac into Lake Michigan. The Frenchmen piloted down the western coast of the lake, entering Green Bay. La Salle had previously sent a second trading party ahead to the bay and managed to find their camp with their store of furs. La Salle loaded the hides on the *Griffin*, ordering the navigator to take them to St Ignace, while he and fourteen men took four canoes to explore the shoreline of Lake Michigan. He had earlier been given a peace pipe by a native chief and used it to enter Indian villages as a friend, trading for food and reconnoitring their lands. In late October, they reached the bottom of the lake and paddled north along the eastern shore.

The Frenchmen canoed up the lake, establishing their camp close to the St Joseph River. La Salle had previously arranged to meet Tonty at the river, but he was a few weeks late. While they waited, the cavelier and his men built a stockade they called Fort Miami. Land was cleared and the French constructed an earthwork fortification 40 feet long and 30 feet wide, surrounded by a log palisade. On 20 November, Tonty finally arrived with his twenty soldiers. Several days later, La Salle, Tonty and thirty explorers set out in eight canoes for the Mississippi River, leaving several men to defend the fort on Lake Michigan.

The French canoed up the St Joseph River to present-day South Bend, Indiana, where they had been told by the Indians of a portage to the Kankakee River. They carried their canoes and supplies overland for 5 miles through the wilderness before continuing their journey on the Kankakee. The travellers navigated down the waterway as it grew broader, passing through an open country of tall grasses with few trees. After travelling for a month, they finally reached the Illinois River on 1 January 1680. The explorers continued paddling south-west on the Illinois, reaching the site of modern-day Peoria, Illinois, where they discovered a settlement of the Illinois tribe. La Salle approached the shoreline cautiously and slowly raised the peace pipe over his head in a show of friendship. Speaking through an interpreter, he asked for permission for his men to spend the winter on their lands assuring the elders if allowed to stay they would help defend the village against an attack with their muskets.

When the chief gave his approval, the Frenchmen started to build a fortress named Crevecoeur several miles away. While working on the stockade, the labourers heard numerous stories from the Illinois of huge monsters, lizards and demons that lived on the Mississippi River's banks. La Salle ignored the tales, but six of his workers became so frightened they deserted the camp, while others attempted to convince him to return north. After finishing construction of Fort Crevecoeur, La Salle ordered his men to begin building another bark like the *Griffin*. Realizing the expedition lacked the skilled workers and equipment to complete the ship, he decided to return to Lake Michigan with five men and bring back the necessary sails, rigging and labourers, while Father Louis Hennepin was ordered to explore to the west, searching for possible routes to the Mississippi River. Tonty was to remain at the fort and continue construction on the vessel.

While La Salle was trudging through the wilderness toward the Niagara River, Tonty kept his men occupied working on the bark, but soon many began to desert. As Tonty remained at the fort, the Iroquois travelled west into Illinois lands in the summer, threatening to attack the tribe with over 1,000 warriors. When Tonty learned of their approach, he joined the Illinois to defend their settlement. During the following clash he was wounded and taken prisoner. Tonty spoke to the enemy chief, reminding him of his pledge of peace to the governor-general of Canada, and the Iroquois, fearing reprisals from the muskets and cannons of the king's soldiers, released Tonty with a warning to return to the French. The next day, he and his few remaining men left the Illinois village for Fort Miami.

The French cavelier and his men left Tonty at Fort Crevecoeur on 1 March 1680, travelling overland on foot through the ice-covered wilderness. They made their way up the still frozen Illinois River, pulling their canoes and supplies on sleds. After walking for more than three weeks, the French party reached Fort Miami, where La Salle learned that the *Griffin*, along with its valuable cargo of furs, had been sunk. He refused to wait at the fort for the ice to melt, and after resting for a few days set out for present-day Detroit across the Michigan Peninsula to Lake Huron. They struggled through the snow-covered woodlands, their clothing torn to shreds by the sharp thorns and brambles. As they trudged eastward across unknown territory, the French hunted for food, avoiding the hostile Indians who lived on the Michigan Peninsula. Finally, the exhausted explorers arrived at the strait between Lake Huron and Lake Erie. Two of the Frenchmen were too sick and weak to continue, and La Salle, with the last healthy man, fashioned a canoe to cross Lake Erie. They paddled across the lake, reaching the French trading outpost on the Niagara River after travelling over 600 miles.

Remaining at the outpost for a few days, the cavelier then travelled on to Fort Frontenac, arriving on 6 May after a journey of over two months. At the fortress he learned that his creditors in Montreal were selling his property to pay his debts. He then set out for Montreal, where he held negotiations with new investors. He convinced many of them that trading with the Indians to the west had a vast profit potential, and was able to raise additional funds to renew his explorations. With the money secured, La Salle returned to Fort Frontenac with fresh supplies, equipment, trade goods and a crew of labourers.

When La Salle reached the fort, he was told by the local Frenchmen that Fort Crevecoeur had been deserted by his men, who followed his trail to Fort Miami and the Niagara trading post, burning the buildings. He learned that twelve of the deserters were now travelling across Lake Ontario in three canoes with the intention of murdering him. La Salle gathered nine loyal workers and canoed to Quinte Bay at the eastern end of the lake to ambush the approaching deserters. When he suddenly appeared in front of the first two boats with loaded guns, they quickly surrendered. The traitors in the third canoe were later intercepted and two men killed during the ensuing clash. The renegades were clapped in irons and sent to prison.

On 22 August, La Salle set out to rebuild the ship at Fort Crevecoeur with a new crew of carpenters, iron workers and woodcutters. Retracing his earlier route, he reached the Illinois settlement as early winter began to set in. After the French found the ruins of the fort, they spent several days searching the area for Tonty. The cavelier returned to Fort Miami to spend the winter with his men after failing to locate his loyal lieutenant.

During La Salle's many discussions with the Count of Frontenac, they decided to expand the French Empire in North America by colonizing the Mississippi River and its tributaries. However, the Iroquois tribes in the region were a constant threat against French expansionism, and the cavelier devised a plan to unite the Great Lakes Indians against the Iroquois Nation. In May 1681, he held a grand gathering of the tribes under a council oak tree near the site of modern-day South Bend, Indiana. He distributed gifts to the chiefs and elders, telling them of the great power of the French king, who wanted his children to live in peace with each other. La Salle proposed that the different tribes accept the protection of the mighty king and band together in friendship. Together they could present a united front against future Iroquois attacks and ensure peace in their country. Chiefs and elders from the Mohicans, Miami, Shawnee and Illinois agreed to the grand federation, bringing peace for the next few years between the various Great Lakes tribes and keeping the Iroquois in their own territory. Following his meeting with the Great Lakes tribes, La Salle journeyed up Lake Michigan to the Jesuit Mission at St Ignace, hoping to find news of his friend Tonty. When the cavelier arrived at the mission, he found Tonty waiting on him.

La Salle returned to Montreal to satisfy the growing concerns of his investors and prepare for his journey of exploration down the Mississippi River to its outlet into the Gulf of Mexico. The creditors had received no return on their investments and were demanding La Salle repay some of their money. He was finally able to quell their concerns by agreeing to leave a will assigning his property and future earnings to his backers. By signing the legal document, he gave up all potential monetary gain from his expedition. He also met governor-general Frontenac in Montreal, discussing his venture down the Mississippi River to the Gulf of Mexico. He spent several months in the town, holding frequent meetings with Frontenac and purchasing supplies and equipment for the journey, also recruiting twenty-seven Frenchmen and twenty-five Native Americans for the epic trek. A missionary from the Recollets named Father Zenobe Membre also volunteered for the expeditionary force.

In the early autumn of 1681, La Salle left Montreal, making his way overland to Lake Huron with his expeditionary party of explorers and American Indians. After continuing on to Lake Michigan, they moved down the eastern shore, spending a few days at the French trading post while Tonty and several men went ahead to modern-day Chicago to ready the provisions and equipment for the portage to the Illinois River. At the fort, La Salle held another meeting with the chiefs who had earlier gathered at the oak tree conference to ensure their continued loyalty to the French crown.

On 28 December, the French cavelier and his exploration party of Frenchmen and Indians joined Tonty and began the quest for the mouth of the Mississippi. After transporting their supplies, equipment and canoes overland by sleds, they followed the ice-covered Illinois River south-west to its confluence with the Mississippi. The great river was still frozen solid, compelling La Salle to wait for the ice to melt. Within a few days he began hearing loud cracking sounds as the frozen water started to break up, multiple splits appearing in the ice over the next few days. As winter receded, the ice melted faster and the river began to clear. The flotilla of canoes was finally placed in the Illinois River in early February 1682, and the explorers floated into the rapid current of the Mississippi, heading south.

They canoed downriver, passing high cliffs to the east and vast open prairie lands to the west. After travelling about 20 miles, they encountered the silt-laden waters of the Missouri River, which crashed violently into the Mississippi. The combined force of the rivers threatened to overturn the canoes as the Frenchmen and Indians struggled to stay afloat. Pushed further south, the current became more calm and the explorers continued with little trouble. Three days later, they passed the Ohio River as it joined the Mississippi near current-day Cairo, Illinois. The river now began to change direction, going south and then swinging east and west. By late February, La Salle and his men arrived at present-day Memphis, Tennessee, where the pathfinders and Native Americans went ashore to hunt the abundant wild game. All of the hunters returned to the camp except the gunsmith, Prud'homme. La Salle refused to abandon his man, spending the following ten days looking for him before resuming the journey. As the travellers went around a bend in the river, they suddenly found Prud'homme floating alive on a tree trunk used as a raft.

The French flotilla paddled further downriver as the weather became warmer, the banks now covered with dark green vegetation. In the swamplands of the south, the French had their first encounter with alligators, which inhabited the river banks and grew to over 12ft in length. All along the route was an infinite variety of wild flowers growing on the shoreline, abundant deer, bear and buffalo inland and many kinds of fish in the river, including catfish and gar. The men of the expeditionary force learned to fear the gar, which was renowned by the local Native Americans for its razor sharp teeth and fierce attacks. At night, they had to endure the loud croaking sounds of thousands of frogs, bellowing of alligators and constant buzzing of swarms of mosquitoes. Throughout the first half of their journey, the Frenchmen, Nika and Great Lakes natives met few river Indians, who remained hidden in the wilderness. However, when the explorers passed below the Arkansas River, they confronted a belligerent band of warriors from the Arkansas tribe. As the Indians approached the French, who were crouching behind a hastily constructed fort, La Salle held up the peace pipe in his hand in a sign of friendship, and amicable relations were soon established. The trailbreakers were invited to the Arkansas village, and La

Salle and his men stayed for several days, attending a grand feast and questioning the chief and elders about the course of the river to the south and location of Spanish soldiers. The cavelier held a ceremony at the settlement, erecting a cross with the emblem of Louis XIV, officially claiming the territory for the French crown. A royal decree was drawn up and, following a musket salute, the explorers shouted, 'Long Live the King.'

The Frenchmen and Indians from the north paddled on downriver, holding more peaceful meetings with the local natives as La Salle repeatedly performed the ceremony claiming the land for Louis XIV. The Native Americans were friendly, sharing their food and lodges with the strangers. The French and their native allies were able to find food along the way, but as they canoed further south the wild game and birds disappeared, and they were forced to eat foul-tasting alligators. Soon even the alligators became more scarce, and the men grew increasingly hungry, with only a small supply of cornmeal for provisions. Continuing downriver, the explorers spotted three Indians in a canoe. As they approached the Indians, the warriors beached their canoe and ran away. When the explorers looked inside the small boat, they found some bones and meat. They quickly ate the meat before realizing it was human flesh.

By early April 1682, La Salle began to detect the presence of the gulf, as the air and river water had a smell of salt. As the Frenchmen and Great Lakes Indians paddled south, the river suddenly divided into three branches. La Salle decided to split his exploration party, sending Tonty down the middle artery and Jean Bourdon d'Autray via the left passageway, while he searched the tributary to the right. About 3 miles ahead, the blue waters of the Gulf of Mexico opened before the three groups. La Salle and his men had become the first Europeans to journey down most of the length of the Mississippi River. Before returning to the spot where the waterway separated into three channels, the explorers ventured out into the gulf, ensuring it was deep enough for ships to travel up the Mississippi. When the search party returned to the split in the river, La Salle had a tree cut down and made into a mast. A pole was erected on 9 April with a sign stating that 'Louis the Great King of France and Navarre, Reigns Here.' The notary drew up legal papers officially claiming the river, its many tributaries and people for the French throne. The vast territory was named Louisiana by La Salle in honour of the king. The decree gave France an empire that stretched from the Canadian Arctic in the north to the tropical coast of the Gulf of Mexico in the south. Before leaving the gulf, La Salle drew numerous charts of the region and took measurements to determine its exact location for map-makers in France.

The expeditionary force did not take time to reconnoitre the area around the Gulf of Mexico, and La Salle set out for New France. As the Frenchmen and their Great Lakes Indian allies passed through the territory of the Oqinipassa tribe, they were suddenly attacked by a large band of warriors with their bodies painted red and black. The explorers quickly erected a small fort and managed to fend off the charge of the Oqinipassa natives with their muskets and pistols. They resumed their trek, but during the journey upriver found little food, forcing them to trade for corn with the river Indians. Many of the French became ill due to the limited diet, including La Salle. He became seriously ill with a high fever, and was forced to stop at the fort built during the search for Prud'homme. Tonty and the men were sent on to the mission at St. Ignace, while the cavelier was cared for by Father Zenobe Membre and Nika. The priest took care of La Salle for forty days before he was strong enough to slowly make his way back upriver. By mid-July, the explorer and priest had reached the Illinois River and canoed up the waterway before travelling overland to Lake Michigan. Once on the lake, the two men completed the final phase of their expedition to the Jesuit mission.

When La Salle, Nika and Father Membre reached the mission, they were met by Henri Tonty. From his trusted lieutenant he learned that his patron and friend Count Frontenac had been relieved by Joseph-Antoine de la Barre, who planned to replace him as commander for the frontier forts and trading posts. To make matters worse, La Barre was a strong sponsor of the Quebec and Montreal merchants and supported their belief that colonization of the west served no purpose. La Salle was now without his principal backer and deprived of investors willing to fund his venture to settle the Mississippi River Valley. His only hope was to return to France and induce Louis XIV to issue a licence to him for the expansion of the French Empire in North America.

In November 1683, cavelier La Salle and his constant companion, Nika, sailed across the North Atlantic to France, arriving the following month. To convince the king of the merit of expansion into western Canada, he planned a new expedition to the New World with enough men to build a large fort at the mouth of the Mississippi River, giving France control of the waterway. When La Salle reached Paris, he found two new allies from the Sulpician Order, who strongly supported a greater French presence in North America at the expense of Spain. The two Sulpician abbots modified La Salle's plan to now use the fort on the Mississippi as a military base to attack Spanish outposts in Mexico and the Gulf of Mexico. The abbots used their influence and contacts at court to secure an audience with the king. When they met

Louis XIV, La Salle showed him a map that greatly distorted the course of the Mississippi River, depicting it veering far to the west. He further enhanced the likelihood of royal approval by telling the king that the Indians from the oak tree confederation would aid in a campaign against Spain. France and Spain had recently declared war, and the king envisioned the fort as a base to disrupt Spanish interests in Mexico. In March 1684, La Salle was issued a charter to establish a new colony, given command over the men and forts needed to protect the project and reappointed governor for the fortifications previously constructed in western New France.

The French crown included in its licence to the cavelier two ships, *Bella* and *Joly*, and with money from the king two additional vessels were chartered, the *Aimable* and *St Francois*. As news of the expedition spread, La Salle had little trouble recruiting the men, women and children for his new colony. Included among over 300 colonists were nearly 150 soldiers and sailors and 150 settlers. The expeditionary fleet was assembled at La Rochelle, and set sail for North America on 1 August.

After a two-month journey across the Atlantic on overcrowded ships in hot, oppressive conditions, and with tainted food, the French finally neared the island of Hispaniola in the Caribbean Sea. As the vessels steered closer to the shoreline, the *St Francois* was captured by Spanish privateers and its valuable cargo of provisions and equipment lost. La Salle was still suffering from his earlier illness contracted on the Mississippi, and became increasingly sick with the news of the ship's seizure. While he lay sweating and suffering from hallucinations, some of his sailors and soldiers deserted, joining the Spanish privateers. La Salle was compelled to remain at the port of Santo Domingo for nearly two months before he was well enough to continue the voyage. Finally, in late November, the French fleet put back to sea, navigating to the north-west into the Gulf of Mexico.

The three ships sailed the waters of the gulf for most of December before spotting land. The French travelled along the coastline, searching for a river outlet large enough to be the Mississippi. La Salle's previous measurements of the opening's location were inaccurate, and he could not find the river. He continued searching, but navigated too far to the west before deciding to land his expeditionary force at Matagorda Bay near current-day Port Lavaca, Texas, over 300 miles from the Mississippi River. In mid-January 1685, the settlers, soldiers, equipment and supplies were brought ashore. While the Frenchmen set up a camp with tents and makeshift huts, the three vessels were kept several miles off-shore to avoid destruction by sudden changes in the wind's direction. Despite the precautions, in March the flotilla was struck by a violent storm and the *Aimable* was driven aground and sunk. As work on the encampment continued, in early spring the *Joly* was sent back to France for additional men and supplies, leaving only the *Bella* for La Salle and his colonists. When the captain of the *Joly* reached Paris, he attempted to convince the French minister of colonies to send more settlers, provisions and equipment to La Salle, but the crown was involved in war against Spain and no money was available.

After the departure of the *Joly*, the Frenchmen began building a stockade called Fort Saint Louis several miles inland, while La Salle took fifty soldiers with five canoes to search east for the Mississippi River. During La Salle's absence, conditions at the camp grew worse, the settlers suffering from hunger and disease, with several dying every week. Relations with the local Indians from the Karankawa tribe were amicable at first, but after several warriors were punished for stealing, the natives began to unleash attacks against the settlers while attempting to drive them away by burning the grass fields surrounding the outpost. To protect against a surprise attack, guards were posted around the encampment with loaded muskets.

La Salle returned to Fort Saint Louis after travelling over 200 miles by canoe along the coast without locating the Mississippi. During his absence the last remaining ship was destroyed in a winter storm, so the French settlers and soldiers were now without a means to return home or send for supplies and reinforcements. The cavelier arrived at the fort exhausted and ill, and was compelled to spend several months regaining his health from the ordeal. While La Salle was recuperating, he decided to renew his quest for the Mississippi. After recovering his health he took a second expedition north-east to look for the mouth of the Mississippi, setting out with twenty Frenchmen. They trudged through the wilderness on foot in late April 1686 searching for the outlet, but were forced to return to Fort Saint Louis when many of the explorers became ill, including La Salle. When they finally reached the settlement in August, only eight of the original twenty men were still alive. Surviving at the fort was difficult for the French, with constant hunger and disease, and by the end of 1686 only thirty-seven of the initial 300 colonists remained alive.

With little chance of relief from France, La Salle was forced to renew his search for the Mississippi River as the only means of rescuing his surviving settlers. After once again recovering his health, in January 1687 he took Nika and eighteen soldiers and settlers, setting out to the east on foot. During the journey they traded with the Indians, hunted and gathered berries and roots for food, slowly making their way through eastern Texas. As they trekked further into the wilderness, dissension erupted among the men. Several, led by Pierre Duhaut, began plotting to kill La Salle, blaming him for putting their lives in jeopardy. On 19 March, they ambushed the cavelier and Duhaut shot him as he walked through the tall grass, killing him instantly. The murderers stripped him of his clothes, leaving La Salle to the wolves and wild dogs. After the death of La Salle, the search party continued to trudge north-east, finally reaching the Mississippi and following it upstream to the Illinois River before joining Henri Tonty at the French fort and trading post near Lake Michigan. The remaining colonists at Fort Saint Louis were either killed by the Karankawa Indians or by attacks from Spanish soldiers, while the fort was burned to the ground.

SELECTED SOURCES:
Coulter, Tony, *La Salle and the Explorers of the Mississippi.*
Crompton, Samuel Willard, *Robert de La Salle.*
Johnson, Donald S., *La Salle – A Perilous Odyssey from Canada to the Gulf of Mexico.*
Muhlstein, Anka, *La Salle – Explorer of the North American Frontier.*
Payment, Simone, *La Salle – Claiming the Mississippi River for France.*

Vitus Bering

Vitus Bering's first journey to the Far East in 1725 for the Russian court of Tsar Peter I, the Great, had established the existence of a strait between the North American continent and Asia. Eight years later, he was named to lead the Great Nordic Expedition by Empress Anna, with instructions to travel along the western coast of North America until reaching territory controlled by a European power. He set out with an expeditionary force of several thousand sailors, soldiers, carpenters, iron workers and scientists, making the long, hard, 6,000-mile overland trek to Siberia. Following the construction of the *St Peter* and *St Paul* ships in eastern Asia, he set sail from the Kamchatka Peninsula on 4 June 1741 with 152 men, navigating east across the northern Pacific Ocean. After steering to the south-east for fifty-three days, the Russian lookout high in the *St Peter's* rigging spotted land on 16 July. Vitus Bering pushed on and anchored his vessel off the rugged shoreline of an island in the current-day Gulf of Alaska, discovering the western coast of the North American continent. He sent a search party ashore to explore the new land, while the expedition's naturalist walked about the island, making notes on the natural resources, plants and wildlife. Following a brief stopover on the island, the Russian ship piloted to the north, mapping the shorelines of Alaska Bay, the Alaskan Peninsula and parts of the Aleutian Islands, establishing Russia's claim to the new territory.

Vitus Jonassen Bering was born in Horsens, Jutland, Denmark, in early August 1681, the son of Anne Pedderdatter Bering and Jonas Svendsen, a local customs official and Lutheran churchwarden. On the maternal side of his family, Vitus was related to several distinguished relatives who had served the Danish crown as advisors and judicial officials. He spent his youth in the port town, developing an interest in going to sea by talking to the many Danish and foreign sailors, travellers and merchants who gathered around the harbour. Jonas Svendsen earned a modest income as a town official, enabling Vitus to acquire a basic education. Two of Vitus' half-brothers attended the University of Copenhagen, but he was more interested in pursuing a maritime career. In 1696, when his half-brother, Svend, was sent to India, he signed-on with the expedition as a cabin boy, gaining his first experiences as a sailor. Following the voyage to India, he continued to work on various vessels, sailing for Danish and Dutch captains while learning the skills of a seaman, navigator, astronomer and map-maker. Vitus served on Danish whalers in the North Atlantic, visited the Danish Antilles and journeyed to the Spanish colonies in the Caribbean and English settlements along the North American coast, before travelling to Asia to the Dutch East Indies, which is now Indonesia.

As Vitus Bering developed into a skilled sailor and leader, he was appointed to the Dutch naval officers' academy in Amsterdam. After graduation, he served as a ship's officer on a Dutch expedition to their colony in the East Indies. When Bering returned to Amsterdam in 1703, he was introduced to the Russian admiral, Cornelius Ivanovich Cruys, who had been recruited by Tsar Peter the Great to build the imperial naval fleet. After speaking with Cruys, the 22-year-old Danish mariner was offered a commission in the Russian navy as a sub-lieutenant. As an experienced seaman, Bering rose steadily through the navy's ranks and in 1707 was promoted to lieutenant and lieutenant-captain three years later.

Bering had joined Peter the Great's navy during the Great Northern War against Sweden, but was denied the opportunity to lead seamen into battle, serving in several non-combat commands in the Baltic Fleet. He was named captain of a schooner delivering building materials for the construction of the defences at the new capital of St Petersburg. After serving in the Baltic Fleet, Lieutenant-captain Bering was transferred to the Azov Sea Fleet and stationed on the northern shoreline of the Gulf of Taganrog in southern Russia at the port of Taganrog. While with the southern fleet, Bering continued to command transport vessels, sailing to ports in the Black Sea and Sea of Azov. In 1711, after Sultan Ahmed III led the Ottoman Turks to victory over Russia and its Moldavian ally in the Pruth River campaign, the tsar chose Lieutenant-captain Bering to save one of his prize warships from capture, ordering him to pilot the *Munker* from the Sea of Azov to safety in the Baltic Sea. Bering navigated the vessel across the Black Sea, through the dangerous Bosporus Straits into the Mediterranean and up the western coast of Europe to Russia. The lieutenant-captain remained in the Baltic Fleet, serving with distinction, and in 1715 was advanced again to the rank of captain fourth-grade.

While the conflict with Sweden dragged on, Bering was ordered to take the *Pearl* from Copenhagen across northern Scandinavia to Archangel on the White Sea, and after delivering the vessel he captained the newly constructed fifty-two-gun *Selafail* from the shipyard to the port at Tallinn in the Gulf of Finland. After transferring the warship, Bering was reassigned to the fortress at Kronshlot on the Sea of Finland, and was involved with the protection of the sea approaches to St Petersburg against an attack by Sweden. The following year, he took part in a combined naval expedition with the fleets of Russia and Denmark, sailing to Bornholm Island in the Baltic Sea and threatening to raid Sweden. He remained in the Baltic theatre of operations and was occupied at several ports directing the transfer of supplies and equipment from ships that were too large to dock at the shallow harbours. Continuing to serve with the Russian navy, Captain Bering participated in numerous expeditions in the Baltic Sea against the enemy, and later served as ranking naval officer at Tallinn supervising the operations of the seaport.

Bering was married to Anna Christina Pulse in October 1713 at Viborg, Russia. From a wealthy merchant family, she was the eldest of four siblings. During their thirty-eight years of marriage, the Berings had nine children, four of whom survived into adulthood. Throughout his career in the navy, when Bering was transferred to numerous posts, Anna frequently travelled with him to foreign and distant ports, establishing a home and caring for their children.

Following the end of the war against Sweden in 1721, Bering expected to receive a promotion to captain first-class in recognition of his services to the imperial throne. Numerous upgrades were made by the Russian Admiralty, but he was passed over, despite his many years of distinguished duty in the imperial navy. Many officers junior to Bering were advanced in grade and he was humiliated by his lack of promotion. At the encouragement of Anna, whose younger sister was engaged to a rear admiral, Bering submitted his request for retirement. In late February 1724, his retirement was accepted by the Admiralty and in acknowledgement of his twenty-two years in the navy he was granted the rank of captain first-class. Bering, his wife and their two sons soon left St Petersburg, travelling to her home at Viborg. However service at sea was the only life Bering knew, and after five months of inactivity he visited the Admiralty to request a return to active duty. After receiving the endorsement of Tsar Peter, the application was approved and in August he re-entered the navy, retaining his rank of captain first-class.

Soon after reporting to the fleet, Bering was appointed commander of the ninety-gun warship *Lesnoe* and took up his duty station in the icy waters of the Baltic. While he sailed his vessel with the fleet, Peter the Great began finalizing his plans to send an expeditionary force to the eastern end of his vast empire to reconnoitre the unexplored Pacific coastline. After seizing control of the eastern slopes of the Ural Mountains, the Russians had swept across Siberia to the Pacific Ocean in the first half of the seventeenth century. Gaining sovereignty over the territory, the regime issued an edict barring western European kingdoms from entry into Russian waters in the northern Pacific. Tsar Peter was eager to explore the land between the Kamchatka Peninsula and Spanish settlements in North America for future Russian colonization, and was interested in determining if a land bridge existed between the Americas and Asia. On 23 December 1724, he ordered the Admiralty to prepare an expedition to the Far East. When the Tsar made his request, he indicated his preference for a captain with experience sailing in North American waters. Bering had previously travelled to colonies in the Caribbean and on the American east coast. Several days later, a list of proposed officers to lead the reconnaissance was given to the tsar, with Bering's name at the top. At the end of the month, he was notified of his appointment as commander of the First Kamchatka Expedition.

As the Admiralty assembled the expeditionary force, Lieutenants Martin Spangberg and Aleksei Chirikov were chosen as executive officers for the project, and by mid-January 1725 thirty-four men had been selected from the Baltic Fleet. Bering was authorized by the Admiralty to take only essential items on the long journey across Russia, and supplies unavailable at Kamchatka were packed, including cannons, anchors and navigational instruments.

While the final preparations for the journey continued, on 28 January Peter the Great died at St Petersburg and was succeeded by his wife, Empress Catherine I. Before Bering departed from the capital for the East, the new empress pledged full support for the venture. Chirikov and twenty-six men had already left St Petersburg, travelling toward Vologda with supplies loaded on horse-drawn sleds. During his final discussions with the empress, Captain Bering was instructed to build one or two ships in Kamchatka, map the territory to the north of the peninsula and search for land that was joined to America. On 6 February, Bering and Spangberg left the Admiralty in St Petersburg with two navigators and three sailors, joining Chirikov at Vologda just over a week later. The unified expeditionary force pushed on, crossing frozen lands to the fort at Tobolsk, at the confluence of the Tobol and Irtysh rivers. At the desolate outpost, which had earlier served as the capital of Siberia before its conquest by the Russians, the captain recruited thirty-nine soldiers from the imperial garrison, while hiring carpenters, coopers and blacksmiths to supplement his work crew for the construction of his ships at Kamchatka. The Russians remained at Tobolsk until mid-May, and after purchasing four flat-bottomed riverboats outfitted with masts and sails set out for their next destination, the large town of Yakutsk in eastern Russia on the Lena River. The search party followed the well-established water route to the east, sailing on the Ob River toward Yakutsk. On the Ob, the travellers were forced to propel their boats forward with oars and barge poles. The expedition continued to the east on the Ket River, and after a portage reached the town of Yeniseisk. At this outpost, Bering acquired additional labourers, horses and carts, despite strong opposition from the garrison's administrator. With his men now rested and resupplied, Bering set out again, moving along numerous rivers by flatboats and arriving at the Russian settlement of Ilim. From the fort he was forced to advance overland for 80 miles by horse-drawn carts to Ust-Kut, where the Russians journeyed down the Lena River by boats for two weeks, finally docking at Yakutsk in June.

Yakutsk, a sizeable town with over 4,000 inhabitants, was a major port on the Lena River. Bering pressed the town's administrator for the soldiers, craftsmen and horses needed to reach the harbour at Okhotsk, on the north-western coast of the Okhotsk Sea, before the onset of winter. Only when the captain threatened to blame the governor for the failure of the expedition did he receive additional labourers and draft animals. While Chirikov remained at the town until the spring, stockpiling additional provisions and supplies, on 7 July a body of over eighty men led by Spangberg started transporting several tons of equipment and food to the east on the rivers by flatboats, while Bering and two other groups travelled overland by horse.

The expedition struggled through the desolate, dense forest of pines, larches and spruces, plagued with constant shortages of food in the forbidding country. During the hard and dangerous trek, many men deserted, stealing food and horses, and when Bering reached Okhotsk in October only a remnant of his expeditionary force remained. In early January 1726, Spangberg finally made his way to the town with several soldiers following a nightmarish trudge through the snow-covered wilderness, in frozen temperatures with little food. Two weeks later, a contingent of sixty stragglers stumbled into Okhotsk, barely alive. The journey to the town through the terrible Russian winter had decimated Bering's expedition, and those at Okhotsk would have starved to death if Chirikov had not arrived from Yakutsk in the spring with a supply of provisions. While at the town, Bering decided to build a boat to cross the Sea of Okhotsk to the Kamchatka Peninsula. In the summer he put his surviving carpenters, caulkers and ironmen to work building the vessel, christened the *Fortuna*. On 22 August, the Russians boarded the ship, sailing across the Sea of Okhotsk to the western coastline of the peninsula, landing at the port of Bolsheretsk.

Disembarking from the *Fortuna*, Bering assembled his soldiers, sailors, craftsmen and labourers and began the advance across the peninsula to the small village of Lower Kamchatka Post on the Pacific coast. The peninsula was lightly defended by Russian troops, and during their journey across it Bering's men had to be on guard against surprise ambushes by local natives. After reaching the fort at Bolshaya, he sent Spangberg ahead by boat to the coast with part of the reconnaissance party, while Bering, with a second group, moved overland with tons of supplies and equipment on sleds pulled by native labourers and dogs. Chirikov had been left behind at Bolshaya, and the following spring of 1727 his men joined Bering with the remaining baggage at Lower Kamchatka Post, completing the nearly three-year journey of 6,000 miles from St Petersburg to the Pacific Ocean.

Before the onset of winter, Bering sent work parties up the Ashik River to cut larch trees suitable for the construction of a ship. After the timber was collected it was hauled to the Kamchatka River by dogs and labourers. By the time the lumber was cut, the freezing winter weather had arrived and Bering's expeditionary force spent the next few months at the village of Klyucha. In the spring of 1728, construction of the vessel began. By the beginning of May, the planking of the ship was started, and in June the interior was caulked and tarred. On the evening of 9 June the newly named *Archangel Gabriel* was launched, with a crew of forty-four sailors and soldiers. The vessel was held together with nails and iron, and was nearly 60 feet long and 20 feet wide. The twin-mast *Archangel Gabriel* was armed with four cannons and three falconets, while a small shallop for travel close to the shore was attached to the rear. After the vessel was loaded with tons of provisions and supplies, it slowly made its way down the Kamchatka River on 13 July in a heavy fog. The following morning, under fair weather, the sails were unfurled and the *Archangel Gabriel* sailed out into the Pacific.

Bering navigated the vessel to the north-east keeping close to the shoreline. As the mariners sailed up the coast, the peninsula was mapped and landmarks noted in the logbook. On 7 August, the small shallop was sent ashore to explore inland and refill the water caskets. The expedition continued piloting to the north, spotting whales, porpoises and walruses swimming near the vessel. During the voyage, several bands of natives paddled their kayaks out to the ship and Bering questioned them about the geographic features of Kamchatka and along the polar waters ahead. By mid-August they were approaching 65°North latitude, with the open sea still in front of them.

Unknown to Bering, his ship was entering the strait later named after him, and the continent of North America was only about 56 miles to the east. On 13 August, he summoned Chirikov and Spangberg to his cabin, asking them if they believed that with the Asian coastline now swinging to the west, that North America was separated from Asia by the sea ahead. Both lieutenants replied in writing, suggesting that they continue to steer further north for at least another fourteen days to confirm the absence of a land bridge to America. Bering, concerned about becoming beached and trapped on an unknown outcropping of the peninsula during a dark foggy night, decided to return south to the Kamchatka River and search for a safe harbour to spend the winter before the weather turned cold and icy.

The Russian captain continued to steer to the north for two more days, sighting no land to the east, and in the mid-afternoon of 15 August Bering ordered the *Archangel Gabriel* to begin the return voyage after reaching a latitude of 67° 24' in the freezing polar waters. By 18 August, they had passed St Lawrence Island, previously discovered on the way north. Two days later, the vessel was approached by over forty natives in four canoes. The Indians knew about the arrival of the Russians from the west and had come to trade their meat, fish, pelts and walrus tusks for European goods. Bering again questioned them about the region's terrain, but due to language difficulties discovered little of value. On 25 August, the expedition was battered by strong winds and the vessel tossed and rolled by rough seas, snapping the foremast. They piloted on with only the mainsail, and on 30 August were struck by another violent storm, the torn sails and rigging crashing to the deck. Bering ordered the anchor dropped to keep from drifting, while the crew worked to replace the ripped sails. The weather slowly cleared and Bering resumed the voyage down the coastline under calmer skies. On 2 September the lookout sighted the Cape of Kamchatka and the following day the sailors navigated up the mouth of the Kamchatka River, ending the fifty-day journey to search for the land bridge to America.

Following their return from the north, Bering ordered his crew to prepare the *Archangel Gabriel* and *Fortuna* for winter. The sails and rigging were hauled down and stored, while the ships were repaired and placed in the care of the local governor. At the village Bering learned of the death of Empress Catherine I and the assumption of the Russian crown by Peter II, grandson of Peter the Great. The soldiers and sailors settled into their winter quarters and were occupied in good weather with maintenance and repairs to the vessels' sails, riggings, plankings, decks and masts. The first frost occurred in early October, and by the end of the month the river had started to freeze.

While at the Russian settlement, Bering spoke to numerous natives and was repeatedly told that on clear days they could see land across the sea to the east. He assumed from their descriptions that the territory was the coast of America, and in the spring planned an eastern voyage to look for the undiscovered land. As the weather slowly turned warmer, the ships were prepared to sail, with provisions and equipment loaded in the holds. In early May 1529, the ice in the river broke up and Bering ordered the *Fortuna* to return to Bolsheretsk by rounding the southern tip of the Kamchatka Peninsula, while the *Archangel Gabriel* put to sea. Late in the month, the crew of forty sailors and soldiers began boarding the ship, and taking advantage of favourable currents and tide navigated into the northern Pacific on 5 June, setting a course to the east to renew the search for North America. During the following two days, the mariners steered in calm seas with a light breeze, but on 8 June the winds suddenly grew stronger, ripping the foresail, as the vessel pitched and rolled. Bering continued eastward with only the mainsail pushing the *Archangel Gabriel* forward. After travelling over 100 miles without sighting land, the captain lost hope of discovering America, ordering the crew to return to the Kamchatka Peninsula and thus ending the First Kamchatka Expedition's quest for the North American continent. On 1 July, Bering began the homeward journey to St Petersburg, rounding the bottom of the peninsula and rejoining the *Fortuna* at the fort of Bolsheretsk. After additional flour, dried meats and salt were loaded, the two vessels sailed across the Sea of Okhotsk reaching the port of Okhotsk on the Russian mainland on 24 July.

From Okhotsk, Bering sent his navigator, Richard Enze, with six men overland to begin building boats and rafts at the Iakitsk settlement to travel on the Lena River during the next stage of the homeward journey. On 29 July, the captain set out with the main party, ten days later reaching Iudoma Cross. After a short pause, he continued to the west, travelling on several rivers before reaching Iakitsk and rejoining Enze on 29 August. On 10 September, the expeditionary force sailed up the Lena River, finally arriving at the fort of Peledui as ice began to form in the river. Remaining at the outpost until the waterway froze in late October, the soldiers and sailors resumed their journey on horseback, riding over the solid ice.

By early December, the returning explorers had arrived at the modern-day town of Yeniseisk on the left bank of the Yenisei River, and began their trek across the steppes to Tobolsk via the Irtysh River. The soldiers, who had earlier joined Bering's expeditionary force, returned to their former duties in the town, and the sailors and navigators continued west on sleds over the same route they had taken five years before. On 23 February, Bering left the main party, travelling ahead by sled through the frozen Russian wilderness with four men, reaching St Petersburg on 28 February 1730, completing the five-year expedition of exploration.

Captain Bering was occupied for the next ten days finalizing his two reports and numerous maps for the Admiralty, and on 10 and 12 March submitted his assessments of the expedition. In the first account he summarized the activities of the journey, and followed it with a detailed description of the venture, writing about the accomplishments and hardships experienced and the failure to discover a land bridge to America, concluding with a list of recommendations for promotion. He described some of the native tribes encountered, writing about their villages, foods, religions, appearance and clothes. Bering later received a promotion to captain-commander and was awarded 1,000 rubles. He had expected an advancement in rank to rear admiral and was dissatisfied with the lower grade. When Bering pressed the Admiralty for the higher rank, his request was forwarded to the new empress, Anna, but it was denied.

While Bering was in the Far East, in January 1730 Tsar Peter II had died from smallpox and the niece of Peter I ascended to the Russian crown as Empress Anna. She had spent her adult life at the courts in Germany, and following her coronation the Supreme Privy Council dominated by the Russian aristocrats was abolished. She restored the weak Senate and appointed Germans to important offices in her cabinet. With the government under the control of foreigners, it was vital to remain in St Petersburg to court the favour of the western European ministers. Soon after meeting with the Admiralty, Bering began developing a new proposal to return to Kamchatka and build larger ships to renew the quest for North America, while moving his family to the capital to be closer to the influential members of the imperial court.

As a result of the Kamchatka expedition and his profitable fur trading activities in Siberia, Bering had become wealthy and leased a large, lavish residence in St Petersburg with a staff of servants. With his new rank of captain-commander, he was now part of the nobility and Anna Bering used their new status to advance her husband in the social life of the Russian court. Anna Bering was attractive, and with a quick wit and charm she rapidly becoming popular with powerful government officials. She developed a close relationship with the Austrian ambassador, who represented Russia's closest European ally in the imperial seat of government, giving Captain-commander Bering access to important bureaucrats. With his renown from the Kamchatka expedition and his growing influence with the administration, Bering began to finalize his new proposal to return to the Far East and search the north-eastern Pacific for the coastline of the North American continent.

After Empress Anna secured the imperial crown, the seat of government was returned to Moscow, but the Admiralty remained in St Petersburg. Bering was compelled to travel to Moscow to present his new proposal for the second expedition to the administration. After submitting his plans to the regime, he found a valuable supporter in Ivan Kirilov, who envisioned the venture as an expansion of the Russian Empire and a means of opening the wealth of Siberia to further development. Through Kirilov's influence, the Russian Senate approved Bering's undertaking in December 1730. While the Senate, guided by Kirilov, drew up the goals of the expedition, in January 1731 Bering returned to St Petersburg. As presiding officer in the Senate, Kirilov set out the areas that Bering was to explore to enhance Russia's presence in the north Pacific, stressing the need to visit not only the North American coastline but also to resume the mapping of the north-eastern shores of Asia, establish contacts with Japan and Korea and continue south to the Spanish colonies. In June, the Senate approved the inclusion of an academic legation that was to investigate items of scientific interest. The Russian Academy of Sciences named academicians to study natural history, make astronomical observations and examine native cultures. The academy included in the scientific party two landscape painters, an instrument maker, five surveyors, six assistants, a surgeon and fourteen soldiers, adding over thirty more men who Bering was to shelter, transport and feed. In the following year, the Russian government was relocated again to St Petersburg, and Bering now added his personal input to the planning process. In mid-October 1732, the Admiralty issued Bering his instructions for the second Kamchatka expedition, ordering him to travel overland to the Pacific coast and construct two double-masted ships on the Kamchatka River for the exploration and charting of the area above the peninsula to 67° North latitude searching for the shore of the North American continent. He was placed in command of one of the vessels, while Chirikov was to take charge of the second. He was ordered to continue looking for the American coastline if necessary into the late summer, before returning to Kamchatka, despite the dangers of ice floes.

On 28 December 1732, the Senate submitted its instructions for the second Kamchatka venture to Empress Anna for her approval. After receiving her authorization, in early 1733 the Great Nordic Expedition began leaving St Petersburg, with Spangberg leading the first party and Chirikov moving to Tobolsk with the main body of eight lieutenants, their wives, children and approximately 500 sailors, soldiers and labourers to transport the tons of equipment and supplies. Bering departed for the east on 29 April, joining Anna and his two youngest children en-route, overtaking the expedition at the Volga River. They continued travelling toward the east coast by boats on the Volga and Kama rivers, and when freezing weather arrived in late autumn used sleds to resume their journey to Tobolsk. The scientific contingent was the last to leave St Petersburg, finally arriving at Tobolsk in January 1734. The demands for suitable dwellings and food for an additional 600 people put a terrible strain on the unprepared inhabitants of the town. Bering met frequently with the local governor, demanding equipment, carpenters and skilled craftsmen to build a sloop to sail on the Lena River, requisitioning 1,500 workers for the expedition.

While the men began constructing the sloop, in late February Bering and his family left Tobolsk over frozen trails for Irkutsk with a small party. After reaching the town they sailed down the Lena River in October to the major river port town of Yakutsk in eastern central Russia, as Chirikov made his way with the main party over the same route followed eight years earlier, travelling eastward by river boats in the summer and sledges in the snows of winter. The captain-commander remained at Yakutsk during the winter, and in June Chirikov rejoined him. While waiting for the main body of men to arrive, Bering ordered his skilled workmen to build two ships for the exploration and mapping of the north-eastern coastline of Asia. When the *Yakutsk* was completed and equipped, Lieutenant V. M. Pronchishchev was placed in command. In late June 1735, he steered the vessel down the Lena River and in the following year reconnoitred the Asian coast only to 77° North. The expeditionary force failed to complete the survey, and spent the winter at the mouth of the Lena River preparing to renew the project in the spring. However, the lieutenant died of scurvy and Bering sent the second vessel, *Iskutsk*, to complete the mapping. As the crew of the *Iskutsk* wintered along the coast, disease spread among the sailors, killing nearly forty of them and forcing the abandonment of the voyage. When the Admiralty demanded maps of the entire region, Bering ordered a third expedition to trudge overland to chart the eastern Asia coastline, finally completing the reconnaissance in 1743.

Captain-commander Bering spent three years at Yakutsk making arrangements for the sea voyage to search for the North American continent, occupied procuring skilled craftsmen and labourers, while stockpiling equipment and supplies from the surrounding forts and settlements. While Bering remained at the river port, he was mired in a sea of administrative details, struggling with the lack of cooperation from the Siberian governors for provisions, workmen and materials and the area's foundries for the production of cannons and ammunition. Spangberg had earlier led the expedition from St Petersburg with the heavy equipment, including iron products and shipbuilding materials, passing through Yakutsk to Okhotsk to begin preparations for the arrival of the expeditionary force. At Okhotsk, Spangberg and his workers started building barracks, houses and ships for Bering's force. As preparations for the expedition continued at the port, Bering's relationship with the academicians grew increasingly strained as they made demands for better accommodation and greater comforts. Several years had passed since the departure from St Petersburg, and Bering had not yet reached the Pacific coast. He was now receiving criticism from the Admiralty, threatening to bring charges against him and reduce his rank. Bering defended himself, sending letters to the members of the Academy assuring them of his unrelenting loyalty, persistence and dedication to the expedition.

Finally, in the summer of 1737, Bering had the initial phase of preparations for the voyage finalized and moved his headquarters to Okhotsk on the coast of the Sea of Okhotsk, rejoining Spangberg. In the following months, his men, supplies and equipment were transferred to the port or distributed to various forts and towns in the region. He was occupied at Okhotsk building houses for the officers and their families, barracks for the seamen, soldiers and craftsmen, a large dock and numerous buildings for storage, while also erecting a church. When the captain-commander reached the port, he found two new ships, the *Archangel Michael* and *Hope*, in the harbour waiting for him, along with the repaired *Fortuna* and *Archangel Gabriel*. Spangberg had also begun construction on two larger vessels, the *St Peter* and *St Paul*, for the American expedition. While work on the ships continued, the scientific party sailed in the sloop to Bolsheretsk to begin its investigation of the region's natural resources and native cultures. Bering wrote that, 'The place is new and desolate with no vegetation and no timber in the vicinity.' Despite its difficulties, the geographic location was ideal for a harbour and Bering was determined to overcome its disadvantages.

Bering remained at Okhotsk for the next three years, preparing to sail to the North American coast. Work on the *St Peter* and *St Paul* continued, while provisions and equipment were stockpiled. During this time the captain-commander remained in disfavour with the Russian Senate and Admiralty, which complained about the lack of progress and threatened to discontinue the expedition. Bering had to contend with the complaints and protests of the area's governors, who continually ignored his request for labourers and supplies.

Before leaving St Petersburg, the captain-commander had been ordered to send a reconnaissance party south to map the coastline of northern Japan, and Spangberg sailed down the Russian shore in three ships in 1738. After reaching the Kuril Islands, the Russian vessels became separated in a dense fog, and without the leadership of Spangberg only about thirty of the fifty-six islands were charted. He returned the following year with four ships and 200 sailors and soldiers, surveying the northernmost of the four main islands, Hokkaido, and part of the eastern coast of Japan's largest island, Hondo. Two of his vessels made contact with local seamen, becoming the first Russians to meet with the Japanese. Spangberg's two expeditions added greatly to Europe's knowledge of the cartographical features of this part of the northern Pacific.

The material requirements for Spangberg's voyages to Japan had exhausted the provisions and stores at Okhotsk, and it was again necessary to stockpile new supplies from the farms and factories of eastern Siberia. Bering sent demands for the required items to the local government officials. To facilitate delivery of the goods, the roads were improved and additional workers hired, while the Siberian authorities exhibited greater cooperation and energy than before. By 1740, Bering had gathered the required supplies and finalized preparations for the journey to North America. As work on the expedition continued, in March 1740 George William Steller arrived from St Petersburg, joining the expedition as the Russian Academy's representative. During the expedition, Steller assembled a collection of specimens, including numerous species of birds, fish and mammals. He recorded his observations of the lands' fauna and described in detail many animals, including the fur seal, sea otter, sea eagle, elder, cormorant and sea cow in his book *The Beasts of the Sea*, which was published after his death in 1751.

In June 1740, the *St Peter* and *St Paul* were finally launched from the port at Okhotsk. The twin ships had been constructed with a main and foremast, and were 90 feet long and 23 feet wide. Each vessel carried fourteen mounted cannons, and bunks and hammocks for seventy-six men, not including the captain. In the bright sun of early summer under passing white clouds, the Great Nordic Expedition's fleet of eight vessels sailed from the harbour, all built under the direction of Captain-commander Bering.

Following the departure of Anna Bering and their two children on the long journey back to St Petersburg, on 8 September 1740 Bering steered his small fleet of five ships from Okhotsk harbour, sailing across the Okhotsk

Sea to Avacha Bay on the eastern coast of the peninsula of Kamchatka to spend the winter months. The flotilla was made up of the *St Peter* and *St Paul* along with two smaller transports and a sloop for the scientific party. When the expeditionary force reached the bay, the men were ordered by Bering to construct a fortified stockade in Niakina Cove. A log fort was built, with barracks for the men and cabins for the officers, while a small church was also erected. During the crossing from Okhotsk, a large quantity of biscuits was lost at sea, and to conserve food for the American voyage, additional provisions for the nearly 200 Russians were brought from the town of Bolsheretsk over 100 miles away. Local Cossacks were hired to transport the goods and they used dogsleds handled by natives to haul the food. When the natives rebelled at their harsh treatment by the Cossacks, launching attacks against the Russian settlements, the departure of the expedition was delayed until early June 1741.

During May 1741, the *St Peter* and *St Paul* were loaded with provisions and supplies for six months at sea. The *St Peter* was commanded by Bering and the *St Paul* by Lieutenant Alexei Chirikov. Bering's ship was manned by seventy-seven sailors and soldiers, while Chirikov's carried a crew of seventy-six men. Following a prayer service, the two vessels raised their anchors on 4 June, setting a course to the south-east, with the Russian flag of horizontal white, blue and red stripes flying from the mast, to first search for the island of Gamaland, which appeared on numerous maps given to Bering by the Admiralty. According to many European cartographers and navigators, Gamaland was a large landmass rich in gold and silver located north of Japan, and had been discovered in the early seventeenth century by the Portuguese captain, Juan de Gama. The Russian mariners kept a steady course to the south-east, sailing over 600 miles toward the uncharted island. According to the chart of Joseph N. Delisle, they should have already found the island, and with only open seas ahead of them Bering decided to turn about and steer north-east. Shortly after the two ships changed direction, the Russians were struck by a sudden storm and fog on 20 June. During the squall, the *St Peter* and *St Paul* became separated. After remaining in the area for two days looking for Chirikov, Bering ordered his crew to resume the reconnaissance for Gamaland, navigating to the 45° North latitude without locating the mythical landmass. He resumed his voyage, piloting alone across clear open waters with fair winds. While the expeditionary force travelled steadily to the north-east, Bering became ill from exhaustion and the effects of scurvy, and was forced to stay in his cabin. On 16 July, after crossing the 58° and 28' North latitude, the lookout high in the rigging spotted an uncharted landmass after fifty-three days at sea. As the *St Peter* sailed closer to the land, Bering saw an island with a rugged coastline and a high, snow-capped mountain, later named St Elias, rising inland. The Russians had finally discovered the western coast of North America by navigating from the west.

The imperial ship steered slowly to the north, contending a strong headwind, anchoring on 20 July off an island Bering called St Elias, modern-day Kayak Island. From the vessel, the coast of the mainland was visible to the east, steep snow-crested mountains emerging in the distance. The captain-commander sent a search party of sixteen men ashore to explore and refill the water caskets. The expedition's academician, George Steller, accompanied the contingent of seamen and soldiers, studying Kayak Island's natural resources and cataloguing an array of plants, animals and bird species during his ten hours ashore. While the scientist was occupied on the island, the main body of Russians searched nearby Wingham Island, finding signs of the presence of Native Americans.

On the morning of 21 July, Bering issued orders for the crew to weigh anchor and set out to sea, despite the protests of Steller, who wanted to continue investigating the numerous species of animals and plants on the islands. With a strong eastward wind driving the *St Peter*, they steered to the south-west. They continued to sail a steady course for the following five days in mist and rain showers, and by the morning of 26 July were off the coast of Kodiak Island. Bering navigated his vessel past Kodiak as the weather turned stormy, with steady rain, dense fog and fierce winds. On 2 August, the lookout spotted another island, later named Chirikov, located 100 miles south-west of Kodiak in the Gulf of Alaska. The landmass was about 40 square miles, with sandy beaches, freshwater lakes and rolling hills of grasslands. As the ship resumed its course to the south-west, following the coastline of the Alaskan Peninsula, on 4 August, near a latitude of 56°, the seamen sighted the treeless Semidi Islands spread over 15 miles. During their voyage, the Russian mariners discovered five of the archipelago's nine major islands, and as they sailed through the chain of rocky landmasses noted the many sea otters, whales, sea lions, seals, porpoises and large varieties of sea birds. Bering continued on past the Semidi Islands, but was then struck by strong headwinds.

After making little progress on his current course, Bering ordered the crewmen to turn north-west into the present-day Bering Sea. The Russian Academy's scientist noted in his logbook the presence of sea otters, seals and whales swimming close to the ship as the weather turned rainy and foggy. Bering continued to sail north-west as the vessel encountered contrary winds and rough waters. The *St Peter* rolled and pitched, while fierce waves slammed into its sides. While the sailors struggled against the violent weather in the unexplored area of the Aleutian Islands, sixteen men fell ill with scurvy as it spread among the crew. Bering had earlier been affected with the disease, and after over two months at sea the scurvy returned. As his health deteriorated, he was confined to his cabin. In the prolonged absence of their captain, the ship's officers met on 10 August, deciding to end the mapping of the Alaskan coastline and return to Avacha Bay over 1,600 miles away by following the fifty-third latitude west. They wrote a charter explaining their reasons for ending the expedition, signed by all the officers and crewmen.

The ship continued sailing north-west against strong headwinds in foggy seas, but on 27 August they were forced to change course, steering due north in search of freshwater to refill the caskets, which were now found to be inadequate to reach port. Two days later, the *St Peter* neared the fifty-fifth parallel, driven by a strong western wind under blue skies, when land suddenly appeared on the horizon. While Bering's illness grew increasingly worse, the crew steered toward the treeless, rocky and barren Shumagin Islands, a large chain of fifty islands off the south-western coast of the Alaskan Peninsula. The ship now headed north-east toward the nearest landmass, present-day Nagai Island, which extended 30 miles from north to south. The vessel's anchor was lowered and, after daybreak, a landing party of eleven Russians, including Steller, went ashore in the longboat to refill the empty water barrels and explore inland. The seamen quickly located a freshwater pond at the northern end of Nagai, spending the following two days filling more than fifty water caskets, while the scientist searched the island collecting various plants. As Steller and the mariners began returning to the *St Peter*, a violent storm suddenly erupted and they struggled back to the ship through large waves and rough seas. While Steller reconnoitred the island, he had collected gonberries, crowberries and various grasses, and after returning to the vessel made a medication for the men with scurvy. A few days later, the victims of the disease began to feel better, with many of the symptoms of scurvy disappearing, and by 4 September Bering was able to walk on deck and retake active command of the expedition.

While the Russians were occupied on Nagai, a second contingent of seamen and soldiers rowed in a longboat to nearby Turner Island, where a fire had been seen the previous night. As they approached the beach, their boat was thrown against the rocks by fierce waves. The men reached the shore unharmed, but their longboat was destroyed. Bering was forced to send the second longboat to rescue the six stranded crew.

In early September, Bering sailed close by Bird Island, anchoring in the protected inlet. While the crew stayed at the island, in the late afternoon of 4 September, two sealskin kayaks paddled toward the ship. When they neared the *St Peter*, the two Indians shouted to the Russians and waved their arms toward the shore. As the natives moved closer, they pointed to their mouths, while scooping up seawater signalling that the sailors could have food and water with them. The Aleut natives then took a long pole with two falcon feathers at the top, throwing it toward the ship. Bering ordered several items placed on a plank and tossed to the Indians. The Native Americans again gestured toward the beach, where seven other Indians could now be seen by a fire. The captain-commander accepted the invitation, and ten mariners and soldiers along with Steller and an interpreter boarded the longboat, rowing toward the shore. The waters near the island had many hidden rocks, and not willing to risk damaging the boat, three men were instructed to wade ashore. After reaching the sandy beach, they were taken to the campfire and given pieces of blubber to eat. The Indians continued to encourage the remaining Russians in the surf to join them, but with darkness now approaching the sailors on the shore were ordered back to the longboat. Two men made it to the boat, but the interpreter was taken captive. The commander of the reconnaissance party ordered muskets fired over the Aleuts' heads to scare them. When the Indians fell to the ground, the interpreter broke free, running to the water and wading to the waiting seamen. The Russians quickly returned to the ship, ending the expedition's first encounter with Native Americans. The following day, the natives again paddled to the ship, trading two caps and a rod with attached multi-coloured feathers for an iron kettle and sewing needles.

After remaining in the Shumagin Islands for eight days, Bering sailed southward back to the 53° North latitude on 6 September to resume his voyage to the west. For over two weeks he made steady progress to the south-west, slipping below the fifty-third parallel, as the ship was struck with frequent storms and dense fog. The crew had trouble taking position observations due to the lack of sun at noon, and there was constant fear of shipwreck on an unseen landmass due to continuing fog, haze and rain. On 11 October the sky cleared, and with the sun now visible a more accurate reading of the latitude was made, showing the expedition had drifted to 48° North. The weather stayed fair and mild for the next ten days as the men navigated west. As the vessel steered toward the Kamchatka Peninsula, conditions on the *St Peter* were barely tolerable with the crewmen suffering from bad water, lack of food and exhaustion, while Steller's medications became scarce and scurvy soon returned. Captain-commander Bering was ill again with the disease and confined to his cabin, his health steadily deteriorating. On 25 October, the lookout spotted an island, present-day Amchitka in the western Aleutian Islands at a latitude of 51° North. Conditions on the ship worsened and the Russians were unable to explore the newly discovered landmass. As Bering continued toward the west, he found additional small islands from the Aleutian Archipelago. In early November, the weather turned damp and raw, with sharp eastern winds, while men were now dying weekly. On 4 November, the lookout sighted an elevated coastline at 53° North and news quickly spread among the crew that Avacha Bay was ahead. The sick and nearly dead crawled to the deck to see the port, but after moving closer to the shore no familiar landmarks were observed and the mariners were bitterly distraught.

The Russians piloted toward the unknown landmass, dropping anchor half a mile from shore and spending the night in a bay under a nearly full moon. In the early morning the weather began to turn stormy, with strong winds and heavy seas. The ship was severely damaged and the mainmast rendered useless. After the gale, Bering called a meeting with his officers and crew to decide whether to continue to Kamchatka with the foresail or anchor the vessel in a safe bay spotted 15 miles away. Bering favoured sailing on to Kamchatka but the soldiers and sailors voted to end the expedition and take shelter on the island later named after their captain-commander.

In the late afternoon of 6 November, the *St Peter* sailed slowly south-west into the broad bay with a strong north wind. As the ship approached the beach, an anchor was thrown out but its cable soon broke and they floated dangerously toward the reef surrounding the island. A second anchor was dropped but its cable also snapped and the *St Peter* crashed into rocks. Steller later wrote that he heard men shouting, 'Oh, we are done for! Oh, God, our ship! A disaster has befallen our ship!' The surf suddenly lifted the vessel over the reef and 600 yards from the beach it hit the bottom in 24 feet of water. After four months, the Russian expedition of exploration to the North American continent ended with sixty-six survivors resting on the deck of the battered ship.

In the early afternoon of 7 November, Lieutenant Sven Waxell and George Steller led an expeditionary force ashore to explore the island, locate fresh drinking water and find a safe site to locate the camp. They discovered a rocky and uninviting land with a treeless interior and snowless mountains, rich in wildlife with abundant Arctic foxes, sea otters, seals, sea lions and birds. The search party found a protected area and built a small encampment with huts of driftwood to spend the night, while Steller searched for plants and grasses. During their first day on the island, the crewmen killed several grouse and Steller located some edible plants. A few men returned to the ship, taking fresh food to Bering and the sick seamen and soldiers.

The following day was spent hunting for food and looking for new plants, while construction of a more permanent settlement for the crew began. The condition of the sick had deteriorated, and many died as they were taken from the *St Peter* to the beach and placed in tents made from sails. Bering was rowed ashore on 10 November and given a tent on the beach. In the evening he met with Steller, discussing their likely location and ways to save the ship. The next morning he was moved on a stretcher to a dugout hut next to Steller's. Those healthy enough to work built a hospital for the scurvy victims and brought the remaining provisions from the vessel. On 28 November, the *St Peter* was driven ashore by strong winds and rough seas, its keel buried 8ft deep in sand.

By early December, the whole crew was lodged in five underground huts near a freshwater stream. The ship's provisions were soon exhausted and the men were dependent on meat and plants from the island for their food as the snowy Siberian winter set in. Nine sailors and soldiers had died during and immediately after the landing on the beach, while seven more deaths had occurred by the end of November.

During the first week of December, Bering's condition grew worse from the constant hunger, cold, exhaustion and grief, and he refused to see anyone. On 8 December, the 60-year-old Vitus Bering died two hours before the sun rose over the desolate, windswept island. A wooden coffin was made and after a brief religious service he was buried near his shelter. A wooden cross was later erected over his grave.

After spending the winter on Bering Island, on 9 April 1742, Lieutenant Waxell, who had assumed command of the expedition, met with the survivors and offered them three options for their return to Avacha Bay. After considering the choices, the men decided to build a small ship from the wreckage of the *St Peter* and sail back to the bay. Work on the vessel started and by mid-July the hull was finished. Construction of the new ship, also named *St. Peter*, was completed in mid-August and the vessel launched. On 14 August, the remaining seamen and soldiers began the voyage to the Kamchatka Peninsula. Nearly two weeks later, they reached the harbour on the Russian mainland. Soon after their arrival, the survivors learned that Chirikov's *St Paul* had reached port on 12 October 1741 after discovering the current-day Prince of Wales Island and navigating north-west along the Alexander Archipelago, locating the future Russian port of Sitka. After sailing through the archipelago, the *St Paul* seamen had piloted to the west, past the Kenai Peninsula, Kodiak Island and Adak Island in the Gulf of Alaska, as Chirikov set a course for the Kamchatka Peninsula and Russia.

SELECTED SOURCES:
Brebner, John Bartlet, *The Explorers of North America 1492-1806.*
Frost, Orcutt, *Bering – The Russian Discovery of America.*
Kushnarev, Evgenii G., *Bering's Search for the Strait – The First Kamchatka Expedition.*
Lauridsen, Peter, *Vitus Bering – The Discoverer of Bering Strait.*
Steller, Georg Wilhelm, *Journal of a Voyage with Bering, 1741-1742.*

Daniel Boone

By 1775, Daniel Boone had gained widespread repute as an experienced explorer and frontiersman, and was hired by the Transylvania Company to mark out a route through the Appalachian Mountains from Kingsport, Tennessee, to the Kentucky River in the north central region of the present-day state of Kentucky. In March that year, Boone set out with thirty axe men to fashion a rough path through the wilderness and mountains, providing a trail for the settlement of Kentucky by the colonists from Pennsylvania and western Virginia. The course of the Wilderness Road went west from the Anderson Blockhouse near the Holston River, through Moccasin Gap, across the Clinch River and over the Powell Mountains at Kanes Gap. Boone's workmen carved out a rough pathway to the south-west through the Cumberland Gap, pushing on to the Kentucky River. Day after day, Boone and his workers cleared trees, underbrush and overhanging foliage on the roadway. After its completion, the Wilderness Road became the principal artery for the settlement of the American heartland, over 300,000 pioneers trudging over the trail that Daniel Boone had explored and built.

Daniel Boone was born on 2 November 1734 on his family's farm in Berks County, Pennsylvania, on the western frontier of the British colony, the sixth of eleven children born to Squire and Sarah Morgan Boone. Squire Boone had emigrated from England to William Penn's colony in Pennsylvania in 1712, and was employed as a weaver and part-time blacksmith. The Boones were Quakers and were held in high esteem by their church and community. Through his Quaker frugality and labour, Squire Boone earned enough money to purchase a farm, and young Daniel spent his youth working in the fields and tending herds of cattle. He took every opportunity to disregard his duties and trek through the surrounding woodlands, learning to hunt, trap and the art of survival. When Daniel was 12, his father gave him his first musket, and he quickly developed into an expert marksman. As Daniel grew older, he frequently went on long hunts, travelling into the mountains for several weeks, becoming a skilled hunter and woodsman. He received little formal education but was taught the basics of reading and writing by a family member, though never completely mastering spelling and grammar.

DANIEL BOONE

The French court and the kings of England had long sponsored the exploration of the North American continent, asserting their rights to vast tracts of land. Through the discoveries of cavelier Robert La Salle, the French claimed possession of the Ohio River Valley, while the English maintained that the region was the property of their crown under the terms of the 1609 Virginia Charter. France regarded Ohio as a vital part of its Mississippi River Empire and had built a network of forts to protect its territory from encroachment. As the Boone family became prominent members of the Quakers and their community in Berks County, in 1730 the British began constructing trading posts in the Upper Ohio Valley in defiance of the French, quickly coming into conflict with their rivals. As the dispute over control of the Ohio Valley escalated, in October 1753 the governor of Virginia sent George Washington to Fort Le Boeuf in north-western Pennsylvania to demand the French abandon the headwaters of the Ohio River. The French replied that they planned to take full possession of the country and had no intention of withdrawing.

While the British and French continued to struggle for control of the Ohio Valley, the Boones sold their properties in Berks County in 1750, relocating to the Yadkin Valley in central North Carolina after two of Squire's children married non-Quakers and the family was forced to leave the religious order. Squire Boone purchased over 600 acres of land in current-day Davie County and built a new house for his family. The farm was located on the western frontier and surrounded by dense forests abundant in deer, bear and other game. Daniel had little interest in pursuing a career as a farmer, spending his days hunting and exploring the wilderness country, supplementing the family's income by selling his fur pelts.

In 1754, Daniel Boone joined the North Carolina militiamen to fight against the French in the Ohio Valley as part of George Washington's army, acquiring his first experiences as a soldier. Washington was sent into the disputed area of the Ohio Valley by the British colonial government to establish a crown presence against the French-claimed country. He led his militiamen to the confluence of the Allegheny and Monongahela rivers near current-day Pittsburgh. The colonial troops built a small stockade named Fort Necessity, but were soon driven off in July by the attacks of the French and their Indian allies in the first battle of the seven-year French and Indian War. Boone was part of the small unit sent by the North Carolina government to reinforce Washington, but arrived too late to participate in the fighting.

The British regime remained determined to enforce its territorial rights to the Ohio Valley, and in early 1755 ordered Major General Edward

Braddock to move against the French with two regiments of regulars. When Braddock's infantrymen, augmented with colonial militia, marched against the French at Fort Duquesne near present-day Pittsburgh, the 20-year-old Daniel Boone was serving in the North Carolina Provincials as a wagoner. Braddock's advance from Fort Cumberland in north-western Maryland began on 2 April, with Boone trailing behind the army and artillery with the wagons. During the nights he sat around the campfire talking to his fellow wagoners. He became friends with John Finley, from whom Boone heard fascinating stories about a new territory to the west called Kentucky, with fertile lands of bluegrass and plentiful deer, buffalo and many other game animals, that could be reached through the Cumberland Gap. The tales of Kentucky excited Boone's imagination, firing his desire to travel to the region.

As the British approached the French stockade during the morning of 9 July, with drums and fifes playing martial songs in the bright summer sun, they were attacked by warriors from the Ottawa and Potawatomi tribes hidden in the dense forest on both sides of the trail, while French troops blockaded the pathway ahead. The professional British redcoats attempted to fight as European soldiers, but were cut down by the Indian warriors from behind trees and rocks. When Braddock was mortally wounded during the fighting, Washington took command and ordered a withdrawal. Boone was positioned in the rear with the wagons and equipment, but when the retreating British and militiamen ran through his camp, he jumped on a horse to ride to safety as the Indians charged through the woodlands, yelling and waving their bloody tomahawks. Following the defeat of the British at the Battle of the Monongahela, Boone spent little time in Virginia before making his way back to his father's farm in western North Carolina.

Shortly after his return to Davie County, Daniel Boone renewed his acquaintance with Rebecca Bryan, whom he had first met in the autumn of 1753. Rebecca was described by her contemporaries as a handsome 17-year-old standing nearly as tall as Daniel, with a dark complexion and black hair and eyes. He invited Rebecca to pick cherries with him, and during their time together accidently cut a hole in her apron with his hunting knife Rebecca ignored the incident and Boone considered her reaction as an indication that she had the temperament and qualities for a good wife. Following a courtship that lasted less than a year, they were married at Salisbury, North Carolina, on 14 August 1756 by Squire Boone, who was serving as a justice in the County Court of Pleas. During their fifty-six years of marriage, they developed a close and loving relationship. After their wedding they lived for a brief period in a log cabin on the Boone farm before relocating several miles away to Sugar Tree Creek, settling on Bryan family property. Boone worked as a farmer, while making frequent hunting expeditions in the autumn and winter to supplement his income with the sale of fur pelts.

As Boone lived a quiet life on the frontier at Sugar Tree Creek, the war between the British and French raged on in the Ohio Valley. The Cherokee tribe had agreed to support the British war effort after the promise of many gifts. When the presents were not delivered, the warriors deserted the army and began raiding the border settlements in Virginia and North Carolina, igniting the Anglo-Cherokee War. When the attacks of the Indian war parties intensified in 1758 following the brutal murder of twenty natives by the settlers in retaliation for earlier raids, Boone and his family were compelled to flee to safety in the formidable fortification at Fort Dobbs, North Carolina.

While at Fort Dobbs, Boone again joined the North Carolina Provincials, serving in the army of Brigadier General John Forbes as a wagon master. In the autumn of 1758, Forbes moved his redcoat infantry and colonial militia against the French at Fort Duquesne, with Boone bringing up the wagons in the rear of the column. The British forces advanced directly toward the French fortification through the rough wilderness trails approaching Fort Duquesne in October. The small garrison was greatly outnumbered by Forbes' army and the Frenchmen abandoned the fort, burning it as they retreated toward Canada. The British troops took possession of the smoldering ruins, renaming it Fort Pitt. During the military operation against the fort, Boone killed his first Indian. As he was leading the wagons over the Juniata River bridge, a warrior ran out of the woodlands, attacking him with a knife. Boone grabbed the Indian, throwing him onto the rocks below the bridge.

After the capture of Fort Pitt, Boone moved his family from Fort Dobbs to Culpeper County, Virginia. He supported his wife and children there by delivering tobacco crops from local farmers to market and working part-time as a labourer. Before Boone left North Carolina, he had purchased over 600 acres on Bear Creek from his father and returned there during the winter of 1759 to supplement his income by hunting for deer, beaver and otter pelts as the conflict with the Cherokees continued. During a temporary pause in hostilities, Boone made his first journey across the Blue Ridge Mountains, reaching as far west as current-day Washington County in eastern Tennessee. While on the expedition, he carved the message 'D. Boone cilled a Bar on tree in the year 1760'. Following his return to Davie County, he travelled to Culpeper, selling his furs to the local merchants, earning substantially more than from farming.

In the late summer of 1760, Boone returned to North Carolina to enlist in the army of Colonel Hugh Waddell, who had been ordered to launch a relentless armed campaign to subjugate the Cherokees. The colonials unleashed a fierce attack against the Indians, burning their crops and villages. Boone took part in the offensive, fighting against the Cherokees and forcing them to sign a peace treaty. He was present on 19 November 1760 when the Cherokee chiefs signed an agreement pledging to end hostilities and restore trade.

Soon after the militia was disbanded in North Carolina, Boone led an expeditionary party of Davie County settlers through eastern Tennessee, exploring the headwaters of the Yadkin River and making their way into south-western Virginia near White Top Mountain. The trailblazers climbed to the crest of the 5,500 feet mountain with its commanding view to the west toward Kentucky. Thoughts of Kentucky likely rushed into Boone's mind from the mountain top, reigniting the earlier stories he had heard of the region. After reconnoitring the Holston River into Tennessee, Boone and his men returned home to Culpeper in the spring of 1761.

From Culpeper, Boone travelled back to his farm on Sugar Tree Creek and planted his fields with wheat, corn and tobacco. After harvesting his crops in the autumn, he returned briefly to Culpeper, bringing Rebecca and his children back to North Carolina. Boone continued to make hunting excursions lasting several months, trudging through the Great Smoky Mountains and becoming familiar with the mountains, valleys, rivers and streams. While he farmed his lands, hunted and trapped game for their pelts, gangs of British colonial bandits swept into the county, stealing horses, cattle, tools and equipment. Most of the outlaws were former farmers who had turned to robbery to make easier money. The settlers in the region banded together to form groups of regulators, who aggressively pursued and punished the criminals. Boone joined the regulators and participated in several punitive raids against the robbers' camps. When a neighbour's daughter was kidnapped and held for ransom, he led the vigilantes to the bandits' compound to rescue the young girl. Boone, with a force of regulators, attacked the camp of the rogues, capturing several men and recovering large quantities of stolen goods. The prisoners were taken to the jail in Salisbury for prosecution.

As the area around Bear Creek became increasingly populated and Boone had to travel further into the forest to find good hunting, he and Rebecca sold part of their land in late February 1764. While Boone made plans to relocate his family to a less civilized area to the west, five of his friends from the militia visited him in the summer of 1765 on their way to explore Florida. The territory had recently been ceded to the British regime by Spain, and the crown was giving large tracts of land to new immigrants in the panhandle region to encourage settlement. Boone decided to leave with his friends and combine his annual autumn hunt with a reconnaissance of the Florida country. He was joined by his younger brother, Squire, and brother-in-law, John Stuart, and in August the eight men set out, promising Rebecca to be back in time for Christmas.

The expeditionary party rode south of Salisbury before heading south-east to Savannah and then along the Savannah River into eastern Florida. After crossing the St John's River at Cowford, they travelled the last forty miles to St Augustine. As the frontiersmen explored the panhandle, they found much of the country was swampland and quagmires. They only discovered rich soil close to the rivers, but several hundred yards inland it became too sandy for farming. They trudged across the panhandle, hunting as they travelled. During the journey to the west, the search party continued to pass through areas of barren sandy hills, marshes and swamps. Along the banks of the rivers, they saw rich green foliage with abundant coloured flowers but few locations suitable for farming. In several sections of the route they came across only little wild game and suffered from hunger, while enduring relentless attacks from hordes of insects and avoiding the numerous alligators. When Boone and the men became lost in a dense swamp, they were rescued by a band of Seminoles, who took them to their village, providing food for the hungry strangers. After finally reaching Pensacola, the explorers traded their pelts to offset part of the cost of the expedition, while making inquiries about acquiring tracts of land. Boone found the territory around the Gulf of Mexico appealing, with its feel of a frontier, and before leaving the town he purchased a lot in Pensacola.

The eight travellers set out for home in October, making their way through modern-day Alabama and east through the large virgin pine forests of Georgia. After leaving Fort Moore in Augusta, they followed their earlier trail, reaching western North Carolina four months after their departure. On 25 December, Boone opened the door to his cabin at Sugar Tree Creek, surprising his family. During the Christmas dinner he described his journey to the Florida Panhandle, entertaining his wife and children with descriptions of the unfamiliar alligators, large flocks of seabirds, strange fish, forbidding swamplands and the blue waters of the Gulf of Mexico. When Boone told Rebecca that he had purchased a town lot and planned to move his family to Pensacola, she refused to leave her friends and many relatives or take her children to that inhospitable place. Boone was forced to accept her decision, abandoning his plan to relocate to northern Florida.

In 1763, France and Britain signed the Treaty of Paris, ending the French and Indian War, with the British gaining possession of the country east of the Mississippi River. The British regime ended the war financially impoverished, and to reduce overseas expenses issued the Proclamation of 1763, limiting new settlements in North America to the area east of the Appalachian Mountains. While the proclamation satisfied the interest of the king's government, its American colonials had no intention of being excluded from the rich farming land and profitable hunting territory over the mountains. The region west of the Appalachians known as Kentucky became the focus of many colonists, including Daniel Boone.

Following his return from Florida, Boone spent the spring and summer cultivating his crops of corn and wheat at Sugar Tree Creek, and after harvesting made his annual long hunting expedition into the woodlands. In the spring of 1767 he moved his family to a new farm at Beaver Creek near the Yadkin River, planting and tending his fields. After the harvest, Boone decided to explore Kentucky, and with two other trailblazers set out in the autumn. They journeyed into Virginia, hunting along the Clinch River to its source, and crossed the Appalachian Ridge to reach the Big Sandy River. The hunters followed the river north-west for over 50 miles until they found a salt lick, where the soil had been impregnated with salt seeping up from underground deposits, attracting buffalo herds, near present-day Prestonburg, Kentucky. While at the lick, Boone and his friends were struck by a fierce, unrelenting snowstorm and compelled to remain for the winter. They spent their time hunting and trapping the wild game, while Boone killed his first buffalo around the salt lick. In the spring, the pathfinders returned to their farms on the Yadkin River without realizing they had entered Kentucky.

During the winter of 1768, Boone was visited by John Finley, who had first stimulated his interest in Kentucky during their fireside talks while serving in the militia. Finley had recently returned from a highly successful hunting expedition along the Ohio River, but now needed a guide to take him overland to Kentucky. He told Boone about a trail called the Warriors' Path that the Cherokees used to attack their enemies in the north. On the Indians' way north, they passed through an unknown gap in the Cumberland Mountains into Kentucky, and Finley needed Boone's help in locating the passageway to the hunting forests. Despite the dangers of encountering hostile Indians, Boone immediately volunteered to go on the journey. In early

May, after planting his crops, Boone, Finley and four other men set out to discover the route to Kentucky.

The trailbreakers, carrying their muskets, powder horns and hunting knives, set out with their equipment and supplies loaded on fifteen packhorses, travelling north-west along the course of the Yadkin River. Boone took the men over the Blue Ridge Mountains, and after passing through several gaps reached the Holston River. After following the river they changed direction to the south-west, crossing the Moccasin Gap into the Clinch River Valley. The explorers continued west to the Powell River and followed it south, finally reaching the White Rocks of the Cumberland Mountains, which served as the landmark for the passageway into Kentucky. Boone made many journeys into Kentucky, and the news of his discoveries became widely known in the British American colony. After the discovery of the Cumberland Gap by Boone, it became the primary gateway to Kentucky and the Ohio Valley for more than 300,000 settlers before 1810, when the Ohio River came into wider use as a safer and faster route to the west.

Passing through the gap, Boone and the frontiersmen moved north, crossing the Cumberland River and reaching the Sand Gap near present-day McKee, Kentucky. As the group pushed on, they soon spotted the end of the mountains and the rolling country of Kentucky in front of them after five weeks of trudging through the dense wilderness. Once in Kentucky, the explorers established a base camp on 7 June, calling it Station Camp. Soon after the compound was completed, the men began hunting the plentiful deer along the Red and Kentucky rivers while reconnoitring the new territory. To accumulate more animal hides, they formed two shooting parties, and Boone and his brother-in-law, John Stuart, hunted and trapped together in the thick woodlands to the north. During the next six months, they accumulated large caches of skins worth nearly £100. Boone later wrote of his first experiences in Kentucky that 'Nature was here a series of wonders and a fund of delight.'

While Boone and Stuart were hunting, they were surprised by a band of Shawnee warriors led by a chief called Captain Will on 22 December. Kentucky was the traditional hunting grounds of the Shawnees, and they resented the escalating incursions of the British in their lands. As the warriors surrounded Boone and Stuart, waving their tomahawks, the chief demanded to visit their camp. Boone slowly led the Indians back to Station Camp, showing them several small caches of hides and hoping the noise of their movements would alert the other hunters at the main camp. Captain Will insisted on being taken to the encampment, and Boone reluctantly complied. When they reached Station Camp, the other British had fled into the woods in terror and the Shawnees seized all the animal skins, horses, supplies and guns, leaving them only an old musket and several rounds of ammunition. As the chief rode away, he shouted to the pathfinders, 'Now brothers, go home and stay there.'

As the Shawnees rode off into the woodlands with their deer skins and horses, Boone and Stuart decided to pursue the Indians. During the night, they found Chief Will's campsite and retook several of their pack animals. As they made their way back to Station Camp, the two men were overtaken by Captain Will's warriors and recaptured. They travelled under guard for seven days to the Ohio River before they managed to break their bindings and escape, taking guns and ammunition with them. It took Boone and Stuart several days to return to their base camp, but found it abandoned. They continued south for two more days before overtaking Finley and his companions. To Boone's great surprise, he found his brother, Squire, with the retreating party. Squire had come west to join his brother, bringing additional horses and supplies. With the new pack animals and equipment, Boone along with Squire, John Stuart and Alexander Neely decided to remain in the Kentucky wilderness for the winter, hunting and trapping to avoid returning to North Carolina in debt, while continuing to explore the vast new territory.

Boone and the three other frontiersmen spent the next several months in the dense woodlands, setting their trap lines and hunting. Boone and his brother explored and hunted in the area north of the Kentucky River, while Stuart and Neely travelled to the south. The two brothers built a small log cabin, spending the long cold winter shooting, trapping and exploring in the enormous Kentucky wilderness. In May, Squire Boone loaded the animal pelts on packhorses, returning to western North Carolina to sell the goods. As Daniel waited for his brother's return with additional ammunition and horses, he resumed hunting and reconnoitring the Kentucky Valley and along the Ohio River, while remaining on guard against ambushes by hostile Indians. During his explorations he visited the Blue Licks, marvelling at the immense herds of buffalo that came to the salt fields. When Boone saw signs of Indians, he took cover in the impenetrable canebrake grasses that grew over 20 feet high or hid along the dense swamplands. He had several encounters with hostile warriors, and when trapped on a high bluff was forced to escape by leaping onto a treetop at the bottom of the cliff. Boone greatly enjoyed his life in the forests, writing, 'No populous city, with all the varieties of commerce and stately structures, could afford so much pleasure to my mind, as the beauties of nature I found here.' After spending nearly three months alone in the backwoods, he met his brother as agreed at the old camp site on 27 July 1771. The brothers spent the summer hunting and exploring, and in the autumn Squire returned home again to sell the skins and purchase more supplies. Daniel Boone stayed in Kentucky, searching the new lands and hunting deer, buffalo and bears. In the early winter, when Squire failed to return at the scheduled time, Daniel set out to find him. As Boone trudged eastward through the wilderness on a frigid December day, he saw a large campfire in a clearing and slowly crept forward only to find it was Squire. The brothers continued hunting, while investigating the region around the Cumberland and Green rivers.

After spending the winter in Kentucky, in March 1772 the Boones left the Cumberland Valley and headed home with a large horde of fur pelts. While the brothers were camped for the night near the Cumberland Gap, they were attacked by a band of rogue Indian warriors and forced to flee, abandoning their animal hides. Following the Indian raid, they returned to North Carolina with little gain for the last five months. While the final expedition had ended unprofitably, Daniel Boone had explored much of Kentucky during the past twenty months and knew the territory better than any European.

Following his return to Rebecca and his children, Boone stayed on his farm until early 1773, when he returned to Kentucky for a brief visit. He came home with an increased desire to relocate his family across the mountains. While Boone remained in North Carolina, several new settlements were begun in Kentucky, and fearing the loss of the best lands he began to recruit colonists for his community. He convinced several of his wife's relatives to move to Kentucky, while five neighbour families also agreed to join him. In late September 1773, they set out for their new home in the bluegrass country. The pathway into Kentucky was too narrow for wagons, and the immigrants were compelled to walk single-file with packtrains carrying provisions and supplies. As the pioneers neared Powell's Valley, Boone sent his son, James, and several other men ahead to the outpost in the Clinch Valley to tell them of their coming. After making contact with the settlers, James Boone and his party started back to rejoin his father. At dawn on 9 October, they were attacked by a band of Indians and most of the pathfinders brutally killed. James Boone and Henry Russell were both shot in the hip and slowly tortured to death as their bodies were repeatedly slashed and stabbed by the Native Americans with their knives and tomahawks. The news of the slaughter caused widespread fear among Boone's immigrants, and they decided to end their attempt to establish the settlement in Kentucky.

After the failed attempt to begin a new life in Kentucky, Boone and his family returned to North Carolina. As he stayed on his land, the Shawnees and Cherokees unleashed a series of savage raids against the British settlers along the frontier. The brutality was especially fierce in the region beyond the mountains, and in the summer of 1774 Boone and another experienced woodsman were sent by the colonial government to persuade the remaining frontiersmen in Kentucky to flee. They set out on 26 June, travelling over 800 miles in sixty-two days and warning many Kentuckians of the looming danger. The expedition into the bluegrass country reignited Boone's determination to establish a settlement in the region.

Shortly after his return to western North Carolina, Boone was named a lieutenant in the colonial militia and ordered to raise a company of soldiers to fight the warring Indians. He enlisted a small contingent of men and was sent to reinforce the defences of the Clinch River Valley against Shawnee and Cherokee raiding parties. Boone was actively involved in the pursuit of marauding Indians, and was promoted to captain for his leadership and bravery. The conflict against the Native Americans was finally resolved with the British colonials' victory at the Battle of Point Pleasant, fought near the confluence of the Ohio and Great Kanawha rivers. The Indians from the Shawnee and Mingo tribes led by Chief Cornstalk attacked the Virginia militiamen on 10 October 1774, attempting to stop their advance into the Ohio Valley. After a fierce fight lasting most of the day, Cornstalk was forced to withdraw, allowing the colonists to march into the Ohio Valley. Following the defeat of the Shawnee and Mingo tribes at Point Pleasant, Captain Boone was discharged from the militia in late November.

With peace now restored to the frontier, Judge Richard Henderson renewed his plans to purchase twenty million acres of land from the Cherokees, most of the modern-day state of Kentucky. He formed the Transylvania Company with a group of investors, buying the region with the objective of creating the fourteenth colony. After the defeat of the Cherokees, he held talks with their chiefs and convinced them to sell the land for £10,000. Boone had been earlier hired by Henderson to explore the territory, and after the treaty with the Cherokees was signed at Sycamore Shoals on 17 March 1775, was instructed to recruit a work party of thirty wood cutters to create a passageway through the wilderness to Kentucky.

Later that month, Boone and his thirty axe men departed from Long Island on the Holston River, and began cutting a trail for packhorses to the west from a narrow footpath. They blazed the roadway through Powell's Valley and the Cumberland Gap before swinging north-west to the Rockcastle River.

Day after gruelling day, the woodsmen cleared out trees, underbrush and thick canes. Despite the signing of the peace treaty with the British, not all Indians accepted its terms, and at dawn on 24 March Boone's camp was attacked by a rogue band of hostiles. During the brief fight, the frontiersmen rushed into the woods for safety, but two were killed and one wounded. Work on the trail continued, and by 6 April Boone reached the Kentucky River, completing the initial phase of the Wilderness Road that would eventually extend from Virginia to the Ohio River.

Soon after reaching the Kentucky River, Boone decided to stay in Kentucky and begin construction of his settlement, called Boonesborough, on a stretch of flatland south of the river. The isolated outpost was protected by a stockade, and several log cabins were built for the pioneers. While Boone was erecting the fort, Richard Henderson was slowly following the Wilderness Road with additional frontiersmen, supplies and provisions. On 20 April he reached Boonesborough, but found it too small to accommodate the additional settlers, and the site was moved by 300 yards. Land was cleared and the 200 feet long and 100 feet wide Fort Boone was constructed, with log walls and a blockhouse at each corner.

While the British pioneers in Boonesborough constructed their settlement, prepared for Indian raids and established a representative governing body, war was breaking out between British troops and American colonists along the Atlantic coast. As the hostilities intensified, the crown began supplying and encouraging the Indian tribes in the north-west and south to attack colonial settlements. Despite the growing threat of war, Boone refused to abandon his dream of a Kentucky community, and in mid-June returned to western North Carolina to bring his wife and seven children back to Boonesborough. After reaching home, he remained with his family for several weeks before travelling back to Kentucky with Rebecca, his children and over thirty new recruits, arriving in early September. While Boone was in North Carolina, the Transylvania Company began selling tracts of land for 50 shillings per 100 acres, and the new farmers started clearing the fields and planting corn and wheat, while raising cattle, hogs, poultry and horses.

As the war along the Atlantic coast spread and Indian attacks in the west intensified, many of the new Kentuckians abandoned their lands to return to the east. The Boone family remained at Boonesborough, Daniel continuing to work for the permanent establishment of the settlement. In recent months there had been only several small skirmishes with the Native Americans, and the frontier families grew less cautious. On 14 July, Jemima Boone and the two Callaway sisters went canoeing alone on the Kentucky River. As they paddled slowly down the river, the current grew stronger and pushed them toward the shore. When they reached the riverbank, several Shawnee and Cherokee Indians covered in war paint broke through the long grass and bushes, grabbing the girls and taking them captive, despite their repeated screams. They were forced to travel with the war party as it moved deeper into the wilderness. The girls tried to slow their abductors' progress, while leaving markers for rescuers to follow. When Jemima and the Callaway sisters failed to return home, a search party was quickly organized, Boone leading the men and overtaking the rogue natives after three days. As the Indians camped to cook the meat from a recently slain buffalo, the search party silently crept forward, opening fire with their muskets and killing two hostiles. They then rushed the camp and in the ensuing confusion freed the three girls.

While the settlers at Boonesborough struggled to survive in the wilderness, Richard Henderson continually pressed his claims for the recognition of his Kentucky purchase from the Cherokees before the Virginia House of Burgess, but in December 1776 the delegates declared the region as the westernmost county of Virginia. While Henderson was dealing with the legislators, in the American west the Indians, with the support of the British, were escalating their attacks against colonial settlements, with the pioneers fleeing to North Carolina and Virginia in increasing numbers for safety. In early 1777, Indian raids against Fort Boone increased, and in late April the Shawnees, led by Chief Blackfish, advanced against the stockade with a force of over 100 warriors. They surprised a work party outside the fort, killing one man, as Boone and three other frontiersmen rushed forward to their rescue. The Kentuckians were quickly surrounded by Blackfish's warriors, and Boone ordered his men to charge through the Native Americans and run to the fort. During the ensuing melee, Boone battled wave after wave of charging hostiles, barely escaping death several times, but managed to fight his way back to the safety of the blockhouse.

Unable to take the stronghold by storm, Blackfish decided to pull back into the woodlands, but before leaving he sent his Shawnees to burn the farms and crops and slaughter the livestock, leaving the Kentuckians with only meat from hunting as food. While the Indians abandoned their direct assaults against the stockade, they remained in the nearby wilderness, continuing to unleash surprise raids. Faced with the threat of starvation, Boone and his men were forced to hunt in the forest, in danger of attack by the Shawnee on every expedition. The settlers needed salt to preserve the meat, and in early January 1778 Boone and thirty pioneers left to collect the preservative from the Lower

Blue Licks. As they extracted salt from the water, in early February Boone went hunting. After killing a buffalo, he was surprised by four Shawnee warriors and taken prisoner. He was led to their main camp and turned over to Blackfish and Captain Will. Boone talked with the two chiefs, learning they were preparing to attack the work party at the salt licks. He convinced the chiefs that the woodsmen would surrender if promised fair treatment and exemption from running the gauntlet. The following morning, Blackfish's men surrounded the salt lick and Boone persuaded the Kentuckians to submit. The pioneers were taken to the Indians' camp at Old Chillicothe near the Old Miami River, where Boone and half of the frontiersmen were adopted by the Shawnees. During the ceremony, Boone became the son of Blackfish.

Boone and the other captured pioneers remained at the Indian camp for the next four months, living and hunting with the warriors and their families. In March, the pioneers accompanied Blackfish to Detroit, where the ten non-adopted men were turned over to the British for a large bounty. The British governor, Henry Hamilton, courted Boone's favour, trying to influence him to support the crown's cause in North America. After returning south with the Indians, Boone learned that the Shawnee, Mingo and Delaware tribes were planning to launch a relentless attack on Boonesborough. Fearing his wife and family to be in dire danger, Boone slipped away from a hunting party in mid-June, escaping on a stolen horse. He travelled over 160 miles to the fort in four days. He found that during his prolonged absence, Rebecca had returned to her father's farm in North Carolina with her children, leaving only the recently married Jemima. With the settlement threatened with imminent attack, Boone decided to remain at the stockade and prepare the defences.

Throughout the summer of 1778, the pioneers laboured to strenthen the walls of the fort, finish two blockhouses and reinforce the main gate, while harvesting the corn crop. While work on the stronghold continued, in early September 500 hostiles with their faces covered in bright war paint surrounded Fort Boone. The Native Americans besieged the fortification for eleven days as thundering war cries echoed across the battlefield. The Indians fired wave after wave of flaming arrows into the stockade, but the sixty defenders continued to fight back with their muskets. To give the impression of a larger garrison, Boone had the women dress in hunting clothes and walk about with muskets. The Shawnees and their allies' attempts to scale the walls, set fire to the fort and dig a tunnel were all thwarted by Boone's frontiersmen.

As the settlers continued to hold out, Blackfish offered to negotiate with

Boone. During the meeting with the chief, Squire Boone tried to bluff the Indians into leaving by telling them George Rogers Clark was leading an army to rescue those besieged in Boonesborough. The negotiations with Blackfish were resumed the next day as Daniel Boone and his brother continued to stall the chief. When the talks failed, Blackfish's men attempted to seize the Boone brothers, but they fought free and ran toward the fort's gate. In the melee, Daniel was struck a glancing blow to the back of the head by a tomahawk and Squire was hit in the shoulder by a musket ball. Following the break-up of the negotiations, Blackfish ordered his warriors to storm the fort, but their attacks were repeatedly repelled by the deadly musket fire of the defenders. During the night of 17 September, the Shawnees and their allies unleashed their largest attack, firing arrows, shooting muskets and hurling flaming torches into the fort, but they were thrown back by the Kentuckians' resolve. When the late summer dawn filtered through the trees the following morning, the Indians had disappeared. Two settlers were killed and four wounded during the eleven-day siege, while nearly forty hostiles were slain.

Soon after the Shawnees abandoned their siege of Fort Boone, Colonel Richard Callaway brought formal charges of collaboration with the British against Daniel Boone. Calloway accused Boone of voluntarily surrendering his men at Blue Licks and conspiring with the British to abandon Boonesborough. Following an investigation and court-martial hearing, Boone was completely exonerated of the charges and promoted to the rank of major for his loyal services in the militia. After his acquittal, he returned to western North Carolina in late 1778, finding Rebecca and his children living with his father-in-law, Joseph Bryan. He stayed with his in-laws for nearly a year before setting out with his wife, children and members of the Boone and Bryan families back to Kentucky.

While Boone was away in North Carolina, settlers began surging back into Kentucky following George Rogers Clark's victory with forty-seven soldiers and volunteers over a superior force of British and Indians at Fort Vincennes on 23 February 1779. Emboldened by Clark's defeat of the enemy, an estimated 20,000 pioneers settled in Kentucky during the year. On the morning of 22 September 1779, the Boones and their friends set out for Boonesborough, arriving safely a month later. Daniel Boone's property rights issued by the Transylvania Company were now invalid following the Virginia Assembly's denial of Richard Henderson's claim to the land, and soon after arriving at the fort he appeared at a hearing to establish lawful title to his 1,400 acres. After his ownership was verified, he spent the harsh winter of

1780 with its frequent snowstorms and freezing weather - at the settlement, and in the spring sold his farm, planning to buy warrants for new land. In early 1780, he set out for Virginia to purchase the permits, his saddlebags packed with a large sum of money. Boone made his way to James City, Virginia, where he spent the night at an inn, placing the saddlebags in his room. When Boone woke the next morning, the cash was gone and he had lost everything he had worked for in Kentucky. He suspected the innkeeper had initiated the robbery, but could not prove the accusation and was forced to return to his family at Fort Boone impoverished.

During Boone's absence, the Indians had again escalated their raids against the Kentuckians in support of the British war effort. The British governor of Detroit sent his agents into Kentucky to encourage the hostiles to harass the Americans, and in mid-June 1780, Captain Henry Bird led a contingent of British regulars and Shawnee warriors into Kentucky, quickly overrunning four frontier outposts. The Native Americans increasingly ignored Bird's orders, and many of their prisoners were tortured to death or made slaves. Following Boone's return to Kentucky, he had to fend off several attacks by Shawnee war parties during hunting expeditions.

As the Shawnees continued to raid the settlements with increasing brutality, in late July Boone joined George Rogers Clark in a retaliatory raid against their villages on the Miami River. Clark, with a large force of over 1,000 men, unleashed brutal assaults against the Indians, burning their villages and committing atrocities in revenge. The sorties failed to end the Indians' attacks, and Boone was compelled to fight in several more skirmishes to end their hostilities.

In late 1780, the Virginia legislature divided Kentucky into three counties and Daniel Boone was pressed into service in the newly created district of Fayette. He was appointed to various offices, serving as sheriff, deputy surveyor, lieutenant colonel of the militia and finally representative to the state assembly. In early 1781, he travelled to Richmond to attend the meetings of the legislative body. However, with the approach of British troops the assembly was compelled to reconvene at Charlottesville in May. While the delegates met, British troops led by the notorious Banastre Tarleton advanced against the town, forcing the representatives to flee. Boone and several other men stayed behind to save the official records, and as they departed from Charlottesville, a patrol of dragoons took them prisoner. After questioning by Tarleton, the Americans were confined to a coal house under guard. Several of Rebecca's relatives were loyalists serving with Tarleton and they arranged Boone's release. He rejoined the legislature later in May at Staunton, remaining until the following month before returning to Kentucky. In November, Boone again journeyed to Virginia for the new legislative session, staying until January 1782. By late February, Boone was back in Boonesborough, occupied during the winter supplying food and clothing for the settlers with the meat and hides from his many hunting expeditions, and in the spring planting his fields with corn and tobacco.

In early 1782, British officials in Detroit again supplied arms and encouraged the Indians to raid settlements in Kentucky. There were numerous bloody attacks, with many Kentuckians brutally tortured and killed. In August, Boone led a detachment of men from Boonesborough to the relief of the defenders at Bryan's Station. As the reinforcements advanced toward the stockade, the Shawnees, Cherokees, Delawares, Miamis, Mingos and loyalists led by British captain William Caldwell abandoned their assault against the fort, after burning the crops and killing the livestock. Boone and his militiamen joined other volunteers from two outposts at Bryan's Station, and the combined force of nearly 200 soldiers pursued the hostiles. The Kentuckians moved quickly through the wilderness, and as they followed the Indians' trail Boone grew increasingly suspicious of an ambush. When the Americans approached the Lower Blue Licks, near the Licking River in north-eastern Kentucky, Boone wanted to cross the river further upstream but the frontiersmen were anxious to attack the marauders and moved forward. As they manoeuvred down a small hill, they were struck by the crushing fire of natives hidden in a ravine. The pioneers were soon surrounded, and Boone ordered his troops to break through the enemy's line and run to the river. While Boone advanced toward the river, his son, Israel, was killed and he was forced to leave him, swimming across the Licking River to escape. The shattered American force sustained about seventy-five casualties, inflicting only small losses on the enemy. After the militiamen made their way back to Bryan's Station, Boone took part in a retaliatory expedition in the autumn but failed to decisively defeat the British soldiers and Indians. Nevertheless, the sortie resulted in the break-up of the Native American alliance, reducing the strength and effectiveness of their future attacks.

On 19 April 1783, the Treaty of Paris was signed between Britain and the Americans, ending the Revolutionary War and creating the United States of America. The British stopped supporting and providing arms to the Indians, but the natives' ruthless raids against Kentucky continued for several more years. As the terms of the treaty were being finalized, Boone moved his family to the present-day town of Maysville in north-eastern Kentucky on the Ohio River. New settlers used the river to travel into Kentucky, and Boone established an inn and general store, selling supplies and equipment to the pioneers, while trading ammunition, whiskey and tools for animal hides with the hunters and trappers. At the small settlement he became a deputy surveyor for Fayette and Lincoln counties, receiving half of the acres surveyed for providing a clear title to the buyers. However, Boone's claims were frequently challenged because of his failure to complete the documents or properly register them, resulting in numerous lawsuits. When all the disputes were finally settled in court, he lost title to most of his property. Despite his mounting legal problems and debts, Boone's prominence and reputation as a frontiersman and woodsman became legendary when a brief biography entitled *The Adventures of Colonel Daniel Boone* was published in 1784 by John Filson as an appendix to his book *Discovery, Settlement and Present State of Kentucky*.

As the East Coast Americans intensified their migration across the Appalachian Mountains, Indian raids against the Kentucky settlers escalated. In late May 1786, a large war party attacked the pioneers near the convergence of the Ohio and Kentucky rivers. A retaliatory sortie was launched a few months later, with Boone joining the detachment of Colonel Benjamin Logan. The soldiers moved against the Shawnee villages on the Miami River, catching the warriors by surprise. As the Indians fled into the dense woodlands, they were aggressively pursued by the Kentuckians. During the fighting, the warrior who had earlier tortured to death Boone's son, James, was killed. The military campaign against the Indians continued into 1787, when a peace agreement negotiated by Boone was signed. He had earlier contracted with the Virginia government to supply the needs of Indian prisoners, and netted a handsome profit after the signing of the treaty by providing goods to the captives.

Boone stayed at Maysville managing his businesses, while spending several months on hunting and trapping expeditions. However, legal problems continued to mount, and in 1791 he left Maysville, relocating to Mount Pleasant in current-day West Virginia. The Boones stayed at Mount Pleasant for the next four years, with Daniel occupied supplying goods to the local militia, also serving again in the Virginia legislature and participating in long hunting expeditions. He moved his family back to Kentucky in 1795, settling at Brushy Fork near Blue Licks. The allure of Kentucky among those living in the Atlantic states had remained strong, and thousands of easterners streamed into the territory. Kentucky was admitted to the Union in 1792 as the fifteenth state, and Boone became increasingly constrained by the influx of new settlers, while retaining his dream of owning property. He sent his son, Daniel Morgan Boone, to explore the Missouri Territory in the autumn of 1797. Before he departed Boone asked his son to meet the Spanish authorities to inquire about their terms for acquiring land. After reconnoitering the area north of the Missouri River named Femme Osage, Daniel Morgan called on Don Zenon Tradeau, the Spanish lieutenant governor for Missouri. At the son's request, he wrote a letter to Daniel Boone on 24 January 1798, promising him a large tract of land. By the autumn he had returned to Kentucky, reporting to his father that Missouri was a fertile territory with plentiful game and the Spanish eager to attract more colonists. Daniel had lost most of his property to court decisions and decided to relocate his family to Missouri, where Spanish officials would welcome him as an enticement to attract additional settlers.

Rebecca Boone left Kentucky in September 1799 with her children and several relatives in a 60 feet dugout canoe fashioned out of a poplar tree, while Daniel and two other men drove the livestock overland. When the Boones reached Cincinnati, Daniel was asked why he was leaving Kentucky. 'Too crowded, I need more elbow room,' was his reply. During the journey, they were joined by additional family members, and after travelling down the Ohio River and paddling up the Mississippi, the Boones reached St Louis in October. The pioneers were greeted by the new lieutenant governor, Carlos D. Delassus, in a grand welcoming ceremony. The Spanish authorities were pleased to have the renowned Daniel Boone in Missouri, granting him an 850-acre tract of land, while each new settler received between 340 and 500 acres, depending on the size of their family. Boone and his wife first lived with their son, Daniel Morgan, on his farm 60 miles north of St Louis before erecting their own log cabin. He and Rebecca built a maple sugar mill on his youngest son's property and began earning an income by producing and selling sugar.

In July 1800, Carlos Delassus appointed Daniel Boone magistrate for the Femme Osage area. He now served as judge, sheriff and military leader for the region, while continuing to act as disburser of property to newly arrived settlers. While Boone functioned as governor for Femme Osage, in October 1800 the Louisiana Territory, covering fifteen modern-day American states and two Canadian provinces, stretching from Louisiana in the south to North Dakota and Montana in the north, as well as portions of Alberta and Saskatchewan, originally claimed by the French regime, was ceded back to it by the Spanish. The official transfer was delayed until 1803, and during the interim period French officials paid little attention to their far-off colony, allowing Boone to govern without interference. Besides his fees as magistrate, Boone found the hunting and trapping in Missouri highly profitable, and despite his age, he led numerous expeditions to collect beaver, otter and deer pelts.

Boone greatly enjoyed his first years in Missouri, but in March 1803 the United States purchased the massive Louisiana Territory from the French after Spain officially ceded it to first consul Napoleon Bonaparte. Initially, the Americans made few changes in the government of the Missouri Territory, Boone continuing to serve as magistrate for Femme Osage. During the Spanish administration, he had failed to properly register his property deeds and in December 1809 the American Land Commission denied his rights to the land. In danger of losing his farm again, he wrote to his influential friends in Congress, seeking their intervention. While waiting for the final vote from Congress, Boone and Rebecca temporarily relocated to a room in St Charles, where he had access to a doctor to treat his painful arthritis. When the decision was announced by Congress in 1814, Boone lost all of his property except the original 850 acres granted by the Spanish on his arrival, and fifteen months later he was forced to sell the farm to satisfy his creditors in Kentucky. In the wake of the loss of his land, the Boones were forced to live with their children for the remainder of their lives.

In 1811, Indian attacks against the settlers in Missouri began to escalate under the growing encouragement and influence of the British, who were again increasingly moving toward open hostilities with the Americans. After war was declared the following year, the 78-year-old Boone volunteered for service in the army, and was outraged when his offer was refused. He did serve in the war effort as a sentry, guarding outposts. In mid-March 1813, Boone was grief-stricken by the death of his wife of fifty-six years, burying her on a hilltop overlooking the Missouri River. During the War of 1812, he was forced to flee to safety from the farms of his children on several occasions when the Indians threatened to unleash raids into his area.

By early 1815, the War of 1812 between America and Britain had been resolved, and with its vast plains of fertile lands, numerous rivers, plentiful wild game and Indian raids now on the decline, a new era of mass migration was ushered into Missouri. The settlers followed Boone's footsteps over the Wilderness Road to the Ohio River, and then by flatboats to the Mississippi River and Missouri. In the years between 1810 and Boone's death in 1820, the population of Missouri tripled to over 60,000. In the following years, the great migration across the Appalachian Mountains continued, with settlers pushing across the Great Plains and Rocky Mountains to the Pacific Ocean, following the pathway of Daniel Boone.

As America initiated its great movement to the west, Boone, despite being in his 80s, continued to hunt and explore, travelling over hundreds of miles in the west. He spent his winters in the wilderness, trapping beavers and otters, earning a large sum of money for his pelts. Boone later went back to Kentucky, using his earnings from hunting to repay many of his creditors. Following his return to Missouri, he canoed up the Missouri River to the future state of Kansas, exploring the country while hunting and trapping furs. Boone resumed his expedition, reaching the Platte River and likely visiting the Yellowstone Territory.

In the autumn of 1817, Daniel Boone went hunting again with his grandson, James, and several other men. During the journey, the weather turned bitterly cold and Daniel was forced to return to his granddaughter's cabin at Loutre Lick, near present-day Mineola in north-eastern Missouri, where he became seriously ill. He spent the next few months slowly recovering his health. By the summer of 1818, Boone was well enough to travel to Kentucky, where he finally repaid his last creditors, coming back to Missouri virtually penniless. As the years took their toll on the nearly 86-year-old Boone, he was forced to remain around the farm of his son, Nathan. In June 1820, the artist Chester Harding visited the farm, painting a portrait of Colonel Boone. At first he refused to sit for the painting, but his daughter, Jemima, persuaded him to change his mind. Ever since the aborted 1817 hunting expedition, Boone had frequently been ill with fevers, while his eyesight and hearing had deteriorated. While at Nathan's farm, Daniel Boone became feverish and went to bed in a small room at the front of the stone house. As his condition worsened, in the early morning of 26 September 1820, he told his gathered family that, 'My time has come.' Daniel Boone died just after dawn. He was initially buried alongside Rebecca on a hill above the Missouri River, but in the autumn of 1845 the remains of the Boones were exhumed and reburied in Lexington, Kentucky.

SELECTED SOURCES:
Brown, Meredith Mason, *Frontiersman – Daniel Boone and the Making of America.*
Cavan, Seamus, *Daniel Boone and the Opening of the Ohio Country.*
Faragher, John Mack, *Daniel Boone – The Life and Legend of an American Pioneer.*
Lofaro, Michael A., *Daniel Boone – An American Life.*

Sir Alexander Mackenzie

On 9 May 1793, Alexander Mackenzie, with seven Canadians and two Indian guides, set out from Fort Fork on the Peace River in a 25 feet long canoe to search western Canada for a water route to the Pacific Ocean. Following an arduous journey of 1,200 miles lasting more than two months, on the evening of 19 July Mackenzie's expeditionary force saw the Pacific, becoming the first explorers to cross the North American continent north of Mexico. Three days later, he made a mixture of vermilion and melted grease to write on a large rock, 'Alexander Mackenzie, from Canada, by land, the twenty-second of July, one thousand seven hundred and ninety-three.' The fabled Northwest Passage had finally been completed by canoe and portage across uncharted mountains, rivers and valleys, opening western Canada to exploration, commerce, settlement and development of its natural resources.

Alexander Mackenzie was born in 1764 at the fishing port of Stornoway on the Isle of Lewis in the Scottish Hebrides, the second son of Kenneth and Isabella Maciver Mackenzie. Soon after his birth, the Mackenzie family relocated to a farm several miles away in the agricultural village of Melbost. The Mackenzies had a long history of service to their clan as soldiers and civil officials. Kenneth Mackenzie was an army officer, successful merchant and, as a prominent chieftain in the clan, was awarded sizeable land holdings. Alexander attended the local school, learning to read and write, while studying English, French and the classics. Growing up on the rugged Scottish island, he was an adventurous boy who enjoyed fishing, swimming and engaging in mischievous games with other children.

Shortly after Alexander Mackenzie's birth, Scots began leaving the poverty, unemployment and hardships of their homeland in large numbers, seeking a better life across the Atlantic Ocean in America. Over 20,000 men, women and children departed from the Highlands during the first ten years of Alexander's life. Following the death of his mother sometime before 1774, and in search of greater opportunity, the 12-year-old Alexander Mackenzie was taken to New York City by his father. In November 1774, the Mackenzies boarded the emigrant ship, *Peace and Plenty*, leaving Stornoway Bay for the shores of America, arriving in early 1775. Kenneth Mackenzie's brother, John, and brother-in-law, John Maciver, had earlier sailed to the British colony, establishing a highly profitable mercantile business in New York. After landing in New York, the Mackenzies stayed with their relatives while the city was on the verge of armed rebellion against the British crown. In the spring of 1775, with the threat of war escalating, Kenneth Mackenzie and John Maciver joined the king's army and were appointed to the rank of lieutenant in the Royal York Regiment of New York. Following the enlistment of his father and uncle, Alexander was sent to live with two aunts near Johnstown in the royalist enclave of the Mohawk Valley.

Alexander Mackenzie remained with his aunts in Johnstown for three years, initially attending local schools. When the Revolutionary War erupted in April 1776, he joined the royalist militia, serving in the town's company. As a soldier, Mackenzie defended the Mohawk Valley against incursions by the rebels, taking part in the fighting while learning to survive in the wilderness. Despite the efforts of the loyalists, the insurgents increasingly gained control of the area, burning the villages and farms and forcing Mackenzie and his aunts to flee to safety at the British haven of Montreal in Canada.

The British had gained control of Canada under the terms of the 1763 Treaty of Paris, which ended the French and Indian War. Montreal, located on the St Lawrence River, was at the centre of the Canadian fur trading business. After attending school for a year, Mackenzie was hired by the countinghouse firm of Finley and Gregory as a bookkeeper. He spent the next five years working in the company's headquarters and warehouses, occupied with the routine duties of an auditor, preparing reports, filing papers, copying letters and learning the accounting practices. During his years with Finley and Gregory, he acquired an understanding of government regulations, the financial secrets of fur trading and the practices and tactics of rival firms, while mastering every aspect of the business. As part of his job, Mackenzie made numerous journeys to the firm's far-flung outposts in western Canada. During his trips, he studied the region's rivers, mountain ranges, valleys, vegetation, wild animals and the customs and ways of the Native Indians.

Mackenzie had worked hard and diligently to learn the fur trading business, and in 1784 his accomplishments were recognized by the firm. The two partners entrusted him with a small portfolio of goods, sending him to Detroit to begin his fur trading career. At Detroit, he favourably impressed the company and was offered a minority partnership in the organization. In the spring of the following year, he was assigned to the fur trading centre at Grand Portage on the western shore of Lake Superior. Grand Portage was an important base of operations for Finley and Gregory, serving as a trans-shipping point to the east. The outpost was located at the western limits of

English authority, and had a reputation for lawlessness and turmoil. Grand Portage was established by the North West Company at the mouth of the Pigeon River, which by 1784 had become the wilderness capital of the fur trading business, developing into a meeting place for firms to transport supplies and equipment from Montreal and hunters to bring their furs from the woodlands to sell. At the beginning of winter, the local Indians came to the fort to be outfitted for the trapping season on credit. The amount of debt accumulated by the trappers was calculated in terms of adult beaver pelts. A musket cost fourteen skins, a blanket six and an axe or trap two. The post was protected by a 6 feet high palisade with a bastion and heavy gate. Located inside the stockade was the great hall, houses, barracks, shops, warehouses and a stone powder magazine.

Shortly after reaching Grand Portage, Mackenzie was assigned by the firm's partners to the outpost in the Isle-a-la-Cross region of north-western Saskatchewan to assume the duties of Joseph Frobisher as head fur trader. Isle-a-la-Cross was a small village and fort on a peninsula of the Churchill River. The fort served as the administrative centre for the English River District of the fur trading companies, and an important supply depot on the route of the hunters and trappers. Mackenzie journeyed to the west, using the area's many rivers to reach his new posting. He continued his accounting duties at the frontier depot, keeping records and directing operations, while sending the firm's agents on expeditions to collect pelts from the local Indians and search for additional sources of furs. His predecessor had earlier established the tactic of intercepting natives as they travelled east to Hudson Bay to trade their goods with the Hudson Bay Company, convincing them to exchange them nearby at Frog Portage. Taking charge at the Churchill River depot, Mackenzie continued to follow this policy, dispatching his men to divert and trade with the Indians. Several rival businesses had sent brokers into the Isle-a-la-Cross country, and to outmanoeuvre his competitors Mackenzie built a series of small outposts in the wilderness to expand the territory covered by his agents.

While at Isle-a-la-Cross, Mackenzie made friends with a Chipewyan chief called the English Chief, who was the head of the largest tribe trading their pelts at the fort. When the English Chief arrived at the fort in April 1786, his appearance with over forty warriors virtually ensured a successful season for Mackenzie's outpost. The chief was familiar with the geography and various native tribes along the Churchill River, and Mackenzie talked at length with him, learning the topography of the many rivers, mountains and valleys to the west. He further discovered the safe routes to travel through the rugged terrain, while acquiring an understanding of the different Indian alliances and power struggles. The English Chief was well known to the explorers and traders, and Mackenzie greatly valued his knowledge and friendship, considering him the individual with the most knowledge about travelling in the wilds of western Canada.

As Mackenzie and his fellow fur traders continued to expand the operations of the company into western Canada, they came into increasing conflict with agents from the North West Company. He later wrote in his *General History*, 'After the severest struggle ever known and suffering every oppression which a jealous and rival spirit could instigate, after the murder of one of our partners, the loss of another, and the narrow escape of one of our clerks, who received a bullet through his powder horn in the execution of his duty, the North West Company were compelled to allow us a share of the trade.' The two companies had been illegally transporting gallons of whiskey and wine out of Montreal to entice the Indians into trading with them. When news of the resulting violence by the natives caused by their drinking sessions reached government officials in Quebec, they threatened to withhold the annual licences necessary to trade unless the companies acted together. In the summer of 1787, the partners from the two businesses, including Mackenzie, met at Grand Portage, agreeing to take the Gregory, McLeod and Company traders into the North West Company. The North West was a federation of several firms in the fur trading business, who agreed to turn the buying and selling of animal pelts into a highly profitable monopoly. Wintering partners in the firm were called Nor'Westers, and had a reputation for their unrelenting opposition to non-members of the firm, threatening their competitors with violence, raiding their supplies and using force or liquor to convince the Indians to deal with them.

Shortly after becoming a Nor'Wester in 1787, Mackenzie was assigned to the Athabasca River region in present-day Alberta, western Canada. He was sent to the company's fur-rich Athabasca District as second-in-command to the experienced and highly successful Nor'Wester, Peter Pond. When Mackenzie was ordered to spend the winter season with Pond, he gave instructions for his men to prepare the canoes and pack the supplies, muskets and ammunition for the 2,000-mile journey to the northwest. He left the supply depot at Grand Portage, journeying several miles overland to his waiting flotilla of boats on the Pigeon River. The canoemen were dressed in their working clothes of deerskin leggings, loose-fitting shirts and moccasins, with long hair to the shoulders to protect against the multitude of insects, and were ready to begin the gruelling journey. The mostly French-Canadian canoeists were well-known for their physical endurance and stamina, and were expected to paddle fifteen hours a day, with only two breaks for meals and several short rest periods. After examining the canoes and Indian trading goods of metal tools and knives, muskets, ammunition and liquor, Mackenzie ordered his trailbreakers to load the boats and set out on the expedition to Fort Athabasca by way of the Pigeon River.

The first leg of the journey was the most difficult, travelling over 600 miles through what the British called the North-west Road, a scattered and confusing network of lakes spread across the wilderness. From the Pigeon River, the men moved along the North-west Road, crossing the shallow waters of Lake Winnipeg to its north-western corner, where they entered the mouth of the Saskatchewan River after making a long, hard portage. The Canadians moved up the river paddling against the current, while avoiding the outpost of their Hudson Bay Company rival. After passing their competitor, the expeditionary force trudged north to join the Churchill River. Mackenzie and his pathfinders spent several weeks canoeing up the waterway, finally arriving in the Athabasca territory and Pond's woodland outpost on 21 October 1787.

During the annual meeting of the North West Company's senior traders at Grand Portage, Peter Pond had agreed with the firm's managing partners to stay one more season at Fort Athabasca before relinquishing control of the department to Mackenzie in 1788. The new Nor'Wester spent the next months learning from Pond how to manage the day-to-day operations of the company, while visiting the outposts and meeting with the numerous Native American tribes. During Pond's nine years at the fur trading centre, he had established a far-reaching network of smaller outposts north of Lake Athabasca and formed trading agreements with the local Chipewyan, Slave, Beaver, Dogrib and Yellowknife tribes. The region contained two large rivers, and their many tributaries created easy accessible routes for the firm's agents to contact the scattered Indians. The waterways and snow forest served as a natural breeding ground for the large numbers of fur-bearing animals, making the Athabasca area the most profitable of the North West Company's trading posts.

While Mackenzie gained experience in managing the trading centre under Pond's direct supervision, he also spent many long nights discussing the region's topographic features with him. Pond had explored the Athabasca area extensively, and gave details of his discoveries and travels to Mackenzie. He had made maps of the rivers, mountains and valleys, while becoming increasingly interested in the unknown territories to the west and the possible existence of a North-west Passage to the Pacific Ocean and a water route to the Arctic Ocean. Pond heard stories from the natives that the Peace River ran from its source in the Rocky Mountains, and was part of a water system that drained north-west through Lake Athabasca and the Great Slave Lake to a great frozen sea. He had studied James Cook's maps and papers from his voyage to the Pacific in search of an outlet for the North-west Passage, becoming convinced that a large estuary on one of the charts marked the end of a great river from the east. Peter Pond believed the river on James Cook's maps that marked the end of the North-west Passage had to originate in the Athabasca territory to the north of the trading centre. Included in Pond's numerous maps was a drawing of a large waterway flowing to the Pacific north-west, marked as Cook's River. From his many discussions with Pond, and after studying his charts, Mackenzie became obsessed with the discovery of the North-west Passage to the Pacific. He was determined to lead an expeditionary force from Athabasca, confident it would be a profitable venture for the North West Company.

In January 1788, Mackenzie began making plans for his journey of exploration to the west. In order to leave his trading centre for an extended period, he needed a confident and trusted replacement, asking his cousin, Roderick, who also worked for the North West Company, to transfer to Athabasca. Roderick Mackenzie at first refused to come to Athabasca, but after his cousin told him that the project would be abandoned if he did not agree, the offer was accepted. Shortly after Roderick Mackenzie's arrival, his Nor'Wester cousin sent him to supervise the construction of a new depot on the southern shore of Lake Athabasca. As fur trading with the local Chipewyan Indians had accelerated in recent years, Mackenzie decided to build a new fort named after the tribe to expand trading opportunities along the Peace River. Roderick chose a strategic site for Fort Chipewyan, and following its completion the English firm's traders had a highly profitable first season buying and selling furs.

By late summer 1788, with Roderick now in charge at Fort Athabasca, Alexander Mackenzie devoted all his efforts to recruiting the men and acquiring the equipment and supplies for the passage down the modern-day Mackenzie River to the Pacific Ocean. In mid-December he moved to Fort Chipewyan, and was occupied during the following months with the preparations for the summer expedition, studying maps and talking with traders and local Indians about the territory to the west. Acting under the authority of the North West Company, Mackenzie was making the journey for financial reasons to find a less expensive and easier way of transporting the enormous amounts of Indian trading goods to the various outposts in the north-west of Canada. The cost of transportation was a significant expense to the company, and Mackenzie was determined to increase the profit margins. He later wrote in his book *Voyages from Montreal*, 'Transportation to and from the most distant parts of Athabasca occupies an extent of from three to four thousand miles through upwards of sixty large lakes and numerous rivers, and the means of transport are by slight bark canoes. It must also be observed that these waters were intercepted by more than two hundred rapids, along which the articles of merchandise are chiefly carried on men's backs and over an hundred and thirty carrying places, from twenty five paces to thirteen miles in length.'

At 9 am on 9 June 1789, Mackenzie set out from Fort Chipewyan with four French-Canadian trailbreakers, two of whom travelled with their Indian wives, and a German named John Steinbruick in one of the three birchbark canoes. The English Chief with two of his wives was in the second boat, while the third was manned by two of the chief's followers. The Chipewyans were along to serve as hunters and interpreters. Mackenzie's canoe was larger than the other two, measuring 32 feet in length. His boat carried a crew of four paddlers, and was designed to hold a cargo of over twenty packets of trade goods, along with personal items and an emergency supply of corn and dried meat pounded and compressed with fat. All three canoes were outfitted with masts and canvas sails, punting poles and tow lines. Before leaving the fort, Mackenzie rechecked the boats and equipment, ensuring all ordered items were onboard the canoes.

The North West Company's expeditionary force began the journey from the north-western end of Lake Athabasca, paddling north to join the Slave River at its confluence with the Peace River. During the first day, the expedition party travelled nearly 36 miles, but the following day they covered 80 miles. After setting up his camp for the night, Mackenzie usually led his Indian hunters in a search for game animals and birds for the evening meal. They hunted the plentiful geese, ducks and deer, or fished the rivers and streams for whitefish. While Mackenzie hunted in the wilderness, the canoes were carried ashore and the explorers spent considerable time recaulking the seams and joints or making other needed repairs.

After entering the Slave River, travel was slowed by frequent rapids and waterfalls, but Mackenzie pushed his trailbreakers onward through the wilderness terrain. They were compelled to make six portages around the obstacles, carrying their canoes and supplies overland for a total of 2½ miles. After completing 30 miles through the difficult landscape, he made camp after 5 pm with his men exhausted from the day's paddling and carrying the equipment. The following day, the weather grew increasingly volatile with strong headwinds, snow and rain. As the storm grew stronger, Mackenzie was forced to order his men to remain at the camp. When the weather cleared, Mackenzie's party continued down the Slave River, working from 3 am until 9 pm in the long daylight of the sub-Arctic summer. In the early days of the journey, snow often fell, and during the four-hour night the men woke to find the river frozen. Despite the snow, freezing rain and strong headwinds, early on 9 June they reached the Great Slave Lake, discovering it covered with ice except along the shoreline. Mackenzie was forced to wait several days for the rain and robust winds to begin breaking up the ice. He resumed the expedition, slowly pushing north from lake island to island, reaching the mainland on 23 June. It was dangerous crossing the lake, and the canoeists had to carefully paddle around the many ice floes, avoiding tearing holes in the skins of the birchbark boats. In spite of the cold temperatures, the expeditionary force was tormented by the multitude of mosquitoes, compelling Mackenzie to remark later that, 'They visited us in greater numbers than we would wish as they are very troublesome guests.'

Shortly after landing on the north shore of the Great Slave Lake, the pathfinders met several Indians from the Yellowknife tribe. Mackenzie questioned them about the location of the river that flowed out of the lake's western end. The natives only wanted to trade their beaver pelts for English metal goods, and the men became engaged in lively bartering. However, Mackenzie continued to talk to the Yellowknife warriors about the site of the river and they finally provided a guide to take him there. The Indian first led them to a large bay, but they did not find a river. The following day he showed Mackenzie's party another bay, but it also had no outflowing river. With the Yellowknife guide continuing to lead the explorers, they spent several more days in fruitless searches. Unknown to Mackenzie and his explorers, the local Yellowknife warriors believed an evil monster guarded the river's entrance, and only when the English Chief threatened to kill the guide out of frustration would he finally lead them to the location of the waterway.

Finally, on 29 June, the expeditionary party entered the westward-flowing Mackenzie River, a powerful current and strong breeze from the east driving it downriver under sails. Mackenzie set his latitude at 61° 47' North, the approximate location of Cook's River on Peter Pond's charts. By early July, the explorers had journeyed down the river for over 250 miles. Mackenzie was now expecting to see the Rocky Mountains any day, and follow the waterway to the Pacific Ocean through a pass in the mountains. During the journey, he made careful notes in his journal describing the area's rich soil, dense woodlands, types of vegetation and abundance of wild animals, while again mentioning the swarms of mosquitoes.

As the English party sailed and paddled down the river, as the early fog slowly disappeared on the morning of 2 July, Mackenzie and his men saw a large mountain ahead. He later wrote that, 'At nine we perceived a very high mountain which appeared on our nearer approach to be rather a cluster of mountains, stretching as far as our view could reach to the southwest, and whose tops were lost in the clouds.' Thus far the outward journey had followed Pond's maps and descriptions of the region, but after canoeing down the waterway for several more days the river began to swing more to the north near the current-day Camsell Bend, the canoes travelling parallel to the line of snowy mountains. Mackenzie noted in his logbook the disappointing change of direction, but decided to continue following the river in the hope it would again turn westward toward the Pacific.

On 5 July, Mackenzie went ashore to speak with a band of local Dogrib and Slave warriors. When he asked them how far the great sea was, they told him it would take several winters to reach the body of water to the west. When the English Chief heard the news, he threatened to leave the search party and return to his homeland. Mackenzie was forced to intervene, convincing his friend and his followers to remain with the expedition. The following day the journey was renewed and the explorers continued to meet more Slave and Dogrib warriors, who were unwilling to act as guides for the voyage north, telling Mackenzie's men stories of horrible devils that lived further downriver. He finally bribed a Dogrib with an iron kettle, axe and knife to join the expedition as guide.

When Mackenzie took his latitude readings on 10 July, he calculated that they were at 67° and 47' North, which was further toward the Arctic Ocean. The reading only confirmed that he was nowhere near Cook's River or any of its tributaries, making it certain that it could not be a route to the Pacific. Mackenzie wrote in his logbook, 'Being certain that my going further in this direction will not answer the purpose of which the voyage was intended, as it is evident these waters must empty themselves into the Northern Ocean.' The Nor'Wester questioned his guide about additional rivers in the area, but he knew of no others. According to the Indian, they would reach the northern sea in less than ten days. Mackenzie decided to push on, 'To the discharge of these waters, as it would satisfy peoples [sic] curiosity tho' not their intensions.' With food supplies beginning to run low and the short Arctic summer soon ending, his men urged him to turn back now, but Mackenzie prevailed upon them to resume the journey.

As the trailbreakers paddled northward, the Mackenzie River began to widen and flow through numerous channels, which were formed by islands, creating a large delta area. Mackenzie and his men spent the next few days in the river delta, struggling through dense fogbanks and avoiding dangerous ice floes that could easily rip holes in their canoes. The water remained fresh, but it ebbed and flowed with the tide, suggesting the expedition had reached the Arctic Ocean. As the explorers journeyed across the delta, they saw numerous Eskimo camps on the islands, but they darted away refusing to talk to them. On 14 July, Mackenzie established his camp on an island in the delta he called Whale Island, present-day Garry Island, named for the large number of white whales seen in the vicinity. During the night the water rose, flooding the encampment, and Mackenzie finally realized his search party had reached the Arctic Ocean.

While the North West Company's expedition paddled along the shoreline of the Arctic Ocean, Mackenzie attempted several times to make contact with the local Eskimos, but was never able to speak to them. On 16 July, he made a last search for the Eskimos among the delta's islands before deciding to return to Fort Chipewyan. The short Arctic summer was nearly over, and with his food supplies almost depleted he needed to backtrack up the Mackenzie River as quickly as possible to avoid the onset of winter.

The journey back to Athabasca was now a race against the freezing weather before the expedition became stranded by icefields in the wilderness for the winter. Mackenzie pushed his men hard, testing the limits of their endurance and stamina. They were forced to travel against the strong current, and day after day when no progress could be made by paddling the explorers spent long hard hours pulling the canoes through shallow waters, stumbling over slippery rocks. During the return voyage, the weather varied greatly from one day to the next, shifting from oppressively hot to biting cold. Despite the hardships, the explorers averaged 30 miles a day upriver. On the way home, Mackenzie stopped briefly just beyond the entrance of the Great Bear River to explore the burning lignite beds, while further upriver he found pieces of petroleum wax, suggesting the presence of oil deposits.

Despite the failure to locate the North-west Passage to the Pacific, Mackenzie still believed in its existence, and during the return journey to Fort Chipewyan began planning for a new expedition to the west. As they trudged slowly up the Mackenzie River, he continued to visit the local Indian villages, talking to the warriors about the rivers and mountains to the west. From the natives at a Dogrib encampment, he heard stories about a long river on the other side of the mountain range that flowed into a vast lake. The area was populated by a race of evil giants, who made large canoes and trapped a red beaver. From the river natives' descriptions, Mackenzie believed the giants were fur traders from Russia and the red beavers were sea otters. While talking to the Indians at another village, a warrior sketched a map showing a fort at the mouth of a large river. The drawing was interpreted by Mackenzie as showing Cook's River and a fort built by the Russians that Peter Pond had earlier discussed with him named Unalaska.

As Mackenzie continued to delay the departure to meet with other river Indians, the English Chief became concerned that he would be encouraged to change direction back to the west and renew the search for the passageway to the Pacific, despite the approach of winter. They were eager to return to Athabasca and were increasingly aggravated by the delays. The dissension among the crewmen affected their relationships, and they began to argue among themselves, even abusing the natives and stealing from them. Mackenzie was still determined to collect as much information as possible, and took a small canoe to explore by himself and talk to more river Indians. However, the tribes had left the river region for the annual caribou hunt, and he could not locate any natives to speak to. Still undeterred, he climbed a high mountain near the Camsell Bend to search for the western waterway from the peak, but saw no rivers. When all his attempts to find new information failed, Mackenzie was forced to resume the journey upriver to home.

By mid-August, as the North West Company's expedition reached the Great Slave Lake following a difficult journey, the weather began to turn colder, with frequent rain and hail. During the lake crossing in a violent storm, Mackenzie's large canoe took on too much water and nearly sank. In spite of the many obstacles, the explorers pressed on up the river, and were near the confluence with the Peace River when it started to snow on 10 September and the ground froze hard at night. After reaching the river, Mackenzie's men hurried to Fort Chipewyan and on the afternoon of 12 September, as a light snow fell, they reached the stockade to complete a voyage of just over 3,000 miles in 102 days.

Despite successfully making a journey of exploration covering the entire length of the second largest river on the North American continent, exploring the coastline of the Arctic Ocean and discovering the northern range of the Rocky Mountains, Mackenzie was disappointed by his failure to reach the Pacific Ocean. When he attended the annual conference of the Nor'Westers at Grand Portage in the following year, his expedition was largely ignored. While he had not met the goal of the Pacific Ocean project, Mackenzie was rewarded at the meeting by the North West Company with a second partnership share in the firm.

At Fort Chipewyan, Mackenzie soon began preparing for a second expedition to search for the North-west Passage, while working with Roderick to expand the company's fur trading business along the Mackenzie River. During the first venture he had little trouble determining his approximate latitude, but had no instruments to calculate the longitude. Recognizing his inadequacies as a geographer, he travelled to Montreal in 1791 and boarded a ship for England to study map-making, astronomy, mathematics and navigation during the winter and spring. While in London, he learned how to use the latest astronomical instruments and purchased the best ones for his next expeditionary force. During his stay in England, he attended Cambridge University, studying geography in preparation for the journey to the west. He spent time speaking to fur trading merchants, while reading all the accounts of James Cook's voyage along the Pacific coast, studying the terrain features. He returned to Fort Chipewyan in the late summer of 1792 with an expanded understanding of how to determine the longitude, bringing a sextant, compass, chronometer, azimuth and telescope to use in establishing his location.

Before sailing from England, Mackenzie sent word to Roderick at Fort Chipewyan to begin construction of another fort far up the Peace River to serve as a forward base of operations for the journey to the Pacific. Following his return to the fort, he finalized his preparations for the Pacific Ocean undertaking, and set out across Lake Athabasca on 10 October. Two days later he began travelling up the Peace River to spend the winter months at the new encampment. After paddling 250 miles to the west, his expedition reached what was called Fort Fork at the union of the Peace and Smoky rivers, arriving on 1 November as the first snows began to fall. The construction party sent earlier by his cousin had cut timber into planks and worked on the fortifications. Using the precut planks, Mackenzie set his men to work building log cabins, storehouses and the fort's walls, hiring nearby Indians to hunt beaver to send back to Roderick at Fort Chipewyan. He spent the winter with his six French-Canadian paddlers and Alexander Mackay, who served as his second-in-command. During the winter, the fort was regularly visited by local Indians. The natives were from the Beaver and Rocky Mountain tribes, who were renowned in the region for their hunting skills, prompting Mackenzie to take two of them on the Pacific trek as hunters and guides.

On the evening of 9 May 1793, Mackenzie's expeditionary force left Fort Fork, heading west up the Peace River. They journeyed in a single large canoe that was 25 feet long and 4 feet 9 inches wide. In the boat were provisions, muskets, ammunition, baggage and goods as gifts for the Indians, a total of

3,000 pounds, according to Mackenzie's later accounts. Despite the weight of the canoe, two men could carry it for 3 or 4 miles over an easy portage without resting.

Despite the freezing weather and leaks in the canoe, the first ten days on the Peace River passed without incident. Mackenzie noted the beauty of the countryside, writing in his logbook, 'The magnificent theatre of nature has all the decoration which the trees and animals of the country can afford it. The whole country displayed an exuberant verdure.' His Indian hunters had little trouble finding game, bringing elk and buffalo to the encampments for meals. On 12 May, the expedition party camped with a band of Mountain Indians, who told Mackenzie that it was possible to reach a large westward-flowing river beyond the mountain range with only a short portage. The news greatly lifted the spirits of the explorers.

Several days after leaving the Mountain Indians' camp, the expedition entered a section of the Peace River that was a succession of rapids, cascades and waterfalls stretching for 22 miles, with much of the way through a narrow canyon reaching over 1,000 feet high in some places. Ignoring his guides' advice to portage around the obstacles, Mackenzie ordered his pathfinders to continue upriver. Due to the many swift-running rapids, they were soon forced to pole and tow the heavy canoe from the shoreline for several miles, struggling against slippery rocks in the water and loose ones on the narrow banks of the canyon. As the explorers then paddled west, the river turned into a steady flow of whitewater, compelling the men to portage 10 miles over six days to avoid the dangerous waters.

Shortly after leaving the Peace River canyon, their progress was slowed by the strong river current and pathfinders were forced to make frequent stops to repair the canoe and replace broken equipment. During the long days, the explorers struggled against the fast current, pulling their paddles stroke after stroke, while the biting sub-Arctic winds swept against their faces and chilled their bodies. As the trailblazers journeyed to the west, snow-capped mountain tops began to appear on either side of them on the horizon. Despite the spring season, the weather remained cold and the men still had to wear their heavy coats. The mountain ranges slowly grew larger, and Mackenzie knew they had reached the Rocky Mountains. By the end of May, the expeditionary force had passed through the Rockies. Despite frequent rainstorms, a slow advance and cold weather, they continued the upriver voyage and finally reached the point where the Parsnip and Finley rivers came together to form the Peace River. The canoemen wanted to take the Finley River to the south, but remembering that an old Indian had told him to travel up the northern tributary, Mackenzie followed that advice and ordered them to take the current-day Parsnip River.

During their first day on the Parsnip River, the expedition could only travel 3 miles due to the strong current, delays to make repairs and choppy waters. The men grew increasingly disgruntled at the endless work and slow progress, compelling Mackenzie to intercede to calm their discontent and discouragement, writing, 'I delivered my sentiment in such a way as to convince them that I was determined to proceed.'

After struggling upriver for eight days, Mackenzie became anxious to locate the portage that the old Indian had told him would lead to a great river. His doubts mounted as they continued to paddle to the west, but on 9 June they came upon a band of Sekani warriors. After befriending the natives, Mackenzie asked them about the passageway to a large sea. Taking a piece of bark, one of the Sekanis drew a map showing a route across several lakes, with frequent portages, to a small river that led to a large body of water.

Armed with this new information, the expedition set out again with their spirits lifted, and following several days on the Parsnip the river grew narrower and shallower, becoming no more than a stream. The travellers soon found the first lake that the Sekani had described, and started across the waterway. The canoe now floated easily over the water, made high by the melting snow. At the far end of the small lake, Mackenzie located a well-used and beaten down Indian trail, following it to the present-day Pacific Lake. During the trek to the second lake, Mackenzie and his expeditionary force crossed the Continental Divide, becoming the first Europeans to do so this far north. Mackenzie knew that the waterways would now run to the west and the Pacific Ocean.

The explorers crossed the Pacific Lake and began paddling down a stream. they found at the far end. Just after the brilliant orange and red rays of the sun broke over the eastern horizon and filtered through the dark green leaves of the sub-Artic forest, Mackenzie had his men ready to begin another long day that could last until eight or nine o'clock at night. As they continued on the waterway, they encountered fallen trees, large boulders and rapid currents. The trailblazers were compelled to clear away trees, underbrush and debris, slowing their progress. Navigating the stream, they were forced to carefully guide their canoe around dangerously sharp rocks that could easily rip a hole in the bottom of the boat's thin birchbark cover. As they paddled on, a sudden surge of current drove the canoe sideways, slamming it into boulders. Before they could regain control of the boat, it suffered a shattered stern and bow and multiple holes across the bottom. After reaching the creek's shore and establishing an encampment, Mackenzie spent the next two days making repairs, patching the large gashes with birchbark and using oilcloth to fill the smaller holes.

The trailbreakers resumed their journey on 15 June, making only 3 miles through the many fallen trees, dense underbrush, thick fog and heavy rains. The following day they portaged around several waterfalls, crossing through swamplands in hip-deep mud and travelling only 2 miles. The next day the misery continued as they made their way back to the stream. Reaching the waterway, they paddled downstream until they were again forced to portage around impassable obstacles. Late in the evening, the explorers finally reached what appeared to be a navigable waterway. The expedition had arrived at the headwaters of the Fraser River, and in the morning the men set out down the river, driven by its strong current. By late June, the canoe had become so unmanageable from the earlier damage that Mackenzie had to abandon it and build a new one.

As they journeyed on, Mackenzie made frequent stops to talk to the local Carrie Indians. He found the natives friendly and eager to direct him to the Pacific. From the Carries he learned that the Fraser flowed for many miles to the south before finally turning west. He had grown increasingly convinced that the waterway was not Cook's River after comparing his current latitude calculations of 52° North to Peter Pond's estimations of 56° based on Captain Cook's maps. Mackenzie was determined to reach the ocean that summer, deciding to abandon the river and head overland on an Indian trail that ran west. He had heard from the natives that they used the pathway to trade their beaver, bear and fox pelts to foreigners in huge ships. When Mackenzie first disclosed to his men that they were backtracking to reach the trail, they were reluctant to agree, but after telling them that if necessary he would continue alone, they gave their approval.

Mackenzie led his men back upriver, and by early July they had reached the trail to the Pacific that the Carrie Indians had earlier told them about. He convinced a Carrie warrior to join the expedition and serve as guide to the coast. During the overland trek, the trailbreakers carried their muskets and ammunition on their backs, along with 90 pounds of provisions and supplies, while Mackenzie's load consisted of dried meats, personal arms and scientific instruments weighing 70 pounds. Near the junction of the Frazer and West Road rivers, the expeditionary force set out to the west, following the well-beaten Indian pathways. After travelling through the West Road Valley, they trudged up the Ulgako Creek, a tributary of the West Road, advancing to the Tanya Lakes. Pressing on, the pioneers began to meet Indians who wore

English coins on their ears, which they said they had acquired on the coast from foreign men in great white ships. As they continued to follow the pathway, they climbed into the Pacific Coastal Range that stretched along the west coast of the North American continent from Alaska to central Mexico in a series of mountain ranges. Late on 17 July, after hours of climbing, they crossed through a narrow pass, now known as the Mackenzie Pass, at 6,000 feet. They descended the western side into a deep gorge, encountering warriors from the Bella Coola tribe at their village. Mackenzie noted in his logbook that the Indians lived in large wooden longhouses, 100 feet long and 40 feet wide, that were raised 10 feet off the ground on wooden poles to protect against flooding from the Bella Coola River. The longhouses were divided into separate sections for several families, with a communal room in the centre. The Bella Coola men, women and children were well dressed in fine clothes, and Mackenzie was greatly surprised by the detailed workmanship of their materials. From his observations of the Indians, he believed they were greatly dependent on the nearby rivers and sea for their sustenance. He talked at length with the Bella Coola, learning they had earlier travelled to the coast and traded with strangers from two ships. From their descriptions of the men, Mackenzie was certain they had met with James Cook, convincing him he was now near the ocean.

During his numerous discussions with the natives, the Scotsman persuaded several of them to act as guides to the Pacific Ocean. Using a Bella Coola canoe, they set out down the west-flowing Bella Coola River, soon reaching another settlement. From the village the trailblazers finally saw the Pacific for the first time. Mackenzie wrote in his journal, 'I could perceive the termination of the river and its discharge into a narrow arm of the sea.' As they canoed further down the Bella Coola River, the explorers encountered local Indians, who made threatening gestures at them with their weapons. The English sea captain and explorer, George Vancouver, had visited the area six weeks earlier, and Mackenzie later learned his seamen had had a confrontation with them, causing the Pacific coast natives to become hostile.

On the night of 21 July, the explorers slept on a large rock in Dean's Channel, and in the morning Mackenzie mixed some vermilion with melted bear grease, writing on the stone, 'Alexander Mackenzie, from Canada, by land, the twenty-second of July, one thousand seven hundred and ninety-three.' Fearing further hostility from the Pacific coast Indians, he decided to end his explorations and begin the return to Fort Fork, completing the journey to the Pacific of more than 1,200 miles by water and land in seventy-four days. Mackenzie later wrote in the preface to the *Voyages from Montreal* that his second expedition was 'To determine the practicability of a commercial communication through the continent of North America between the Atlantic and Pacific Oceans, which is proved by my second journey.'

Mackenzie started the journey to Fort Fork on 23 July after a grand send-off from the Bella Coola tribe. After leaving the Indian settlement, the explorers were compelled to scale the several thousand feet of canyon walls onto the Pacific Coastal Range. Following an exhausting climb, Mackenzie and his men travelled through the mountains day after day, following their earlier route, and by 28 July were back at their Tanya Lakes encampment. They had buried a cache of dried meats for their return to the east, and found the provisions untouched. The next morning, they continued toward the fort, and reached the Fraser River on 4 August. At their previous camp near the river, the explorers located the canoe they had hidden and set off up the river, which was swarming with salmon. As the paddlers navigated upriver and made numerous portages, they arrived at the site where their canoe had crashed into boulders and fallen trees. During the journey, Mackenzie's ankles became so swollen that he had to be carried by two of his men across the Continental Divide.

By mid-August, they were again on the Parsnip River, gliding down the waterway in a strong current. The river's flow now became so powerful that they covered in a single day the distance it had taken them to travel upstream in a week. Mackenzie continued to push his men hard to the south, passing through the Rocky Mountains onto open plains, where they found plentiful wild game and frequently ate elk and bear at their evening meals. The pathfinders reached the confluence of the Parsnip with the Peace River, following it toward Fort Fork. At 4 pm on 24 August, the expedition rounded a bend in the river and the fort came into view. Mackenzie later wrote that, 'We threw out our flag, and accompanied it with a general discharge of our fire-arms.' The outbound journey to the Pacific Ocean had taken seventy-four days, but it required only thirty-three days to return to the fort over the same rugged territory.

While Alexander Mackenzie had travelled across the continent to the Pacific Ocean, he had failed to find a navigable waterway to the coast but still hailed the expedition as a brilliant triumph. The personal physical and mental exertion of the journey had taken its toll on him, and after reaching Fort Chipewyan he was exhausted and suffered from depression. The Scotsman told his cousin that he was unable to concentrate, spending his days absorbed in self-reflection. He became determined to leave the wilderness of the west, but had no intention of abandoning the highly profitable fur trade. The undertaking across the continent had generated a desire in him to expand the fur business across western Canada and on to China and Japan. To accomplish that goal he supported a reorganization of the fur industry, with greater consolidation and cooperation between the North West Company and its competitors.

While Mackenzie promoted his plans for expansion of the fur business, meeting with government officials in Montreal and talking to the directors of the North West Company, he was offered a partnership in the firm of McTavish, Frobisher and Company, which had been recently formed by shareholders from the North West Company. He spent the next four years in Montreal engaged in the purchasing of supplies for sale to the traders and marketing their furs. He became part of the city's society, frequently attending elegant dinners, supper parties and gala balls. At the company he continued to encourage a broader trading strategy, strongly supporting the needs of the wintering partners and coming into conflict with his partners. In late October 1799, he left Canada onboard the merchant ship *Desire*, heading for England.

Mackenzie took up residence in London, where he was hailed as the conqueror of the Canadian wilderness. He had long delayed the publication of his expedition's journals, and while in London began writing his accounts of the journeys to the Arctic and Pacific oceans. When the book entitled *Voyages from Montreal* was published in December1801, it was an immediate success and enhanced the Scotsman's popularity with the British court and people. He was later knighted by King George III in recognition of his expeditions in Canada that opened the resources of the interior to further exploration, trade and settlement. He quickly became a favourite guest of London's prominent hostesses.

Without an active role in the marketing of Canadian furs, Sir Alexander Mackenzie quickly grew restless in London, returning to his plans for the expansion of trading companies in Canada. He prepared a detailed proposal for Lord Robert Hobart, Secretary for English Colonies, promoting the creation of a new London-based Fishery and Fur Company that would control a large part of the North Pacific Coast under government protection. After studying the report, Lord Hobart wanted first to arrange the consolidation of all the Montreal fur companies, sending Mackenzie to Canada in March 1802 to negotiate with the businesses. He spent several months trying to forge a union between the firms, but in October 1802 wrote to Hobart that a merger was impossible at this time.

During the spring of 1800, Mackenzie had briefly returned to Montreal to participate in the formation of a new fur trading firm, the XY Company, also called Alexander Mackenzie and Company. Following its creation, the business aggressively challenged the larger and better-funded North West

Company. During the confrontation between the two companies, the abuse and corruption of the Indians reached new levels. However, in 1804 the forceful head of the North West Company died and his successor, a personal friend of Mackenzie, proposed the union of the two firms to put an end to the excessive cost of their competition. Mackenzie supported the offer and the agreement was signed. When the North West Company was reorganized, Mackenzie was denied any part in the management of the business, becoming a silent partner.

While Mackenzie remained a partner in the revised North West Company, without a management role he became discontented and was persuaded to enter politics. He was elected as a representative for Huntingdon County to the Assembly of Lower Canada in June 1804. He had little interest in government, and in the autumn of 1805 went to live in London, returning to Canada only briefly several times. During his four years in office, he attended only one session of the Assembly.

From his London residence, Mackenzie stayed active in the fur trading business, and in 1808 attempted to purchase control of the Hudson Bay Company. He aggressively pursued the venture, but in May 1811 was outmanoeuvred and his future involvement in fur trading was now only as a consultant. He returned to Scotland in April 1812 and was soon married to his 14-year-old cousin, Geddes Mackenzie. From the earnings of his book and fur trading, he purchased the Avoch Estate in Scotland, and he and Lady Mackenzie spent the social season in London, living the remainder of the year on their large estate. During his later years he became occupied with civic affairs in his Scottish village. Sir Alexander and Lady Mackenzie had a daughter in 1816, and two sons followed in 1818 and the following year.

By 1819, Sir Alexander Mackenzie's health began to seriously decline. He likely suffered from Bright's disease, which reduced the functions of the kidneys. A change in diet along with increased rest extended his life for another year, but on 12 March 1820, while returning to Avoch by stagecoach, he died at the age of 56 at a roadside inn. His body was transported to Avoch and interred at the local church on 20 March.

SELECTED SOURCES:
Brebner, John Bartlet, *The Explorers of North America.*
Gough, Barry, *First Across the Continent – Sir Alexander Mackenzie.*
Smith, James K., *Alexander Mackenzie.*
Xydes, Georgia, *Alexander Mackenzie and the Explorers of Canada.*

Meriwether Lewis

Shortly after the American acquisition of the vast Louisiana Territory from France in 1803, the Corps of Discovery Expedition was commissioned by President Thomas Jefferson to explore, map and search for the North-west Passage to the Pacific, while establishing the presence of the United States in the area. To lead the expeditionary force into the unknown country, the president appointed his secretary, Captain Meriwether Lewis, as commander. In the spring of 1804, the Americans crossed the Mississippi River to begin the voyage up the thick and muddy waters of the Missouri River into the Louisiana Territory in a 55 feet keelboat. Under Lewis' command, the arduous and perilous journey across the continent and return to St Louis lasted from May 1804 until September 1806, and gave the nation a vivid description of the region's wide-ranging and diverse geography, Indian cultures, animals and vegetation, while producing the first charts of America's newly purchased land.

Meriwether Lewis was born on his family's plantation of Locust Hill in Albemarle County, Virginia, on 18 August 1774, the son of William and Lucy Meriwether Lewis. The young Meriwether grew up in the affluent region of Virginia, and was close neighbours with the families of the Jeffersons, Madisons and Randolphs. Meriwether Lewis came from a family with many illustrious relatives, who had served with distinction in the French and Indian and American Revolutionary wars. William Lewis fought for the colonials during the revolution, dying in 1779 from pneumonia while on active duty. The death of his father, along with the redcoats' looting of Albemarle County, created in the young Meriwether a lifelong anti-British sentiment. Six months after the death of her husband, Lucy Lewis married Captain John Marks, moving her family with him to Georgia in May 1780 and settling in the Goose Pond community of Oglethorpe County in the northeastern section of the colony. While living in the Broad River area of the county, Meriwether Lewis was occupied hunting and fishing in the woodlands, developing into a skilled hunter and outdoorsman, while learning how to survive in the wilderness. He studied the county's natural history, investigating the local vegetation and wildlife, while nurturing an interest in edible plants. In Georgia he had numerous contacts with the local Native Americans, supporting their claims to their traditional tribal lands against the encroachments of the colonists.

Until the age of 13, Lewis received little formal education, but in 1787 he was sent back to Virginia to live with his uncle, Nicholas Lewis, and was tutored by private teachers, studying mathematics, grammar, Latin and natural science. After the death of his father, Lewis had inherited the family's property as the oldest son, and with the help of his uncle began managing the operations of the farm, while continuing his education. During the next few years he had three different tutors, but in 1792 was forced to abandon his studies and devote himself to the care of his mother and siblings following the death of his stepfather. In the autumn, he returned to Georgia, bringing his mother, brothers and sisters back to Locust Hill. Now at the age of 18, Lewis was head of the family and responsible for over twenty slaves and 2,000 acres of land. During the next two years he was occupied with the management of the plantation, cultivating and harvesting crops of corn, wheat and tobacco, while raising herds of cattle and sheep. From Locust Hill he acquired additional property for farming, buying 1,800 acres on the Red River in Montgomery County and two smaller parcels. While Lewis had to give up his plans to attend William and Mary College, he retained his desire to further his education and was absorbed with the study of geography and exploration. He read all the recent books and journals on the topics, and was especially fascinated by the voyages of Captain James Cook to the Pacific Ocean and his search for the North-west Passage, studying the subjects extensively during the nights at Locust Hill.

However, by 1794, Meriwether Lewis had grown increasingly unhappy and dissatisfied with the monotony of managing his plantation, longing for adventure and excitement. When President George Washington issued a call for troops to quell the Whiskey Rebellion, Lewis volunteered for military service in the Virginia militia company.

The frontier farmers in western Pennsylvania became angered by the enactment of a new tax against the whiskey they produced and sold, revolting against the Federal government in 1794 and refusing to pay the levy. They assaulted revenue agents, tarring and feathering them, while burning their homes. As the violence escalated, Washington called for 13,000 militiamen to enforce Federal law in August. When news of the call to arms reached Locust Hill, Lewis was among the thousands who volunteered for service in the mustering army, considering the rebelling farmers as traitors. He enlisted in the Virginia Volunteer Corps as a private. An army of 13,000 men from the states of Vurginia, Maryland, New Jersey and Pennsylvania was recruited, and following a brief training period advanced into western Pennsylvania in two columns to confront the insurgents. As Lewis and his fellow soldiers approached Pittsburgh, the insurrectionists began to flee for safety to Spanish Louisiana, ending the Whiskey Rebellion. The successful enforcement of Federal authority in western Pennsylvania strengthened the sovereignty of the young republic, while solidifying the laws of the government. During the campaign against the rebels, Lewis enjoyed his life as a soldier, writing to his mother that 'he and his mates were each cutting a most martial figure'. His only regret was that the rebellion had collapsed so quickly.

As a soldier in the First Army of the United States, Lewis had been issued a newly designed uniform of dark blue waistcoat with scarlet facings and standup collar with turn backs of white wool. His trousers were long-legged overalls covering the tops of his boots and buttoned above the waist, while the hat was rounded and covered with a bearskin. He was given a red waterproof backpack, wooden blue canteen and a cartridge box holding twenty-four rounds of ammunition. The Virginia private was armed with a surplus French musket from the Revolutionary War, with a fixed bayonet.

Following the end of the Whiskey Rebellion, Private Meriwether Lewis had no desire to return to the daily routine of farming, preferring to remain with the small volunteer force in Pittsburgh, patrolling and policing western Pennsylvania. In November, he received a promotion to ensign in the Virginia militia, spending the winter months on the Monongahela River 15 miles upriver from Pittsburgh, writing to his family at Locust Hill, 'I am in perfect health. I am delighted with the soldier's life.' Lewis' term of enlistment was for six months, but he elected to stay in the army and in May 1795 was reassigned to the command of General Anthony Wayne, joining the Second Sub-Legion in the Ohio Territory. General Wayne had earlier reorganized the American Army into a force of legions. Each legion was made independent, with its own infantry units, cavalry and artillery pieces.

During the following months, the ensign was occupied with the peacetime duties of an army officer, caring for the welfare of his men and keeping the peace with the hostile Indians on the frontier, while training his soldiers into a disciplined fighting unit, engaging in marksmanship exercises, endless marches, drills and mock battles. After serving in the Second Sub-Legion for a short period, he was reassigned to the Fourth Sub-Legion at Fort Fayette, which was located near the Allegheny River upstream from the ruins of Fort Pitt and was protected by wooden pickets 12 feet high. Inside the stockade, the troops built two double-storey barracks for 200 men, separate officers' housing, three blockhouses and a powder magazine.

In mid-1795, Ensign Lewis's normal routine was interrupted when he was charged by a fellow officer with engaging in provocative speech and gestures, challenging him to a duel to the death. After the accusations were read to him at his court-martial, Lewis replied with a resounding, 'Not Guilty'. When the testimony was reviewed by members of the court-martial board, they issued a verdict of not guilty and he was immediately returned to active duty. In the aftermath of the trial, Lewis was reassigned to the Chosen Rifle Company of sharpshooters commanded by Captain William Clark, who would become his closest and most trusted life-long friend. Lewis remained under Clark's command in the Chosen Rifle Company for only six months before the captain resigned from the army. As an officer in the rifle company, Lewis travelled extensively through the western territories, completing a detailed reconnaissance of Ohio in 1796 and delivering messages from General Wayne across the wilderness to Pittsburgh with a small escort force. He was transferred to the First Infantry Regiment in November 1796, continuing his routine peacetime duties monitoring the activities of the mountain Indians and training his men.

Ensign Lewis had been on active duty for over three years, and in May 1797 was granted an extended leave, returning to Locust Hill. Shortly after reaching his plantation, he travelled south to Georgia to arrange the transfer of his mother's remaining slaves from the Broad River property to Virginia. From Georgia he went west to Kentucky and Ohio, securing land claims for his mother's stepchildren, and while in the territories purchased 2,600 acres of land for himself. When Lewis returned to the army, he was sent to Fort Pickering on the Mississippi River as commanding officer of an infantry company. The fort had been constructed at Chickasaw Bluffs in current-day western Tennessee as a deterrent to future Spanish expansion up the waterway, and to enforce American sovereignty over the local Cherokee Indians. Lewis was occupied at the frontier fort by leading patrols into the woodlands to monitor the activities of the Cherokees and Spanish, while continuing to train his troops. When the fort commanding officer suddenly died from malaria, Lewis assumed his command and became responsible for the defence of the stockade, securing rations, supplies and arms, and the welfare and training of the soldiers.

Lewis stayed at Fort Pickering until early 1799, when he was transferred to Charlottesville, Virginia, for service as a recruiting officer. While in Virginia, on 3 March 1799, he was promoted to lieutenant after five years in the army. After performing the duties of enlistment officer for over a year, in September 1800 Lieutenant Lewis returned to duty on the frontier and was stationed at the fort at Detroit. It was a presidential election year, and Lewis strongly supported his fellow Virginian and friend, Thomas Jefferson, against the incumbent John Adams. As an outspoken Republican, the lieutenant's vigorous political arguments resulted in frequent clashes with the Federalists. Shortly after reaching Detroit, Lieutenant Lewis was appointed regimental paymaster for the western posts. He travelled extensively throughout the trans-Appalachian frontier, up and down the Ohio River on a keelboat, stopping at numerous river towns, while riding overland to forts in the south. He maintained copious records as part of his duties, building a reputation for accuracy and thoroughness. On 5 December 1800, Lewis was promoted to captain.

While Captain Lewis remained on the frontier as paymaster, in February 1801 the nation's Electoral College met to choose the next president. After the electoral votes were counted, a political crisis was created when Thomas Jefferson and Aaron Burr each had seventy-three votes and Adams received sixty-five. The tie threw the election to the House of Representatives, and following a second deadlock vote, Jefferson was finally elected the third President of the United States in mid-February.

Captain Lewis had chosen a career in the army and fully expected to remain on active duty in the years ahead. However, on 23 February 1801 he received a letter that was to propel him into national prominence and create an important place for him in the history of his country. In his mail was a personal letter from President Jefferson inviting him to serve as his private secretary. He was the president's first choice because of his knowledge of the western territories and army. Four days later, Lewis responded, notifying the president, 'I most cordially acquiesce and with pleasure accept the office … Not a moment has been lost in making the necessary arrangements in order to get forward to the city of Washington with all possible dispatch.'

Meriwether Lewis set out for Washington immediately, but his arrival was delayed by spring rains and impassable roads. He reached the capital on 1 April, but Jefferson had gone to Monticello. After resting a few days, he continued on to Virginia to meet with the president. The two men soon returned to the capital, where Lewis was kept busy assisting the president with his correspondences, copying reports, managing the household staff and arranging state dinners. He lived in the White House, regularly eating his meals with the president, and had his room in the present-day East Room. When Jefferson held discussions with his chief advisors, Lewis attended the meetings. As private secretary, he learned about national diplomacy, statesmanship and state policy at the highest levels of government. Lewis regularly attended White House dinners and was exposed to foreign diplomats, scientists and prominent authors and poets in a cultured and refined environment. During his two years in the White House, Lewis advanced his scientific education and knowledge of geography, Indian cultures and American wildlife.

During the presidential campaign of 1800, Thomas Jefferson had promoted the reduction of the army as a means to reduce Federal expenditures. With Lewis' knowledge of the army, the president assigned him the task of reviewing a roster of the officers, classifying each one on his leadership, military skills and politics. A system of eleven symbols was created and Lewis set to work going through the officer corps list. When Jefferson selected the men for dismissal, he gave higher preference to their military qualifications than political party, yet the majority of Federalists rated acceptable or below were discharged from service.

By the beginning of the nineteenth century, the population of the United States was just over five million, mostly settled on the eastern seaboard, and the nation extended west from the Atlantic Ocean across the Appalachian Mountains to the Mississippi River and north for 1,000 miles from the Gulf of Mexico to the five Great Lakes. The territory west of the trans-Appalachian Mountains was largely unknown, and Jefferson had earlier proposed several times sending an exploration and scientific party across the continent to the Pacific Ocean. The western region was a vast unexplored land, but the English were aggressively moving south from Canada into modern-day North Dakota, the Spanish had settled colonies in the American south-west, Russia was building outposts in Alaska and the French under Napoleon Bonaparte were reclaiming the territory from the Mississippi River to the Rocky Mountains. President Jefferson strongly believed in the existence of a Northwest Passage across the continent, which would make trade with the Orient easier and more profitable. He was certain the country that discovered and controlled the waterway would gain possession of the North American continent, and was determined to acquire the vast riches of the area for the United States.

Now as president, Jefferson began planning the project, and in 1802 met privately with Lewis to suggest he lead the expeditionary force. Lewis quickly accepted the offer, but before he could begin preparations for the journey, the president had to secure the funds from Congress. He sent a secret message to the legislature, petitioning the money to expand trading outposts into the west and purchase additional Indian lands. In the request, he said an expedition would travel up the Missouri River and establish a network of new trading contacts with the local Native American tribes. The members of Congress, eager to limit British commercial activities in the region, voted to approve the requested funds.

To better prepare Lewis for the expedition up the Missouri River and across the continent, President Jefferson sent him to meet with renowned scholars in the fields of botany, zoology, astronomy, mineralogy and Indian history. His education also included courses in medicine, preservation of plant and animal samples, the use of scientific instruments to determine longitude and latitude, and the study of fossils. The president later wrote a set of detailed instructions for Lewis, describing his goals and stressing the importance of the project. He also gave Lewis permission to choose a second-in-command to assist with the management of the men and supplies, map-making and writing of the detailed journals. He was also instructed to make contact with the Indians and study their culture, religion, housing, food and societies. To fill the important position, Lewis asked his army friend, retired Captain William Clark, to join the Corps of Discovery.

While Lewis was meeting with his tutors in Philadelphia, he spent time purchasing supplies and equipment for the expedition, acquiring scientific instruments for navigation, tents, tools, clothing, provisions, arms and ammunition, along with gifts for the Indians in the western tribes. By mid-June he had bought $3,500 of supplies, and the army began transporting the cargo to the Ohio River staging area.

As Lewis prepared to return to Washington for the journey to the west after studying months in preparation for the expedition, news reached him from the capital that President Jefferson had signed a treaty with France, giving the United States full sovereign powers over New Orleans and the entire Louisiana Territory. The purchase of the vast unknown area now expanded the expedition's importance. In January 1803, the president had sent James Monroe and Robert R. Livingston to Paris to negotiate the purchase of New Orleans and its environs, but Napoleon Bonaparte offered to sell the entire Louisiana region for $15 million. Jefferson questioned his legal authority to sign the treaty, but nevertheless agreed, acquiring 828,000 square miles of what later became all or parts of fifteen states for three cents an acre.

While Lewis was in Washington and Philadelphia, William Clark had established a training camp 18 miles upriver from St Louis at the confluence of the Mississippi and Missouri rivers. Later in 1803, Lewis travelled west from Washington, joining Clark at Camp Dubois. During the winter of 1804, the nearly fifty recruited men were occupied drilling under Clark's supervision, while Lewis procured additional provisions and supplies and met with local traders, who were involved with fur trading with the Indians on the Missouri River. In early March, Lewis and Clark went by boat to St Louis to attend the formal ceremonies marking the transfer of the Louisiana Territory to the United States.

Following several brief delays, on the late afternoon of 14 May 1804, the Corps of Discovery Expedition set out from the training camp with forty-eight men in a keelboat that was 55 feet long, 8 feet wide and fitted with a mast and twenty oars, while two smaller flatboats followed. On the first day of the expedition, with the flag of the United States flying from the stern, the two captains sailed across the Mississippi and began the voyage up the thick muddy waters of the Missouri, making only 4½ miles. As they navigated upriver against the strong current and headwinds, Lewis' crews stopped at several small river towns and were welcomed by the friendly inhabitants. On 25 May, the explorers reached the small village of La Charrette, the last American settlement on the Missouri. During the early days of the journey there were frequent rainstorms and the boatmen struggled to manoeuvre the keelboat against the river's swollen waters. They had to use their long poles to push the boat forward or pull it with ropes from the river's banks. The swarms of mosquitoes that flew around their faces and hands were a constant source of irritation as they fought to steer around sandbars, drifting logs and low-hanging tree branches. The men suffered from dysentery, snakebites and painful skin sores. Lewis attempted to treat them with his rudimentary medical training received in Philadelphia. The expeditionary force had its first fatality near present-day Sioux City, Iowa, where Sergeant Charles Floyd died from what Lewis called 'Bilious colic'. The trailblazers celebrated the Fourth of July with a volley from their muskets and an extra ration of whiskey. The recruited men were rough and undisciplined frontiersmen, and during the summer several were court-martialled for sleeping on duty, drunkenness, disobedience and insubordination.

While the expedition struggled on against the weather and current of the Missouri River, the surrounding terrain began to change. Except for along the river's banks, the region was now virtually treeless, turning into open grasslands of rolling hills that stretched into an endless horizon, the Great American Plains. In his journal, Captain Lewis described the sweeping landscape, 'The scenery already rich, pleasing and beautiful was farther heightened by immense herds of buffalo, deer and elk which we saw in every direction feeding on the hills and plains.'

As part of his instructions from President Jefferson, Lewis was directed to take detailed notes of the animals and vegetation in the west, especially those not known on the Atlantic coast. During the journey, he took samples of the soil and completed daily observations of the weather. Plants were collected, dried and stored in safe containers to be later taken back to the president. Killed wild game was skinned and their hides, horns and skeletons preserved, while some were stuffed. The Corps of Discovery brought back to the east a total of 178 previously unknown plants and 122 animals. Lewis recorded the discoveries in his logbook, drawing many sketches of the new flora and fauna. Among the many different animals found were the bighorn sheep, mountain goat, coyote and grizzly bear, along with diverse types of trout and grouse. Unfamiliar flora, including varieties of pine, yew, spruce, honeysuckle and snowberry, were detailed in the expedition's register. As a result of his explorations, Lewis later had several plants named after him. In early September, he encountered another unfamiliar animal, which came to be called the prairie dog. Lewis' explorers spent most of a day capturing one of the creatures alive as a gift for Jefferson. He wrote in his journal, 'I called it the barking squirrel. Its form is that of a squirrel but they bark at you as you approach them.'

Lewis and his Corps of Discovery had contact with few Indians on the lower Missouri River. He had been instructed by President Jefferson to make contact with the tribes and establish trading relations, while collecting information about their customs, ways of living, foods, religions, dwellings and physical appearance. When the expedition reached current-day Nebraska and South Dakota in mid-August, Lewis and Clark began to encounter warriors from the Yankton Sioux. The two captains met with a large delegation of Sioux at Calumet Bluff overlooking the Missouri River in modern-day Nebraska on 30 August. They showed the Yanktons some of the expedition's scientific instruments and fired a musket to impress them. To win their friendship and display the wealth of their 'great father', the explorers gave the Sioux gifts of sewing needles, coloured beads, tobacco, cloth and mirrors, while handing out peace medals with Jefferson's likeness on the front and two hands bound together in peace on the back. The Native Americans were told their lands were now part of the United States and they were presented with signed certificates naming them friends of the nation. Lewis read a speech, telling the Yanktons, 'The great chief of the seventeen great nations of America, impelled by his parental regard for his newly adopted children on the troubled waters has sent us out to clear the road and make it a road of peace.' In the evening, the Sioux performed a tribal ceremony for the men, dancing around the campfire with drums beating, giving speeches describing how many enemy scalps they had taken in battle.

The following night they held a second ritual, smoking from the pipe of peace.

As Lewis and Clark prepared to navigate further up the Missouri, the chiefs again met with the two captains, telling them they were willing to travel to see the new great father if the Yanktons were given additional presents. They also wanted to trade their animal pelts with the strangers for American-made goods. Before Lewis and Clark left the chiefs, they were warned by Chief Half Man that the next tribe up the river was the Lakota Sioux, who would not be friendly. The Lakotas were the dominant warriors on the Great Plains, terrorizing the local tribes and controlling the flow of European trade along the upper Missouri River by intimidating the French and Spanish fur traders.

When the expedition departed from the Yankton village, the keelboat and two flat-bottom boats sailed and rowed upriver into present-day South Dakota. The explorers first encountered the Lakotas in late September. Lewis and Clark agreed to meet with the chiefs on a sandbar island on the river. The soldiers were dressed in their Army uniforms and the American flag was raised on a pole in preparation for the meeting. The Indians began gathering along the river banks at mid-morning, as thirty warriors led by three chiefs arrived for the ceremony. The chiefs were given medals, knives and several other trade goods, along with an American flag. The natives wanted more, telling the pathfinders they must stop now or leave one person with them before they could go on. Lewis tried to frighten the Lakota with his military power, ordering his men to parade with their arms in front of the Indians and fire volleys from their muskets. However, the chiefs were unimpressed and insisted the Corps of Discovery go no further upriver. To quell the escalating hostilities, the three chiefs were shown around the keelboat, but tensions still mounted. When the party reached the shore, the warriors tried to take the rowboat and Clark began to argue with a chief, drawing his sword. The frontiersmen raised their muskets and Lewis, who had remained on the keelboat, loaded the cannon. Clark told the Lakotas, 'We must and would go on … we were not squaws but warriors.' As the natives on the shoreline prepared to fire their arrows, Chief Black Buffalo intervened, telling the Americans that his only request was that the women and children from the village be allowed to visit the large boat before they departed. The appeal was quickly granted, and the trailblazers spent the next three days showing the Lakotas the keelboat before resuming their voyage upriver.

By late October, the Corps of Discovery had reached present-day North Dakota after a strenuous journey of nearly 1,600 miles and six months on the river. The weather turned colder and ice began to appear in the river. When the expedition left St Louis in mid-May, Lewis had expected to reach the headwaters of the Missouri before the river froze, but it was now certain he would soon have to establish a winter encampment. As the boatmen continued to navigate north-west, he began searching for a suitable site to spend the winter months. On 27 October, he reached the lands of the friendly Mandan tribe and decided to build his fort close to their five earthen-lodge villages. As snow began to cover the ground, Lewis met with the chiefs of the tribe, passing out medals and other gifts. Following his meeting with the Mandans, he was invited to erect his camp across the river from their settlement near the mouth of the Knife River. The men set up their tents and started construction of the two lines of log cabins. While the frontiersmen worked on the stockade, Lewis met with the French-Canadian fur trapper Toussaint Charbonneau, hiring him and his young Shoshone wife, Sacagawea, as interpreters. She had been captured by the Hidatsas during a raid against her tribe at the headwaters of the Missouri, and Lewis believed she could direct him to her village in the spring. On 13 November, snow fell more heavily and the river began to freeze. Lewis pushed his men to finish the encampment, and by late November they were ready to move into their new quarters. The crude stockade was built with two lines of log huts, enclosed at one end by two storehouses. A line of stakes was positioned at the open end to encircle the fort. For added security, four sentries were stationed around the fort by day and night.

During the winter, Lewis and Clark were occupied hunting wild game to supplement the expedition's food supply and visiting the five villages of the Mandan and the neighbouring tribe. Unable to travel on the frozen river until spring, Lewis had the opportunity to closely study the ways of the Mandan people. He spent time at the Indians' lodges, writing an account of their culture, appearance, dress, foods, laws, religion and dwellings, while describing the winter landscape and weather and drawing detailed maps of the region in his logbook. By December, the weather had turned dangerously cold with temperatures dropping to minus forty-five degrees. The conditions became so bad that Lewis was forced to temporarily suspend hunting. The frontiersmen celebrated Christmas Day firing rounds from their muskets into the air, drinking several rounds of brandy and dancing to the music of a fiddle and tambourine. On 1 January 1805, they visited a Mandan village, taking their fiddle and tambourine to mark the New Year dancing with the Native Americans. In the afternoon, the Mandans brought in buffalo and deer meats for their visitors and gave them presents of animal robes. Several days later, the explorers were invited to attend the Mandan ceremony to call back the buffalo herds to the area. Two days later, after attending the ritual, Lewis and his trailblazers were asked to join the warriors in their buffalo hunt. When they reached the prairie, the Americans found it covered with buffalo and the Indians shooting at them from their horses with their bows and arrows.

During the Corps of Discovery's stay with the Mandan tribe, Lewis' medical skills were frequently called into service. He treated frostbitten feet and fingers, various wounds and venereal disease in several of his men. In mid-February, he was summoned to the lodge of Charbonneau and his wife. Sacagawea was having a difficult delivery with her first baby, and Lewis administered a drink of water with crushed rattlesnake rattles, which someone had suggested as a remedy. Lewis later wrote, 'Whether this medicine was truly the cause or not I shall not undertake to determine but she had not taken it more than ten minutes before she brought forth.' The child was a boy and named Jean-Baptiste by his father.

By mid-March, the long winter was ending and the ice on the Missouri rapidly melting under the warming sun. Lewis and Clark began preparations to renew their journey to the Pacific, talking to the chiefs about the lands to the west. The Indians drew a map on the lodge's floor, using mounds of dirt to show them the terrain features. They were told about a large waterfall and great range of shining mountains. From the descriptions, Lewis estimated the Corps of Discovery Expedition could reach the Pacific Ocean and return to the Mandan settlement before the next winter.

Before starting out up the Missouri again, Lewis sent the keelboat back to St Louis and planned to travel upriver in six canoes and two dugouts. The keelboat was loaded with boxes and trunks filled with items collected during the first year. Specimens of plants, animals, Mandan corn, various minerals, soil samples and cages with a live prairie dog, magpie, birds and grouse were placed in the hold. Several containers were packed with logbooks describing the various tribes, terrain, weather and estimates of the prospects for future trading, along with numerous maps. Lewis sent a personal letter to President Jefferson telling him, 'At the moment, every individual of the party are in good health and excellent spirits, zealously attached to the enterprise and anxious to proceed. With such men I have everything to hope, and but little to fear.'

On 7 April 1805, the Corps of Discovery Expedition continued toward the Pacific, while sixteen men steered the keelboat downriver toward St Louis. The canoemen paddled west day after day against the river's current, into a strong headwind and dust storms, reaching current-day Montana in mid-spring. The farther the explorers travelled upriver, the shallower the waters became. During the journey, they saw bighorn sheep for the first time in an area that was plentiful with elk, deer, antelope, beaver and herds of buffalo. The Americans had plenty of meat to eat but buffalo became their favourite food. The pathfinders had numerous encounters with the huge and ferocious grizzly bears that they had earlier been warned about by the Mandans.

As the expedition continued to canoe westward, the two captains mapped the territory, naming new rivers, streams and mountains. On 9 May, they entered a different area of the river, now named the White Cliffs of the Missouri. They paddled through 5½ miles of bare white sandstone cliffs nearly 300 feet high, that had been carved by exposure to the weather and water into nearly perpendicular pillars and walls, whose strata stood out like streaked bands. After passing through the White Cliffs, the river became shallower still and the pathfinders were compelled to pull their canoes from the shore in chest-high cold water. Pine trees were more common in this region, and buffalo gave way to mountain sheep and elk. On 2 June, the river split into two channels, and the captains could not determine which one was the Missouri. The northern tributary was mostly muddy, like the Missouri, while the southern fork was swifter and clearer. On 4 June, Lewis travelled up the northern branch for four days, exploring the territory, as Captain Clark navigated the other fork, finding a westward-moving waterway. To the north, Lewis discovered endless plains and a river that flowed away from the Pacific. After rejoining Clark, Lewis decided to take the lower branch, but the men still thought the muddy arm was the Missouri. Remembering that the Mandans had told him of a great waterfall on the upper Missouri, Lewis set out on foot with four frontiersmen to look for the falls to end their scepticism, leaving Clark in command of the remaining expeditionary force. On the morning of 13 June, he heard the sounds of constant thunder and saw clouds of mist rising in the distance. After pushing on for 7 miles, the search party found the Great Falls of the Missouri, standing 300 yards wide and 80 feet high. Lewis wrote of the sight, 'To gaze on the sublimely grand spectacle forms the greatest sight I ever beheld … From the reflection of the sun on the spray or mist which arises from these falls there is a beautiful rainbow produced, which adds not a little to the beauty of this majestically grand scenery.' He quickly sent a messenger back to Clark, telling him to join him with his men and boats. While waiting for Clark, Lewis reconnoitred the area, finding additional waterfalls and rapids.

After first learning of the Great Falls, Lewis and Clark had planned to make a short overland portage around the waterfalls, but following his investigation they were forced to prepare for a nearly 20-mile trek through dense and rocky terrain under a scorching summer sun. To carry the heavy equipment and supplies, they built carts of cottonwood. During the journey there were frequent summer thunderstorms with large hailstones, strong winds and heavy rains. The men struggled on through the rugged wilderness day after day. They were constantly harassed by clouds of gnats and mosquitoes, while the threat of attack from grizzly bears and rattlesnakes was a constant worry. In early July, the Corps of Discovery Expeditionary Force finally ended the arduous portage around the rapids and waterfalls, after nearly a month. While the explorers spent several days recovering from the ordeal, they celebrated their second Fourth of July in the woodlands with music, dancing and extra rations of buffalo, beans and dumplings, along with the last of the whiskey.

The following morning, they resumed their expedition, pushing their dugouts and canoes into the Missouri. The course of the river began to turn south and not west, to the disappointment of Lewis and Clark. As the men paddled on, in mid-July they entered Shoshone territory, but despite finding signs of Indians, none were seen. The region was now familiar to Sacagawea, who assured Lewis that this was the river where her people lived. Encouraged by her words that they were advancing in the correct direction, the captains pushed their men forward up the river. On 25 July, after having traveled 2,500 miles, the explorers reached the headwaters of the river, where three smaller waterways joined together to form the Missouri. Lewis named the three branches the Gallatin, Madison and Jefferson.

The Jefferson River seemed to flow south-west, and the trailblazers paddled up the waterway. On 28 July, Sacagawea showed Lewis and Clark the encampment where her tribe had their lodges and she was captured five years before. The Jefferson was a swift and shallow river, and they struggled to make progress against the waterway's current. They had still not made contact with the Shoshone, whose help was vital to the success of the expedition. Finally, on 9 August, Lewis decided to travel overland with three frontiersmen and search the interior for the Native Americans, leaving the ill Clark in charge of the expeditionary force. Two days later, they saw an Indian warrior on horseback several hundred yards away, but as they slowly advanced he rode off. Lewis sent a man ahead to follow the Shoshone's tracks, and he was able to locate a well-worn pathway. They pursued the Shoshone over a ridgeline, making their way west. On 13 August, they encountered three native women gathering food. When the explorers approached them, one of the Indians ran back to her village to warn her people. More than sixty mounted warriors soon rode toward them, as Lewis walked to the Indians with an American flag blowing in the breeze and holding out presents. The Shoshone took the gifts and embraced the strangers as friends, taking them to their settlement. Using sign language, Lewis explained to the chief that there were other men following and they needed horses. The chief agreed to come with them to their river encampment.

In mid-August, Lewis and his party reached the river, and as they walked forward Sacagawea saw the Shoshones and 'Danced for joy', as Clark wrote in his journal. Soon they began negotiating with the chief for the required horses. When they sent for Sacagawea to translate, she recognized the chief as her brother. With his sister acting as interpreter, her brother agreed to sell them all the horses they needed. The Shoshones were eager to trade for American-made goods and willing to sell their animals at low prices.

After the horses were purchased, Lewis talked to the chief about the rivers and terrain to the west, learning the region was impassable by water. They would now have to travel by horse over an old Indian trail through the mountains. The expedition remained with the Shoshones for only a few days before setting out with twenty-nine horses and one mule. The explorers, along with Charbonneau, Sacagawea and her son, crossed through a steep pass before riding into the valley of the Bitterroot River, with snow-capped mountains visible in the distance. On 10 September, the Corps of Discovery camped near current-day Missoula, Montana, where Lewis rested his men, resupplying his provisions with fresh wild game for the arduous trek over the mountains.

The following day, the Americans began their ascent into the Bitterroot Range of the Rocky Mountains. They struggled through a maze of rocky peaks and valleys, the horses becoming exhausted and frequently slipping down the hills. The food started to run out and the further west they travelled, the higher the mountains became, extending as far as they could see. Snow began to fall as Lewis and his men trudged up and down the jagged mountain sides day after day in the biting cold. Provisions were nearly exhausted, compelling the trailblazers to kill one of the horses for food. They were half-starved and began to suffer from diarrhoea, skin rashes and other signs of malnutrition. Eventually, on 22 September, the expedition stumbled half-dead out of the Bitterroot Mountains of northern Idaho.

As the Corps of Discovery trudged on toward the Pacific Ocean following their 140-mile portage, they saw in the distance an extensive open plain. They slowly and painfully made their way to the area, rejoicing when they found a village of the Nez Perce tribe along the Clearwater River. The Native

Americans had never seen a white man before, but greeted Lewis and his men as friends. Chief Twisted Hair of the Nez Perce provided shelter and salmon, camas roots and bulbs for the strangers to eat as they slowly began to regain their strength. After resting and recovering their health, the explorers began building dugouts to resume the expedition down the Clearwater River. Twisted Hair showed the men how to make a canoe by hollowing out the interior of cut pine trees by using fire. Before leaving the Nez Perce, the Indians provided maps for Lewis and Clark, and agreed to keep their horses until the spring. With the chief now acting as guide, the expeditionary force set out again on 7 October in five dugouts.

With the river's current now at their back after crossing the Continental Divide, the canoeists averaged over 20 miles a day. As they paddled and floated down the Clearwater, the Indians were along the river's banks, catching and drying salmon, which served as their primary sustenance. In mid-October, Lewis' band of men entered the Snake River. During the journey, the chief and Sacagawea met first with the local Indians to ensure a friendly welcome for the strangers. Lewis reinforced his reception by giving the natives peace medals and trade goods, while also providing tobacco and fiddle music. The country around the river was barren and wild game scarce, forcing the Americans to trade with the Indians for food.

On 16 October, after ten days of paddling down the Clearwater and Snake rivers, the Corps of Discovery Expedition reached the Columbia River in present-day southern Washington. As they journeyed down the waterway, they were greeted by large crowds of friendly Yakima and Wanapam Indians on the banks. After joining the Columbia from the Snake, the combined rivers widened to over a mile, the strong current now driving the canoes rapidly toward the ocean. The expedition reached the Cascade Mountains on 22 October, and the river turned into a 55-mile stretch of rapids, falls and cascades. They manoeuvred through some of the whitewater, but were forced to portage around others. Several days later, Lewis saw the snow-capped volcanic peak of Mt Hood off in the distance, confirming that the Corps of Discovery was entering lands previously explored and mapped by Europeans. Near the mountain pass, he saw Indians wearing clothes and carrying blankets made in Europe. At the end of October, the men neared the last river obstacle and as they portaged around the cascades, they saw their first sea otters. They were now in the tidewaters of the Pacific Ocean.

As the explorers paddled down the Columbia, Lewis continued to write about the Indian tribes the expedition encountered. He recorded in his journal that the river tribes depended greatly on dried salmon as their primary food source, fuel and trade goods. The local natives lived in large houses made from mats, owned many canoes and wore less clothing than the mountain and plains Indians. The region was completely different from the arid grasslands, and with frequent rains from the Pacific the men saw magnificent dense forests with trees larger than they had ever seen. As the trailblazers travelled on toward the west, they observed thousands of waterfowl, with huge flocks of geese, seagulls and ducks.

On 7 November, the dugouts set out down the river in a dense mist and fog. With limited visibility, Lewis hired a local Indian dressed in a sailor's coat to guide the expedition to the ocean. As he led the corps toward the coast, a huge ocean-generated storm blew across the land for over a week, creating endless cold rain, high winds and flood tides, which made travel slow. The wet and exhausted explorers struggled on the river for nearly two weeks, manoeuvring past dangerous logs, with churning waters, strong winds and high waves, while suffering from the lack of food and fresh water. Lewis and Clark made camp on the north shore on 15 November, and looking across the river's mouth they could finally see the Pacific Ocean. Captain Clark wrote in his journal, 'The emence [immense] Seas and waves roar like an emence fall at a distance and this roaring has continued ever since our arrival. Its waters are foaming and perpetually brake with emence waves on the sands and rocky coasts, tempestuous and horiable.'

After travelling over 4,000 miles, the Corps of Discovery had reached its destination, and a decision now had to be made where to spend the coming winter months. Lewis gathered his men and gave them four options. When each member of the corps voted, it was decided to establish the winter encampment on the south side of the Columbia River. Lewis and Clark spent several days searching for a suitable site for the camp, choosing a thick grove of pine trees several miles from the coast near current-day Astoria, Oregon. On 8 December, they began clearing the land and constructing the fort, named Fort Clatsop after a coastal Indian tribe. The men worked long hard days in cold rain, hail and periods of snow. The walls of the cabins were in place by 14 December, and late in the month they moved into the huts. The explorers' clothes had rotted in the wet weather, and the food spoiled, making living conditions unpleasant. On Christmas Day, they were compelled to eat dried fish, and had no whiskey to celebrate the New Year, only water.

Lewis put the men to work boiling seawater for salt, preserving elk meat in the smokehouse, making candles and clothes, while trading with the Indians for fish and roots. While the trailbreakers worked, Clark drew new maps of the western territory and Lewis wrote in his logbook about the area's plants, animals, Indian tribes and terrain features. At Fort Clatsop, the Pacific storms continued through the winter and the men suffered from frequent fevers and illnesses. The local Clatsops and Chinooks made repeated visits to the fort to trade, but were less friendly than the Mandans and demanded higher prices. During the winter, Lewis expected a ship to arrive from the east to replenish his supplies and take a copy of the journal to Jefferson, but none was ever seen. In late March, he decided it was time to return east after five months at Fort Clatsop.

They loaded their dugout canoes, and set out up the Columbia River for the east at 1 pm. The explorers now paddled against the strong current, making little headway. The salmon had not started their annual runs upriver, making it difficult to find food. The river Indians charged high prices for their dried salmon, quickly depleting Lewis's supply of trade goods. As the snows in the mountains melted, the waters in the river rose, making their passage even more difficult. As the Corps of Discovery journeyed on, Lewis was distraught at the lack of progress, becoming ill-tempered and impatient. He finally ordered his men to trade their canoes to the natives and buy horses to travel overland. While the corps moved east across the wilderness, the captains traded their medical skills for food, treating the Native Americans for wounds, boils, broken bones and sore eyes.

By early June, the expedition was again in Nez Perce country in present-day northern Idaho. The Americans were eager to continue their journey, but the snows had not melted in the Bitterroot Mountains, forcing them to remain with the Indians for five weeks. While waiting for the mountain passes to clear, the men were occupied with preparations to cross the rugged mountains, engaging in physical games to rebuild their stamina and strength. The explorers lacked trade goods to buy food from the Indians, but the Nez Perce gave them several horses to eat. Despite the warnings of the Native Americans that it was too early to cross the mountains, the frontiersmen were anxious to set out. They rode to the east into the Bitterroots, but after travelling into the higher elevations they encountered banks of snow over 12 feet high. They attempted to push through the passes, but after two tortuous days in the biting cold were compelled to turn back. Lewis and Clark waited another week in the foothills before re-entering the mountains with several Nez Perce guides. The snow in some places was still over 6 feet high, but they continued to move onward, and by the end of the month were descending the Bitterroot Range.

After passing through the mountains, the two captains decided to divide the expedition and explore more of the Louisiana Purchase. Clark set out for the Beaverhead River, while Lewis, with a smaller party, travelled north to reconnoitre the overland shortcut to the Great Falls of the Missouri River, which the Indians had earlier described. He later planned to search the upper regions of the Marias River in north-western Montana. The captains agreed to meet a month later at the confluence of the Yellowstone and Missouri rivers.

Lewis began the trek northward down the Bitterroot River on 3 July with nine men in several canoes, before turning east several days later up the Big Blackfoot River. They followed the river until it turned into a small stream. The frontiersmen traded a few American-made goods to the Indians for horses and resumed their journey following a native trail to the Great Falls of the Missouri. The territory was rich in wild game, and they freely ate buffalo, elk and deer. Lewis reached the falls in mid-July, and after exploring the area decided to investigate the Marias River to the north, looking for the boundary of the Louisiana Purchase. After reaching the northern section of the waterway near the border with Canada, he tried to take celestial readings to determine his longitude and latitude, but cloudy skies prevented an exact calculation. It was now late July, and Lewis started back to rejoin Clark.

On the morning of 26 July, the search party rode south toward the Two Medicine River. As the Americans ascended onto a plain, in the afternoon they saw a band of Blackfeet warriors in the distance. Lewis had heard about the bellicose tribe and had tried to avoid contact with it. He had the American flag unfurled, and the men slowly approached the Indians. When they got to within 100 yards of the natives, the captain rode ahead to meet a lone Blackfoot, who had left his war party. He dismounted and shook hands with him, as the other explorers and Blackfeet joined them. Lewis gave the warriors some tobacco and peace medals, while proposing they camp together. The Indians accepted the offer, and during the evening they shared their food with the Americans, smoked the tobacco and answered Lewis' questions about their tribe and its trading relationships with the British.

As the morning sun broke over the horizon, lighting up the prairie, Lewis was roused from his sleep by the shouts of his sentry. The American was fighting with an Indian who was trying to take his musket, and during their struggle killed him with his knife. With the pathfinders distracted by the altercation, the other Blackfeet warriors started rounding up the explorers' horses. When Lewis saw the horses being stolen, he ran after them, threatening to shoot if they did not stop. As an Indian turned toward him, the captain fired his musket, killing him. The remaining warriors fled to the north, while the explorers saddled their animals and rode hard and fast to the

Missouri River. When they finally reached the waterway, the frontiersmen rode down the shore and astonishingly, as they rounded a bend, saw men from Clark's expeditionary force in their canoes. They put their baggage in the boats and paddled downriver, reaching Clark's camp on 12 August.

The reunited expedition travelled down the Missouri River, reaching the Mandan settlement two days later. At the village, Lewis settled with Charbonneau, paying him $500 33⅓ cents for his services. He stayed with the Indians for three days, convincing the chief of the Mandans, Sheheke, to return with him and meet President Jefferson. The Americans set out for St Louis on 17 August, leaving Charbonneau, Sacagawea and Jean Baptiste behind. As they passed through Lakota territory in their dugouts, Clark saw Chief Black Buffalo on the riverbank, shouting at him, 'You have treated all the white people that have visited you very badly and we view you as bad people.'

Travelling with the powerful current, they made over 50 miles a day. On the way to St Louis they met numerous fur trappers and traders heading upriver, exchanging new information about the territory ahead for tobacco, whiskey and news from the United States. On the afternoon of 20 September, the expedition arrived at La Charrette, and three days later Lewis and Clark reached St Louis, where they were greeted by 5,000 wildly cheering inhabitants, ending their two-and-a-half-year expedition into the Louisiana Territory. Later that day, after finding lodgings, Lewis wrote to the president, 'It is with pleasure that I announce to you the safe arrival of myself and party at 12 o'clock today. In obedience to your orders we have penetrated the Continent of North America to the Pacific Ocean.'

Soon after arriving in St Louis, Lewis disbanded the Corps of Discovery and paid the men for their service. Several months later, each explorer was awarded double pay and 320 acres by Congress, while the two captains each received 1,600 acres. Remaining in the west, Lewis began to plan the writing of his account of the expedition detailing the journey to the Pacific. In the autumn, Lewis and Clark set off for Washington to meet with President Jefferson, and as they advanced east they were greeted as national heroes and honoured with gala parties and balls at each town they passed through. Lewis finally reached the capital with chief Sheheke, his wife and son on 28 December, while Clark was delayed several weeks by his marriage to Judith Hancock in Virginia.

In early January 1807, Lewis met with Jefferson at the White House, and during their time together described the Corps of Discovery's journey to the Pacific. He spread the maps on the floor and the president closely examined them. While no record of the meeting was made by Jefferson or the captain, it is likely the president had many questions for the explorer, given his interest in the geography of the area, the customs, appearances, villages, foods and ways of the Indian tribes in the territory and the potential for trade and new American settlements. The president was anxious for Lewis to start writing his manuscript of the expedition.

Unbeknown to Lewis, the president had nominated him to fill the post of governor for the Upper Louisiana Territory, and on 9 March the petition was approved by Congress. After his appointment, Lewis returned to St Louis and took up his office. Lewis, a man of action who was accustomed to adventure and life in the wilderness, was ill-suited to political office. As governor, he struggled with the endless stacks of paperwork. He was compelled to resolve land claims, settle disputes between trading companies and deal with partisan politics. While in St Louis, Lewis began speculating in land sales, but without any prior business experience he made bad decisions, losing money as his debts escalated. After several months in office, he began to drink heavily and started taking opium as his life spiralled out of control.

While Lewis struggled with the governorship, he was pressed by Jefferson to write his report on the journey of the Corps of Discovery. Despite the president's urging, Lewis was unable to begin work on the manuscript and stopped answering the president's letters. When a new administration came into the White House in 1809, the government began questioning some of Lewis' expenditures and he decided to travel to the capital to clear his name. As he prepared to leave St Louis, his creditors harassed him as he left, driving him into a deeper state of despair.

As the depression intensified during the ride to Washington, Lewis twice attempted suicide. The governor was held by local officials until he appeared well enough to continue his journey. In mid-October he reached a small inn at Grinders Stand near Nashville, Tennessee, and stopped for the night. During the early morning, he shot himself twice, dying shortly after sunrise on 11 October 1809, aged 35.

SELECTED SOURCES:
Ambrose, Stephen E., *Undaunted Courage – Meriwether Lewis, Thomas Jefferson and the Opening of the American West.*
Brebner, John Bartlet, *The Explorers of North America – 1492-1806.*
Dillon, Richard, *Meriwether Lewis – A Biography.*
Duncan, Dayton, *Lewis and Clark – The Journey of the Corps of Discovery.*

Conclusion

Driven by Christopher Columbus' discovery of a New World across the Atlantic Ocean, a wave of explorations to the west erupted as the royal courts of Europe challenged for dominance in North America. During the following centuries, the Spanish gained a firm hold in the south of the continent, while the English and French struggled for pre-eminence in the north. When the Age of Exploration ended in the eighteenth century, North America had been explored and new settlements were rapidly spreading across the continent to the Pacific Ocean. The lands first discovered by Columbus resulted in the creation of twenty-three independent nations by the beginning of the twenty-first century that reached from the Arctic Circle of Canada to the jungles of Central America. The spirit of exploration did not end, but continued into the following centuries as the explorers placed their flags on the North and South Poles and began the quest to conquer outer space and Neil Armstrong's walk on the moon in July 1969 and continued with the manned expeditions to the International Space Station, unmanned land rover and orbiting satellite probes of Mars and flyby and orbital missions to Saturn, Jupiter, Uranus, Neptune and Pluto. In 2018 the American National Aeronautics and Space Administration will launch the Parker Solar Probe to survey the sun's outer corona travelling to within 3.9 million miles of the surface.

Maps of the Explorers

Sixteenth Century Map of the
Eastern Coastline of North America

Voyages of the Early Explorers

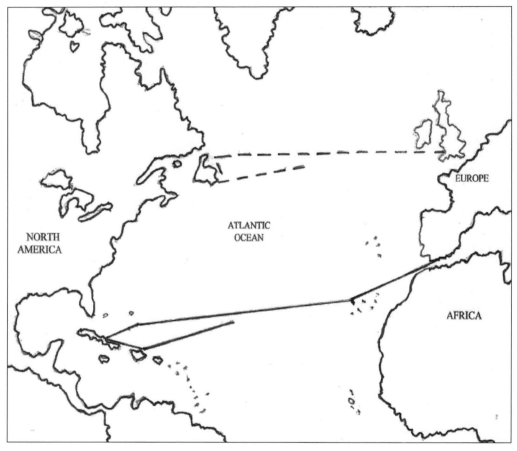

Routes of the Explorers

Columbus 1492 ——
Cabot 1497 ———

Voyages of the Early Explorers

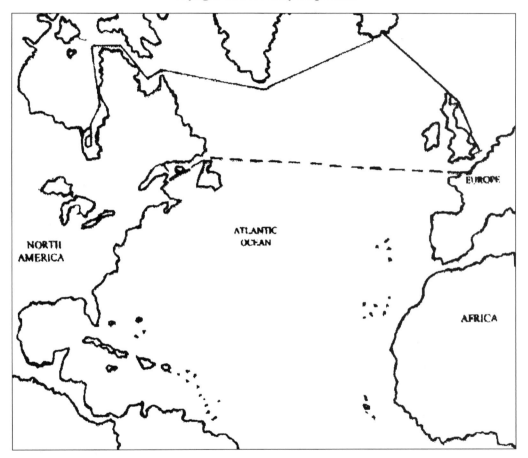

Routes of the Explorers

Hudson 1610 ——
Cartier 1534 ‒ ‒ ‒

1650 European Colonies in America

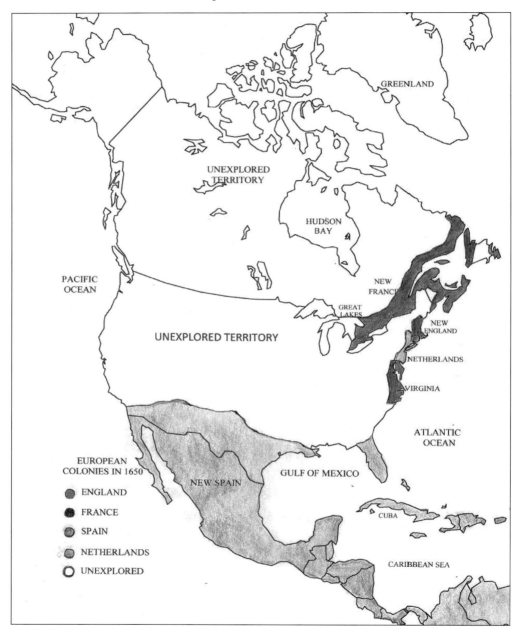

GREENLAND

UNEXPLORED
TERRITORY

HUDSON
BAY

PACIFIC
OCEAN

NEW
FRANCE

GREAT
LAKES

NEW
ENGLAND

UNEXPLORED TERRITORY

NETHERLANDS

VIRGINIA

ATLANTIC
OCEAN

EUROPEAN
COLONIES IN 1650

GULF OF MEXICO

NEW SPAIN

ENGLAND

FRANCE

SPAIN

CUBA

NETHERLANDS

UNEXPLORED

CARIBBEAN SEA

1750 European Colonies in North America

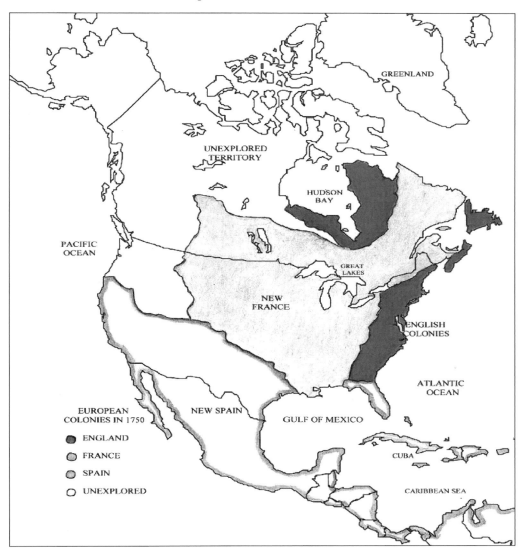

Bibliography

Abbott, John S.C., *Hernando Cortez – Makers of History*. New York and London: Harper & Brothers Publishers, 1901.

Albornoz, Miguel, *Hernando De Soto Knight of the America*. New York and Toronto: Franklin Watts, 1986.

Ambrose, Stephen E., *Undaunted Courage – Meriwether Lewis, Thomas Jefferson and the Opening of the American West*. New York: Touchstone, 1996.

Armstrong, Joe C.W., *Champlain*. Toronto, Ontario, Canada: Macmillan of Canada, 1987.

Barbour, Philip L., *The Three Worlds of Captain John Smith*. Boston: Houghton, Mifflin Company, 1964.

Beazley, Raymond., *John and Sebastian Cabot – The Discovery of North America*. New York: Burt Franklin, 1898.

Bolton, Herbert E., *Coronado – Knight of Pueblos and Plains*. New York, London, Toronto: McGraw Hill Book Company, Inc., 1949.

Brebner, John Bartlet, *The Explorers of North America*. Cleveland and New York: The World Publishing Company, 1964.

Brown, Meredith Mason, *Frontiersman – Daniel Boone and the Making of America*. Baton Rouge: Louisiana State University Press, 2008.

Butts, Edward, *Henry Hudson – New World Voyage*. Toronto: Dundurn Press, 2009.

Cavan, Seamus, *Daniel Boone and the Opening of the Ohio Country*. New York and Philadelphia: Chelsea House Publishers, 1991.

Coulter, Tony, *Jacques Cartier, Samuel de Champlain, and the Explorers of Canada*. New York and Philadelphia: Chelsea House Publishers, 1993.

Coulter, Tony, *La Salle and the Explorers of the Mississippi*. New York and Philadelphia: Chelsea House Publishers, 1991.

Crompton, Samuel Willard, *Robert de La Salle*. New York: Chelsea House Publishers, 2009.

Dalton, Anthony, *Henry Hudson – Doomed Navigator and Explorer*. Victoria, Vancouver and Calgary: Heritage House Publishing Company Ltd, 2014.

Danisi, Thomas C., and Jackson, John C., *Meriwether Lewis*. Amherst, New York: Prometheus Books, 2009.

Day, A. Grove, *Coronado's Quest*. Berkeley and Los Angeles: University of California Press, 1964.

Dillon, Richard, *Meriwether Lewis – A Biography*. New York: Coward-McCann, Inc., 1965.

Duncan, David Ewing, *Hernando de Soto. A Savage Quest in the Americas*. New York: Crown Publishers, 1995.

Duncan, Dayton, and Burns, Ken, *Lewis & Clark – The Journey of the Corps of Discovery*. New York: Alfred A. Knopf, 1997.

Faragher, John Mack, *Daniel Boone – The Life and Legend of an American Pioneer*. New York: Henry Holt and Company, 1992.

Favor, Lesli J., *Francisco Vasquez De Coronado*. New York: The Rosen Publishers Group, Inc., 2003.

Fernandez-Armesto, Felipe, *Columbus*. Oxford and New York: Oxford University Press, 1992.

Firstbrook, Peter, *The Voyage of the Matthew*. London: BBC Books, 1997.

Fischer, David Hackett, *Champlain's Dream*. New York, London, Toronto and Sydney: Simon & Schuster, 2008.

Frost, Orcutt, *Bering – The Russian Discovery of America*. New Haven and London: Yale University Press, 2003.

Gerson, Noel B., *The Glorious Scoundrel – A Biography of Captain John Smith*. New York: Dodd, Mead & Company, 1978.

Gough, Barry, *First Across the Continent – Sir Alexander Mackenzie*. Norman and London: University of Oklahoma Press, 1997.

Greene, Meg, *Jacques Cartier – Navigating the St Lawrence River*. New York: The Publishing Group, Inc., 2004.

Harrisse, Henry, *John Cabot – The Discoverer of North America and Sebastian His Son*. London: Benjamin Franklin Stevens, 1896.

Horgan, Paul, *Conquistadors in North American History*. New York: Farrar, Straus and Giroux, 1972.

Hunter, Douglas, *Half Moon and the Voyage That Redrew the Map of the New World*. New York, Berlin and London: Bloomsburg Press, 2009.

Johnson, Donald S., *La Salle. A Perilous Odyssey from Canada to the Gulf of Mexico*. New York: Cooper Square Press, 2002.

Kushnarev, Evgenii, G. *Bering's Search For The Strait*. Portland: Oregon Historical Society, 1990.

Lauridsen, Peter, *Vitus Bering – The Discovery of Bering Strait*. Freeport, New York: Books for Libraries Press, 1990.

Legare, Francine, *Samuel de Champlain*. Montreal, Canada: XYZ Publishing, 2003.

Levy, Buddy, *Conquistador Hernan Cortes, King Montezuma, and the Last Stand of the Aztecs.* New York: Bantam Book, 2008.

Lofaro, Michael A., *Daniel Boone – An American Life.* Lexington, Kentucky: University of Kentucky Press, 2003.

Marks, Richard Lee, *Cortes, The Great Adventurer and the Fate of Aztec Mexico.* New York: Alfred A. Knopf, 1993.

Morison, Samuel Eliot, *Admiral of the Ocean Sea. A life of Christopher Columbus.* Boston, Toronto and London: Little Brown and Company, 1970.

Morison, Samuel Eliot, *Christopher Columbus – Mariner.* New York: Signet Books, 1955.

Morison, Samuel Eliot, *Samuel De Champlain – Father of New France.* Boston and Toronto: Little, Brown and Company, 1972.

Morison, Samuel Eliot, *The European Discovery of America.* New York: Oxford University Press, 1974.

Morison, Samuel Eliot, *The Great Explorers.* New York and Oxford: Oxford University Press, 1978.

Morris, John Miller, *From Coronado to Escalante: The Explorers of the Spanish Southwest.* New York and Philadelphia: Chelsea House Publishers, 1992.

Mountjoy, Shane, *Francisco Coronado and the Seven Cities of Gold.* Philadelphia: Chelsea House Publishers, 2006.

Muhlstein, Anka, *La Salle – Explorer of the North American Frontier.* New York: Arcade Publishing, 1994.

Payment, Simone, *La Salle – Claiming the Mississippi River for France.* New York: The Rosen Publishing Group, Inc., 2004.

Phillips, William D., and Phillips, Carla Rahn, *The Worlds of Christopher Columbus.* Cambridge, New York, Fort Chester, Melbourne and Sydney: Cambridge University Press, 1992.

Potter, Philip J., *Monarchs of the Renaissance.* Jefferson, North Carolina, and London: McFarland & Company Publishers, 2012.

Sandler, Corey, *Henry Hudson – Dreams and Obsession.* New York: Kensington Publishing Corp., 2007.

Sedgewick, H.D., Jr, *Samuel de Champlain.* Boston and New York: Houghton, Mifflin and Company, 2013.

Sherman, Josepha, *Henry Hudson – English Explorer of the Northwest Passage.* New York, The Rosen Publishing Group, Inc., 2003.

Smith, James K., *Alexander Mackenzie.* Ontario, Canada: Fitzhenry & Whiteside Limited, 1976.

Steller, Georg Wilhelm, *Journal of a Voyage with Bering, 1741-1742.* Stanford, California: Stanford University Press, 1988.

Vaughan, Alden T., *American Genesis – Captain John Smith and the Founding of Virginia.* New York: Little, Brown and Company, 1975.

Wagner, Heather Lehr, *Hernan Cortes.* New York: Chelsea House, 2009.

Wepman, Dennis, *Hernan Cortes.* New York, New Haven and Philadelphia: Chelsea House Publishers, 1986.

Whitman, Sylvia, *Hernando de Soto and the Explorers of the American South.* New York and Philadelphia: Chelsea House Publishers, 1991.

Woog, Adam, *Jacques Cartier.* New York: Chelsea House, 2010.

Xydes, Georgia, *Alexander Mackenzie and the Explorers of Canada.* New York and Philadelphia: Chelsea House Publishers, 1992.

Young, Jeff C., *Hernando De Soto – Spanish Conquistador in the Americas.* Berkeley Heights, New Jersey: Enslow Publishers, 2009.

Index